Criminal Evidence
Principles and Cases
FIFTH EDITION

Thomas J. Gardner
Attorney at Law
And former Assistant District Attorney

Terry M. Anderson
Creighton University School of Law

THOMSON
★
WADSWORTH

Australia • Canada • Mexico • Singapore • Spain
United Kingdom • United States

To Eileen Gardner, for her courage
and fortitude

THOMSON
™
WADSWORTH

Publisher: Eve Howard
Acquisitions Editor: Jay Whitney
Technology Project Manager: Susan DeVanna
Editorial Assistant: Paul Massicotte
Marketing Manager: Dory Schaeffer
Project Manager, Editorial Production: Cheri Palmer
Print/Media Buyer: Kris Waller
Permissions Editor: Kiely Sexton
Production Service: Robin Lockwood Productions

Text Designer: Carolyn Deacy
Photo Researcher: Roberta Broyer
Copy Editor: Jennifer Gordon
Illustrator: Thompson Type
Cover Designer: Yvo Riezebos
Cover Image: Davis Freeman/gettyimages
Compositor: Thompson Type
Printer: Phoenix Color Corp

Printed in the United States of America

2   3   4   5   6   7   07   06   05   04

For more information about our products, contact us at:
Thomson Learning Academic Resource Center
1-800-423-0563
For permission to use material from this text, contact us by:
Phone: 1-800-730-2214
Fax: 1-800-730-2215
Web: http://www.thomsonrights.com

Library of Congress Control Number: 2003110246
ISBN 0-534-61551-1

Wadsworth/Thomson Learning
10 Davis Drive
Belmont, CA 94002-3098
USA

Asia
Thomson Learning
5 Shenton Way #01-01
UIC Building
Singapore 068808

Australia/New Zealand
Thomson Learning
102 Dodds Street
Southbank, Victoria 3006
Australia

Canada
Nelson
1120 Birchmount Road
Toronto, Ontario M1K 5G4
Canada

Europe/Middle East/Africa
Thomson Learning
High Holborn House
50/51 Bedford Row
London WC1R 4LR
United Kingdom

EXPLANATORY NOTE

In this text the authors have presented the principles of the law of evidence which are generally applicable in state and federal courts in the United States. However, because of local statutes or court decisions, it is not unusual for in-dividual states to have evidentiary rules which vary from those generally applicable elsewhere.

For that reason, students and law officers should consult with their legal advisors before assuming that the general principles of evidence appearing in this text represent the law of their jurisdiction.

Brief Contents

Contents

CHAPTER 3

Using Evidence to Determine Guilt or Innocence 34

CHAPTER 4

Direct and Circumstantial Evidence and the Use of Inferences 53

PART II

Witnesses and Their Testimony

PART III

When Evidence Cannot Be Used Because of Police Mistakes or Misconduct

CHAPTER 14

Obtaining Physical and Other Evidence 249

CHAPTER 15

Obtaining Evidence by Use of Search Warrants, Wiretapping, or Dogs Trained to Indicate an Alert 277

PART IV

Crime-Scene, Documentary, and Scientific Evidence

Preface

In 1791, just four years after the writing of the U.S. Constitution, the original thirteen states ratified the first ten amendments to that Constitution. These amendments, known today as the American Bill of Rights, were two hundred years old in 1991. They represent concerns of our Founding Fathers that the strong, central federal government would usurp individual rights then enjoyed in the American colonies. The first American Congress had considered more than 145 proposed amendments, but sent only twelve of these to the states for ratification. The Bill of Rights has established the core of basic individual rights in the United States.

The Bill of Rights, as interpreted by the U.S. Supreme Court and state courts, has historically been the basis for the rules of evidence used in criminal trials throughout the United States. Today, most states and the federal government use the Federal Rules of Evidence found in Appendix B of this text. The remaining states use rules of evidence similar to the Federal Rules of Evidence. These rules incorporate more than two hundred years of judicial and legislative debate as to what should be used in the courts of the fifty states and of the federal government. Today, as in 1791, the Bill of Rights sets the standards for rules of evidence. For this reason, this book focuses on the Bill of Rights and cases interpreting the Bill of Rights.

In criminal trials, rules of evidence have as their goal securing a defendant's constitutional right to a fair trial. What is meant by a "fair trial" can vary over many years. What was considered a fair trial in the 1692 Salem, Massachusetts, witchcraft trial is no longer a fair trial in any democratic nation in the world today. In 1692, nineteen persons were executed in Salem as witches and 150 more were jailed on evidence that would not be permitted today under the Bill of Rights.

Rules of evidence are not only important for protecting the fundamental rights of a person accused of crimes, but are also necessary in seeking to assure the interest of the American public through efficient and effective functioning of the American criminal justice system. However, a necessary trade-off exists between the protection of individual rights and judicial efficiency. Understanding this trade-off adds greatly to the student's appreciation of the dynamics of the criminal justice system.

NEW TO THIS EDITION

Gardner and Anderson present the key rules of evidence, the rationale behind these rules, and the applicability of these rules in criminal matters in a manner that is not encyclopedic or overwhelming to the student. The text's excellent coverage of current issues, unique photo and art program, accessible writing style, clear explanations, and numerous pedagogical aids help students understand complex legal topics more so than any other text on the market. The authors utilize fascinating, high-interest, news-based examples to help students understand and retain concepts. A true evidence book, the text includes both brief and lengthier case excerpts to help students develop critical thinking skills and expose them to legal reasoning. The Fifth Edition offers these additional remarkable features:

- InfoTrac®College Edition exercises are added at the end of each chapter.

- Expanded discussion of key topics such as racial profiling—as it applies to consensual searches, search and seizure, entrapment, judicial federalism, reasonable suspicion, and entering evidence at trial, among others.

- New cases that have been added to better illustrate hearsay.

- Comprehensive coverage of the law of evidence.

- An increased depth of coverage on key topics, including expanded presentation and discussion of court cases, while still maintaining a briefer text than others currently available for this course.

- A completely updated *Instructor's Resource Manual* includes learning objectives, chapter outlines, key terms, relevant cases, answers to the discussion questions, and a test bank.

- Chapter 11 is new and entitled, "Evidence Is Admissible If Obtained During an Administrative Function Under the 'Special Needs' of Government." Learn where government employees, not usually from law enforcement, get authority to "search and seize."

Once again Appendix A of the text contains the Bill of Rights and applicable section of the U.S. Constitution. Appendix B presents most of the Federal Rules of Evidence used in federal courts and in the courts of most states. Both the U.S. Constitution and the Federal Rules of Evidence are cited frequently in this text, and thus are an integral part of the material. Also the Glossary has been greatly expanded, and its comprehensiveness will aid in student mastery and retention of terms.

The result of our efforts in preparing this Fifth Edition is, we believe, a text that is devoted to only the law of evidence, but in a manner that is improved from both a substance and an organizational perspective. We hope our readers will reach a similar conclusion. The length of the book has been contained as well in this edition. We believe a shorter edition to be more suitable for a typical semester or quarter class in this subject.

ACKNOWLEDGMENTS

We would like to thank the reviewers of the Fifth Edition for their suggestions: David Jones, University of Wisconsin, Oshkosh; Taiping Ho, Ball State University; Craig Hemmens, Boise State University; Raymond Kessler, Sul Ross State University; Walter Lewis, St. Louis Community College at Meramec; Michael Meyer, University of North Dakota; and Tim Bragg, Mississippi County Community College, Arkansas. We also wish to thank Robin Lockwood for her excellent work in the production of this text.

I

Introduction to Criminal Evidence

1

History and Development of the Law of Criminal Evidence

Ⓐ HISTORY OF THE RULES OF EVIDENCE

One cannot understand the **rules of evidence** applicable in criminal trials today without some appreciation of the historical development of those rules. Evidentiary rules are the gates through which information flows into our criminal courtrooms; the size and shape of the gate has varied over the life of the United States and other English-speaking nations.

The United States and England share a common judicial heritage. Most of the early rules of evidence were made by English courts, and some were made by English Parliaments. These early rules of evidence were brought to the American colonies and used by the first English settlers. The same rules were used by other English-speaking colonies, such as Canada and Australia, and were known as **common-law rules of evidence.**[1] Because of this common heritage, many similarities exist even today in the law of evidence used in English-speaking countries. The following account of the first murder trial in the American colonies would also describe the court proceedings used in other English colonies.

> The first reported murder in the American colonies occurred in 1630. John Billington, one of the original band of 102 Pilgrims to sail on the Mayflower, waylaid a neighbor and killed the man by shooting him with his blunderbuss. As the colonies had no written criminal laws, Billington was charged with the English common-law crime of murder and tried using the English common-law rules of evidence and criminal procedure. After a prompt trial and conviction, Billington was sentenced to death and hanged.[2]

Rules of evidence are an important part of all criminal justice systems, just as rules are important in baseball, football, and basketball games. In a democracy, rules of evidence are important not only in safeguarding the rights of accused persons to a fair trial but also in seeking to ensure the interests of the public in the proper functioning of the criminal justice system. Some rules of evidence are highly controversial and cause arguments over what these rules should be and what would best serve the overall needs of society.

Early Methods of Determining Guilt or Innocence

In its essence, a criminal charge against a person is either admitted or denied. If denied, rules must be created to determine the truth or falsity of the denial. Our earliest rules of evidence were not so much rules about trials but about proof. When has the accused's guilt (or innocence) been proved?

In 1066, when the Normans conquered England, determining guilt or innocence by the use of procedures known as **ordeals** was a common practice. A person of noble birth or who was titled could demand trial by battle to determine his guilt or innocence. Winning a sword fight would prove innocence, whereas losing would show guilt. Since the loser would often be killed or seriously injured, the case would ordinarily be disposed of by the outcome of the battle.

The guilt or innocence of a common person would be determined by other types of ordeals. The nineteenth-century English judge Sir James Stephens described these ordeals in his *History of the Criminal Law of England*:

> It is unnecessary to give a minute account of the ceremonial of the ordeals. They were of various kinds. The general nature of all was the same. They were appeals to God to work a miracle in attestation of the innocence of the accused person. The handling of hot iron, plunging the hand or arm into boiling water unhurt, were the commonest. The ordeal of water was a very singular institution. Sinking was the sign of innocence, floating the sign of guilt. As any one would sink unless he understood how to float, and intentionally did so, it is difficult to see how anyone could ever be convicted by this means. Is it possible that this ordeal may have been an honourable form of suicide, like the Japanese happy despatch? In nearly every case the accused would sink. This would prove his innocence, indeed, but there would be no need to take him out. He would thus die honourably. If by accident he floated, he would be put to death disgracefully.[3]

The ordeals adjudicated guilt by appeals to God (or the supernatural). The mind of a person in the Middle Ages was conditioned to believe in frequent divine intervention in human affairs and was thus content to leave questions of guilt or innocence to such intervention.

However, in England this all changed when, at the Lateran Council of 1215, clergy were prohibited from taking part in ordeals. Without the clergy, of course, one could not be sure God had ordained the result of the ordeal. Indeed, in the reign of King John (1199–1216), the ordeal went from being the standard of proof to complete disappearance.

In its place came the oath and oath-helpers. Although still an appeal to divine guidance, the oath, in which the accused swore before God his innocence, began the journey toward trial by jury. To support his oath, the accused gathered oath-helpers to swear to his innocence. Over time, these oath-helpers began to swear not to the ultimate guilt of innocence of the accused but to facts relevant to his guilt or innocence. They became witnesses.

At the same time, itinerant justices holding court around England began impaneling groups of local residents into presentment juries, the purpose of which was to inform the justices of crimes committed by other residents. The accused then put himself on the oath of his fellow residents. Over time, it came to be realized that those serving on the **presentment jury** should not serve on the smaller, petit, jury. By the fourteenth century, the origins of our grand jury and trial jury system were firmly established in English law.

As the use of presentment and petit jury became widespread in England, rules developed to control and direct the task of those juries. Then, as now, the presentment jury had few evidentiary limitations. The petit jury, however, became charged not only with determining the guilt or innocence of the accused but also with finding the facts upon which its determination depended. Once the jury was established as a fact-finding body, rules of evidence controlling how facts could be presented to the jury began developing.

In the long period between the fourteenth century and our own, rules governing the introduction of facts into criminal trials developed slowly and inconsistently. For example, even though hearsay evidence was regarded as unreliable even in the early thirteenth century,[4] such evidence was still widely permitted in the American colonies. Other nonjudicial forces helped move the nature of criminal trials and rules of evidence forward.

Ⓑ MAGNA CARTA AND HABEAS CORPUS

Together with the evolution of methods of proof came important limitations on the power of the sovereign, the English monarchy. In twelfth-century England, people lived under a system in which they could be jailed on anonymous accusations of wrongdoing; or they could be seized on mere suspicion or on the whim of a government official. English kings suppressed political opposition by jailing any person who dared criticize the Crown or the government. Absolute loyalty was compelled by the arrest of anyone suspected of antigovernment sentiments or statements.

Because of these abuses by English kings, the great barons of England revolted against the Crown. After many years of fighting, King John met with the barons in 1215 at a field in Runnymede, England. An agreement between the parties to stop the fighting resulted in the king and the barons signing a document called **Magna Carta,** or the Great Charter. Among other clauses, Magna Carta stated that there would be no criminal "trial upon . . . simple accusation without producing credible witnesses to the truth therein" and that "no freeman shall be taken, imprisoned . . . except by lawful judgment of his peers or the law of the land."

Magna Carta was a historic first step toward democracy and the establishment of minimum standards for arresting and imprisoning people accused of crimes. Under this new concept of law, no one could be taken into **custody** on mere suspicion, on whim, or without substantial good cause. Magna Carta began the development of the concept in law that there had to be probable cause, or "reasonable grounds to believe," to justify arresting or holding a person in custody.

Magna Carta deeply affected the drafters of the American Declaration of Independence:

> The event became the rallying cry of individual liberty in England during the 17th century, and so influenced the Founding Fathers of our country that the Seal of the Magna Carta was emblazoned on the cover of the *Journal of the Proceedings of the First Continental Congress,* held in Philadelphia on September 5, 1774, where our forefathers laid the foundation stone of individual liberty in the United States.[5]

Another important milestone in the protection of personal liberties was the development of the *writ of habeas corpus.* This famous writ is believed to date to the fourteenth and fifteenth centuries. The writ of habeas corpus was and is a safeguard against the illegal or improper holding of a person against his or her will. The word *writ* means a "writing," and **habeas corpus** is a Latin term meaning "have the body." This writ, when signed by a judge, is served upon the governmental official who has custody of a person and orders that official to appear before the court and show cause for holding the person.

Magna Carta and habeas corpus are not only very important legal concepts in the English-speaking world but also have had an important impact in other parts of the world. Magna Carta began the concept that a person cannot be jailed or held without just cause. The writ of habeas corpus was the earliest legal procedure by which illegal or improper jailing or detention could be challenged in a court of law. If a person is being held without just cause and legal authority, the judge presiding at the habeas corpus hearing must then order his or her release.

The American Founding Fathers guaranteed the right of habeas corpus in the U.S. Constitution. ARTICLE I, SECTION 9, of the U.S. Constitution provides that "The privilege of the Writ of Habeas Corpus shall not be suspended, unless when in Cases of Rebellion or Invasion the public Safety may require it."

The original thirteen states, and all those that subsequently joined the union, did the same. Some states strengthened the constitutional guarantee by statutes, such as Wisconsin statute 782.09, which provides that "any judge who refuses to grant a writ of habeas corpus, when legally applied for, is liable to the prisoner in the sum of $1,000." Other statutes impose penalties for "refusing papers" ($200), "concealing" or "transferring" the prisoner ($1,000 or six months imprisonment), and "reimprisoning party discharged" ($1,250 and misdemeanor violation).

The famous English writer Sir William Blackstone wrote that habeas corpus is "the most celebrated writ in the English law." Chief Justice Marshall of the U.S. Supreme Court called the writ a "great constitutional privilege," and the U.S. Supreme Court has stated a number of times that "there is no higher duty than to maintain it unimpaired."

C THE AMERICAN DECLARATION OF INDEPENDENCE

When students are asked where their personal freedoms come from, they will often answer that personal freedoms come from government. This answer was correct hundreds of years ago, when it was believed that kings received their authority to rule from God. What few personal rights the ordinary person had in those days came from the ruler. This was known as the **divine right of kings.** Generally accepted and promoted throughout the world in the Middle Ages, this doctrine stated that monarchs received absolute authority to govern from God and that their subjects had only such personal freedoms as fit their status under their sovereign. This theory, actively promoted by those in power, helped them rule and maintain control over their subjects.

Early American documents show that the American colonies did not accept the European concept of the divine right of kings. The 1641 Massachusetts Body of Liberties commenced by discussing the "free fruition of such liberties, Immunities and privileges . . . as due every man."[6] The 176⁵ Declaration of Rights spoke of "inherent rights and liberties," "freedom of a people," and "the undoubted rights of Englishmen."[7]

The American Declaration of Independence of 1776 specifically repudiated the doctrine of the divine right of kings, pointing out that personal freedoms do not come from government or kings. Every Fourth of July, we celebrate the signing of the document that established the following propositions:

- That the United States was independent from Great Britain, detailing the "history of repeated injuries and usurpations" of the king of Great Britain who sought to establish "an absolute Tyranny over these States"

Some of the Abuses that Led to the Signing of the Declaration of Independence

The American Declaration of Independence, celebrated each year on the Fourth of July, lists more than twenty-five abuses by the "King of Great Britain" against the American colonies. It was these abuses that caused the colonies to declare their independence from Great Britain. About two-thirds of the abuses concerned legislative, commercial, and tax abuses. The following is a brief summary of the remaining one-third of those abuses and the constitutional provisions adopted by the new nation to remedy them.

Abuses Concerning Liberty, Freedom, and the Judiciary	Correction of the Abuse in the U.S. Constitution
"He has made Judges dependent on his will alone . . ."	ARTICLE III, creating an independent judiciary
"He has kept among us in times of peace Standing Armies . . . [and] has quartered large bodies of armed troops among us"	Third Amendment to the Bill of Rights
He ". . . protect[s] [the armed troops], by a mock trial, from punishment for any Murders which they should commit on the Inhabitants . . ."	The establishment of an independent judiciary, an elected president and Congress, and the use of grand juries
". . .depriving us in many cases, of the benefits of Trial by Jury"	". . . the accused shall enjoy the right of a . . . trial . . . by an impartial jury" (Fourth Amendment)
He ". . . transport[s] us beyond the Seas to be tried for pretended offenses."	The right to an "indictment by a Grand Jury" and right to be tried in "the State and district where the crime shall have been committed . . ." (Fifth and Sixth Amendments)
"He has plundered our seas, ravaged our Coasts, burnt our towns, and destroyed the lives of our people."	The establishment of an independent judiciary, an elected Congress and president, and the use of grand juries
"He is at this time transporting large Armies of foreign Mercenaries to compleat the work of death, desolation and tyranny . . ."	Limiting the powers of the president and the Congress to those specifically set forth in ARTICLES I and II, and the protection of the Third Amendment

- That "Governments are instituted among Men, deriving their just powers from the consent of the governed"
- That "all men are created equal, that they are endowed by their Creator with certain unalienable Rights, that among these are Life, Liberty, and the pursuit of Happiness"

Ⓓ THE U.S. CONSTITUTION AND THE AMERICAN BILL OF RIGHTS

When the American Founding Fathers met in Philadelphia in 1787, many of the wrongs of the past had been eliminated. For example, trial for witchcraft had been

The signing of the U.S. Constitution from a painting in the Smithsonian Institute in Washington, D.C.

abolished, and people accused of crimes no longer had to prove their innocence by ordeal or battle. The delegates set about writing a constitution for the new American democracy that would embody the spirit of the Declaration of Independence and would create a workable, practical government to serve the people. They stated their goals in the preamble to the new U.S. Constitution:

> We the People of the United States, in order to form a more perfect Union, establish justice, insure domestic Tranquility, provide for the common defense, promote the general Welfare, and secure the Blessings of Liberty to ourselves and our Posterity, do ordain and establish this Constitution for the United States of America.

The U.S. Constitution sought to protect the privilege of habeas corpus and prohibited such abuses as the passing of bills of attainder and ex post facto laws. The right of trial by jury was protected, and *corruption of blood* (punishing a family for the criminal acts of another family member) was forbidden. The drafters of the Constitution knew that such abuses had occurred in England and were determined that they would not occur in the new American nation.

As a further protection, the Constitution provided that all federal officials, including the president of the United States, could be removed upon "Impeachment for, and Conviction of, Treason, Bribery, or other high Crimes and Misdemeanors" (Art. II, Sec. 4).

When the Constitution was presented to the states for ratification, it was criticized as not going far enough in protecting the people from possible abuses by the new federal government. The people understood their state governments and believed they could control them, but they were suspicious of the new central government. As a result, prior to ratification of the new Constitution, it was agreed that additional protections would immediately be added to the Constitution. The U.S. Constitution was ratified in 1788 and ten amendments, now known as the **Bill of Rights,** were added in 1791.

In a 1991 U.S. Supreme Court opinion, Justice Scalia pointed out that "most of the procedural protections of the federal Bill of Rights simply codified traditional common law privileges (that) had been widely adopted by the states." Justice Scalia used the following quote from 1878, which stated that "the law is perfectly well settled that the first ten amendments to the Constitution . . . were not intended to lay down any novel principles of government, but simply to embody certain guarantees and immunities which we had inherited from our English ancestors."[8]

The Bill of Rights (see Appendix A) originally applied only to the federal government. Beginning in 1961 the U.S. Supreme Court began the process of making the Bill of Rights applicable to the states through the Fourteenth Amendment. (See the case of *Mapp v. Ohio* and the material in Chapter 9 on the use of the American exclusionary rule.)

Ⓔ BASIC RIGHTS UNDER THE U.S. CONSTITUTION TODAY

The United States celebrated the two hundredth anniversary of the American Constitution in 1988. This remarkable document, which includes the Bill of Rights, has received worldwide attention and has been a model for use in many countries. It sets forth the foundation and requirements for the law of criminal evidence used throughout the United States.

The people of the United States may change, abolish, or modify any part of the Constitution they wish; polls show, however, that the great majority of Americans want to keep the Constitution and the Bill of Rights intact. The following summarizes some of the most basic rights protected or created by the Bill of Rights.

The Presumption of Innocence Until Proven Guilty

One of the most deeply rooted traditions of modern Anglo-Saxon law is that an accused is innocent until proven guilty **beyond a reasonable doubt.**[9]

Besides the **presumption of innocence** until proven guilty, the United States also uses an accusatorial system of justice. In 1961 the U.S. Supreme Court stated that "ours is an accusatorial and not an inquisitorial system—a system in which the State must establish guilt by evidence independently and freely secured and may not by coercion prove its charge against an accused out of his mouth."[10]

Ancient Wrongs that Influenced the American Criminal Justice System

Wrong	Resulted In	Led to the Following Development	U.S. Constitution
The practice of English kings jailing persons for no good reason, on mere suspicion or on simple accusation by another.	The English civil war of the late 1100s and early 1200s, which was settled by King John signing Magna Carta ("great charter") in 1215.	Magna Carta provides that there will be no criminal "trial upon . . . simple accusation without producing credible witnesses to the truth therein." Magna Carta led to the development of the great English Writ of Habeas Corpus, which requires law officers to show probable cause to a court in order to hold a person in custody.	The Fourth Amendment requires probable cause to arrest and to issue a search warrant. Habeas corpus is guaranteed by ARTICLE I, SECTION 9, of the Constitution.
The use of torture and coercion to obtain confessions.	The English Parliament abolished the inquisitorial court, the Star Chamber, in 1640s. [See *Miranda v. Arizona,* 384 U.S. 436 (1966).]	The development of the privilege against self-incrimination and right to remain silent while in police custody.	The Fifth Amendment contains privilege against self-incrimination, and the Sixth Amendment the right to an attorney. The *Miranda* rule is not a constitutional requirement but is a court-created procedural safeguard.
The use of general warrants, which gave British officials power to search anywhere and anything they wished.	This practice was discontinued in England but continued to "bedevil" the American colonies.	The continued practice of the British to search "where they pleased" was the "most prominent event" that led to the Declaration of Independence and the American Revolutionary War. [*Stanford v. State of Texas,* 85 S.Ct. 506, 510 (1965).]	The Fourth Amendment forbids "unreasonable searches and seizures" and requires probable cause and search warrants.
The practice of English courts of convicting persons on hearsay and written statements or from persons who did not appear in court and who were not identified to the accused.	This practice was used to "frame" Sir Walter Raleigh in 1603 and send him to prison for treason.	The hearsay rules and the requirement that the government prove criminal charges with witnesses who testified in court in the presence of the accused.	The Sixth Amendment makes it a requirement that ". . . the accused shall enjoy the right to be confronted with the witnesses against him . . ." ARTICLE II, SECTION 3, of the Constitution prohibits conviction for treason except on "the testimony of two witnesses."
Charging a person with a trumped-up criminal charge and then putting pressure on the jury to convict the person.	William Penn was charged in this manner in 1670. When an English jury would not convict him, the jury was held for two days without food, water, or toilet facilities.	When the jury would not give in to the pressures of the judge and the king, they were fined for their conduct. This case was important in the development of a system of independent juries. William Penn left England and founded the state of Pennsylvania.	Persons charged with crimes have a right to "an impartial jury" (Sixth Amendment) and "due process of law" (fundamental fairness requirement of the Fourteenth Amendment).

The Right to a Speedy and Public Trial

The Sixth Amendment provides that "the accused shall enjoy the right to a speedy and public trial." A defendant may waive the right to a speedy trial with the permission of the court. The federal government and many states have enacted statutes that state the time within which a trial must be held. The federal government requires a trial within seventy days for a felony and within sixty days for a misdemeanor, unless the requirement for a speedy trial is waived.

The Right to an Indictment

About half of the states follow the system imposed upon the federal government by the Fifth Amendment requiring a grand jury **indictment** for a "capital, or otherwise infamous crime." In the other states, elected prosecutors (district attorneys or state attorneys) make the decisions about whether to charge and what crimes to charge. Defendants charged by a district or state attorney have the right to a preliminary hearing if they are charged with a felony.

The Right to a Fair (Not Perfect) Trial

In a long trial, mistakes will probably be made. The U.S. Supreme Court and state courts have repeatedly held that "the law does not require that a defendant receive a perfect trial, only a fair one."[11]

A defendant convicted in a trial where harmless error has occurred has received a **fair trial,** but not a perfect trial. However, if the error were harmful, reversible, or plain error, the defendant has not received a fair trial and is entitled to a new trial or to have the criminal charges dropped.

A defendant is not entitled to a new trial if it is shown that the error was harmless beyond a reasonable doubt. The U.S. Supreme Court held that "the test for harmfulness is whether there is a reasonable possibility that the improperly admitted evidence contributed to the conviction."[12]

For example, the use of a confession obtained by force would be **reversible error** (**harmful** or **plain error**) when the conviction rested only on this evidence. But if the crime charged were bank robbery and ten eyewitnesses testified and the bank's video also showed the defendant robbing the bank, an appellant court might hold that the use of the coerced confession was **harmless error.**

The Right to Assistance of Counsel

Persons charged with a state or federal crime (or juveniles where a delinquency petition has been filed against them) have the Sixth Amendment right to counsel. If the defendant (or juvenile) cannot afford an attorney, one will be provided by the state or federal government.[13]

The Right to Be Informed of Charges

A defendant charged with a crime has a right to be informed of what he or she is alleged to have done and what specific crime or crimes are being charged. The Sixth Amendment provides that "the accused shall enjoy the right . . . to be informed of the nature and cause of the accusation."

The Right of the Defendant to Compel Witnesses

The Sixth Amendment provides that "the accused shall enjoy the right . . . to have compulsory process for obtaining witnesses in his favor. . . ." If there are witnesses who can help a defendant's case, the accused may compel their appearance by use of subpoenas. Such witnesses, however, could be very uncooperative. They could make efforts to avoid service by a subpoena, fail to appear in court, state that they do not remember or did not see or hear the incident. They could also use the Fifth Amendment privilege against self-incrimination.

The Right of the Defendant to Testify

In criminal cases, many defendants enter not-guilty pleas and then place the burden on the government to come forward with sufficient credible evidence to prove guilt beyond a reasonable doubt. A defendant may take the witness stand and testify in his or her own defense. Most defendants, however, do not testify for various tactical reasons. The most important of these reasons is that a defendant who testifies is then subject to cross-examination, which could be disastrous to the defendant's case. Therefore, many defense lawyers do not want their clients to take this serious risk.[14]

The Right of the Defendant to Confront and Cross-Examine Witnesses

The Sixth Amendment provides that "the accused shall enjoy the right . . . to be confronted with the witnesses against him. . . ." The U.S. Supreme Court pointed out that the famous London trial of Sir Walter Raleigh in 1603 was one of the reasons for including the confrontation clause in the Sixth Amendment of the Bill of Rights.

Sir Walter Raleigh was a favorite of Queen Elizabeth. When Elizabeth died in 1603, James I became king of England. James feared and disliked Raleigh and wanted to get rid of him. Raleigh was charged with treason. The statements and writings of unidentified persons, plus hearsay, were used to convict him. Because most of the witnesses against Raleigh were not present in court, there was no confrontation, and Raleigh could not cross-examine witnesses.

The Right of Privacy

The Fourth Amendment forbids unreasonable searches and seizures by officers of the federal and state governments. Therefore, law officers must have a search warrant or must show that a search or seizure is justified by an exception to the search warrant requirements.

The historic roots of the Fourth Amendment go back to Magna Carta and the development over the centuries of the **probable cause** requirement. In 1965 the U.S. Supreme Court traced events that led to the American Revolution against British rule:

Vivid in the memory of the newly formed independent Americans were those general warrants known as writs of assistance under which officers of the Crown had so bedeviled the Colonists. The hated writs of assistance had given customs officials blanket authority to search where they pleased for goods imported in violation of British tax laws. They were denounced by James Otis as "the worst instrument of arbitrary power, the most destructive of English liberty, and the fundamental principles of law, that ever was found in an English law book" because they placed "the liberty of every man in the hands of every petty officer." The historic occasion of that denunciation in 1761 at Boston has been characterized as "perhaps the most prominent event which inaugurated the resistance of the colonies to the oppressions of the mother country." "Then and there," said John Adams, "was the first scene of the first act of opposition to the arbitrary claims of Great Britain. Then and there the child Independence was born."[15]

The Right to an Impartial Jury

The Sixth Amendment of the U.S. Constitution guarantees defendants the right to "an impartial jury of the State and district wherein the crime shall have been committed. . . ."

SUMMARY

Rules of evidence are the gates through which information flows into courtrooms in both civil and criminal cases. Guilt or innocence in criminal cases was determined a thousand years ago by trial by battle, if you were titled or belonged to the nobility, or by an ordeal, if you were a common person.

In the 1692 Salem, Massachusetts, witchcraft trials, nineteen persons were convicted of being witches and were put to death on evidence that would not be permitted in the courtrooms of any democracy today.

Original copies of Magna Carta can be seen on display in the National Archives Building in Washington, D.C., or in the British Museum in London. This writ (writing) was the first step toward a democracy in the English-speaking world in the year 1215. The American Declaration of Independence, the U.S. Constitution, and the American Bill of Rights followed.

PROBLEMS

Refer to Appendix A, which contains the Bill of Rights and applicable sections of the U.S. Constitution, and answer the following questions about rights and privileges in the United States. You may also have to use the index for further information on a few of the questions.

AVAILABLE ANSWERS:

a. This is a right or privilege protected by the U.S. Constitution.

b. This is *not* a right or privilege protected by the U.S. Constitution.

A PERSON CHARGED WITH A CRIME HAS A RIGHT TO:

1. A perfect trial.

2. A speedy trial.

3. A private (not public) trial.

4. The assistance of a lawyer for his or her defense.

5. Compel witnesses to appear in his or her defense.

6. Not be tried more than once for the same offense and same conduct.

7. Due process of law (fundamental fairness).

8. An impartial jury.

9. Not take the witness stand in his criminal trial (right to remain silent).

10. Make false statements in court under oath.

11. See and hear witnesses as they testify in court.

12. Cross-examine witnesses.

13. Be informed of the charge or charges.

14. Be tried in the county in which the crime was committed.

15. An unbiased judge.

16. A defense lawyer who believes the defendant to be innocent.

17. Reasonable bail if bail is set.

ALL PERSONS HAVE THE FOLLOWING RIGHTS OR FREEDOMS:

18. Freedom to say, print, or write anything and everything he or she wishes (absolute freedom of speech)

19. Freedom from any and all government searches

20. The right to have *Miranda* warnings given when in police custody

21. The right to a habeas corpus hearing if held illegally or improperly

22. Freedom of movement without interference by a government official unless there is lawful authority

23. The right to remain silent when a person is an important material witness to a serious felony and is not incriminating himself

24. Freedom to move from one state to another or from one city to another city

25. The right to block sidewalks or streets as part of a protest

INFOTRAC COLLEGE EDITION EXERCISES

1. Go to InfoTrac College Edition and using the search term "habeas corpus" find the 2002 article in the *William and Mary Law Review*, 'Habeas Corpus and the Antiterrorism and Effective Death Penalty Act of 1996.' This article discusses the history of the habeas corpus writ in federal courts and recent measures taken by Congress and the Supreme Court to limit the use of the writ in federal courts. One of the moving forces behind the 1996 Antiterrorism Act, the article says, was congressional concern that those convicted of the Oklahoma City bombing would use the writ to delay execution. Should federal courts continue to use the habeas corpus writ to review state court criminal convictions? When, and with what limitations?

2. Go to InfoTrac College Edition and using the search term "habeas corpus" find the 1998 article in the *Journal of Criminal Law and Criminology* titled "Getting Out of this Mess: Steps Toward Addressing and Avoiding Inordinate Delay in Capital Cases." In many states, the length of time between imposition of a capital (death) sentence and the execution of the sentence is very long. Often, the delay is caused by multiple appeals by the defendant, which include habeas corpus actions in the federal courts. The author of this article concludes that a death sentence too long delayed is itself a cruel and unusual sentence under the Constitution. Do you agree? Why or why not?

NOTES

1. Common law is sometimes referred to as *unwritten law*. In early England and during American colonial times, legislatures did not meet often to enact statutory law. Courts made most of the laws, usually based on the custom and usage of the community. This judge-made law became known

as *common law.* Since there were few printing presses and few people could read and write, law for the most part in those days was unwritten and carried in the minds of judges, lawyers, and government officials. Today, written law can be found in statutes enacted by legislative bodies, and common law is found in court reports, court transcripts, and other written material.

2. See *Bloodletters and Sudmen: A Narrative Encyclopedia of American Criminals from the Pilgrims to the Present* by Jay Robert Nash (New York: M. Evans & Co., 1974).

3. *A History of the Criminal Law of England,* vol. 1, p. 73 (MacMillan & Co., 1883).

4. F. Pollack and F. W. Maitland, *History of English Law,* 2d ed., vol. 2, p. 622 (Cambridge University Press, 1968).

5. J. Few, *In Defense of Trial by Jury,* vol. 1, p. 1 (American Jury Trial Foundation, 1993).

6. See *The Harvard Classics,* vol. 43, p. 70 (Collier & Son, 1910).

7. See *The Harvard Classics,* vol. 43, p. 157 (Collier & Son, 1910).

8. *Pacific Mutual Life Ins. Co. v. Haslip,* 499 U.S. 1, 111 S.Ct. 1032 (1991).

9. T. Cooley, *Constitutional Limitations,* chap. 10 (4th ed. 1878). Abraham's widely used text makes the statement that all democracies use the presumption of innocence until proven guilty. See Abraham, *The Judicial Process,* 2d ed., p. 101 (Oxford University Press, 1968).

10. *Rogers v. Richmond,* 365 U.S. 534 at 540–41, 81 S.Ct. 735, at 737–40 (1961).

11. *Lutwak v. United States,* 344 U.S. 604, at 619, 73 S.Ct. 481, at 490 (1953).

12. *Chapman v. California,* 386 U.S. 18, 87 S.Ct. 824 (1967), rehearing denied 386 U.S. 987, 87 S.Ct 1283; *State v. Jones,* 575 A.2d 216 (Conn., 1990); and *Schneble v. Florida,* 405 U.S. 427, 92 S.Ct. 1056 (1972).

13. In the 1975 case of *Faretta v. California,* 422 U.S. 806, 95 S.Ct. 2525 (1975), the U.S. Supreme Court recognized the right of a criminal defendant under the Sixth Amendment to act as his or her own attorney. Denial of this constitutional right of self-representation is reversible error unless it is shown that (1) the request was untimely, or (2) the defendant abused the right of self-representation, or (3) the request was made solely for the purposes of delay, or (4) the case is so complex that it requires the assistance of a lawyer, or (5) the defendant is unable to voluntarily and intelligently waive her right to a lawyer. See also *McKaskle v. Wiggins,* 465 U.S. 168, 177 n.8, 104 S.Ct. 944, 950 n.8 (1984).

A convicted defendant who claims he was represented by an inadequate or ineffective lawyer must prove that (1) the lawyer's defense fell below an objective standard of reasonableness and (2) that a reasonable probability exists that, but for the lawyer's unprofessional errors, the results would have been different. [*Strickland v. Washington,* 466 U.S. 668, 104 S.Ct. 2052 (1984).]

When the state is paying the attorney fee, the right to choose one's own attorney is limited in most states and is balanced with the public's need for the efficient and effective administration of criminal justice. The annual cost to taxpayers in a state of 5 or 6 million people for public defense attorneys runs over $30 million. For a discussion of the right to pick an attorney to be paid for with public funds, see *People v. Phelps,* 557 N.E.2d 235 (App., 1990).

When a criminal case will receive considerable public attention, experienced lawyers will either volunteer their services or will accept the public fee for their services. The publicity in the 1992 *Dahmer* case in Wisconsin was worldwide (Dahmer was the bizarre confessed killer of seventeen young men). Many experienced criminal lawyers were interested in handling the case because of the extensive publicity.

14. Witnesses and prosecutors cannot comment on the fact that a defendant in a criminal case has exercised the constitutional right to remain silent. Such comments or statements would in most instances be "reversible" error should the defendant be convicted. Such comments could also be grounds for a charge against a lawyer before a bar association.

In 1993 the U.S. Supreme Court held that "defendant's right to testify does not include a right to commit perjury." However, a defendant who only enters a not-guilty plea does not commit perjury if the defendant is found guilty after a trial. (See Chapter 6, "Witnesses and the Testimony of Witnesses.") *United States v. Dunnigan,* 507 U.S. 87, 113 S.Ct. 1111 (1993). Also see *United States v. Havens,* 446 U.S. 620, at 626, 100 S.Ct. 1912, at 1918 (1980).

15. *Stanford v. Texas,* 379 U.S. 476, 85 S.Ct 506 (1965).

2

Important Aspects of the American Criminal Justice System

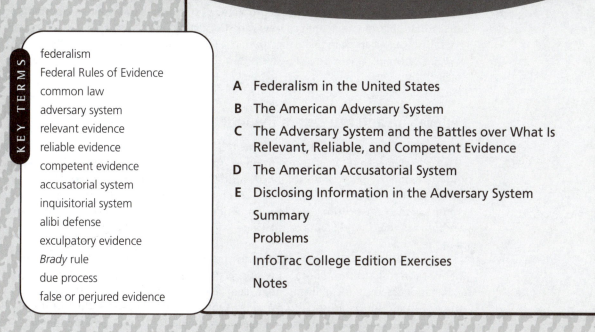

Ⓐ FEDERALISM IN THE UNITED STATES

The United States uses a form of government called **federalism,** which was created at the 1787 Constitutional Convention in Philadelphia. The people of the original thirteen states thought of themselves as being primarily citizens of their state. They knew the political and civic leaders of their local community but knew little of the leaders of the proposed national government because telephones, radio, and motor vehicles did not exist. But a strong central government was needed to provide for national defense, to create a national currency and central banking system, to establish a postal system, to regulate trade with foreign nations, and to establish a taxing system to pay the expenses of the new national government.

The United States was the first country in the world to use a federal form of government.[1] Under a federal system, the central government has the power and authority to handle national problems, whereas the states have the power to regulate local needs and problems. Federalism allows for diversity and flexibility at state and local levels of government. The needs and problems of states such as Maine or Colorado differ from those of states such as New York, California, or Illinois. Under American federalism, states are responsible for public safety and can enact laws that they believe are most effective in providing for public order and an efficient, effective criminal justice system.

Federalism and the Law of Evidence

The keystone of American federalism is the U.S. Constitution. ARTICLE VI of the Constitution provides that "This Constitution . . . shall be the supreme Law of the Land; and the Judges in every State shall be bound thereby. . . ." The powers of the U.S. Congress, the president, and the U.S. Supreme Court are limited to those powers granted in the Constitution. The Tenth Amendment provides that "The powers not delegated to the United States by the Constitution . . . are reserved to the States . . . or to the people."

Each state is sovereign, and the officials of each state have the powers granted to them by the constitution of that state. Each state has its own criminal codes, and each has enacted a code of criminal procedure and evidence. These codes and the rulings of state courts must conform to the requirements of the U.S. Constitution. However, state laws and state court rulings may provide additional rights to the people of the state and to criminal defendants within that state, beyond those extended by the Constitution.

In 1975 Congress enacted the **Federal Rules of Evidence** (Appendix B). Since that time, most states have adopted rules of evidence almost identical to the Federal Rules, with local modifications. However, each state retains the power to interpret and modify those rules of evidence. Thus, the meaning and application of the Federal Rules of Evidence can vary between federal courts and state courts and between the states.

The Federal Rules of Evidence and most state rules of evidence apply in both civil and criminal trials. However, some rules or parts of rules may apply differently in criminal cases.[2]

State and Federal Jurisdiction over Crimes in the United States

The great majority of crimes committed in the United States are violations of state criminal codes. Some crimes are federal offenses in violation of the Federal Criminal Code. A small percentage of criminal offenses are violations of both the Federal Criminal Code and a state criminal code.

Because each state is sovereign and has the power and authority granted to it by its people, it may enforce its criminal laws against anyone who violates them.[3] The federal government is also sovereign, having the power and authority to enforce violations of federal law.

The U.S. Constitution does not grant to the federal government a general police power, nor has there ever been federal criminal common law. All federal crimes therefore have to be statutory crimes enacted by Congress.[4] States have general police power to regulate in providing for domestic tranquility. Common law, both civil and criminal, has always been part of the legal systems of the states. **Common law** refers to the rules developed over years by courts and judges. It is sometimes called unwritten law. Common-law crimes and common-law rules of evidence were used for years during the early history of the United States. Today, criminal codes and rules of evidence are enacted by state legislatures and are found in the codified laws of each state.

To enact federal criminal law, the U.S. Congress must act within the powers granted to it by the U.S. Constitution. Criminal laws may be enacted by the federal government in the following areas:

1. To protect itself, its officials and employees, its property, and the administration of its authorized functions
2. To regulate interstate and foreign commerce
3. To protect civil rights
4. To enact criminal laws for places beyond the jurisdiction of any state, such as the District of Columbia, federal territories, and federal enclaves such as military bases and national parks

Law Enforcement in the American Federal System

There are over sixteen thousand law enforcement agencies in the United States. Most of these are at the local levels of government (cities, counties, towns, and so on). All fifty states have law enforcement agencies working at the state level of government. At the federal level are the federal law enforcement agencies created by Congress to enforce specific federal laws.

Local law enforcement agencies such as police and sheriff departments enforce city and county ordinances in addition to the criminal laws of their state. They bring their cases to city attorneys and state attorneys (district attorneys) for charging and prosecution. Municipal police officers often spend more time in municipal courts on ordinance violations than they spend in state courts appearing in criminal cases. State rules of evidence are used in both municipal and state courts.

Law enforcement agencies working at the state level of government are generally created by state law to enforce state criminal laws or to enforce hunting, fishing,

Estimates of Reported Crimes in the United States

In 2001, the National Crime Victimization Survey (NCVS) reported that 24.2 million violent and felon property crimes were known to the over 16,000 law enforcement agencies in the United States. This figure does not include misdemeanors and offenses charged as ordinance violations throughout the United States. Estimates as to the sources and percentages of crime reporting are:

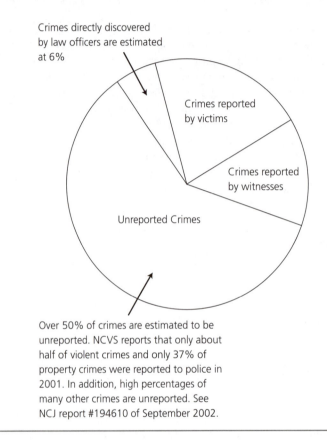

Crimes directly discovered by law officers are estimated at 6%

Crimes reported by victims

Crimes reported by witnesses

Unreported Crimes

Over 50% of crimes are estimated to be unreported. NCVS reports that only about half of violent crimes and only 37% of property crimes were reported to police in 2001. In addition, high percentages of many other crimes are unreported. See NCJ report #194610 of September 2002.

health, sanitation, fire, and other state codes. The usual type of state law enforcement officers are state troopers, state traffic patrol, game wardens, and health, sanitation, and fire inspectors.

Federal law enforcement officers work in the many federal law agencies created by the Congress. They enforce specific federal laws assigned to their agencies and take most of their cases to federal prosecutors for trial in the federal court system. Some of the many federal law enforcement agencies are the Federal Bureau of Investigation, Drug Enforcement Agency, Secret Service, U.S. Customs, U.S. Marshals, and Postal Inspectors.

Ⓑ THE AMERICAN ADVERSARY SYSTEM

In the American court system, the function of the criminal trial is to provide a venue for determining the facts upon which the guilt or innocence of the accused is based. The main actors at the trial are the judge, the jury, the prosecutor, and the defense attorney, Each has a well-defined role to play in the trial. In the American **adversary system,** the prosecutor and the defense attorney assume an adversarial role; that is, they do not seek to establish the facts in cooperation with one another, but in opposition. Each adversary has two goals: Each adversary seeks to present the facts most advantageous to their position, and each seeks to prevent and make it difficult for their opponent to do the same.

This system—which "sets the parties fighting," in the words of former U.S. Supreme Court Justice Jackson—gives the adversaries clearly defined roles. The prosecutor, though obligated to "seek justice, not merely to convict," attempts to have the defendant "found guilty beyond a reasonable doubt by a unanimous jury."[5] The defense counsel's duty is "to represent his client (the defendant) zealously within the bounds of the law."[6]

The two adversaries (the prosecutor and the defense lawyer) approach the facts in the case from entirely different perspectives. Each advocate comes to the trial prepared to present evidence and arguments. The trial judge and the jury come to the trial uncommitted. Within the framework of the rules of evidence and the rules of court procedure, witnesses and evidence are presented. Witnesses are cross-examined and evidence is challenged.

The trial judge presides neutrally at the criminal trial and

> has the responsibility for safeguarding both the rights of the accused and the interests of the public in the administration of criminal justice. The adversary nature of the proceedings does not relieve the trial judge of the obligation of raising, on his own initiative, at all appropriate times and in an appropriate manner, matters which may significantly promote a just determination of the trial. The only purpose of a criminal trial is to determine whether the prosecution has established the guilt of the accused as required by law, and the trial judge should not allow the proceedings to be used for any other purpose."[7]

Because a criminal trial "is in the end basically a fact-finding process,"[8] questions of fact must be determined in all contested criminal cases.[9] The Supreme Court stated in the case of *Tehan v. U.S. ex rel. Shott* that "(t)he basic purpose of a trial is the determination of truth."[10] Therefore, after the adversaries have presented all their evidence and made all their motions and arguments, the trier of fact must then make the determination as to whether the government has carried the burden of proving the defendant guilty beyond reasonable doubt.

The *determination of truth* is the function of the jury. But because the jury must determine that truth based only on the often-conflicting versions presented by the adversaries, the system has elaborate rules to control how those versions of the truth are presented. The purpose of the rules of evidence is to ensure that each adversary's version of the truth is put before the jury by relevant, reliable, and competent evidence.

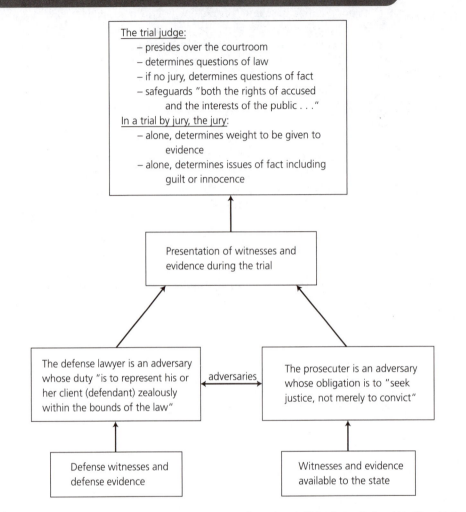

The trial judge:
- presides over the courtroom
- determines questions of law
- if no jury, determines questions of fact
- safeguards "both the rights of accused and the interests of the public . . ."

In a trial by jury, the jury:
- alone, determines weight to be given to evidence
- alone, determines issues of fact including guilt or innocence

Presentation of witnesses and evidence during the trial

The defense lawyer is an adversary whose duty "is to represent his or her client (defendant) zealously within the bounds of the law"

adversaries

The prosecuter is an adversary whose obligation is to "seek justice, not merely to convict"

Defense witnesses and defense evidence

Witnesses and evidence available to the state

[a]In most civil and criminal jury trials, the names and addresses of jurors are available from public records for people with the interest and knowledge of how to go about obtaining them. It does not occur to most people sitting on juror panels that this could be a problem. However, jurors sitting on criminal cases where defendants are potentially dangerous or retaliatory should have some concerns for their families and themselves.

Trial courts can restrict the disclosure of juror information if the court determines that jurors are in need of protection.

Courts have held that factors that could justify restricting jury information could include ". . . but are not limited to: (1) the defendant's involvement in organized crime; (2) the defendant's participation in a group with the capacity to harm jurors; (3) the defendant's past attempts to interfere with the judicial process; and (4) extensive publicity that could enhance the possibility that jurors' names would become public and expose them to intimidation or harassment." *United States v. Darden,* 70 F.3d 1507, 1532 (8th Cir. 1995); *United States v. Ross,* 33 F.3d at 1520.

© THE ADVERSARY SYSTEM AND THE BATTLES OVER WHAT IS RELEVANT, RELIABLE, AND COMPETENT EVIDENCE

Each adversary (prosecution and defense) seeks to present the facts that are most advantageous to their position. Each adversary also seeks to prevent and make it difficult for their opponent to do the same.

The battle over what is relevant, reliable, and competent evidence is often disputed between the parties. To be admissible, evidence must be relevant, reliable, and competent. If evidence is not relevant, or not reliable, or not competent, it is not admissible and cannot be used in a trial.

Relevant Evidence

Relevant evidence is direct or circumstantial evidence[11] that has "any tendency to make the existence of any fact that is of consequence to the determination of the action more probative or less probative than it would be without the evidence."[12] Non-relevant evidence is inadmissible (see Rule 402 in Appendix B).

EXAMPLES:

- To show that the defendant was benefiting from illegal drug operations, evidence that he purchased expensive cars and jewelry and that his assets (net worth) far exceeded his wages from legitimate employment was relevant.[13]

- To show the defendant knew illegal drugs were in his rental truck, evidence that defendant traveled with his wife in prior drug transportations was relevant and admissible. But evidence that defendant's children had been involved in illegal drug operations was held not relevant and not admissible evidence.[14]

- In a charge of sexual assault, evidence that the defendant operates an X-rated movie theater is not relevant because, even if true, the evidence has no logical basis as tending to increase the probability that the defendant did any acts constituting the sexual assault.

- In a charge of transporting stolen property, evidence that the defendant has gambling addiction is not relevant to that charge. Addiction does not logically support the inference that the defendant lacked the ability to refrain from nongambling crimes.[15]

However, under Rule 403 (see Appendix B) relevant evidence may be excluded and held not admissible if the evidence may (1) unfairly prejudice a party, (2) confuse the jury, or (3) waste the court's time. Trial judges are generally given great discretion in striking the balance between the evidence's probative value and its likely prejudicial or confusing potential.

EXAMPLES:

- In child pornography prosecutions, photographs of the child pornography are highly probative and outweigh prejudicial effects on the jury that views such photographs.[16]

- If the admissible child pornography pictures that were the basis of the criminal charge did not show violent and gruesome sexual practices, then sexually explicit narratives in the defendant's possession that described the violent and gruesome practices were not admissible because of the prejudicial effect that such narratives had.[17]

- In a prosecution for making false statements on a passport application, evidence of the defendant's marriage to a Japanese citizen were held inadmissible because such evidence was likely to confuse the jury and create sympathy for the defendant, who sought a passport to return to his wife in Japan.[18]

Reliable Evidence

Reliable evidence is evidence that possesses a sufficient degree of believability—that is, a likelihood that the evidence is true and accurate. An adult witness's testimony about what he actually saw or heard is generally reliable. A statement by a witness about what another person said she saw or heard is generally unreliable. (This is the hearsay rule, discussed in detail in Chapters 7 and 8.) Unreliable evidence is inadmissible.

Reliable and admissible evidence is needed to justify charging a person with a crime. The U.S. Supreme Court pointed out in the 1986 case of *Holbrook v. Flynn*[19] that central to the right to a fair trial, guaranteed by the Sixth and Fourteenth Amendments, is the principle that "one accused of a crime is entitled to have his guilt or innocence determined solely on the basis of the evidence introduced at trial, and not on grounds of official suspicion, indictment, continued custody, or other circumstances not adduced as proof at trial."[20]

Each state has authority to commence a criminal prosecution if sufficient evidence is available to justify the criminal charge. The U.S. Supreme Court pointed out that the authority of the states "derive from separate and independent sources of power and authority originally belonging to them before the admission to the Union and preserved to them by the Tenth Amendment."[21]

Each state also "has the power, inherent in any sovereign, independently to determine what shall be an offense against its authority and to punish such offenses, and in doing so each 'is exercising its own sovereignty, not that of the other.'"[22]

Under the American federal system, each state has its own constitution, court system, and other governmental units. States have the principle responsibility of maintaining public order within their boundaries.

Competent Evidence

Competent evidence is a catch-all term that includes relevant, reliable evidence that is not otherwise rendered inadmissible. Relevant, reliable evidence may be incompetent for any of several reasons.

Comparing the U.S. Criminal Justice System with Those of Other Industrial Democracies

The United States

Uses a guilty plea and plea-bargaining system to dispose of the vast majority of criminal cases.

Has 70 percent of the world's lawyers. "Let's ask ourselves: Does America need 70 percent of the world's lawyers?" (Vice-President Dan Quayle to the American Bar Association in 1991)

Uses a system of political appointment or election of judges.

Places a great amount of discretion and responsibility in the hands of public prosecutors. (The American prosecutor is unique in the world and is not part of the system that came to the United States from the old English common law system.)

Has created rules that make it more difficult to obtain confessions and admissions to use as evidence.

Has adopted the American exclusionary rule.

Has probably the longest jury selections and the longest trials in the world. See the book *Helter Skelter* of the California Manson trial that went on for nine months with a sequestered jury that could not go home.

Has the highest crime rate and highest illegal drug use of the industrial democracies, which places very heavy loads on the criminal justice system. Over 2 million persons are in American jails and prisons.

Has a growing public dissatisfaction with its legal system. The former President of Harvard, Derek Bok, complained that "there is far too much law for those who can afford it and far too little for those who cannot." Supreme Court Justice Sandra Day O'Connor complained of the decline in professionalism and the "Rambo-style" tactics of some lawyers. The former chairman of the Chrysler Corporation, Lee Iacocca, warned the American Bar Association that civil lawsuits are threatening the competitiveness of American businesses.

Other Industrial Democracies

Do not rely on plea bargaining to the extent that it is used in the United States.

Israel has the next highest number of lawyers; the rest of the world shares the remaining 20–25 percent.

Use career magistrates. Other legal systems are less political and less adversarial generally than the U.S. legal system.

Do not place as much discretion and responsibility in the hands of prosecutors.

Rely more heavily upon obtaining confessions and admissions for use as evidence in criminal trials.

Have not adopted the strict American exclusionary rules; therefore, some evidence that cannot be used in the United States can be used in their criminal trials.

Have criminal trials and jury selection generally done in a much shorter time.

Do not have such high crime rates or as much illegal drug use. Do not use prison as a punishment to the extent that the United States does.

Do not have the problems of too much law, too many lawyers, and not enough justice to the extent that the United States does. Has more public confidence in their police and legal systems.

EXAMPLE: Evidence that a defendant in an armed robbery told the treating physician that the injury occurred during the robbery is inadmissible. Though clearly relevant and reliable, the communication between patient and treating physician is privileged.[23]

EXAMPLE: Evidence seized in violation of the Fourth Amendment's probable cause requirement, though relevant and reliable, is inadmissible under the amendment's exclusionary rule.[24]

The rules of evidence discussed in the balance of this text are thus designed as complements to the adversary system. Though the system encourages the prosecutor and the defense attorney to "fight it out," it limits the tactics in that fight by rules of evidence. By doing so, the jury will see and hear only that evidence that properly should influence its deliberations.

Ⓓ THE AMERICAN ACCUSATORIAL SYSTEM

The United States and most of the English-speaking democracies in the world use the **accusatorial system** in criminal investigations and in criminal trials. The U.S. Supreme Court stated in the case of *Rogers v. Richmond* that

> ours is an accusatorial and not an inquisitorial system—a system in which the State must establish guilt by evidence independently and freely secured and may not by coercion prove its charge against an accused out of his own mouth.[25]

Under the accusatorial system, suspects and defendants have an absolute right to remain silent about matters that could incriminate them. If a defendant chooses to remain silent, the state must carry the burden of proving guilt beyond a reasonable doubt—using evidence obtained elsewhere in a manner that did not violate the rights of the suspect.

Most European countries and other democracies of the world do not use the accusatorial system but use instead a system called the inquisitorial system. Under the **inquisitorial system,** defendants do not have an absolute right to remain silent. In some European countries, special judges become responsible for the investigation of serious crimes and question witnesses and suspects.

While countries using the inquisitorial system rely more heavily on the obtaining of confessions in the solving of crimes, the U.S. Supreme Court expressed a different philosophy in the 1964 case of *Escobedo v. Illinois*[26] and the 1966 case of *Miranda v. Arizona.*[27]

Some of the ways that the American criminal justice system differs from the criminal justice systems of other industrial democracies are pointed out in the boxed material on page 25.

Ⓔ DISCLOSING INFORMATION IN THE ADVERSARY SYSTEM

When a criminal charge has been made (see Chapter 3 for a discussion of the charging process), the prosecution and the defense begin separate investigations of the facts.

As adversaries, neither the prosecution nor the defense is inclined to share information with the other side.

However, the U.S. Supreme Court has placed limits on this unwillingness to share:

> The adversary system of trial is hardly an end in itself, it is not yet a poker game in which players enjoy an absolute right always to conceal their cards until played.[28]

Many of the rules compelling disclosure apply to the prosecution, but some compel a defendant to disclose information to the prosecution.

Notice of Alibi Statutes

In using the **alibi defense,** a defendant is alleging that he or she physically could not have committed the crime that is charged because the defendant was at another place at the time the crime was committed.

> **EXAMPLE:** X is charged with robbery of a liquor store and has been identified by two witnesses and an employee of the store as the man who robbed the store. X uses the defense of alibi and states that at the time of robbery, he was at his mother's home 100 miles away. X's wife and mother corroborate X's story, stating that they were with X at the time of the robbery.

Because an alibi can be easily fabricated, it must be carefully investigated. Probably all states have notice of alibi statutes that require defendants who plan to use an alibi defense to serve notice on the prosecutor before trial. These statutes are meant to safeguard against the wrongful use of alibis and give law enforcement agencies and prosecutors necessary notice and time to investigate the merits of the proposed alibi.

Notice of alibi statutes require a defendant to disclose the place where the defendant claims to have been at the time the crime was committed and the names and addresses of witnesses to the alibi, if known. In the 1973 case of *Wardius v. Oregon,* the U.S. Supreme Court held that if a defendant is compelled to disclose information, the state must also make similar disclosures so that discovery is a "two-way street." The Court held in the *Wardius* case that:

> [In] the absence of a strong showing of state interests to the contrary, discovery must be a two-way street. The State may not insist that trials be run as a "search for truth" so far as defense witnesses are concerned, while maintaining "poker game" secrecy for its own witnesses. It is fundamentally unfair to require a defendant to divulge the details of his own case while at the same time subjecting him to the hazard of surprise concerning refutation of the very pieces of evidence which he disclosed to the State.[29]

The Duty to Disclose Evidence Tending to Show the Innocence of an Accused (The *Brady* Rule)

Exculpatory evidence is evidence that tends to show innocence. The following cases establish the well-recognized rule that a prosecutor has a duty to disclose evidence favorable to an accused upon request, where the evidence is material to guilt or innocence.

Where such evidence is in the exclusive possession of the prosecution, it must be disclosed even when there is no request for disclosure by the defense if such evidence is "clearly supportive of a claim of innocence."[30] For discovery purposes, it has been held that law enforcement officers are part of the prosecution and also have a duty of disclosure.

Brady v. Maryland
United States Supreme Court, 373 U.S. 83, 83 S. Ct. 1194 (1963)

The defendant testified that he participated in the robbery charged but stated that his accomplice had killed the victim. Despite a request for exculpatory evidence from the defense lawyer, the prosecutor withheld a statement by the accomplice admitting the killing but claiming that the defendant had wanted to strangle the victim, whereas the accomplice had wanted to shoot him. After the defendant was sentenced to death by a jury, the case was remanded for retrial on the question of punishment, but not on the question of guilt. The Supreme Court quoted the Maryland Court of Appeals as saying that there was "considerable doubt" about how much good the undisclosed statement would have done the defendant, but that it was "too dogmatic" to say that the jury would not have attached "any significance" to the evidence. The Court held that

> the suppression by the prosecution of evidence favorable to an accused upon request violates due process where the evidence is material either to guilt or to punishment, irrespective of the good faith or bad faith of the prosecution.

Since the 1963 *Brady* case, all states have enacted statutes providing for the discovery of information and evidence by defense lawyers. Although an accused does not have a right to all information available to the prosecutor, he does have the right to information as provided by the statutes of the state and to information required under the **Brady rule.**

Lost, Misplaced, and Destroyed Evidence

Hundreds of thousands of criminal cases are handled every year by thousands of law officers. Sometimes evidence is lost, misplaced, or accidentally destroyed. In investigating a violent crime, an item of clothing or other potential evidence can be overlooked in the concern to render medical assistance to the victim or to apprehend the offender. These problems have occurred over the years and raise the question of the government's duty to collect and preserve evidence that might assist a defense lawyer in defending a client.

In the 1984 case of *California v. Trombetta*[31] and the 1988 case of *Arizona v. Youngblood*[32] the U.S. Supreme Court established rules concerning the government's duty to preserve evidence. In the *Trombetta* case, California law officers followed routine procedure in not saving the breath samples of persons charged with driving while intoxicated, where the chances were very low that the samples would have helped defense lawyers. In the *Youngblood* case, Arizona law officers did not properly refrigerate evidence of a sexual assault. The Supreme Court held that a violation of **due process** has not occurred unless the following is shown:

1. Bad faith on the part of the police or other law enforcement official: The Court held that "unless a criminal defendant can show bad faith on the part of the police, failure to preserve potentially useful evidence does not constitute a denial of due process of law."[33]

2. The evidence also would be of likely significance to the defendant's defense: The Court held that "[the] evidence must both possess an exculpatory value that was apparent before the evidence was destroyed, and be of such a nature that the defendant would be unable to obtain comparable evidence by other reasonably available means."[34]

In both the *Trombetta* and the *Youngblood* cases, the Supreme Court held that there was no bad faith on the part of the law officers and that both convictions were based on other strong, credible evidence.

Following are examples of cases where police negligently lost or destroyed evidence.

- *U.S. v. Dougherty:*[35] The police negligently destroyed most of the seven hundred seized marijuana plants in a case where the accused was charged with possession of one hundred plants.

- *Commonwealth v. Phoenix:*[36] Fingerprints were destroyed in an attempt to raise other latent prints; the defendant had photographs taken before the accident and was not prejudiced.

- *State v. Cain:*[37] The tape recording of the victim's 911 telephone call was destroyed; the court ordered all 911 tapes in Connecticut maintained for a period of one year.

- *Louissaint v. State:*[38] Cocaine seized from the defendant was negligently lost; the defendant had to be charged with attempted trafficking in cocaine, where it is not necessary to prove that the substance involved was actually cocaine.

- *People v. Stallings:*[39] In a murder trial nine years after the killing, it was disclosed that tissue samples taken during the autopsy nine years earlier were accidentally destroyed.

- *State v. Reynolds:*[40] The tape of the police radio broadcast by which the arresting officer learned of the crime and received a description of the suspect was destroyed.

If a *Brady* violation occurs, the penalty will be more severe and will probably lead to a new trial or to complete dismissal of the criminal charges. A *Brady* violation occurred in *Ouimette v. Moran,*[41] where a state prosecutor's chief witness had an extensive criminal record and the state failed to disclose that record, which the defense lawyer needed for cross-examination. A new trial was ordered. A new trial was also ordered where, because of the improper handling of a murder weapon, blood and fingerprint evidence was lost.[42]

Other lesser penalties could include forbidding the state to use some of its evidence, a warning in court, or filing a complaint with the employer of the person causing the problem.

The following is the summary of the *Brady* rule presented by the National Institute of Justice in the May 2002 publication (#NCJ 191717):

- Under the *Brady* rule, the state is required to turn over any and all exculpatory evidence to the defense.

- In most states, "missing" evidence or failure to turn over evidence violates the *Brady* rule only if it is found to have been done in bad faith, which requires a showing that: (a) it was known that the evidence was exculpatory, (b) it was intentionally withheld.

- Potentially useful but not conclusively exculpatory information does not necessary need to be turned over.

- To prevail on a *Brady* claim, the defendant must prove a conscious effort to suppress exculpatory evidence.

Law enforcement officers are part of the prosecution and have a duty of disclosure as does the prosecutor.

Use of False or Perjured Evidence

The deliberate use of **false** or **perjured evidence** in an attempt to obtain a criminal conviction is a crime in itself. Such conduct could also be the basis for a civil lawsuit in which large compensatory and punitive damages could be awarded. The following Supreme Court cases illustrate misconduct by prosecutors.

Mooney v. Holohan
United States Supreme Court, **294 U.S. 103, 55 S.Ct. 340 (1935)**

The Supreme Court made it very clear that a conviction obtained by the knowing use of false testimony or false evidence is a denial of due process of law and will be reversed. The Court held that

> if a state has contrived a conviction through the pretense of a trial which in truth is but used as a means of depriving a defendant of liberty through a deliberate deception of court and jury by the presentation of testimony known to be perjured. Such a contrivance by a state to procure the conviction and imprisonment of a defendant is as inconsistent with the rudimentary demands of justice as is the obtaining of a like result by intimidation.

Miller v. Pate
Unites States Supreme Court, **386 U.S. 1, 87 S.Ct. 785 (1967)**

The Supreme Court reversed and remanded the defendant's murder and rape conviction. The prosecutor referred to and exhibited to the jury a pair of "blood-stained shorts" that were an important link in the chain of the circumstantial evidence case against the defendant. The prosecutor knew but did not tell the jury or defense lawyer that the reddish-brown stains on the shorts were not blood, but paint. The Court held that the prosecution "deliberately misrepresented the truth" and that

> More than 30 years ago this Court held that the Fourteenth Amendment cannot tolerate a state criminal conviction obtained by the knowing use of false evidence . . . . There has been no deviation from that established principle. . . . There can be no retreat from that principle here.

SUMMARY

The United States, Canada, and Mexico use the federal system of government because they are large countries made up of people from different cultures. Most European countries use a unitarian form of government.

The United States uses an adversary system where the prosecutor and the defense attorney present facts (evidence) that are most advantageous to their position. Each of the parties seeks to prevent and make it difficult for the other to do the same. Under the adversary system, there is almost a constant fight over what is relevant, reliable, and competent evidence.

The United States uses an accusatorial system under which there is an absolute right to remain silent if accused of a crime. Most European countries use inquisitorial systems where there is not a total right to remain silent.

Federal and state governments have disclosure statutes where parties to a criminal or civil proceeding are required to disclose information to the other party. Prosecutors (including law officers) must disclose exculpatory evidence, and defense lawyers must give notice if they are going to use an alibi defense.

PROBLEMS

AVAILABLE ANSWERS

a. An accusatorial system

b. An inquisitorial system

c. A totalitarian system

d. All of the above are correct

e. None of the above are correct

1. The United States uses

2. Most European countries use

3. Defendants charged with a crime have an absolute right to remain silent under

4. Under this system, defendants charged with crimes do not have an absolute right to remain silent.

5. Under this system, more confessions are obtained and used as evidence.

6. Under this system, confessions and incriminating statements cannot be used as evidence.

AVAILABLE ANSWERS

a. Relevant evidence

b. Reliable evidence

c. Competent evidence

d. All of the above

e. None of the above

7. To be admissible, evidence must be

8. Most hearsay is not admissible because

9. Testimony that the defendant's son has a long criminal record is not admissible because

10. Evidence obtained by a police burglary of the defendant's home is not admissible because

11. A voluntary confession is not ordinarily admissible because

12. An eyewitness who saw X commit the armed robbery he or she is charged with cannot testify as to what the witness saw because

13. Testimony of a defendant's wife as to a confession to the crime charged is not admissible because

INFOTRAC COLLEGE EDITION EXERCISES

1. Go to InfoTrac College Edition and using the subject search term "federalism" and the subdivision "history" find the 1990 article "Pre-emption: The Dramatic Rise of Federal Supremacy" in the March 1990 *Journal of State Government.* In a federal system of government such as ours, conflicts may develop between state and federal laws. For the system to work, federal law must preempt state law in proper situations. Just what those situations are is the subject of this article.

2. Go to InfoTrac College Edition and using the subject search term "accusatorial system" find the article in the 1997 *Journal of Criminal Law and Criminology* on the right to silence in the accusatorial system. The author discusses the pros and cons of the decision by Great Britain to impose a duty to speak in criminal cases, coupled with the right of the prosecution to comment on and the jury to consider the failure of the defendant to testify. Should we do something similar here? Which side are you on?

NOTES

1. Since the invention of federalism over two hundred years ago, other democratic countries have also adopted forms of federalism, including Canada, Mexico, Australia, and the Federal German Republic. Other forms of government used by democratic nations are: (a) The *unitary form*—used by England, France, Ireland, Norway, and other countries—has one center of power (the central government), which creates smaller units, such as cities and provinces, to provide services. Countries using unitary forms of government are generally small in size and population. (b) The *confederate form* of government, which has been used by the Swiss for over seven hundred years, bands together provinces and states in a loose organization called a confederacy. The United States used this form of

government after the American Revolution until 1791. Because it was not working, the Constitutional Convention was convened in Philadelphia in 1787 to draft a new constitution and to invent a workable system of government acceptable to all thirteen states.

2. See, e.g., Federal Rules of Evidence, 201(g); 404(b).

3. In the 1985 case of *Heath v. Alabama,* 474 U.S. 82, 106 S.Ct. 433, the U.S. Supreme Court ruled that under the dual sovereignty doctrine, a defendant who "in a single act violates the 'peace and dignity' of two sovereigns by breaking the laws of each. . . . has committed two distinct 'offenses.'"

In the *Heath* case, the defendant confessed that he hired two men in Georgia to kidnap his pregnant wife from their Alabama home and kill her. After his wife was murdered in Alabama, the defendant (and the men) were convicted of crimes in both Alabama and Georgia. The Supreme Court affirmed the criminal convictions under the dual sovereignty doctrine, holding that "(t)o deny a State its power to enforce its criminal laws because another state has won the race to the courthouse 'would be a shocking. . . . deprivation of the historic right and obligation of the States to maintain peace and order within their confines.'"

Dual sovereignty also applies when criminal acts violate both state and federal laws. The 1993 trial of four Los Angeles police officers for beating Rodney King is an example. When federal prosecutors were not satisfied with the outcome of the California trial (the officer's acquittals resulted in a large-scale riot in Los Angeles), federal criminal indictments were sought under federal law, and the officers were tried again in a federal court for the same conduct. The second trial resulted in the conviction of two of the officers and acquittal of the other two.

Some states, however, have enacted statutes that forbid criminal prosecution for a criminal act (or acts) already prosecuted in another state or in the federal courts. Wisconsin statute 939.71 is an example of such a statute.

4. See the 1812 Supreme Court case *United States v. Hudson and Goodwin,* 11 U.S. (7 Cranch) 32, and the 1949 Supreme Court case *Krulewitch v. United States,* 336 U.S. 440, 69 S.Ct. 16, where Justice Jackson stated, "It is well and wisely settled that there can be no judge-made offense against the United States and that every federal prosecution must be sustained by statutory authority."

5. American Bar Association (ABA) Standards Relating to the Prosecution Function and the Defense Function, 1.1(c).

6. ABA Code EC 7–1.

7. Page 167 of *General Responsibility of the Trial Judge,* ABA Standards Relating to the Administration of Criminal Justice.

8. *Herring v. New York,* 422 U.S. 853, 95 S.Ct. 2550 (1975).

9. Questions of fact are determined by the fact finder. This would be a jury in a jury trial or the trial judge when a case is tried without a jury.

Questions of law are always determined by the trial judge.

10. 382 U.S. 406, 416, 86 S.Ct. 459, 465 (1966).

11. See Chapter 4, p. 56 for definitions of *direct* and *circumstantial.*

12. Federal Rules of Evidence, sec. 401. Evidence, even though relevant, may be excluded under evidentiary rules like Rule 403 of the federal rules if it is unduly prejudicial or may tend to mislead the jury. This is sometimes referred to as the *legally relevant* test.

13. *United States v. Burgos,* 254 F.3d 8 (1st Cir. 2001).

14. *United States v. Espinoza,* 244 F.3d 1234 (10th Cir., 2001).

15. *United States v. Garcia,* 94 F.3d 57 (2d Cir., 1996).

16. *United States v. Becht,* 267 F.3d 767 (8th Cir. 2001).

17. *United States v. Grimes,* 244 F.3d 375 (5th Cir. 2001).

18. *United States v. George,* 266 F.3d 52 (2d Cir. 2001).

19. 475 U.S. 560, 106 S.Ct. 1340.

20. *Taylor v. Kentucky,* 436 U.S. 478, 485 (1978).

21. *Heath v. Alabama,* 474 U.S. 82 (1985).

22. Idem.

23. See Chapter 6 for a discussion of privileged communications.

24. See Chapter 14, p. 258 for a discussion of the Fourth Amendment exclusionary rule.

25. 365 U.S. 534, 540–41, 81 S.Ct. 735, 739–40 (1961).

26. 378 U.S. 478, 84 S.Ct. 1758.

27. 384 U.S. 436, 86 S.Ct. 1602.

28. *Williams v. Florida,* 399 U.S. 78, 90 S.Ct. 1893, 1896 (1970).

29. 93 S. T. 2208 (1973). See also *Williams v. Florida,* 399 U.S. 78 (1970) and *Taylor v. Illinois,* 484 U.S. 400 (1988).

30. 83 S.Ct. 1194.

31. 467 U.S. 479, 104 S.Ct. 2528.

32. 488 U.S. 51, 109 S.Ct. 333.

33. 488 U.S. 58, 109 S.Ct. 337.

34. 467 U.S. 489, 104 S.Ct. 2534.

35. 774 F. Supp. 1181 (W.D. Wis., 1989).

36. 567 N.E.2d 193 (Mass. 1991).

37. 596 A.2d 449 (Conn. 1991).

38. 576 So.2d 316 (Fla. App., 1991).

39. 570 N.E.2d 820 (Ill. App., 1991).

40. 592 A.2d 194 (N.J., 1991).

41. 942 F.2d 1 (1st Cir., 1991).

42. *Sanburn v. State,* 812 P.2d 1279 (Nev., 1991).

3

Using Evidence to Determine Guilt or Innocence

Ⓐ EVALUATION AND REVIEW OF EVIDENCE

The rules of evidence ultimately decide what evidence will be presented to the judge and jury for evaluation and what evidence will not. However, at various stages of the investigatory and criminal court process, evidence may be evaluated in a variety of settings. In many of these settings, the rules of evidence do not apply. Consider a shoplifting case:

1. Store employees or security personnel would ordinarily be the first to evaluate and judge the information and evidence available to them before detaining a person for shoplifting. Probable cause based on firsthand information by a reliable adult employee is the standard required. Store employees are told, "If you did not see it, it did not happen" and "When in doubt, let him go."

2. After a suspect is detained for shoplifting and the police are called, the officer must then evaluate the available evidence before proceeding. If the evidence is insufficient, the suspect should be immediately released.

3. Evaluations made in points 1 and 2 are often reviewed immediately by superiors (store managers and police sergeants).

4. If the case is presented to a prosecutor (a city attorney or a district attorney), the prosecutor reviews the available evidence to determine whether further proceedings are warranted.

5. If a charge or citation is issued, a defense lawyer in many cases will review the evidence, looking for weaknesses in the case. Insufficient or questionable evidence, use of improper procedure, or lack of probable cause based on firsthand information are some of the weaknesses for which a defense lawyer would look.

6. A motion to suppress evidence and dismiss could bring the matter before a judge. To rule on the motion, the judge would have to review the evidence.

7. Should the defense motion be denied, the case could then be tried before a jury, who would evaluate the evidence and determine guilt or innocence.

8. A convicted defendant can appeal the case and argue to an appellate court that the evidence was not sufficient to support a finding or a judgment of guilt. The appellate court would then review the evidence.

The defendant in the 1984 case of *Lee v. State* did not argue insufficient evidence, but in his appeal argued instead that a shoplifter had to leave a store in order to be convicted of larceny (theft). The Maryland Court of Special Appeals, however, affirmed the defendant's conviction, holding that it was not necessary that a state show that a defendant leave a store to be convicted of shoplifting. Stating that they found no court decision holding otherwise, the court held that once "a customer goes beyond the mere removal of goods from the shelf and crosses the threshold into the realm of behavior inconsistent with the owner's expectations, the circumstances may be such that a larcenous intent can be inferred."[1]

In the process of review and evaluation of evidence, weaker cases are filtered out of the system or lesser charges are used. Not all cases go to court and trial. A merchant might recover the stolen merchandise from a shoplifter and, after warning the person, take no further action. A police officer might take a teenaged shoplifter home to his parents. After the parents have been informed of the incident, the matter may be dropped.

Goals of the Criminal Justice System

The most basic function of any government is to provide for the security of the individual and his property [U.S. Supreme Court in *Lanzetta v. New Jersey,* 306 U.S. 451, 455, 59 S.Ct. 618 (1939)].

The generally recognized overall goals of the criminal justice system are

- To discourage and to deter people from committing crimes

- To protect society from dangerous and harmful people
- To punish people who have committed crimes
- To rehabilitate and reform people who have committed crimes

B THE CRIMINAL COURT PROCESS

In this text, we study the rules of evidence as they apply in formal judicial proceedings, principally jury trials. Included here is a short discussion of the criminal court process. In misdemeanor cases, the process typically begins with the filing of a **criminal complaint** with a magistrate or other judicial official. The complaint can come before or after the defendant is placed under arrest. The magistrate determines only if probable cause exists to believe that a crime has been committed and that the named defendant committed it.

Following issuance of the complaint, a warrant could be issued for the defendant's arrest, if he or she is not already in custody. The **initial appearance** before the magistrate is then promptly held. At this appearance, the charges are read to the defendant, a plea is entered, and bail is set.

If a felony is charged, the next step would be the **preliminary hearing** in states that do not use the indictment system. This is a full adversarial hearing where lawyers are present, evidence is heard, and a judge makes the determination whether probable cause exists to believe the defendant committed the crime charged. Although this hearing is more detailed than initial appearance, it is not a full trial. However, at this juncture a judge may dismiss charges if the prosecution's case is weak. If sufficient evidence is introduced to show probable cause, the defendant is bound over for trial.

In many states and in federal courts, the indictment system is used for felonies instead of public prosecutors issuing criminal complaints. A **criminal indictment** is a list of criminal charges issued by a **grand jury,** which has heard evidence presented by the federal attorney or state prosecuting attorney. The grand jury proceedings are held in secret, are not adversarial, and include only evidence presented by the prosecution.

In states that do not use the grand jury system, a criminal case can commence by the filing of an **information,** which is a statement by the prosecution detailing the basis on which it is believed the defendant committed a crime.

After an indictment or information has been issued, the defendant is *arraigned*. At the **arraignment,** the defendant enters a plea, and the case is bound over to the appropriate criminal court for trial.

Purposes of Rules of Evidence

- **Rules of evidence that are designed to be of assistance to the judge or jury in the search for the truth.** Examples of these rules are:

  Rules that exclude and keep evidence out of court:

  Rules requiring that evidence be relevant, reliable, and competent

  The *opinion evidence* rule

  The hearsay rules

  } These rules of evidence assist in the search for the truth by guarding against unreliable evidence that could be prejudicial, misleading, inaccurate, or distracting.

- **Rules that expedite trials and help move trials along without unnecessary delays:**

  Rules concerning *judicial notice* that relieve parties to a trial of proving uncontested facts that are of common knowledge to the community or are available in a reliable text or other publication

  Rules concerning presumptions and inferences that give directions to judges and juries and also determine in criminal and civil trials which of the parties has the burden of proof and the burden of coming forward with evidence

- **Some rules of evidence are not designed to be of assistance in the search for the truth but have other purposes. These rules often actually hinder the search for the truth:**

  Testimony privilege rules that have been created to protect relationships and interests such as husband–wife, attorney–client, and physician–patient. These relationships have been determined to be of sufficient importance so as to justify sacrificing what might be very reliable evidence from being used in criminal and civil trials.

  The rule of the exclusion of evidence (the *exclusionary rule*) that is used to discourage and deter law enforcement officers from improper or illegal conduct or procedure. This form of "policing the police" sometimes prevents very reliable evidence from being used in criminal trials.

During the period between arraignment, or preliminary hearing, and full trial, the defendant my reevaluate the evidence and either change a simple not-guilty plea or begin plea bargaining. Because of the prevalence of such practices, the following section discuss the plea and plea-bargaining process in greater detail.

C PLEAS A DEFENDANT MAY ENTER TO A CRIMINAL CHARGE

After a defendant has been charged with a criminal offense, the defendant and the attorney must evaluate the evidence available to the state to support its criminal charge. Their evaluation of the evidence could determine what defenses they will or will not use and what plea they will enter. The following pleas are available to defendants:

- *Not guilty*
- *Guilty* This may be a regular guilty plea, or an Alford guilty plea in states permitting the Alford plea.
- *An insanity plea (or defense)* The usual insanity plea is not guilty by reason of mental disease or defect. This plea may be joined with a plea of not guilty. If it is not joined with a not-guilty plea, the defendant then admits committing the offense but pleads a lack of mental capacity.

  A jury or a judge may, if the evidence permits, find a defendant guilty but mentally ill under the statutes of eight states.[2] Such a person is not legally insane but at the time of the offense had serious mental or emotional problems. Under this verdict, prison authorities must provide necessary psychiatric or psychological treatment to restore the offender's mental and emotional health in an appropriate treatment setting.
- *No contest (nolo contendere)* This is permitted if the statutes of a state might allow the plea, subject to the approval of the court. A defendant using this plea would seek to avoid admitting guilt in the hope of successfully denying the truth of the charges in a subsequent civil law suit.
- *Standing mute or refusing to enter a plea* This would ordinarily cause the court to direct the entry of a plea of not guilty on behalf of the defendant.

The Not-Guilty Plea

All defendants in criminal cases are presumed innocent until proven guilty through the use of evidence and witnesses presented during a trial. The burden of proof is always on the state or government.

The level of proof required in criminal cases is proof beyond a reasonable doubt. This level of proof is the highest the law requires in any kind of case. It means that the evidence presented during the trial must convince the finder of fact (jury or judge) of the defendant's guilt to a moral certitude. It does not mean that the evidence must show that the defendant is guilty beyond *any* doubt, nor does it require evidence of absolute certainty of the defendant's guilt. The burden on the state is to prove the defendant guilty beyond any *reasonable* doubt.

Because of the constitutional presumption of innocence, the system of justice used in the United States is an accusatorial system. The accuser must bear the entire burden of proving the charge by the use of competent evidence. The defendant does not have to do anything. The burden is on the state to come forward with sufficient evidence to carry the burden of proof beyond reasonable doubt.

The defendant can remain silent and inactive. Or the defendant can appear as a witness on his or her own behalf and may present evidence showing or tending to show his or her innocence. The defense may also very actively attack or seek to hinder and minimize the state's evidence and case by use of motions before, during, or after the trial.

The defendant can deny performing the acts charged or assert an affirmative defense. In an affirmative defense, a defendant in effect admits to performing the acts charged but claims that he or she had a lawful excuse for doing so and thus is not guilty of the crime charged. To assert an affirmative defense, the defendant must come forward with evidence showing a basis for it.

An example of an affirmative defense is the claim of entrapment. Many states require that a defendant using an entrapment defense admit that he or she committed the criminal act or acts. The defense is that law enforcement officers used excessive or improper inducements that caused the defendant to violate the law. Other affirmative defenses include outrageous government conduct, frame-up, and coercion or duress ("I was forced to do it"). (For an explanation of affirmative defenses, see Chapter 7 of Gardner and Anderson, *Criminal Law: Principles and Cases*, 8th ed., Wadsworth Publishing, 2003.)

The Guilty Plea

In the United States, well over 70 percent of the people charged with felonies plead guilty.[3] The U.S. Supreme Court held in the 1969 case of *Boykin v. Alabama* that "[a] plea of guilty is more than a confession which admits that the accused did various acts; it is itself a conviction; nothing remains but to give judgment and determine punishment."[4]

Most of the guilty pleas are entered because defendants realize that the evidence, which the state or government has against them, will result in a conviction. Defendants therefore enter the guilty plea because of the standard practice of rewarding a defendant who acknowledges guilt in open court with a lighter sentence.[5]

The U.S. Supreme Court has held that the foundations of a valid guilty plea are the defendant's voluntary admission in open court that he committed the acts charged and the defendant's knowing consent to the judgment of guilt without a trial. Because the defendant stands before the court as a witness against himself in entering a guilty plea, the admission of guilt cannot be compelled but must be a voluntary expression of his own choice. And because a defendant's consent to judgment without trial constitutes a waiver of the constitutional rights attending a trial, his consent must be made with knowledge of the waiver of those rights.[6]

It must be shown that a defendant entered a guilty plea voluntarily and intelligently.[7] The trial judge must be convinced by the evidence presented that the defendant did in fact commit the criminal act of which she is charged. There is no constitutional right to plead guilty, but a state may create a statutory right to do so.[8]

In *Boykin v. Alabama*,[9] the Court held that the following rights are waived by a guilty plea.

> Several federal constitutional rights are involved in a waiver that takes place when a plea of guilty is entered in a state criminal trial. First, is the privilege against compulsory self-incrimination guaranteed by the Fifth Amendment and applicable to the States by reason of the Fourteenth. . . .
>
> Second, is the right to trial by jury. . . .
>
> Third, is the right to confront one's accusers. . . .
>
> We cannot presume a waiver of these three important federal rights from a silent record.

THE ALFORD GUILTY PLEA In the case of *North Carolina v. Alford*, the U.S. Supreme Court held that a defendant "may voluntarily, knowingly, and understandingly consent to the imposition of a prison sentence even if he is unwilling or unable to admit his participation in the acts constituting the crime."[10] The **Alford guilty plea** permits a defendant to enter a guilty plea while at the same time protesting his innocence. The Alford plea is not mandatory for states, but most states have adopted it. State judges, however, are generally not obligated to accept an Alford plea. Most judges do accept it because the sentence given would be the same as that given for a regular guilty plea under the state sentencing guidelines.

Most state courts hold that an Alford plea is the "functional equivalent" of a regular plea of guilty.[11] Therefore, defendants who enter a guilty plea, whether an Alford plea or regular guilty plea, have lost almost all rights to appeal. Most courts hold that the only issues applicable are the voluntary and intelligent nature of the plea and the jurisdiction of the court.

Defendants seek to use an Alford plea when they want to avoid the greater sentence they generally face if they take their case to trial and lose. In the 1991 case of *State v. Hansen*,[12] the defendant entered an Alford plea to a second-degree murder charge of killing her husband during one of their many domestic disputes. She acknowledged that there was sufficient evidence to convict her but denied she intended to kill her husband. At the sentencing hearing, she sought to withdraw her Alford plea. The judge refused her motion to withdraw her plea and sentenced her to fifteen years in prison. On appeal, the sentence was affirmed.

The No Contest, or Nolo Contendere, Plea

Most (if not all) states also have statutes permitting the **no contest,** or **nolo contendere, plea.** In most states, as in the federal court system, the plea may be made only with the consent of the trial judge. Some states limit the plea to misdemeanor and ordinance violations.

The no contest plea has been called a troublesome legal creature. In 1974 the advisory committee writing a proposed code of federal criminal procedure noted that the "defendant who asserts his innocence while pleading guilty or nolo contendere is often difficult to deal with in a correctional setting."[13]

In the 1991 case of *State v. Smith*,[14] the defendant elected not to contest the state's case against him and entered a plea of nolo contendere. The Utah Court of Appeals found that the defendant's failure to admit his guilt "also prevented rehabilitative efforts [while he was on probation] and ultimately resulted in his incarceration." The trial judge stated that this is "the first and last no contest plea . . . that . . . I will receive."

Conditional Guilty Plea

Defendants do not have a constitutional right to plead guilty and may be forced to go to trial. But because forcing a defendant to stand trial rarely serves a useful purpose, all states have statutes and case law setting the procedure for accepting guilty pleas. Nor does a criminal defendant "have an absolute right under the Constitution to have his guilty plea accepted by the court."[15] Trial judges have the discretion under the laws of all states to refuse to accept a plea of guilty.

Defendants who enter a guilty plea in any form to a criminal charge lose most of their right to appeal. The U.S. Supreme Court ruled in 1973 that "[w]hen a criminal defendant has solemnly admitted in open court that he is in fact guilty of the offense

The majority of criminal cases coming before courts in the United States end with the defendant entering a guilty plea in open court. All states and the federal government have a number of different forms of guilty pleas. Different types of guilty pleas are the following:

- The *regular guilty plea* is made in open court upon a showing that the defendant did in fact commit the criminal act or acts with which he or she is charged and upon a showing that the defendant voluntarily and intelligently is entering the guilty plea and waiving the right to a trial.

    In this guilty plea and all other guilty pleas, the defendant is subject to the statutory penalties of the state. However, it is a common practice in the United States to reward the defendant entering a guilty plea with a lesser sentence under the sentencing guidelines and practices of the state.

- The *Alford plea* permits a defendant to enter a guilty plea without admitting guilt.

- The *no contest,* or *nolo contendere, plea* allows defendants not to contest the criminal charge or charges against them. Defendants who believe they will be sued in a civil court for their criminal conduct sometimes seek to use this plea.

- The *conditional guilty plea* is used when a defendant seeks to preserve the right to appeal a ruling of the trial judge. A defendant entering any of the other guilty pleas loses practically all rights to appeal many aspects of the case.

with which he is charged, he may not thereafter raise independent claims relating to the deprivation of constitutional rights that occurred prior to the entry of the guilty plea."[16]

To preserve the right to appeal on any issue before a trial court, defense lawyers sometimes use the conditional guilty plea. This might be done, for example, after the defense has failed in a motion to suppress evidence, after an attack on the validity of a search warrant, or following a defense attack on the validity of an arrest. The defendant can enter a guilty plea conditioned upon the defendant's right to appeal the trial judge's ruling.

The Insanity Plea

The plea of not guilty because of mental disease or defect (the insanity plea) is found in the criminal codes of most states. Three states (Idaho, Utah, and Montana) are reported to have abolished the insanity defense. If an insanity plea were entered in a minor criminal matter, the state might agree and join the defendant in requesting the court to find the defendant legally insane. The defendant would very likely then be held for mental observations and treatment for a much longer period than would have been the case had he been convicted of the crime charged.

For these reasons, the insanity plea is used by defendants primarily in murder cases, for which sentences are severe. In using the insanity defense, most defendants also enter a not-guilty plea. The trial would then be bifurcated, with the first part of the trial determining guilt or innocence of the charge and the second part determining whether the defendant was legally insane when the criminal act was committed.

Because there is a legal inference that all people are sane and normal, most states place the burden on a defendant using the insanity plea to come forward with evidence showing that he or she was so mentally diseased or defective that he or she was unable to formulate the mental intent to commit the crime charged.

In 1981 John Hinckley, Jr., was charged with attempting to kill President Reagan. In a wild shooting spree in Washington, D.C., Hinckley seriously wounded the president and three others. At the time of the Hinckley trial, federal courts required the government to carry the burden of proving that the defendant was sane and normal. The government could not produce evidence showing that Hinckley was sane and normal, and therefore under the rule used then, Hinckley was found not guilty because of insanity.

In 1984 Congress passed legislation providing that the federal courts rejoin most of the state courts in requiring defendants using the insanity plea to prove by clear and convincing evidence that the defendant was insane at the time of the crime. Studies show that the success rate by defense lawyers in using the defense of insanity is very low.

Ⓓ PLEA BARGAINING OR SENTENCE BARGAINING

Multiple criminal charges are often issued in criminal or ordinance violations. Defendants who agree to plead guilty in return for the dropping of one or more of the charges are **plea bargaining.** In plea bargains, defendants sometimes agree to help law officers or to appear as a witness in return for concessions from the government.

Sentence bargains are agreements on the sentence a defendant will receive. All sentence or plea bargains are subject to the approval of the trial judge, who may refuse to accept them if the judge concludes the plea agreement is not in the best interests of the public.

In 1967 the President's Commission on Law Enforcement and Administration of Justice stated that "[w]hen a decision is made to prosecute, it is estimated that in many courts as many as 90 percent of all convictions are obtained by guilty pleas."[17]

In appraising the amount and quality of the evidence against a client, the American defense lawyer often turns to plea bargaining if the government has a strong case. The defense lawyer usually informs the client that there is a strong likelihood of conviction and advises "copping a plea."

However, not all guilty pleas are plea-bargained. Many guilty pleas are entered every day in American courts without any assurance from a prosecutor concerning the penalty. Plea bargaining, or sentence bargaining, implies a situation in which a defendant receives (or is assured of) a consideration in return for a guilty plea. Considerations that could cause a defendant to plead guilty are

- Receiving an agreed-upon sentence or penalty instead of running the risk of a more severe sentence.

- Reaching an agreement in a case having multiple charges to drop one or more of the charges, which in most situations are then "read into the record" in court for sentencing consideration.[18]

- Permitting a defendant to plead guilty to a lesser charge.
- Recommending to the court that the defendant receive probation or a suspended sentence.
- Agreement by the prosecutor to drop charges against another person.
- Reducing charges or dropping charges when the defendant agrees to testify as a state's witness (such as a burglar turning state's evidence against a "fence").
- Reducing charges or receiving probation or a suspended sentence when the defendant agrees to compensate the victim for damages or injuries that occurred.
- Receiving probation or a suspended sentence when the defendant agrees to undergo psychiatric, drug, or alcohol treatment when the criminal conduct was caused by any of these conditions. (In some of these situations, the defendant agrees to commit himself to an institution for such treatment.)

Prosecutors list the following reasons why plea bargaining, negotiated pleas, and sentence pleading have become a standard practice in most American communities:

- It clears the court calendar of that case with a rapid trial and punishment.
- Defendants participate and admit their guilt to the charges to which they plead guilty.
- The practice eliminates many appeals.
- The practice provides a certainty of adjudication.
- A guilty plea could be the first step toward genuine rehabilitation.

The President's Commission commented in the 1967 report entitled "The Challenge of Crime in a Free Society":

> Many overburdened courts have come to rely upon these informal procedures to deal with overpowering caseloads, and some cases that are dropped might have been prosecuted had sufficient resources been available. But it would be an oversimplification to tie the use of early disposition solely to the problem of volume, for some courts appear to be able to deal with their workloads without recourse to such procedures. . . .

The main dangers in the present system of nontrial dispositions lie in the fact that it is so informal and invisible that it gives rise to fears that it does not operate fairly or that it does not accurately identify those who should be prosecuted and what disposition should be made in their cases. Often important decisions are made without adequate information, without sound policy guidance or rules, and without basic procedural protections for the defendant, such as counsel or judicial consideration of the issues. Because these dispositions are reached at an early stage, often little factual material is available about the offense, the offender, and the treatment alternatives. No record reveals the participants, their positions, or the reason for or facts underlying the disposition. When the disposition involves dismissal of filed charges or the entry of a guilty plea, it is likely to reach court, but only the end product is visible and that view often is misleading. There are disturbing opportunities for coercion and overreaching, as well as for undue leniency. The very informality and flexibility of the procedures are sources both of potential usefulness and of abuse.

Fast Track Trials and Fast Track Plea Bargains

For years, many states and the federal government have had policies of putting criminal trials that have high public concern on a "fast track." Defendants in these cases must then prepare for an early trial or have the choice of "fast tracking" plea bargaining.

Conferences between defense lawyers and prosecutors are held to accelerate cases that can be settled through plea or sentence agreements. In such a conference, federal prosecutors in California included an additional requirement in a criminal proceeding against Defendant Ruiz. Ruiz had to waive his right to receive impeachment information relating to any informant witness or other prosecution witnesses, and also possible evidence that could have helped Ruiz establish an affirmative defense. Prosecutors were obligated to provide Ruiz with any exculpatory evidence (tending to prove innocence) as required under the *Brady* rule.

Ruiz refused the fast track plea agreement that was offered to him. The government then withdrew the offer and indicted Ruiz. Despite the absence of an agreement, Ruiz pleaded guilty, and at the sentencing hearing asked for the reduced sentence offered in the plea agreement. The trial court refused and sentenced Ruiz to the maximum penalty permitted.

On appeal, the Federal Court of Appeals held that the fast track plea agreement was unconstitutional because it required a defendant to waive the right to receive impeachment and affirmative defense information. In the case of *United States v. Ruiz,* 122 S. Ct. 2450 (2002), the U.S. Supreme Court reversed and held that a guilty plea can be voluntary even if the defendant is not aware of all the information known to the prosecution. However, exculpatory information must be disclosed under the *Brady* rule, but the prosecution need not disclose impeachment and affirmative defense information.

Debates about plea bargaining have been going on for years. The practice was denounced as early as 1875.[19] However, over the years, plea negotiation has continued. Some states have enacted statutes regulating the practice of plea bargaining.

AN OFFER TO PLEAD GUILTY CANNOT BE USED AS EVIDENCE IF THE OFFER IS LATER WITHDRAWN

Both public policy and the judicial system encourage voluntary, intelligent guilty pleas. By admitting guilt in open court, the defendant acknowledges the wrongful conduct, which is the first step in rehabilitation. Guilty pleas also help keep court calendars current.

To encourage guilty pleas, the federal government and many states have statutes such as Rule 410 of the Federal Rules of Evidence and Rule 11 (6) of the Federal Rules of Criminal Procedure that forbid the use of any of the following as evidence:

> evidence of a plea of guilty, later withdrawn, or a plea of nolo contendere, or of an offer to plead guilty or nolo contendere to the crime charged or any

Use of Evidence at a Bail Hearing

The purpose of bail is to assure the defendant's appearance at trial. Bail hearings can become hotly contested—angry confrontations with defense lawyers arguing that high bail punishes a defendant and that defendants can only be punished after trial and conviction.

Another argument of defense lawyers is that high bail amounts to preventive detention. This could trigger arguments about higher court rulings in that state concerning the use of high bail to protect witnesses who might be easily intimidated.

In asking for high bail, prosecutors will generally stress the seriousness of the crime, the viciousness of the criminal act, and the strength of the evidence against the defendant. Because the likelihood of flight by a defendant goes up with the probability of a long prison term, very high bail is often set in murder and other violent crime cases.

Prosecutors will present the past criminal record of the defendant that is not admissible evidence during a trial but is admissible evidence during both bail hearings and sentencing hearings. Defense lawyers must be provided prior to the bail hearing with the defendant's known criminal record (or lack of criminal record).

Evidence of roots in the community could be argued by both sides with evidence as to whether the defendant has a family, close relatives, a good job, owns a home, and his or her age and marital status.

The Eighth Amendment of the U.S. Constitution states that "Excessive bail shall not be required . . ." Therefore, either the defense or the prosecutor could immediately appeal a bail ruling by a lower court and present arguments to a higher court seeking a different bail ruling.

---

other crime, or of statements made in connection with any of the foregoing pleas or offers.

States with similar statutes also prohibit use of such evidence, as the following cases illustrate:

- After a sex crime had occurred, Muniz (the defendant) offered to pay some of the victim's medical expenses. The state of California then charged Muniz with the sex crime. As Muniz's statements were not part of an offer to plead guilty, his statements were held to be admissible as an admission against interest.[20]

- When a plea-bargain agreement was not carried out due to a failure on both sides, the state sought to use incriminating statements the defendant had made during the negotiations. The Supreme Court of Louisiana held the statements could not be used as evidence against the defendant on the basis of "equitable immunity."[21]

- During the sentencing hearing where the state was seeking the death penalty, the state sought to use as evidence the fact that the defendant offered to plea-bargain to avoid the death penalty. It was held that such evidence was inadmissible. (The defendant was nevertheless sentenced to death for murder and robbery by force.)[22]

- Before going to trial, a drug-trafficking defendant wrote a letter to the prosecutor offering to plead guilty in return for sentencing concessions. The letter was held to be inadmissible against the defendant at trial.[23]

ⓕ THE TRIAL

The vast majority of criminal charges result in guilty pleas after plea bargaining. Only about 8 percent of criminal cases in the United States actually go to trial. Of those, about 20 percent are tried before a judge, and 80 percent are tried before a jury.

Prior to the trial, the parties undertake **discovery.** In the discovery process, both the prosecution and the defense gather evidence, through formal questions put to the other side, depositions of witnesses, and examination of documents and records.

As a result of discovery, various *motions* can be filed by the parties, such as to compel discovery, to dismiss for lack of jurisdiction or evidence, or to exclude evidence obtained in violation of a defendant's rights, such as violations of the defendant's Fourth Amendment rights. At this time or at any other time during the trial, the defendant may agree to enter a guilty plea ending the trial. The guilty plea could be based upon a sentence or plea agreement, which would be subject to the approval of the trial judge.

If the trial goes forward, jurors are summoned and selected, and subpoenas are issued to compel witnesses to attend and testify at the trial. Jurors are selected from the community in which the court sits (the *venue*) from lists maintained by the court, such as registered voters. The jury may consist of six to twelve people, depending on the seriousness of the crime charged and state rules.[24]

The prosecution presents evidence first and must establish a **prima facie case**— that is, the evidence must be sufficient to permit a reasonable jury to believe the defendant was guilty beyond a reasonable doubt. A defendant may move for a judgment of acquittal after the close of the prosecution's case. If the judge concludes the evidence is insufficient to support a reasonable jury verdict of guilty beyond a reasonable doubt, the case will be dismissed without going to the jury.

If the case is not dismissed, the defendant presents evidence to either cast doubt on the prosecution's case or to prove an **affirmative defense.** Affirmative defenses include insanity, immunity, entrapment, or double jeopardy. The defendant carries the burden of proving any affirmative defense raised, and the prosecution may offer *rebuttal* evidence to such defense and other new matters brought out in the defendant's case.

After all evidence is in and both sides have delivered closing arguments to the jury, the trial judge issues *jury instructions*. These instructions are the judge's explanation of the relevant law that governs the case. Following the trial judge's instructions, the jury begins its deliberations. They weigh the evidence presented to them during the trial and vote on the issue of guilt or innocence of the defendant.

If the jury reaches a verdict of not guilty, the case is over, and the defendant is discharged from custody. If the verdict is guilty, the defendant may file posttrial motions in the trial court. These motions include motions for *judgment notwithstanding the verdict* (sometimes called **judgment NOV**) or motions for a new trial. Motions for judgment NOV are rarely granted, since the trial judge has usually already heard motions for a *directed verdict* after the close of the prosecution and defense cases. Motions for a new trial meet with better success, since the trial judge may have a better opportunity following the trial to consider errors that occurred during trial.

If the defendant's motions are overruled, the defendant may appeal the criminal conviction and/or the sentence imposed upon the defendant. In state cases, the defendant's initial appeals go through the state appellate process, which frequently

Use of Evidence in the Stages of the Criminal Process

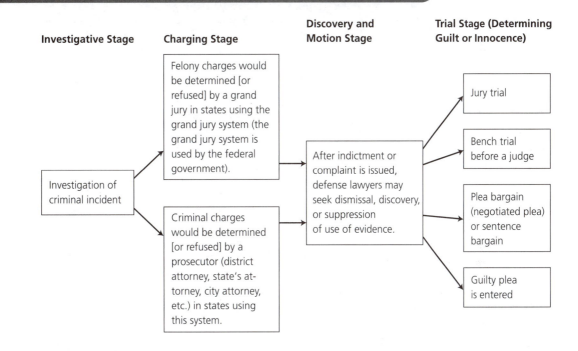

Investigative Stage

Charging Stage

Discovery and Motion Stage

Trial Stage (Determining Guilt or Innocence)

Investigation of criminal incident

Felony charges would be determined [or refused] by a grand jury in states using the grand jury system (the grand jury system is used by the federal government).

Criminal charges would be determined [or refused] by a prosecutor (district attorney, state's attorney, city attorney, etc.) in states using this system.

After indictment or complaint is issued, defense lawyers may seek dismissal, discovery, or suppression of use of evidence.

Jury trial

Bench trial before a judge

Plea bargain (negotiated plea) or sentence bargain

Guilty plea is entered

If it is known (or suspected) that a crime or offense has been committed, law enforcement officers or private persons and investigators would seek evidence of the offense. If competent evidence exists amounting to probable cause to believe that

- a crime (or offense) has been committed and
- that a specific person (persons) committed the offense

then the matter can be taken to a prosecutor.

If it is determined that probable cause exists proving

- corpus delicti (that a crime has been committed) and
- that the suspect was a party to the crime[a]

then a criminal charge or indictment can be issued for charging the suspect with a crime or crimes.

[a]A party to a crime can be (1) the person (or persons) who actually committed the crime; (2) a conspirator who hired, procured, planned, or counseled the crime; or (3) a person (or persons) who aided and abetted in the commission of the crime. Different evidence is required to carry the burden of proving each of the different categories of parties to a crime.

The defense lawyer will seek to discover and obtain evidence helpful to his client. He may also make some or all of the following motions[b] before the court:

- Motion to dismiss because of insufficient evidence, etc.
- Motion to dismiss because of improper procedure, or constitutionality of statue, etc.
- Motion to suppress evidence (statements, physical evidence, identification evidence, or procedure, etc.)
- Motion for discovery of evidence.

[b]A *motion* means an application for an order from that judge or other court.

The decision by the defense whether to try the case before a jury or judge is generally based on the evaluation of the case and the evidence. As weaker cases are filtered out of the system or are charged as lesser offenses, most cases that reach the trial stage are strong governmental cases. In these cases, the defense may attempt to plea-bargain or may enter a guilty plea. Should the state have a weakness in their case at this stage, the state may attempt to plea-bargain.

Sentencing authority is granted to the trial judge by the law defining the crime and by other statues in the state or federal criminal code. The sentencing judge could be further guided by sentencing guidelines enacted by that state's legislature. Reviews of imposed sentences may be made by the following:

- *Trial judge* On motion by the defense attorney, the trial judge will review his or her sentence of a particular defendant and may modify the sentence after hearing arguments presented by both the defense lawyer and the prosecutor.

- *Appeallate courts* (including the U.S. Supreme Court and state supreme courts) On appeal, an appellate court could find that a particular sentence was not within the statutory authority of the trial judge to impose, or that the sentence violated the Eighth Amendment's cruel and unusual clause.

- A state prisoner would ordinarily use a writ of habeas corpus in attempting to get his or her case into the federal courts. To do this, a violation of a right under the U.S. Constitution must be shown. Because there are very few violations (or errors) of this type, few habeas corpus hearings are granted.

- *State parole board or parole authorities* Parole authority is granted by a statute of that state. State statutes might provide that parole eligibility for murder does not commence until after sixteen years—or after twenty or twenty-five years. Whether the convicted person would be released on parole (and the conditions of parole) would then be determined by the parole board.

- *Pardoning power of the president of the United States and state governors* The power to pardon, grant amnesty, or commute a sentence by the president or a state governor is generally broad. Such authority is constitutional with additional statutory power often also provided. ARTICLE II of the U.S. Constitution provides that the president "shall have Power to grant Reprieves and Pardons for Offenses against the United States, except in Cases of Impeachment."[a]

[a]See the case of *Murphy v. Ford,* 390 F.Supp. 1372 (W.D.Mich. 1975), in which a federal district court found that President Gerald R. Ford had the constitutional authority to grant a pardon to former President Richard M. Nixon before Nixon was charged with a crime.

---

includes an intermediate court called a *court of appeals* and a final court called a *state supreme court.*

The state appellate court does not conduct a new trial. Rather, it looks at the evidence to see if it supports the conviction, determines if the judge made any **reversible errors**—such as permitting the use of damaging, inadmissible evidence. The state appellate court also rules on other claims that the defendant may make such as a constitutional violation.

After the defendant has exhausted his or her state court appeals, the defendant may seek review in the federal courts, but only for violation of federal constitutional rights. The defendant may file for a **writ of certiorari** in the U.S. Supreme Court or a writ of *habeas corpus* in the U.S. District Courts.

Writs of certiorari are limited to a review of state court rulings that violate the defendant's rights under the Constitution, such as the right to counsel, fair trial, confrontation of witnesses, and so on. Writs of certiorari are very rarely granted.

Habeas corpus writs, filed with a federal district court, ask that court to determine if the defendant is being held in violation of his constitutional rights. Frequently, constitutional issues not reviewed by the Supreme Court under the certiorari power are raised in habeas corpus writs. The denial of a writ is itself appealable by the defendant through the federal appellate system.

In theory, the habeas corpus writ is the final stop in the criminal process. However, filing successive habeas corpus writs is possible, so it is not accurate to ever say the process is truly complete.

SUMMARY

Many people evaluate and review evidence in suspected or known criminal incidents, and for that reason, they should have a working knowledge of the law of criminal evidence.

Public prosecutors review evidence in cases presented to them and make decisions based on the evidence as to whether to seek or to issue criminal charges. Defense lawyers review evidence to determine what possible defenses are available in view of the evidence.

The plea that a defendant or a defense lawyer enters before a court is based upon the evidence that confronts his or her client. Pleas that may be entered are: not guilty, guilty, Alford, no contest (with the permission of the court), a conditional guilty plea, or the insanity plea.

If the government has a strong case, defense lawyers often attempt to plea bargain. When there is weakness in the evidence against a defendant, prosecutors are likely to charge a lesser crime or to offer a negotiated plea.

Studies show that the majority of criminal cases in the United States result in either a guilty plea without plea bargaining or a guilty plea based upon a plea agreement. The trial judge can reject a prior plea agreement and can set a date for the case to go to trial.

Only about 8 percent of criminal cases in the United States go to trial. Twenty percent of these are tried before a judge, and 80 percent are tried before a jury. For example, thousands of drunk driving cases come before judges every month in the United States. Because the evidence against the average defendant in these cases is so strong, most defendants enter guilty pleas.

PROBLEMS

AVAILABLE ANSWERS

a. Not-guilty plea

b. Guilty plea

c. Alford plea

d. Insanity plea

e. Only a and d of above

1. Most felony cases in the United States are concluded when the defendant enters:

2. When a defendant refuses to enter a plea or stands mute, the court will enter:

3. A defendant who has evidence supporting a strong defense is likely to enter:

4. Defendants have the burden of producing evidence to prove this plea in most states:

5. Which of the pleas listed is a not-guilty plea?

6. A defendant who acknowledges that sufficient evidence exists to convict but denies guilt might seek to enter:

7. All but three states are reported to have statutorized which plea?

8. In drunken driving cases, there are a very high percentange of which plea?

9. To support which plea is a defense likely to seek an expert witness?

10. Defendants entering which pleas have the right to a jury trial in most states?

INFOTRAC COLLEGE EDITION EXERCISES

1. Go to InfoTrac College Edition and using the search term "guilty pleas" find the Fall 2001 article in the *Journal of Criminal Law and Criminology* on withdrawing a guilty plea under Federal Rule of Criminal Procedure 32(e). What limits, if any, should be placed on the right of a criminal defendant to withdraw a guilty plea? What are some of the issues presented by that question? Voluntary nature of the plea? Representation by legal counsel? Actual innocence of the defendant?

2. In connection with the *Irala v. Connecticut* case discussed in note 6 of this chapter, go to InfoTrac College Edition and using the search term "guilty pleas" find the Fall 2001 article in the *New York Defender Digest* discussing the Federal Court of Appeals case permitting an alien facing deportation because of a guilty plea entered in a criminal case to withdraw that plea. How did that case differ from *Irala?* Do you think the Court of Appeals would agree with the decision in *Irala?* Why or why not?

3. Guilty pleas entered in criminal cases have a particularly severe effect in cases where defendants face the possibility of deportation. Go to InfoTrac College Edition and using the search term "guilty pleas in deportation cases" find the May 2001 article in the *California Law Review* discussing deportation consequences and their effect on the withdrawal of guilty pleas.

NOTES

1. 59 Md. App., 28, 474 A.2d 537, 35 CrL 2147 (1984).
2. The states using the verdict of guilty but mentally ill are Michigan, Indiana, Illinois, Georgia, Kentucky, New Mexico, Delaware, and Alaska.
3. Cities studied by the Department of Justice in 1988 that have a high percentage of guilty pleas to felony charges are Bakersfield (93%); Brooklyn (80%); Dallas (80%); Los Angeles (84%); Manhattan (81%); Miami (82%); Queens (82%); Riverside (90%); St. Louis (83%); and San Diego (92%) (February, 1992 NCJ Gov't Doc. #130914).
4. U.S. 238, 242, 89 S.Ct. 1709, 1711–12 (1969).
5. For many years, courts have encouraged guilty pleas by rewarding a guilty plea with a lower sentence. Court time is saved, the overloading of court calendars is minimized, witnesses are not

required to come to court more than once, and the interests of justice are served.

In the 1992 case of *United States v. Jones,* 973 F.2d 928 (D.C., Cir.), the defendant received an additional six-month sentence when he took his case to trial instead of entering a guilty plea. The Federal Court of Appeals held that the procedure did not unconstitutionally burden the defendant's right to stand trial. The present federal sentencing guidelines (U.S.S.G., sec. 3 E 1.1) provide that a sentence may be reduced by two levels "if the defendant clearly demonstrates a recognition and affirmative acceptance of personal responsibility for his criminal conduct."

Guilty pleas are particularly high in misdemeanor offenses such as drunk driving. The evidence in most drunk-driving cases is very strong, and conviction rates in these cases are very high. Many drunk drivers feel genuine remorse for what they have done and admit their guilt to get the matter over with quickly. Some drunk-driving defendants have said, "Why waste money on a lawyer? I'll save money by going into court and pleading guilty."

Many prosecutors have established standard office pleading and sentencing practices, which are explained to people charged with misdemeanor or ordinance violations. For example, people charged for the first time with shoplifting or soliciting for prostitution might be told that it was standard office procedure to permit first-time offenders to plead to a lesser charge, such as disorderly conduct, if they enter a guilty plea. Those who wish to go to trial would be charged with the greater offense.

People charged with ordinance or misdemeanor offenses are also told the standard sentences if they enter a guilty plea. Another standard procedure is the practice of issuing multiple charges to an offense such as drunk driving. In return for pleading guilty to the drunk-driving charge and receiving the standard court sentence, the additional charge or charges are dropped.

6. Federal Rule 11c (3) of the Federal Rules of Criminal Procedure requires the judge accepting a guilty plea to inform the defendant of his constitutional rights at the time such plea is taken. Most states have a similar rule. In *United States v. Vonn*, 535 U.S. 55 (2002), the Supreme Court held that failure to give a defendant such advice permits withdrawal of a guilty plea only if the record as a whole shows the defendant was not informed of those rights. Thus, even though such advice was not given at the plea proceeding, the fact that the defendant was informed of his rights at the first arraignment showed the defendant was aware of his rights when he entered his plea.

The rule that guilty pleas be voluntary does not require that the trial judge inform the defendant of all the consequences of the plea. For example, in *Irala v. Connecticut*, 792 A.2d 109 (Conn. App.Ct. 2002), a defendant entered a nolo contendere plea to a charge that, under federal law, would result in deportation upon conviction. The trial judge informed the defendant

only that conviction of the state crime might have deportation consequences. The defendant subsequently sought to withdraw the plea, but her request was denied. On appeal, the court held that the "voluntary" requirement does not require a judge to inform the defendant of all the "collateral" consequences of a plea.

7. Idem.

8. *United States v. Jackson,* 390 U.S. 570, 584, 88 S.Ct. 1209, 1217 (1968). *North Carolina v. Alford,* 400 U.S. 25, 38 n.11, 91 S.Ct. 160, 168 n11 (1970).

9. 395 U.S. 238, 89 S.Ct. 1709 (1969).

10. 400 U.S. 25, 37, 91 S.Ct. 160, 167 (1970).

11. *Ward v. State,* 575 A.2d 771 (Md. App., 1990).

12. 815 P.2d 484 (Idaho App., 1991).

13. Fed. R. Crim. P 11(b) Advisory Committee's Note to 1974 Amendment.

14. 812 P.2d 470 (Utah App., 1991).

15. *North Carolina v. Alford,* 400 U.S. 25, 38 n.11, 91 S.Ct. 160, 168, n.11 (1970).

16. *Tollett v. Henderson,* 411 U.S. 258, 93 S. Ct. 1602 (1973).

17. "Task Force Report: The Courts," p. 4, President's Commission on Law Enforcement and Administration of Justice (Government Printing Office, 1967).

18. *Read-in* plea bargains are used most often in property offenses such as burglary and forgery when there is repetitious conduct on the part of the defendant. An example of a read-in plea bargain occurred in Milwaukee. A woman was charged with forging 10 checks. She pleaded guilty to two of the charges. The other eight charges were dismissed, and information that she had forged 628 checks was read into the record. The judge sentenced her to the maximum twenty years. As the woman had young children, she stayed in prison long enough to cause the parole board to believe that she would not go back to forging checks again, before they placed her on parole with the warning any further violation would send her back to prison.

19. *Golden v. State,* 49 Ind. 424, 427 (1875), in which the Supreme Court of Indiana labeled a plea arrangement a "corrupt agreement" and compared the procedure to "corrupt purchasing of an indulgence."

20. *People v. Muniz,* 262 Cal. Rptr. 473 (Calif., App., 1989).

21. *State v. Lewis,* 539 So.2d 1199 (La., 1989).

22. *Thomas v. State,* 811 P.2d 1337 (Okla. Crim. App., 1991).

23. *Russell v. State,* 614 So.2d 605 (Fla. App., 1993).

24. Either the defense attorney or the prosecutor may challenge a member of the jury panel for cause and disqualify the person. Challenge for cause could be because the panel member was a friend or relative of one of the attorneys, or because an answer to a question in *voir dire* disclosed prejudice in favor or against a party. The parties are also allowed a limited number of *peremptory challenges,* in which a prospective juror may be excused without showing a cause. In *Batson v. Kentucky,* 476 U.S. 79 (1986), the Supreme Court held that the prosecution could not use these peremptory challenges in a discriminatory manner. An example of a prima facie case showing such discrimination is *Roe v. Fernandez,* 286 F.3d 1190 (2001), where the prosecution used most of its peremptory challenges to strike Hispanic and African American members of the jury.

4

Direct and Circumstantial Evidence and the Use of Inferences

Ⓐ EVIDENCE AND PROOF

What Is Evidence?

Evidence is ordinarily defined as the means of establishing and proving the truth or untruth of any fact that is alleged. Evidence can consist of the testimony of witnesses, physical objects, documents, records, fingerprints, photographs, and so on. The famous English lawyer and writer Sir William Blackstone defined evidence in the 1760s as "that which demonstrates, makes clear or ascertains the truth of the very fact or point in issue, either on the one side or other."

When the quality and quantity of the evidence presented is so convincing and is sufficient to prove the existence of the fact sought to be proved or disproved, the result is proof of the fact. **Proof** is therefore the result of evidence, and evidence is the means of attaining proof. Whether a fact has been proved is determined by the trier of the facts (jury or judge).

In trials, evidence is introduced by the parties to satisfy the *burdens of proof* assigned to them. The burden-of-proof requirement is actually two burdens: the burden of production and the burden of persuasion. The **burden of production** requires the party with the burden on a factual issue to introduce sufficient relevant evidence to prove the fact at issue. Failure to do so means the fact has not been proved, which usually means the person with the burden loses. The **burden of persuasion** requires the party with the burden to produce sufficient evidence to persuade the fact finder that a fact exists.

In criminal trials, both the burden of production and the burden of persuasion rest on the prosecution:

> The Due Process Clause protects the accused against conviction except upon proof beyond a reasonable doubt of every fact necessary to constitute the crime with which he is charged.[1]

Thus, for every element of an offense, the prosecution must produce evidence sufficient to establish the element and also persuade the jury that no reasonable doubt exists about the fact's existence, based on the evidence produced.

Ⓑ THE REASONABLE DOUBT STANDARD

Every essential element of the crime charged must be proved by the government beyond **reasonable doubt** in order to convict and punish a defendant for the crime charged. The requirement of "proof beyond a reasonable doubt" is one of the most familiar legal standards in our society. However, courts and legal scholars have not reached a consensus on the exact definition of that important term. As a result, the instructions trial judges give juries on the standard of proof they must apply to the evidence in order to convict a defendant in a criminal case can vary from state to state, and even from court to court within a state. These differences in instructions have caused the U.S. Supreme Court in several cases to consider if the Due Process Clause has been satisfied by a "reasonable doubt" instruction. Those cases, and the history of the reasonable doubt standard, help to explain the standard's meaning today.

As far back as the seventeenth century, English courts recognized that, in many cases a criminal defendant's guilt could never be known with absolute certainty. That is, a jury could not be sure of a defendant's guilt beyond any doubt, since a chance always existed, no matter how unlikely, that the defendant was innocent. English courts thus instructed juries to find guilt if they were morally certain of that guilt.

In the United States, influenced by decisions like Chief Justice Shaw's of the Supreme Judicial Court of Massachusetts in 1850, judges began instructing juries to find guilt by use of a reasonable doubt standard. Chief Justice Shaw said the following about what constitutes reasonable doubt:

> What is reasonable doubt? . . . It is not mere possible doubt; because everything relating to human affairs, and depending on moral evidence, is open to some possible or imaginary doubt.[2]

In 1970 the Supreme Court held in *In re Winship* that the due process clause requires that the prosecution prove each element of a crime beyond a reasonable doubt.[3] However, the Court did not in *Winship* mandate any particular jury instruction on the exact meaning of "reasonable doubt." In the 1990 case of *Victor v. Nebraska* the Supreme Court held that while jury instructions may attempt to define reasonable doubt, they need not do so; all that the Constitution requires is that "taken as a whole, the instructions properly convey the concept of reasonable doubt."[4]

The instructions must inform the jury that they must judge the guilt of the defendant according to a high degree of certainty. The Supreme Court has identified certain language in jury instructions that does not properly convey the concept of reasonable doubt. In *Cage v. Louisiana* the trial court instructed the jury that reasonable doubt meant "such doubt as would give rise to a grave uncertainty" and "an actual substantial doubt."[5] The Supreme Court held that the instruction suggested to the jury that it must find a greater degree of doubt than the reasonable doubt standard requires.

The Supreme Court has also upheld definitions of reasonable doubt that spoke to the degree of doubt. In *Sandoval v. California* the Court upheld a jury instruction that defined reasonable doubt as "not a mere possible doubt."[6] Thus, from these cases it can be said that reasonable doubt is less than "actual substantial doubt" but more than "a mere possible doubt." A jury should not find a defendant guilty because it did not have "substantial doubt" about the defendant's guilt. However, it should not refuse to find that same defendant guilty simply because a "mere possible doubt" exists about the defendant's guilt.

The reasonable doubt jury instruction proposed by the Federal Judicial Center, and which Justice Ginsburg cited with approval in *Victor v. Nebraska*,[7] has been praised by several commentators.[8] That instruction has the advantage of clearly identifying the quantity of doubt the jury must possess, as well as informing the jury that the standard of reasonable doubt is stricter than the standard of proof used in civil cases. That instruction reads:

> The government has the burden of proving the defendant guilty beyond a reasonable doubt. Some of you may have served as jurors in civil cases, where you were told that it is only necessary to prove that a fact is more likely than not true. In criminal cases, the government's proof must be more powerful than that. It must be beyond a reasonable doubt.

Use of Evidence to Prove a Fact

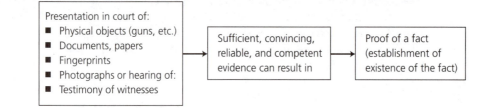

Presentation in court of:
- Physical objects (guns, etc.)
- Documents, papers
- Fingerprints
- Photographs or hearing of:
- Testimony of witnesses

→ Sufficient, convincing, reliable, and competent evidence can result in

→ Proof of a fact (establishment of existence of the fact)

Proof beyond a reasonable doubt is proof that leaves you firmly convinced of the defendant's guilt. There are very few things in this world that we know with absolute certainty, and in criminal cases the law does not require proof that overcomes every possible doubt. If, based on your consideration of the evidence, you are firmly convinced that the defendant is guilty of the crime charged, you must find him guilty. If on the other hand, you think there is a real possibility that he is not guilty, you must give him the benefit of the doubt and find him not guilty.[9]

C DIRECT EVIDENCE AND CIRCUMSTANTIAL EVIDENCE

The U.S. Constitution requires that in all criminal cases the state or the federal government prove each and every essential element of a crime beyond reasonable doubt. This can be done by the use of either **direct evidence** or **circumstantial** (indirect) **evidence;** or, as occurs in most criminal cases, by a combination of both direct and circumstantial evidence.

EXAMPLE OF DIRECT EVIDENCE:

A witness testifies that he or she saw the defendant commit the crime. Further questioning shows that the witness has good eyesight; was close enough to observe the incident; that the lighting was good; that the witness accurately described the defendant to the police and in the courtroom identified the defendant without any doubt. This would be an example of strong direct credible evidence that would be sufficient to convict unless the defense can produce evidence sufficient to impeach the credibility of the witness.

Circumstantial evidence is evidence that indirectly proves a fact in issue. Testimony that the defendant was at the scene of the crime and ran from the scene with a pistol in his or her hand would be circumstantial, or indirect evidence. Inferences have to be drawn for indirect evidence. If it were shown that no one other than the defendant had an opportunity to commit the crime and that the defendant and the victim were heard arguing angrily, the circumstantial evidence against the defendant would be stronger.

While direct evidence can be used to directly prove facts, circumstantial evidence requires the fact finder to draw inferences. An inference is a conclusion that can be drawn from a fact.

Direct and circumstantial evidence are not only used to prove criminal conduct; they must also be used to prove mental elements that are required essential elements of many crimes.[10] Mental elements that must be proved in many crimes of violence include intent, recklessness, and criminal negligence.

In the case of *Commonwealth v. Lee*,[11] the defendant testified that he did not intend to take the victim's life when he pointed a gun directly at the victim and pulled the trigger. In affirming the defendant's conviction, the Pennsylvania Superior Court held:

> [I]t is well settled that the intentional use of a deadly weapon on a vital part of the body raises a permissible inference of malice. . . .
>
> The finder of fact is not required to ignore this inference merely because the defendant testifies that he did not intend to take a person's life. . . .
>
> . . . The law infers . . . from the use of a deadly weapon, in the absence of circumstances of explanation or mitigation, the existence of the mental element—intent, malice, design, premeditation, or whatever term may be used to express it—which is essential as culpable homicide. *See generally* 40 Am. Jur.2d *Homicide* § 265 (1968).

The Inference that People Intend the Natural and Probable Consequences of Their Deliberate Acts[12]

To prove intent, recklessness, malice, or negligence, the law infers that people intend the reasonable, foreseeable consequences of their intentional and deliberate acts. Such inferences must flow rationally from the evidence presented in court. The Federal Court of Appeals, in the 1992 case of *United States v. Ortiz*,[13] pointed out that "jurors are neither required to divorce themselves from their common sense nor to abandon the dictate of mature experience. . . . [A] criminal jury [does not have] to ignore that which is perfectly obvious."

The crimes of attempted murder and assault with intent to cause serious bodily harm or death require proof of the defendant's intent. This intent can be inferred from the defendant's conduct and from the "deadly weapon" doctrine if the defendant uses an object likely to cause death or great bodily harm. A fist could be a deadly weapon if it were used in a way that could easily cause death or great bodily harm to the victim.

What are the natural and probable consequences of the conduct in the following examples? What commonsense conclusions could a fact finder draw as to intent or malice?

- A man drops a 20-pound cement block from a highway overpass, hitting the windshield of a car traveling 60 miles per hour.

- An angry 70-year-old woman hits a 200-pound man with a folded newspaper.

- A strong young man in a rage hits a baby hard in the face with his fist.

- Two men of about equal strength are involved in a fistfight. One of the men hits the other as hard as he can in the face.

Direct and Circumstantial Evidence

Direct evidence is that evidence that proves or disproves a fact in issue without any reasoning or inferences being drawn on the part of the fact finder.

Circumstantial evidence is that evidence that indirectly proves or disproves a fact in issue. The fact finder must reason or draw an inference from circumstantial evidence.

Types of Evidence	Direct Evidence	Circumstantial Evidence
Statements by a suspect or defendant	A full or partial confession by a suspect would be direct evidence.	A statement that the suspect was with the victim a short time before the murder could be used as circumstantial evidence by the state (incriminating statement, but neither a full nor partial confession).
Testimony of witnesses or the victim	Could identify the suspect as the person who committed the crime and be direct evidence.	Could incriminate the suspect by providing evidence that would link the suspect to the crime or would provide evidence showing motive, means, or opportunity for suspect to commit crime (e.g., suspect seen fleeing from crime scene).
Physical evidence	Contraband (drugs, stolen property, concealed weapons, etc.) is direct evidence when a suspect is charged with possession of such evidence.	Otherwise, physical evidence is generally circumstantial evidence (fingerprints, blood stains, weapons used to commit crime, bite marks, etc.).
Evidence obtained as a result of wiretapping or electronic surveillance	Statements directly showing who committed the crime would be direct evidence.	Statements that incriminate but do not directly show who committed the crime would be circumstantial evidence.

Scientific evidence such as DNA and fingerprints are generally circumstantial evidence. See Chapter 18 on scientific evidence.

Conduct that Has Been Used as Circumstantial Evidence to Prove a Defendant's Consciousness of Guilt

General Conduct	Specific Conduct and Cases
Flight and furtive action	The U.S. Supreme Court held in 1968 that "deliberate furtive actions and flight at the approach of strangers or law officers are strong indicia of mens rea (guilty mind)." *Peters v. New York,* 392 U.S. 40, 88 S.Ct. 1889.
Threats directed at a witness in an attempt to discourage cooperation with the police	The Supreme Court of Wisconsin held that "the [defendant's] threat is circumstantial evidence of consciousness of guilt and, hence, of guilt itself." *Price v. State* 154 N.W.2d 222 (1967), review den. U.S. Sup. Ct. 391 U.S. 908, 88 S.Ct. 1662 (1968). Also, *State v. Canaday,* 392 S.E.2d 457 (N.C.App.1990).
Interference with police investigation	Refusal to take blood test or other test when arrested for drunk driving (*South Dakota v. Neville,* 459 U.S. 553, 103 S.Ct. 916 (1983)). Refusing fingerprinting [*Myers v. State,* 427 A.2d 1061, (Md.App.1981)]; eating and destroying evidence [*Sewell v. State,* 368 A.2d 1111, (Md.App. 1977)]; refusal to provide voice or handwriting sample as ordered by court (*United States v. Franks,* 511 F.2d 25 (6th Cir.1975)]; rape suspect in jail shaved pubic hair to prevent sample being taken [*Marshall v. State,* 583 A.2d 1109 (Md.App.1991)]; refusal to take test to determine if suspect had fired gun [*Commonwealth v. Monaba,* 44 CrL 1031 (Pa.Super.1988)]; false and evasive answers [*Player v. State,* 568 So2d 370 (Ala.App.1990)], *Commonwealth v. Lavalley,* 574 N.E.2d 1000 (Mass. 1991)]; use of aliases [*Cabrera v. State,* 576 So.2d 1358 (Fla.App.1991)]; attempted suicide and flight [*State v. Mann,* 582 A.2d 1048 (N.J.Super.1990)]; possession of gun and flight [*Hope v. Commonwealth,* 392 S.E.2d 830 (Va.App.1990)]; hiding to avoid arrest [*United States v. Pallais,* 921 F.2d 684 (7th Cir. 1990)].
Conduct after a crime is committed that has been used as evidence to prove consciousness of guilt	Spending spree and high living after a theft [*United States v. Ewings,* 936 F.2d 903 (7th Cir. 1991)]; "attempt to lick blood" off shirt in murder case [*State v. Arlt,* 833 P.2d 902 (Hawaii App.1992)]; failure to appear for trial [*Langborne v. Commonwealth,* 409 S.E.2d 476 (Va.App.1991.)].

Other cases include the 1896 Supreme Court case of *Allen v. United States,* 164 U.S. 492, 17 S.Ct. 154 (flight and concealment); *Hickory v. United States,* 160 U.S. 408, 16 S.Ct. 327 (1896) (destruction or evidence); *Wright v. State,* 541 A.2d 988 (Md. 1988) (concealing identity); *Hunt v. State,* 540 A.2d 1125 (Md. 1988) (escape or attempt to escape).

When Circumstantial Evidence Alone Is Used to Obtain a Criminal Conviction

In 1954 the U.S. Supreme Court held in the case of *Holland v. United States*[14] that:

> Circumstantial evidence in this respect is intrinsically no different from testimonial evidence. Admittedly, circumstantial evidence may in some cases point to a wholly incorrect result. Yet this is equally true of testimonial evidence. In both instances, a jury is asked to weigh the chances that the evidence correctly points to guilt against the possibility of inaccuracy or ambiguous inference. In both, the jury must use its experience with people and events in weighing the probabilities. If the jury is convinced beyond a reasonable doubt, we can require no more.

In most criminal cases, a combination of direct evidence and circumstantial evidence is used by the government to obtain convictions. However, in some cases, circumstantial evidence alone is used. When only circumstantial evidence is used, many states do not follow the federal rule stated in the *Holland* decision and add requirements like those contained in the following jury instruction used in California:

> However, a finding of guilt as to any crime may not be based on circumstantial evidence unless the proved circumstances are not only (1) consistent with the theory that the defendant is guilty of the crime, but (2) cannot be reconciled with any other rational conclusion. . . .
>
> Also, if the circumstantial evidence [as to any particular count] is susceptible of two reasonable interpretations, one of which points to the defendant's guilt and the other to [his] [her] innocence, you must adopt that interpretation which points to the defendant's innocence, and reject that interpretation which points to [his] [her] guilt.
>
> If, on the other hand, one interpretation of such evidence appears to you to be reasonable and the other interpretation to be unreasonable, you must accept the reasonable interpretation and reject the unreasonable. 1 California Jury Instructions: Criminal (5 Ed. 1988) 23, Section 2.01.

In a few crimes, prosecutors are limited to direct evidence in proving the offenses. For example, ARTICLE III, SECTION 3, CLAUSE 1 of the United States Constitution states that "No person shall be convicted of Treason unless on the Testimony of Two Witnesses to the same overt Act, or on Confession in open Court."

Means-Opportunity-Motive as Circumstantial Evidence

When eyewitness evidence is not available, it has often been stated that investigators and officers should use, as a guideline in investigating crimes, the following questions:

- Who had the means of committing the crime?
- Who had the opportunity to commit the crime?
- Who had the motive to commit the crime?

Evidence that a person satisfied one or all of these circumstances could make that person a suspect, justifying further investigation. For example, when President John F.

Prosecutors may use evidence of motive: "[Motive] is evidence of the commission of any crime" [*United States v. Bradshaw*, 690 F.2d 704, 708 (1982); review denied U.S. Sup. Court, 463 U.S. 1210, 103 S.Ct. 3543 (1983)].

But defendants may also use the lack of motive as evidence: "[T]he absence of motive tends to support the presumption of innocence; it is a fact to be reckoned [with] on the side of innocence" [Supreme Court of California in the 1945 case of *People v. Weatherford*, 164 P. 2d 753, 765 (Calif.). See also *Martin v. United States*, 606 A.2d 120 (D.C. App., 1991)].

Kennedy was killed in Dallas in 1963, strong circumstantial evidence pointed to Lee Harvey Oswald as the assassin. The fact that Oswald fled and then later killed a Dallas police officer provided strong circumstantial evidence that Oswald killed President Kennedy. There was no direct evidence linking Oswald to the Kennedy killing.

Evidence tending to establish a defendant's motive can take a variety of forms. Some are common, such as a financial benefit received by a defendant as a result of the crime, or some personal animosity against a victim held by a defendant. In other cases, motive may be established in more unusual ways. For example, in a 2002 Wisconsin case the prosecution was permitted to introduce testimony establishing a cultural heritage in the Korean culture that members of a family would place family loyalty above other interests. The prosecution argued that the defendant, a Korean American, burned down his father's financially troubled business at his father's request out of loyalty to his father. The cultural tradition was thus used by the prosecution as evidence to show the son's motive.[15]

Defendants may also use circumstantial evidence. A defendant might show that she was 200 hundred miles away at the time the crime was committed, presenting a fact from which a strong inference of innocence could be drawn. Some crimes require a great deal of skill, strength, or physical agility; therefore, a defendant lacking such traits has presented circumstantial evidence tending to prove innocence.

Fingerprints and Shoeprints as Circumstantial Evidence

Fingerprints and shoeprints are circumstantial evidence, and inferences can be drawn from their presence at a crime scene.

> **EXAMPLE:** Your home or apartment is burglarized. Fingerprints of a stranger are found at the site of the forced entry. The prints match those of a person with a long history of committing burglaries. A search warrant for his home results in the police seizure of many items taken from your home. The presence of the stolen articles supports the inference that the fingerprints were made during the crime.

In the 1992 case of *Commonwealth v. Hall*,[16] the Massachusetts Court of Appeals affirmed the conviction of the defendant for burglary, holding:

The presence of a fingerprint at a crime scene is insufficient by itself to support a guilty finding. "The prosecution must couple the fingerprint[] with evidence which reasonably excludes the hypothesis that the fingerprint[] [was] impressed at a time other than when the crime was being committed." *Commonwealth v. Fazzino,* 27 Mass. App. Ct. 485, 487, 539 N.E.2d 1060 (1989). We conclude that the evidence submitted in this case supports a reasonable inference that the defendant placed his fingerprint on the doorknob at the time of the crime.

Circumstantial evidence may produce inferences, and these inferences "need only be reasonable and possible, . . . not necessary or inescapable." *Commonwealth v. Merola,* 405 Mass. 529, 533, 542 N.E.2d 249 (1989), quoting from *Commonwealth v. Beckett,* 373 Mass. 329, 341, 366 N.E.2d 1252 (1977).

While inferences "need only be reasonable and possible," as the court in the above case observed, this means only that the jury is permitted to reach a conclusion using such an inference. The prosecution retains the duty to persuade the jury to make the inference.

Fingerprints were also used as circumstantial evidence to obtain convictions in the 1992 burglary case *Brown v. State* and in the 1991 Georgia auto-theft case *In the Interest of N.R.*[17] The Georgia court held that "[t]here was no evidence of any other explanation of how defendant's fingerprints came to be on the [car window] other than that they were put there during the course of the [theft]."

Shoeprints differ from fingerprints because shoes are not part of the human body as fingerprints are. There must be a showing that the shoe belonged to the defendant. An inference of use by the defendant could be drawn from this showing. The Supreme Court of Illinois affirmed the conviction of the defendant for burglary in the 1992 case of *People v. Campbell,*[18] based on a clear and distinctive shoeprint found in the burglarized home. The court held that this evidence, plus flight and a showing that the defendant had an opportunity to commit the crime, was sufficient to prove guilt:

> While flight by itself is not sufficient to establish guilt, it may be a circumstance to be considered with other factors tending to establish guilt. . . .
>
> This evidence, along with the shoeprint evidence and evidence of opportunity, could properly have been considered as tending to establish defendant as the perpetrator of the charged offense. Again, we note that the weight to be given all the evidence was for the trier of fact to determine.

CONCLUSION

The trial court made a reasoned decision based upon all of the evidence presented at trial. The court properly weighed the evidence, giving full cognizance to its infirmities and the inferences to be drawn therefrom. While we might have weighed the evidence differently, we have neither the authority nor the duty to substitute our judgment. The evidence here, while not of the strongest caliber, does not seem to us so unreasonable as to support a reversal of defendant's conviction for residential burglary.

Everyday Use of Inferences and Deductions

We all draw inferences from observations in our everyday life. From observations you could conclude that a friend is angry or upset; that it is going to rain; that a motorist is driving recklessly; or that a pet is getting old or is sick. The following example illustrates:

You awake one morning to see snow falling in your backyard. In the newly fallen snow are animal tracks across your yard. From your observations and past experiences, you could conclude:

- That a large dog crossed your yard a few minutes earlier

- That the dog was moving slowly from east to west

- That the dog probably belongs to your neighbor to the east who usually lets his dog out every morning

If you had seen the dog cross your yard, you would have direct information regarding the dog. But you did not see or hear the dog, and therefore you made your deductions or conclusions based upon the circumstantial facts available to you. Further investigation could either affirm or rebut the conclusions that you have made.

Inferences Drawn from Other Bad Acts or Other Convictions of Defendants

A defendant charged with a crime must answer for only that crime at his trial. Evidence of prior crimes or other bad acts are generally held to be inadmissible because of the prejudice it could cause in the minds of the jury or fact finder. The court in the 1988 case of *Thompson v. United States*,[19] pointed out that "the jury may condemn the defendant because of his prior criminal behavior and not because he is guilty of the offense charged."

> **EXAMPLE:** The 1991 rape trial of William Kennedy Smith (nephew of Senator Edward Kennedy) received nationwide news coverage. A critical point in the trial was a hearing before the trial judge as to whether three women (a doctor, a medical student, and a law student) would be permitted to testify that Mr. Smith had either raped or tried to rape them. The testimony of the three women could have been devastating and could have changed the outcome of the trial. Trial Judge Mary E. Lupo ruled against the state and would not permit the testimony of the three women. Smith was acquitted.

However, there are exceptions to the rule forbidding evidence of prior crimes or bad acts. Most states have statutes similar to the federal "Other crimes, wrongs, or acts" statute (Federal Rules of Evidence 404 [b]), which provides:

> *Other crimes, wrongs, or acts.* Evidence of other crimes, wrongs, or acts is not admissible to prove the character of a person in order to show that he acted in conformity therewith. It may, however, be admissible for other purposes, such as proof of motive, opportunity, intent, preparation, plan, knowledge, identity, or absence of mistake or accident. . . .

In 1994, Congress passed the Violent Crime Control and Law Enforcement Act.[20] As part of its provisions, this law amended the federal rules of evidence by adding Rules 413, 414, and 415. These rules make admissible in criminal cases evidence of prior sexual assaults (Rule 413) or child molestations (Rule 414) by a defendant charged with those crimes. Unlike the limited use of evidence of "bad acts" under Rule 404(b), evidence introduced under Rules 413 or 414 "may be considered for its bearing on any matter to which it is relevant."[21]

> **EXAMPLE:** Evidence that the defendant had committed child molestation acts twenty years before the crime charged was admissible in present sexual abuse prosecution. The earlier acts were similar to the acts charged, involved the same form of abuse, and both victims were 6- or 7-year-old girls related to the defendant.

Where No Inferences Should Be Drawn

In the following situations, courts have ruled that no inference of guilt may be drawn.

WHERE A DEFENDANT USES THE PRIVILEGE AGAINST SELF-INCRIMINATION An inference of guilt should not be drawn when a defendant or suspect asserts the Fifth Amendment **privilege against self-incrimination.** This includes situations where defendants do not take the witness stand to defend themselves against criminal charges made against them. It also includes other situations, such as the assertion of rights after *Miranda* warnings are given.

In the 1990 case of *U.S. v. Rocha,*[22] the Federal Court of Appeals held that "[t]he Fifth Amendment prohibits a trial judge, a prosecutor or a witness from commenting upon a defendant's failure to testify in a criminal trial."

When police officers appear as witnesses, they should not comment on a defendant's use of the right to remain silent and not answer questions. In the 1989 case of *State v. Marple,*[23] the Oregon Appellate Court held that "[h]ere, defendant invoked his right to remain silent when he refused to answer the officer's question, and his refusal cannot be used as evidence against him."

WHERE INFORMATION IS PROTECTED BY THE RAPE SHIELD LAW Before the enactment of rape shield laws, defense lawyers in rape cases would seek to question victims about their past sex life in hopes that the jury and judge would draw the inference that the woman was sexually promiscuous and likely to consent to sex.

In the 1990 case of *Commonwealth v. Nieves,*[24] the Pennsylvania Superior Court pointed out that "[r]ape shield laws were intended to end the abuses . . . by limiting the harassing and embarrassing inquiries of defense counsel into irrelevant prior sexual conduct of sexual assault complainants."

Rape shield laws enacted by the federal government and probably all states contain exceptions. Federal Rule 412 is found in Appendix B of this text and contains the federal exceptions to the relevance of evidence as to the "alleged victim's past sexual behavior or alleged sexual predisposition."

COURTS RULE BOTH WAYS ON THE CESSATION OF SIGNATURE CRIMES AFTER THE ARREST OF A SUSPECT *Signature crimes* are crimes that are so similar that they bear the mark of a common signature. All large communities have had the terrible problem of serial crimes of some kind. If a suspect is arrested and the serial, or signature, crimes stop, can this be used as evidence?

Although some courts may rule otherwise, the Pennsylvania Superior Court held that such evidence is inherently unreliable. In the 1992 case of *Commonwealth v. Foy*,[25] the court pointed out that there are many reasons why reports of signature crimes could stop: "Further signature crimes may have been committed but never reported to the police. The true culprit may have died, or left the community, or been incarcerated on unrelated charges about the time of the defendant's arrest. Or perhaps the true culprit has decided to refrain from further acts of violence in order to shift suspicion onto the defendant and thereby escape detection."

WHERE A SUSPECT SEEKS TO CONTACT A LAWYER The Federal Court of Appeals held in the 1984 case of *U.S. v. Daoud*,[26] that "[t]he right to counsel is included in the *Miranda* warnings, and as such is covered by the implicit assurance that invocation of the right will carry no penalty."

In seeking legal advice and the assistance of a lawyer, the person may well believe that he or she is guilty of a crime. But an innocent person may also seek legal advice to assist in proving that he or she has not committed a crime. Or the person may only be involved in a minor way in the crime being investigated. The most likely purpose for seeking legal advice or representation is to be informed as to the person's status and what possible exposure may be involved.

Attempting to use evidence that a defendant sought to contact a lawyer would be forbidden by most (if not all) courts. The Maryland Court of Appeals held in the 1990 case of *Hunter v. State*,[27] that:

> Where the request for . . . counsel arises in some other circumstance, as in the case at bar, comment on it has been condemned under principles enunciated in *Griffin v. California*, 380 U.S. 609, 85 S.Ct. 1229, 14 L.Ed.2d 106 (1965). One of the earliest expressions of this rule came in *United States ex rel. Macon v. Yeager*, 476 F.2d 613 (3rd Cir. 1973).

Ⓓ USING DIRECT AND CIRCUMSTANTIAL EVIDENCE

In most criminal cases, both direct and circumstantial evidence is used. Following are some examples of such situations.

Finding Illegal Drugs in a Motor Vehicle

Illegal drugs are found in motor vehicles in a variety of situations. In a lawful stop of a vehicle, a law officer may have seen or smelled illegal drugs. An informant or other source might have provided probable cause to believe drugs were in the vehicle.

If the illegal drugs are in an open position in the vehicle and only the driver is in the car, the inference of knowledge and possession of drugs is easy. When more than one person is in the car, the inference of illegal possession is strongest against the owner and driver of the vehicle. It would be more difficult to obtain a conviction against a passenger in the vehicle, for the inferences of knowledge and possession are weaker. However, the location of the drugs in the vehicle, the amount of illegal drugs found, the criminal record of the passenger, and the passenger's relationship with the driver and owner would all be circumstantial factors in determining whether or not to charge the passenger.

The Federal Court of Appeals, in the 1992 case of *United States v. Gibson*,[28] made the following observations in affirming the conviction of the defendant:

> It is well established in this circuit that in cases involving hidden compartments, reliance may not be placed solely on the defendant's control of the vehicle. In such an instance, possession can be inferred only if knowledge is indicated by additional factors, such as circumstances evidencing a consciousness of guilt on the part of the defendant. Inconsistent stories may constitute substantive evidence of a defendant's guilty knowledge. Circumstantial factors also include lack of knowledge of the name of the true owner and implausible explanations for one's travels. [. . . "nervousness, in certain instances, may also be a factor."]

Proving the Crime of Possession of Illegal Drugs with Intent to Deliver

A defendant apprehended in the act of selling illegal drugs usually can easily be convicted of the offense, since strong direct evidence would then exist to prove selling, transferring, or delivery of the drugs.

When the crime of possession with intent to deliver is charged, the defendant usually has a large quantity of illegal drugs in his or her possession. State and federal governments argue that sufficient circumstantial evidence exists to prove that the defendant had the intent to sell, transfer, or deliver the illegal drugs to others and did not intend all of the drugs for personal use. The crime of possession with intent to deliver has higher penalties than mere possession.[29]

In the 1991 case of *State v. Morgan*,[30] the Supreme Court of North Carolina listed the following cases and circumstances where intent to deliver was inferred from circumstantial evidence:

> A jury can reasonably infer from the amount of the controlled substance found within a defendant's constructive or actual possession and from the manner of its packaging an intent to transfer, sell, or deliver that substance. *See, e.g., State v. Williams,* 307 N.C. 452, 298 S.E.2d 372 (1983) (presence of material normally used for packaging); *State v. Baxter,* 285 N.C. 735, 208 S.E.2d 696 (1974) (amount of marijuana found, its packaging, and presence of packaging materials); *State v. Rich,* 87 N.C.App. 380, 361 S.E.2d 321 (1987) (twenty grams cocaine plus packaging paraphernalia); *State v. Casey,* 59 N.C.App. 99, 296 S.E.2d 473 (1982) (possession of over 25,000 individually wrapped dosage units of LSD); *State v. Mitchell,* 27 N.C.App. 313, 219 S.E.2d 295 (1975), *cert. denied,* 289 N.C. 301, 222 S.E.2d 701 (1976) (possession of considerable inventory of marijuana

plus other seized, "suspicious" items). *See also State v. James,* 81 N.C.App. 91, 344 S.E.2d 77 (1986) (cocaine of small quantity packaged in multiple envelopes); *State v. Williams,* 71 N.C.App. 136, 321 S.E.2d 561 (1984) (less than one ounce marijuana packaged in seventeen small bags); *State v. Francum,* 39 N.C.App.429, 250 S.E.2d 705 (1979) (quantity of LSD unspecified, but found in plastic bags inside larger plastic bags).

Other circumstantial evidence used to prove intent to deliver is mentioned in the 1991 case of *United States v. Solis,*[31] where drugs were found in Solis's luggage:

> As counsel for Ms. Solis conceded on appeal, her intent to distribute the cocaine found in her luggage was at issue. The government had to establish that intent through circumstantial evidence. Evidence of Ms. Solis' actions and of the other articles in her possession was therefore relevant on the issue of whether she intended to distribute the contraband. For instance, evidence of repeated trips to Anchorage, paid for in cash by or on behalf of a woman living on Social Security, certainly provides important pieces to the government's evidentiary puzzle. The simultaneous presence of beeper numbers helps complete the picture—*if* the trier of fact is aware of the role that beepers often play in the conduct of illegal drug trade. The government was entitled to demonstrate through the use of expert testimony that someone traveling with two kilograms of cocaine under the conditions we have described would find access to beepers a useful means of effectuating the transportation and eventual distribution of her deadly cargo.

In addition to beepers, guns are also used as tools of drug traffickers and can be used as circumstantial evidence from which fact finders can infer intent to deliver. The federal court in the 1989 case of *United States v. Carstens*[32] held that "courts have recognized that any gun is a 'tool of the trade' for drug traffickers. The presence of weapons is evidence of . . . intent to distribute controlled substances."

In the 1991 crack-house case *United States v. Bruce,*[33] the court described the crack-house scenario as follows:

> If guns are strewn around a "crack house" in which drugs are stored, it might be inferred that the guns are there to protect the occupant's "possession." In such a case, the guns are "used" in relation to the drug trafficking crime of possession with intent to distribute because they are intended to protect the stash of drugs that will subsequently be distributed. And although actual distribution is a separate crime, courts have treated evidence of the use of guns in such a house for protection of the distribution function as equivalent to protection of possession.

Proving Physical and Sexual Abuse of Children

Many child abuse cases must be proved using circumstantial evidence because direct evidence is not always available. In many instances, the child is unable to tell what happened, and the offender does not ordinarily disclose the truth. Inferences are therefore very important in proving child abuse cases.

Where an adult has sole custody of a child and it is shown that the injury was not accidental or self-inflicted, a jury may infer that the adult inflicted the injury. In the

1989 case of *Commonwealth v. Earnest*,[34] the Superior Court of Pennsylvania relied on this rule, allowing:

> an inference of guilt where a child suffers a fatal injury while an adult has sole custody of the child. *Commonwealth v. Nissly,* 379 Pa.Super. 86, 549 A.2d 918 (1988). In *Nissly,* the defendant was not the only adult in the house when the fatal injury was inflicted but the inference of guilt was still applicable as the defendant was the only adult with the child when the injury had to have occurred. As in the instant case, the fact finder found the injury was not accidental or self-inflicted, therefore, the evidence was sufficient for the conviction, as we find it is here.

In the 1991 case of *Campbell v. Commonwealth*,[35] the victim was a 3-year-old child. The Court of Appeals held that:

> the trial judge could have inferred from all the facts and circumstances that the defendant intended to do exactly what he did—beat the child with such force that it left his back and side extensively marked and bruised. Further, the trial judge could have found that the probable and natural consequence of this act, given the force with which the blows were applied and the location of the marks near Cecil's spinal column and right kidney, was disfigurement or disablement of the child. . . .
>
> A three-year old child with no way to defend himself, except by screaming and crying, received a brutal beating from the much stronger defendant. We conclude that the trial judge could have inferred from all the evidence that this beating was delivered with the intent to disfigure or disable the child.
>
> For the foregoing reasons, therefore, we affirm the defendant's conviction of malicious wounding.

Some sexual abuse statutes require proof of *forcible compulsion.* When the victim is a child, the child will often submit to the advances of adults who have parental or similar authority over the child.

The highest courts in Pennsylvania, North Carolina, and Alabama permit an inference of forcible compulsion where sexual intercourse or abuse is shown even if no physical force was used and no threats were uttered by the adult. In adopting this inference in the 1991 case of *Powe v. State*,[36] the Supreme Court of Alabama held:

> We note that our holding is limited to cases involving the sexual assault of children by adults with whom the children are in a relationship of trust. The reason for the distinction between cases involving children as victims and those involving adults as victims is the great influence and control that an adult who plays a dominant role in a child's life may exert over the child. When a defendant who plays an authoritative role in a child's world instructs the child to submit to certain acts, an implied threat of some sort of disciplinary action accompanies the instruction. If the victim is young, inexperienced, and perhaps ignorant of the "wrongness" of the conduct, the child may submit to the acts because the child assumes the conduct is acceptable or because the child does not have the capacity to refuse. Moreover, fear of the parent resulting from love or respect may play a role as great or greater than that played by fear of threats of serious bodily harm in coercing a child to submit to a sexual act.

Proving that the Defendant Was the Driver of a Motor Vehicle

Thousands of drivers on American highways have had their driver's license suspended or revoked. Many others do not have a valid driver's license or are driving under the influence of drugs or alcohol. In the year 2001 alone, 17,448 people were killed and a half a million people were injured as the result of drunk or drugged driving. Experts state that four out of five people killed on highways and streets are killed by drunk or drugged drivers.

Proof beyond reasonable doubt that the defendant was driving the vehicle is required and is central to the conviction of the defendant in many moving vehicle trials. The following cases illustrate only a few of the many kinds of cases coming before American courts every year, where inferences drawn from circumstantial evidence are used to determine who was driving the vehicle in question.

Mirro v. United States
(Unpublished 4th Cir. Fed. Ct. App.) Review denied,
U.S. Supreme Court 44 CrL 4005 (1988)

When a truck was stopped, a military police officer testified that he saw the defendant climb out of the driver's seat of the truck while another person took his place. This testimony was held sufficient to support the inference that the defendant was the driver of the truck. The defendant was convicted of drunk driving. The Supreme Court refused review.

State v. McGlone
Supreme Court of Ohio, 570 N.E.2d 1115 (1991)

An intoxicated person found in the driver's seat of a motor vehicle parked on private or public property with the key in the ignition is "operating" the vehicle and can be convicted of drunk driving.

State v. Mills
Iowa Court of Appeals, 458 N.W.2d 395 (1990)

After police officers determined that a vehicle's owner had a suspended driver's license, they made the inference that the owner was driving the vehicle illegally. It was held that they had reasonable suspicion to make a stop of the vehicle in the absence of evidence showing that someone else was driving the car. A substantial amount of cocaine was found in a plastic bag at the defendant's feet after a pat-down for weapons.

The defendant was convicted of possession of cocaine with intent to deliver. His conviction was affirmed in view of the large amount of cocaine and a large amount of money found in his sock and in his shoe.

Ⓔ PROVING CORPUS DELICTI BY DIRECT OR CIRCUMSTANTIAL EVIDENCE

In all criminal cases, the state or government must prove that (1) a crime has been committed by someone (**corpus delicti**) and (2) the defendant(s) committed the offense. Most states have adopted a definition of corpus delicti similar to that used by the Supreme Court of California in the 1991 case of *People v. Jennings*.[37] "The corpus delicti of a crime consists of two elements, the fact of the injury or loss or harm, and the existence of a criminal agency as its cause."

The corpus delicti of most crimes is ordinarily proved by direct evidence, as when the victim or a witness tells the police of the crime. The corpus delicti of other crimes are proved by physical evidence; for example, the corpus delicti of a burglary is shown by a broken window and missing valuables. The corpus delicti of a murder could be proved by a dead body with a knife in the chest. The following examples illustrate common corpus delicti problems.

> **EXAMPLE:** A suspicious fire destroys a building housing a business that was in serious financial trouble. Investigators suspect arson but cannot prove corpus delicti (that the fire was deliberately started). The insurance company is unhappy because of the large amount of insurance. It can be shown that the owner of the building and business had the means, opportunity, and motive for "torching" the building, but if the state cannot prove corpus delicti, it cannot charge the owner with a criminal offense.

> **EXAMPLE:** All cities in the United States have "missing persons." Some of these people may be living elsewhere and people who have deliberately cut all ties with their family and friends. Families and friends of a missing person may believe the missing person has been murdered. Before criminal charges can be filed, corpus delicti must be proved.

As a general rule, corpus delicti must be established beyond a reasonable doubt.[38] Corpus delicti may be proved by a combination of direct and circumstantial evidence or by either alone. When an attempt is made to prove corpus delicti by circumstantial evidence, the general rule is that the evidence must be so conclusive as to eliminate all reasonable doubt in concluding that a crime was committed. The following case illustrates:

Epperly v. Commonwealth
Supreme Court of Virginia, 224 Va. 214, 294 S.E.2d 882 (1982)

An 18-year-old college girl (Gina Hall) was last seen leaving a dance with the defendant. Her body was never found to prove conclusively that she was murdered, but her blood-soaked clothing was found. Her car was also found, and there was evidence of a violent struggle at a house on Claytor Lake, where the defendant was seen after the dance. Dog-tracking evidence was admitted at the defendant's trial, corroborating some of the allegations of the state about her whereabouts after the dance. The defendant also made incriminating statements that were admitted as evidence. In holding that the state carried the burden of proving corpus delicti, the Supreme Court of Virginia affirmed the defendant's conviction, ruling that:

> The court instructed the jury that the Commonwealth must first prove that Gina was dead and that her death was caused by criminal violence. The instruction told the jury that these elements might be proved "either by direct evidence or by proof so strong as to produce the full assurance of moral certainty." Defendant agrees that this instruction correctly states the law, but argues that the evidence was insufficient to warrant the jury's finding the existence of the corpus delicti. . . .
>
> In homicide cases, the corpus delicti must consist of proof (1) of the victim's death and (2) that it resulted from the criminal act or agency of another. . . . Although this is the first such case to come to this Court in which the victim's body was not found, we have long held that the corpus delicti may be proven by circumstantial evidence.
>
> We think the evidence was sufficient to warrant the jury in finding, to the full assurance of moral certainty, that Gina Hall was dead as the result of the criminal act of another person. The jury was entitled to take into account, in this connection, her sudden disappearance, her character and personal relationships, her physical and mental health, the evidence of a violent struggle at the house on Claytor Lake, her hidden, blood-soaked clothing, and the defendant's incriminating statements—particularly his reference to "the body" before it was generally thought she was dead.

In 1990 the Supreme Court of North Carolina affirmed the first-degree murder conviction of the defendant in the case of *State v. Franklin*,[39] holding that:

> [when a] body is found with marks of violence upon it, as was the case here, such evidence establishes *corpus delicti.*
>
> Evidence of *corpus delicti* coupled with the testimony of a cell mate relating inculpatory statements made by the defendant is sufficient to support a conviction.
>
> In this case, according to Woolard, defendant said that he had killed a girl, had been questioned about it, and had gotten away with it. He further told Woolard that the reason he had killed the girl was because she owed him money. The evidence shows that defendant had previously been questioned about Jean Sherman's disappearance but had not been charged with her murder. The evidence further conclusively shows that Jean Sherman owed defendant money for the cocaine she had stolen on the night before her disappearance. All of this evidence, taken as a whole, is sufficient to take the case to the jury, which was then entitled to evaluate its weight. We conclude that the State's evidence, when viewed in the light most favorable to the State, is sufficient to withstand defendant's motion to dismiss. This assignment of error is overruled.

Ⓕ THE SUFFICIENCY-OF-EVIDENCE REQUIREMENT TO JUSTIFY A VERDICT OR FINDING OF GUILT

One of the most common grounds for appeal of a jury verdict or a judge's finding of guilty is that of insufficiency of evidence (**sufficiency-of-evidence requirement**). In this appeal, the defense argues that there was not sufficient evidence to support the verdict or finding of guilt beyond a reasonable doubt.

A jury's verdict or a judge's finding must be supported and based on legal and substantial evidence. Mere possibilities, suspicion, or conjecture will not support a verdict or finding of guilt. If the evidence is inherently incredible or is contrary to common knowledge and experience or established physical facts, it will not support a finding of guilt.

Either direct or circumstantial evidence will support a finding of guilt if the evidence is legally sufficient to prove all of the essential elements of the crime charged. The Court of Special Appeals of Maryland held in the case of *Metz v. State*[40] that "we feel that the test for sufficiency is the same whether the evidence be direct, circumstantial, or provided by rational inferences therefrom."

The following cases illustrate sufficiency of evidence issues, which have come before appellate courts.

Burkhart v. State
Supreme Court of Nevada, 107 Nev. 797, 820 P.2d 757 (1991)

The defendant was convicted after a jury trial of the crime of kidnapping based on the following conduct: The defendant approached a child (Mathew) who was standing near his parents in a Nevada gambling casino. The defendant touched the child twice and then "it appears that (defendant) may have momentarily grabbed a jacket that Mathew was wearing." After the third contact, Mathew's parents, who saw and heard all that happened, notified casino security. This evidence was permitted to go to a jury and the jury inferred that the evidence justified a conviction of kidnapping. The Supreme Court of Nevada reversed the conviction, holding that

> there was no testimony which would have allowed the jury to infer what appellant intended to do with Mathew. The undisputed evidence showed that appellant ceased his final contact with Mathew as soon as Mathew indicated that he did not wish to go with appellant. Further, all of the contacts took place in the hallway of a public facility, within easy view of Mathew's parents. The first two contacts were innocuous enough that Mathew's parents made no effort to intervene. Even after Mathew's parents called security, appellant calmly remained in the casino.
>
> Finally, it appears that appellant had no ready means available to take Mathew away from the casino, unless it is to be argued that appellant in-

tended to ride away with Mathew on appellant's bicycle. No rational juror could have inferred from this evidence that appellant seized Mathew with the specific intent to detain him against his will. Any inference as to appellant's specific intent must have been based on unbridled speculation.

In re Woods
Illinois Court of Appeals, 20 Ill.App.3d 641, 314 N.E.2d 606 (1974)

Identification evidence of the defendant's involvement in a robbery was suppressed and could not be used because of improper procedures. The only remaining evidence that could be used was his presence at the scene of the crime and the fact that he ran away. In holding that this evidence was insufficient to support the defendant's conviction, the court ruled that:

> [m]ere presence at the scene of the crime is insufficient to establish accountability . . . , and we believe that presence at the scene together with flight, in the absence of other circumstances indicating a common design to do an unlawful act, does not establish accountability.

Ⓖ THE USE OF PRESUMPTIONS AND INFERENCES

Presumptions

McCormick on Evidence (West Publishing, 1992) writes that the term "presumption is the slipperiest member of the family of legal terms." This statement was made because the term is used in so many ways by different courts.

The following is an example of a jury instruction that must be given to juries in criminal cases. The **presumption** stated in the jury instruction is ordinarily referred to as the "presumption of innocence." However, some writers and McCormick prefer the term "assumption of innocence."

> The law presumes every person charged with the commission of an offense to be innocent. This presumption attends the defendant throughout the trial and prevails at its close unless overcome by evidence which satisfy the jury of his (or her) guilt beyond a reasonable doubt. The defendant is not required to prove his (or her) innocence.

Is the above presumption "rebuttable" (meaning that it can be "overcome" by evidence showing otherwise)? Yes, it can, but the state must carry this burden "throughout the trial."

Is the above presumption "mandatory" (meaning that the jury must "presume" or "assume" the innocence of the defendant "unless overcome by evidence which satisfy the jury of . . . guilt beyond a reasonable doubt"). Yes, it is mandatory.

Other Classifications of Evidence

Corroborative evidence	Corroborative evidence is evidence that adds weight or **credibility** to a case. In many instances, corroborative evidence is important in carrying the burden of persuasion in the mind of the fact finder. For example, in rape cases, corroborative evidence is important to reinforce the testimony of the victim.
Prima facie evidence	The term *prima facie* is Latin for "at first sight" or "on the face of it." Prima facie evidence is that amount of evidence or that quality of evidence that is sufficient in itself to prove a case. When the state presents a prima facie case, the defense must respond or accept a very serious risk of conviction. A prima facie case is then a very strong case with sufficient evidence to obtain a conviction.
Conclusive evidence and conflicting evidence	Conclusive evidence is evidence from which only one reasonable conclusion may be drawn. The term *conclusive evidence* is sometimes used in statutes where the legislature requires evidence so strong as to conclusively prove the fact or issue. The term *conflicting evidence* is usually used to indicate a situation where evidence both proving and disproving a fact or issue has been presented; and, depending on the weight and credibility accorded the evidence, the fact finder could find either way.
Cumulative evidence	Cumulative evidence is additional evidence of the same kind that proves the same point as evidence already presented. However, evidence from a different source or evidence of a different kind is not cumulative even though it tends to prove or disprove the same fact or issue. (See the U.S. Supreme Court case of *Hamling v. United States,* 418 U.S. 87, 94 S.Ct. 2887, discussing cumulative evidence.)
Positive and negative evidence	Most evidence is positive evidence, in that it is presented in positive terms. Some evidence, however, is presented in negative terms and is referred to as negative evidence. For example, a motorist testifying that he saw a "Construction Ahead" sign on the road would be positive evidence. However, another motorist testifying that he did not see any signs is negative evidence. The sign may have been there, but the motorist did not see it. (See 32 C.J.S. Evidence 1079 for discussion and case citations.)
Testimonial evidence	Testimonial evidence is testimony of a witness in court, under oath and subject to cross-examination.
Tangible evidence	Tangible, or physical, evidence refers to objects, such as weapons, drugs, or clothing, that are used as evidence. Some tangible evidence is *contraband* (that is, objects that are illegal to possess, such as illegal drugs or stolen property). Other physical or tangible evidence is what was formerly called *mere evidence.* The defendant could lawfully own objects such as a ski mask, sunglasses, or a jacket, but the objects are used as evidence because the victim identifies the offender as wearing such objects at the time of the crime. Mere evidence is returned to the defendant after being used as evidence. Contraband is never returned to the defendant.
Demonstrative evidence	See Chapter 16 on demonstrative evidence and exhibits such as diagrams, charts, and photographs of a crime scene or traffic accident.
Scientific evidence	See Chapter 18 on scientific evidence, which is the product of crime laboratories and coroner's laboratories.

Res Ipsa Loquitur as an Inference

The phrase, doctrine, or rule **res ipsa loquitur** ("the thing speaks for itself") is used in both civil and criminal law. *McCormick on Evidence* (West Publishing, 1972) points out that this doctrine is an inference that permits but does not require a jury to draw a conclusion:

EXAMPLE: In a sexual or physical assault case where the victim has been terribly injured, photographs of the battered victim are introduced into evidence with a medical person who attended the victim verifying the accuracy of the photographs.

Whether the photographs are contested or not by the defense, the prosecutor can argue that the photographs speak for themselves in presenting strong evidence proving that the criminal harm and wrong that is charged in the criminal action did occur (proof of corpus delicti).

The only issue then remaining before the court and jury is the identity of the perpetrator. The defense lawyer could agree that corpus delicti has been proved and take the position that "Yes a terrible crime has occurred, but my client did not commit the crime and is innocent."

The terms *conclusive* or *irrebuttable presumptions* are used and are defined in different ways by different writers and different courts. The old common law presumption that a child under the age of 7 is incapable of committing a crime can be called an irributable or conclusive presumption as it cannot be overcome by evidence showing otherwise. A state could statutorize this presumption as a law, but most states leave the concept in its common law form.

The Supreme Court of Pennsylvania[41] and the Supreme Court of Indiana[42] defined the legal significance and nature of a presumption as follows:

> [A] presumption of law is not evidence nor should it be weighed by the fact finder as though it had evidentiary value. Rather, a presumption is a rule of law enabling the party in whose favor it operates to take his case to the jury without presenting evidence of the fact presumed. It serves as a challenge for proof and indicates the party from whom such proof must be forthcoming. When the opponent of the presumption has met the burden of production thus imposed, however, the office of the presumption has been performed; the presumption is of no further effect and drops from the case.

Inferences

Inferences are reasonable conclusions or deductions that fact finders (juries or judges) *may* draw from the evidence presented to them. Fact finders should use good common sense and their knowledge of everyday life in their reasoning process.

While a *presumption* is an assumption that the law expressly directs that the trier of fact *must* make, an *inference* is a conclusion that a jury or judge *may* make based upon the evidence presented.

Persons charged with a crime have a constitutional right to a jury trial. Juries in criminal trials, therefore, must decide all issues of fact presented by evidence in the trial. If a jury instruction interferes or infringes upon the jury's obligation to determine and decide issues of fact, a violation of the defendant's right to jury has occurred.

A violation of the defendant's right to a jury occurred in the case of *Sandstrom v. Montana*.[43] The U.S. Supreme Court held that an instruction to a jury that "the law presumes that a person intends the ordinary consequences of his voluntary acts" shifted the burden of proof in Sandstrom's criminal case to the defendant. Because the state must prove all essential elements of the crime charged, the burden-shifting presumption as to the intent of the defendant violated his due process rights.

Juries may infer that a defendant intended "the ordinary consequences of his or her voluntary act," but they cannot be told by a judge in a jury instruction that they have to presume this.

SUMMARY

In criminal trials, both prosecutors and defense lawyers use evidence either to prove or disprove facts that are in issue. The prosecution always has the burden of production of evidence and the burden of persuasion to prove the defendant guilty beyond reasonable doubt.

Direct evidence (if available) may be used to either prove or disprove facts in issue. Circumstantial evidence may also be used. Circumstantial evidence requires the fact finder to draw inferences from evidence that is presented.

In most criminal cases, both direct and circumstantial evidence are used. However, a defendant may be convicted on circumstantial evidence alone. Circumstantial evidence is most often used to prove the mental element, which are essential elements of many crimes. For example, the requirement of specific intent in the crime of murder is most often proved by inferences drawn from the proven conduct of the defendant.

Inferences are conclusions or deductions that a jury or a judge as the fact finder may draw from the evidence presented. Legal presumptions are rules of law that establish which party has the burden of proof in the production of evidence and the burden of persuasion.

PROBLEMS

1. A New York state trooper saw a car traveling at an excessive rate of speed on the New York Thruway. The officer overtook the speeding vehicle and stopped it. Four men were in the vehicle, two in the front seat and two in the back seat. As the officer was asking the driver for his license and the vehicle registration, the officer smelled burning marijuana. The officer then saw an envelope marked "Supergold" lying on the floor of the car between the two men in the front seat.

The evidence that was available to the officer would permit him to draw an inference as to which of the men possessed the marijuana. Did the evidence and the inference drawn from the evidence establish probable cause to arrest the driver? Or the two men in the front seat? Can it be inferred from the evidence that probable cause existed to arrest all four men? Explain. [*New York v. Belton*, 453 U.S. 454, 101 S.Ct. 2860 (1981)]

2. A guard at the state prison in Walpole, Massachusetts, heard loud voices coming from a walkway. The officer immediately opened the door to the walkway and saw "an inmate named Stephens bleeding from the mouth and suffering from a swollen eye. Dirt was strewn about the walkway, which the officer viewed to be further evidence of a scuffle." The officer saw three inmates, including an inmate named Hill, jogging away together down the walkway. There were no other inmates in the area, which was enclosed by a chain-link fence. The officer concluded that the three men acted as a group in assaulting Stephens. There was no evidence as to who actually beat Stephens. Was there sufficient evidence to punish Hill as one of the three men involved in the assault by taking away his good-time credits? Explain. [*Superintendent, Mass. Correctional Institution, Walpole v. Hill*, 472 U.S. 445, 105 S.Ct. 2768, 37 CrL 3108 (1985)]

3. Kent Hansen was sitting on a public park bench close to a man who was smoking a marijuana cigarette. When an officer in plain clothes saw the marijuana cigarette and smelled burning marijuana, he arrested both men. The officer did not see Hansen holding or smoking the marijuana cigarette. Could the officer properly infer from the information he had that Hansen was an active participant in the use or possession of the marijuana? Should Hansen's conviction be affirmed? Give reasons for your answer. [*State of Arizona v. Hansen*, 573 P.2d 896 (Ariz. App., 1977)]

4. An experienced law enforcement officer used the following incident as an example for classes. The officer's wife was babysitting for

their 3-year-old grandson while the parents were away. No one else was in the house when the grandmother put the child to bed for an afternoon nap. A short time later, while the grandmother was in the basement, she heard a crash and ran back upstairs. When she entered the child's room, she saw the window drapes lying across the bed and on the floor. Because the child had the means and opportunity of pulling the drapes down, the grandmother said to the child, "Why did you pull the drapes down?" The child looked his grandmother in the eye and replied, "You didn't see me do it, and you can't prove that I did it."

List the evidence available to the grandmother that caused her to conclude that the child pulled the drapes down. Indicate whether this was direct or circumstantial evidence.

If this situation was presented to a jury, would they be justified in drawing the same conclusion that the grandmother did? Would a jury's verdict of guilty be sustained by the trial court and the appellate court in that there was sufficient evidence to sustain the jury's finding?

5. To prove tax evasion in most cases, the government shows an income upon which tax has not been paid.

In Holland's case, the government showed that Holland's net worth was increasing yearly far beyond the income he was reporting to the government and paying taxes on, but they could not prove where he was getting most of his yearly income. A jury drew inferences of tax fraud from this and convicted Holland of tax evasion based on the "net worth method," as was done with the gangster Al Capone in the 1920s.

Can circumstantial evidence and inferences support a criminal conviction that Holland was not reporting and paying taxes on income from unknown sources? Does the showing that Holland's net worth grew year after year justify this conviction? [*Holland v. United States*, 348 U.S. 121, 75 S.Ct. 127 (1954)]

INFOTRAC COLLEGE EDITION EXERCISES

1. Go to InfoTrac College Edition and using the search term "circumstantial evidence" find the October 21, 2002, article in *Time* magazine "Body of Evidence." This article presents a short summary of how a crime scene is "worked" by law enforcement personnel and also a description of the kinds of evidence one might expect to find at a crime scene.

2. Go to InfoTrac College Edition and using the search term "reasonable doubt standard" find the 1996 *Supreme Court Review* article titled "The Supreme Court, Dr. Jeckyll, and the Due Process of Proof," by Larry Alexander. This article discusses the history of the reasonable doubt standard and a critique of its application in a Montana murder case. Assume a defendant commits a crime while intoxicated. While not a defense to the crime, should the intoxicated state of the defendant be relevant to elements of the crime, such as the defendant's ability to formulate the specific intent to kill? If evidence of such intoxication is excluded, does that effectively shift the burden of "beyond a reasonable doubt" from the state to the defendant? What does the author conclude? Do you agree?

3. Go to InfoTrac College Edition and using the search term "corpus delicti" find the 2000 *Florida Bar Journal* article titled "The Anatomy of Florida's Corpus Delicti Doctrine," by Tom Barber. How does one meet the corpus delicti requirement? Is it a requirement of constitutional magnitude, or do states have flexibility in framing the doctrine? What is the relationship of corpus delicti to the admission of extrajudicial evidence, such as confessions by a defendant?

NOTES

1. *In re Winship,* 397 U.S. 358, 364 (1970).
2. *Commonwealth v. Webster,* 59 Mass. 295, 320 (1850). In *Apodaca v. Oregon,* 406 U.S. 404, 412 (1972), the Supreme Court noted that following *Webster,* courts in the United States began using the "reasonable doubt" standard in criminal cases.
3. *In re Winship,* supra.
4. *Victor v. Nebraska,* 511 U.S. 1 (1994).
5. *Cage v. Louisiana,* 498 U.S. 39, 40 (1990).
6. *Sandoval v. California,* 511 U.S. 1, 6 (1994).
7. *Victor v. Nebraska,* supra, at 23 (Ginsburg, Justice, concurring).
8. Elisabeth Stoffelmayr and Shari S. Diamond, "The Conflict Between Precision and Flexibility in Explaining 'Beyond a Reasonable Doubt,'" 6 *Pyschol. Pub. Pol'y & L* 769 (2000).
9. Federal Judicial Center, *Pattern Criminal Jury Instructions,* 21 (1988).
10. The Supreme Court of Louisiana pointed out that "[s]pecific intent to kill or inflict great bodily harm can easily be inferred where an individual discharges a firearm pointed directly at a victim from a short distance." [*State v. Noble,* 425 So.2d 734 (La., 1983)]. The Supreme Court of Indiana approved of the following jury instruction in the case of *Henderson v. State,* 544 N.E.2d 507 (1989), where intent to steal had to be proved to convict Henderson of burglary:

> [Y]ou may infer that a person is presumed to intend the natural and probable acts, unless the circumstances are such to indicate the absence of such intent. When an unlawful act, however, is proved to be knowingly done, no further proof is needed on the part of the state in the absence of justifying or excusing facts.

The Supreme Court of North Carolina affirmed the first-degree murder conviction of the defendant in the 1990 case of *State v. Porter,* 391 S.E.2d 144. To prove intent to kill, the defendant's statement, "I meant to kill the s-of-a-b-" (direct evidence) was used, as was the fact that he "pumped three rounds into the body" of his girlfriend (circumstantial evidence of intent).

State of mind in attempted murder or assault in the first degree can be shown by circumstantial evidence, as was done in the 1991 case of *State v. Turner,* 587 A.2d 1050, where the Connecticut Appellate Court held:

> "The intent of the actor is a question for the trier of fact, and the conclusion of the trier in this regard should stand unless it is an unreasonable one." *State v. Avcollie,* 178 Conn. 450, 466, 423 A.2d 118 (1979), cert. denied, 444 U.S. 1015, 100 S.Ct. 667, 62 L. Ed.2d 645 (1980).
>
> The jury was free to credit the testimony that the defendant pointed the loaded gun at Russell, pulled the trigger, and that the gun clicked but did not fire. Crediting this testimony, we cannot say that an inference that the defendant intended to inflict serious physical injury on Russell was either unreasonable or illogical. "'It was within the province of the [trier] to draw reasonable and logical inferences from the facts proven.'" *State v. Avcollie,* supra, 178 Conn. at 470, 423 A.2d 118. Also, the jury can draw an inference from the facts they found as the result of other inferences. Thus, the evidence presented at trial amply supported the existence of the requisite intent.

In the 1991 case of *Commonwealth v. Chester,* 587 A.2d 1367, the Supreme Court of Pennsylvania held that slashing a victim's throat was sufficient evidence to support a jury's finding that the killing was intentional.

The crime of theft requires proof of a specific intent to steal, which is almost always proven by inferences drawn from the defendant's conduct. In the case of *Morissette v. United States,* 72 S. Ct. 240 (1952), Morissette took rusted bomb casings that had been laying for years in a wooded area. For all his hard work, Morissette made $84. He was charged with theft and argued that he honestly believed the junk to be abandoned, unwanted, and of no value to the government. The trial judge instructed the jury the government did not have to prove criminal intent for this crime and refused to allow Morissette's defense of honest mistake of fact. The U.S. Supreme Court reversed the trial judge ruling that the specific intent to steal must be proven beyond a reasonable doubt and that juries must be properly instructed as to the law.

11. 626 A.2d 1238 (Pa. Super., 1993).
12. The inference that a person who has possession of recently stolen property is the thief is not used in many states. The validity of this inference, however, was tested in the U.S. Supreme Court in 1992. In the case of *Wright v. West,* 112 S. Ct. 2482, the defendant was charged with grand larceny for the possession in his home of many household items stolen from another home two to four weeks earlier.

The defendant was convicted under a Virginia law that permits "an inference that a person who fails to explain, or falsely explains, his exclusive possession of recently stolen property is the thief." The Court affirmed the defendant's conviction, holding that the evidence was sufficient to justify the conviction.

In the 1991 case of *Buchannon v. State,* 405 S.E.2d 583 (Ga.App.), the police stopped the defendant while he was driving a stolen car. The defendant and his passenger both gave false names to the police and had an explanation of the defendant's possession of the stolen car. The Georgia jury did not believe the defendant and convicted him of theft of the car.

Many prosecutors would not have charged theft in the *West* and *Buchannon* cases. Under the law of most states, crimes such as possession (receiving or concealing) of stolen property and operating a motor vehicle without the consent of the owner would be charged, because they would be much easier to prove.

13. 966 F.2d 707 (1st Cir).
14. 348 U.S. 121, 139, 75 S. Ct. 127, 137.
15. *CHV v. Wisconsin,* 643 N.W. 2d 878 (2002), cert. denied, 123 S. Ct. 443 (2002).
16. 590 N.E.2d 1177 (Mass. App.).
17. *Brown v. State,* 837 S.W.2d 457 (Ark.); *In the Interest of N.R.,* 402 S.E.2d 120 (Ga. App.).
18. 586 N.E.2d 1261.
19. 546 A.2d, at 419 (D.C. App.).
20. P.L. 103–322.
21. Federal Rules of Evidence, 413(a) and 414(a).
22. 916 F.2d 219 (5th Cir.), cert. denied, 500 U.S. 934, 111 S. Ct. 2057 (1991).
23. 780 P.2d 772.
24. 582 A.2d 341.
25. 612 A.2d 1349, 52 CrL 1014.

26. 741 F.2d 478 (1st Cir.).

27. 573 A.2d 85.

28. 963 F.2d 708 (5th Cir.).

29. The crime of transfer of an illegal drug also has a higher penalty than the crime of possession of the illegal drug. In the case of *Meek v. Mississippi*, 806 So. 2d 236 (2002), cert. denied, U.S. Sup. Ct., it was held that the interference that the defendant knew that marijuana was in a toilet kit he transferred was reasonable and proper. In the *Meek* case, the defendant was injured in a car crash. A passing motorist attempted to help the defendant, and in the course of doing so the defendant handed the motorist a shaving kit and asked him to "get rid of it." When the police arrived the motorist gave the kit to them. When the kit was discovered to contain marijuana, the defendant was charged with the crime of transfer of marijuana. The court held that the evidence was sufficient to prove the defendant knew the kit contained illegal drugs when he transferred it to the motorist.

30. 406 S.E.2d 833.

31. 923 F.2d 548 (7th Cir.).

32. 747 F.Supp. 528 (N.D. Iowa).

33. 939 F.2d 1053 (D.C. Cir.).

34. 563 A.2d 158.

35. 405 S.E.2d 1 (Va. App.).

36. 597 So.2d 721, 50 CrL 1342.

37. 807 P.2d 1009.

38. See 23 CJS, Criminal Law, 917.

39. 393 S.E.2d 781.

40. 262 A.2d 331, 335 (Md. App., 1970).

41. *Commonwealth v. Vogel*, 268 A.2d 89, 102 (Pa., 1970).

42. *Sumpter v. State*, 261 Ind. 471, 306 N.E.2d 95 (1974).

43. 442 U.S. 510, 99 S.Ct. 2450.

II

Witnesses and Their Testimony

5

Witnesses and the Testimony of Witnesses

Ⓐ QUALIFICATIONS NECESSARY TO BE A WITNESS

Witnesses are essential in all cases. Without witnesses, neither civil nor criminal cases could commence.[1] In order to be a **witness,** a person must satisfy the following requirements:

- *Requirement of personal knowledge*　The witness must have some personal knowledge of the matter before the court. If the governor of a state was in a bank at the time it was robbed, he or she could have enough personal knowledge to be subpoenaed if needed as a witness by either the state or the defense. Unless it is shown that someone has personal knowledge, the person should not be subpoenaed.

- *Requirement that every witness declare that he will testify truthfully*　Most witnesses will take an oath swearing that they will tell the truth. However, the Federal Rules of Evidence (Rule 602) and the Uniform Rules of Evidence also provide for an *affirmation,* which, like the oath, requires "every witness . . . to declare that he will testify truthfully."

- *Requirement of competency*　The usual modern standard for determining the competency of a witness has been stated: "Competency depends upon the witness' capacity to observe, remember and narrate as well as an understanding of the duty to tell the truth."[2]

The General Presumption that Adults Are Competent to Be Witnesses

Because the law presumes that adults are competent, most adult witnesses take the witness stand and testify without being challenged. The competency of a witness may be challenged, but the opposing attorney would have the burden of showing that the witness lacked one or more of the required qualifications.

Competency of witnesses can relate both to the ability of the witnesses to testify about the particular event they witnessed and also to circumstances that cast doubt on the credibility of that testimony. Thus, a witness whose mental state rendered the witness incapable of comprehending the event about which the witness seeks to testify can be judged incompetent. An example of this kind of incompetence might be a witness who was so intoxicated at the time the witnessed event occurred that the witness lacked the capacity to properly observe and remember the event. Where the witness possessed the capacity to accurately observe the event, but subsequently lost the mental faculties necessary to remember and testify about the event, the witness lacks the competence to testify. This could happen where the witness becomes mentally unstable or where some physical condition affects the memory of the witness.

A witness will not normally be judged incompetent based on circumstances that affect only the credibility of the witness. Thus, in *United States v. Bedonie,*[3] a witness was not found incompetent to testify simply because the witness had previously made several prior inconsistent statements. Also, in cases where the prosecutor presents testimony by paid informants, the fact that the informant was paid to testify does not

A child victim in a sexual abuse case testifies in open court. The anatomically correct doll is used to illustrate sexual acts performed on or by the child.

usually render the witness incompetent (*United States v. Cresta*).[4] In these cases, the jury can decide what effect, if any, the circumstances should have on the credibility of the testimony given by the witness.

Children as Witnesses

If a young child is called as a witness, the trial judge will first question (voir dire) the child to determine if the child is competent to testify. The child must be able to remember what occurred, tell about the events, and know that he or she must be truthful. The trial judge will then make a ruling as to the child's competence as a witness. The judge has broad discretion, and a court of appeals would not disturb the judge's ruling unless there was a clear abuse of that discretion.[5]

The Supreme Court of Arizona traced the history of child witnesses in the 1985 case of *State v. Schossow*,[6] where it was held that four children (aged 7 to 9) were competent to testify:

> At common law no child under fourteen years of age was eligible to testify as a witness. Annot., 81 A.L.R.2d 386, 389–90 (1962). It was not until 1779 that the law renounced the rule of absolute disqualification. In *Rex v. Brasier,* 1 Leach 199, 168 Eng.Rep. 202 (1779), the court held that a child less than seven years

Protecting and Helping Child Victims and Witnesses

Being the victim of a crime is a terrible experience, but the crime itself may be just the beginning of the trauma. The child victim is often grilled repeatedly about the crime by a succession of total strangers (police officers, social workers, lawyers, and others). Court appearances could make the nightmare worse, especially for children who are victims of sex offenses. To protect children and minimize emotional damage, states have enacted statutes to help children in the following ways:

- *Testimony by closed-circuit television* when a "child [is] suffering serious emotional distress" was allowed by the U.S. Supreme Court in the 1990 case of *Maryland v. Craig* (497 U.S. 836, 842, 110 S.Ct. 3157, 3162), where this procedure was approved under a Maryland statute. The trial court found that the child witnesses were so traumatized, they could not "reasonably communicate." The U.S. Supreme Court held in *Craig* that the face-to-face right to confront an accusing witness is not absolute and "must occasionally give way to considerations of public policy and the necessities of the case." More than thirty states have statutes permitting this procedure when it is shown that it is needed.

- *Videotaped testimony* in criminal child abuse proceedings is used in more than thirty-five states.

- *Statutes making it easier for children to be found competent* to testify have been enacted in all states to enable children as young as 3 years of age to appear as witnesses.

- *Special hearsay exceptions for child victims* and child witnesses have been enacted by more than thirty states. Such statutes and the regular hearsay exceptions (see Chapter 8) make it easier for adults such as teachers, neighbors, and parents to testify as to statements made by child victims.

Other statutes seeking to help and protect children include the following:

- *Use of anatomical dolls in criminal child abuse cases* to make it easier for the child witness by pointing to body parts as they testify. Some states have statutes, while others use the practice as part of accepted court procedure.

- *Closing the courtroom* to all but necessary parties while a child victim or witness is testifying. Many judges have this power; some states have statutes.

- *Use of leading questions with child witnesses.* Most state judges can permit this, and a few states now have statutes authorizing it.

- *Limiting the length of time a child is in the witness stand.* A few states have statutes, but judges in all states may limit cross-examination under their broad discretion in the conduct of criminal and civil trials.

- *Limiting the number of interviews with child victims.* In 1992 a California grand jury reported that victims were interviewed up to thirty-two times. California and other states now have statutes limiting the number of interviews.

- *Statutes requiring speedy handling* of cases involving child victims have been enacted by more than half of the states.

old was competent to testify "*provided* such infant appears, *on strict examination by the court,* to possess a sufficient knowledge of the nature and consequences of an oath. . . ." The United States Supreme Court followed the *Brasier* rule in *Wheeler v. United States,* 159 U.S. 523, 16 S.Ct. 93, 40 L.Ed. 244 (1895), and held that a five-year-old child was competent to testify in a criminal trial for murder. The Court stated that the decision of this question rests primarily with the trial judge, who sees the proposed witness, notices his manner, his apparent possession or lack of intelligence, and *may resort to any examination* which will tend to disclose his capacity and intelligence.

Today, all states have statutes that enable children as young as 3 years of age to appear as witnesses.

Voir Dire

The phrase **voir dire** is French for "to speak the truth." The term describes the preliminary examination used to determine whether a witness or juror is competent or qualified.

The voir dire of a young child one of the parties seeks to use as a witness would be a series of questions to determine whether the child has the perception, memory, and ability to testify as a witness in that case. The voir dire of an expert witness would consist of questions to determine whether that person qualifies as an expert. The voir dire of jurors would consist of questions to determine whether they are competent and what their interests and biases are. For example, an old friend of the arresting officer or the neighbor of the defendant would not qualify to sit on the jury.

Questioning during the voir dire is often done by the trial judge. However, depending upon the law or practice within a state, the questioning could be done by the attorneys.

Ⓑ CREDIBILITY OF WITNESSES

Methods Used to Keep Witnesses Honest

Witnesses have a serious responsibility to tell the truth. To encourage witnesses to tell the truth and to bring before the court and the jury the facts pertaining to the issues of the case, the following procedures are used:

- Witnesses must take an oath or affirmation that they will tell the truth.
- Witnesses must be personally present at the trial (the defendant's Sixth Amendment right to confront witnesses must be ensured).[7]
- Witnesses are subject to cross-examination.

In addition, witnesses who do not tell the truth run the risk of being charged with *perjury.* If they refuse to testify or refuse to answer questions that are not privileged, they could be found in *contempt of court* and punished.

Credibility and the Weight of Evidence

It is up to a judge or jury, as the trier of fact, to determine whether statements made by witnesses are to be believed and what weight to give them. In determining the credibility and the weight to be given to the testimony of witnesses, the following factors should be considered:

- *Perception* Did the witness perceive (see, hear, smell, and so on) accurately? Did the witness have an opportunity to observe and perceive?

The Jury Trial of William Penn

An important case in the historic development of the power and authority of the jury to independently determine the credibility of witnesses and the weight to be given to their testimony occurred in London in 1670. William Penn (the founder of Pennsylvania) was a peaceful and nonviolent man who was charged with preaching to an unlawful assembly. The basis for the charge was that Penn had addressed his religious group in an orderly church meeting in London. Penn was not of the same religious faith as the king of England. After the trial, the jury refused to convict Penn. They were ordered to reconsider their finding but continued to refuse to convict. The jury was held for two days without food, water, or other accommodations (a fire and a chamberpot, which they had requested). When this did not break them, they were finally released, after being fined for holding to their verdict of not guilty. A plaque can be found today in the Old Bailey (the central criminal justice building in London) commemorating the "courage and endurance" of that jury. An appellate court sustained Penn and the jury in a writ of habeas corpus, holding that juries were not to be punished for failing to make findings as ordered by the trial court.

The Right to and the Purpose of a Jury Today

The Sixth Amendment of the U.S. Constitution provides that: "In all criminal prosecutions, the accused shall enjoy the right to . . . an impartial jury of the State and district wherein the crime shall have been committed. . . ."

> The purpose of a jury is to make available the commonsense judgment of the community as a hedge against the overzealous or mistaken prosecutor [*Taylor v. Louisiana* (1975), 419 U.S. 522, 530]. . . . It is the jury's duty to assess the credibility of witnesses and to weigh the evidence in determining a defendant's guilt or innocence. [See, e.g., *Glasser v. United States* (1942), 315 U.S. 60, 80.]

- *Memory* Has the witness retained an accurate impression of what the witness saw, heard, smelled, and so on? Is the witness's memory of the events accurate?
- *Narration by the witness* Do the testimony of the witness and the language used accurately describe the events?

In determining the weight and the credit to be given to the testimony of each witness, juries and judges as the triers of fact also use their knowledge and experience. Witness statements that are incredible or contrary to commonly known facts do not have to be accepted. The *incontrovertible physical facts rule* (also known as the *physical facts rule*) holds that the fact-finding body will give no weight to witness statements that are inherently incredible, unbelievable, and contrary to physical facts, known physical laws, general knowledge, or human experience.[8]

The reasonableness of witnesses' testimony, their interest or lack of interest in the results of the trial, their bias or prejudice (if any are shown), their clearness or lack of clearness of recollection, and the overall impression obtained by the jury are factors used in determining the weight and credit to be given to the testimony of a witness.

In a jury trial, the jury is the sole judge of the credibility of all witnesses, including the defendant if he takes the witness stand. The jury evaluates the weight and credibility of testimony, free from the influence of the trial judge.

Demeanor as Evidence in Judging Witnesses

Not only are the words of a witness evidence in a trial, but the demeanor of the witness has been held also to be evidence that may be used in determining credibility. In everyday life, we judge other people not only by what they say, but also to some extent by their appearances and their conduct. The following ruling in the 1952 case of *Dyer v. MacDougall*[9] by Judge Learned Hand is sometimes quoted by other courts:

> It is true that the carriage, behavior, bearing, manner and appearance of a witness—in short, his "demeanor"—is a part of the evidence. The words used are by no means all that we rely on in making up our minds about the truth of a question that arises in our ordinary affairs, and it is abundantly settled that a jury is as little confined to them as we are. They may, and indeed they should, take into consideration the whole nexus of sense impressions which they get from a witness. . . .

In the 1991 case of *Michigan v. Sammons*,[10] a Michigan Court of Appeals held that permitting an informant to wear a ski mask at a hearing on whether entrapment occurred violated the defendant's Sixth Amendment right to confront the witness. The court held that the mask prevented the judge from observing the informer's demeanor and adequately assessing his credibility. The U.S. Supreme Court denied review of the case (112 S.Ct. 3015).

C CONSTITUTIONAL RIGHTS OF DEFENDANTS REGARDING WITNESSES

The Right to Compel the Attendance of Witnesses

The Sixth Amendment of the U.S. Constitution provides that: "In all criminal prosecutions, the accused shall enjoy the right . . . to have compulsory process for obtaining witnesses in his favor. . . ."

To ensure the attendance of a witness, a subpoena must be issued. A **subpoena** is a command to the person to whom it is directed to appear on a specified date at a given time and place for the purpose of testifying. In addition, the person may be required to bring documents or other materials that are expected to be useful in the proceedings. A **subpoena duces tecum** would describe the material that the witness is to bring.

The right to the compulsory process to obtain the attendance of witnesses does not mean that the defendant can subpoena anyone at all in order to delay the case and to make the trial a cumbersome process. Only competent witnesses who have a personal knowledge of facts relevant to the case may be subpoenaed.

The Right to Confront and Cross-Examine Witnesses

The Sixth Amendment also provides that "the accused shall enjoy the right . . . to be confronted with the witnesses against him. . . ." The witness not only testifies in open court in the presence of the accused but is also subject to cross-examination by the opposing party.

The U.S. Supreme Court has pointed out that for centuries **cross-examination** has been considered to be one of the safeguards of the accuracy and completeness of testimony by a witness. The U.S. Supreme Court held in the 1974 case of *Davis v. Alaska*,[11] that:

> Cross-examination is the principal means by which the believability of a witness and the truth of his testimony are tested. Subject always to the broad discretion of a trial judge to preclude repetitive and unduly harassing interrogation, the cross-examiner is not only permitted to delve into the witness' story to test the witness' perceptions and memory, but the cross-examiner has traditionally been allowed to impeach, i.e., discredit, the witness. One way of discrediting the witness is to introduce evidence of a prior criminal conviction of that witness. By so doing the cross-examiner intends to afford the jury a basis to infer that the witness' character is such that he would be less likely than the average trustworthy citizen to be truthful in his testimony. The introduction of evidence of a prior crime is thus a general attack on the credibility of the witness. A more particular attack on the witness' credibility is effected by means of cross-examination directed toward revealing possible biases, prejudices, or ulterior motives of the witness as they may relate directly to issues or personalities in the case at hand. The partiality of a witness is subject to exploration at trial . . . We have recognized that the exposure of a witness' motivation in testifying is a proper and important function of the constitutionally protected right of cross-examination.

The Defendant's Right to Testify in His or Her Defense

Defendants have a right to testify in their own behalf. As the U.S. Supreme Court pointed out in the 1987 case of *Rock v. Arkansas*,[12] this right is derived from the Sixth and Fourteenth Amendments. The Supreme Court held the right "is essential to due process of law in a fair adversary process."

Under the old common law, defendants in criminal cases were not considered competent to appear as witnesses in their own trial.[13] Today, all defendants are considered competent to take the witness stand in their own behalf.

However, defendants who take the witness stand to testify in their behalf waive their right to remain silent and must answer questions on cross-examination. Because of the danger of cross-examination and the risk of impeachment, defense lawyers in most instances strongly urge their clients not to risk testifying in their own defense, pointing out the additional danger that a defendant's testimony may "open the door to otherwise inadmissible evidence which is damaging to the case"[14]

In the 1993 case of *United States v. Dunnigan*,[15] the U.S. Supreme Court unanimously and bluntly held that "a defendant's right to testify does not include a right to commit perjury." It is not perjury for a defendant to enter a not-guilty plea and then be found guilty. But it is perjury for a defendant to take the witness stand and lie in a material way. The Supreme Court stated in the *Dunnigan* case that a "defendant who commits a crime and perjures herself in an unlawful attempt to avoid responsibility is more threatening to society and less deserving of leniency than a defendant who does not defy the trial process."[16]

D TYPES OF WITNESSES AND OPINION EVIDENCE

Ordinary Witnesses and Expert Witnesses

Most witnesses are **ordinary** (or lay) **witnesses** who are called to testify about the first-hand information they have regarding the case before the court. Their testimony is ordinarily limited to what they have seen, heard (although hearsay is in most instances excluded), smelled, felt, and, on rare occasions, tasted. Law enforcement officers appear in most instances as ordinary witnesses, although some officers also appear as expert witnesses when they qualify, testifying about fingerprinting, traffic matters, weapons, and so on.

An **expert witness** is a person who has had special training, education, or experience. Because of this experience and background, the expert witness may be able to assist the jury and the court in resolving the issues before them. The party offering a witness as an expert must lay a foundation (that is, ask a series of questions) establishing the witness as an expert in the field in which the expert will testify and offer opinions.

Three questions are presented to a trial court when one of the parties seeks to introduce an expert witness:

- Is the subject on which the expert witness will testify one for which the court can receive the opinion of an expert?
- What qualifications are necessary to qualify the witness as an expert?
- Does the witness meet these qualifications?

When there is a subject on which an expert witness may testify, the trial judge has to determine whether the expert testimony is reliable enough to admit into evidence. The trial judge is given a great deal of latitude and discretion in determining whether a witness qualifies as an expert witness.

To qualify as an expert in some fields (such as, a medical expert), requires years of formal education, training, and a license. Other subjects, such as fingerprinting or handwriting analysis, require other qualifications. Rule 702 of the Federal Rules of Evidence provides that:

> If scientific, technical, or other specialized knowledge will assist the trier of fact to understand the evidence or to determine a fact in issue, a witness qualified as an expert by knowledge, skill, experience, training, or education, may testify thereto in the form of an opinion or otherwise, if (1) the testimony is based upon sufficient facts or data, (2) the testimony is the product of reliable principles and methods, and (3) the witness has applied the principles and methods reliably to the facts of the case.[17]

In discussing the qualifications necessary to be a handwriting expert, the court in the 1938 case of *First Galesburg National Bank & Trust Company v. Federal Reserve Bank*[18] stated that:

> There is no test by which it can be determined with mathematical certainty how much experience or knowledge of handwriting a witness must have in

order to qualify as an expert for comparison. . . . In order that a witness be competent as an expert in respect to handwriting, it is not necessary that he should belong to any particular calling or profession; it is only necessary that the business opportunities and intelligence of the witness should be such as to enable him to have reasonable skill in judging of handwriting.

In the 1973 case of *Miller v. California,*[19] the U.S. Supreme Court held that a police officer qualified as an expert witness to "community standards" in an obscenity case, stating that:

The record simply does not support appellant's contention, belatedly raised on appeal, that the State's expert was unqualified to give evidence on California "community standards." The expert, a police officer with many years of specialization in obscenity offenses, had conducted an extensive statewide survey and had given expert evidence on 26 occasions in the year prior to this trial. Allowing such expert testimony was certainly not constitutional error.

It is the fact finder (jury or judge) who determines the weight and credibility to be given to the testimony of both expert and ordinary witnesses.

Opinion Evidence by Ordinary Witnesses

An ordinary witness is qualified to testify because of firsthand knowledge of an issue before the court. The expert witness has something different to contribute in assisting the trier of fact. Neither type of witness would be permitted to give an opinion as to whether the defendant is guilty or innocent. This determination is for the fact finder to decide, based on the evidence presented.

The testimony of ordinary witnesses usually consists of statements about the facts in a case that have been observed firsthand but may also include opinions and conclusions as to common things that are within the knowledge of the average person. An opinion that the defendant was intoxicated or angry, for example, or as to the value of his property that was stolen or destroyed would be allowed. Rule 701 of the Federal Rules of Evidence provides that:

If the witness is not testifying as an expert, his testimony in the form of opinions or inferences is limited to those opinions or inferences which are (a) rationally based on the perception of the witness and (b) helpful to a clear understanding of his testimony or the determination of a fact in issue.

If it is shown that an ordinary witness was well acquainted with a defendant's or another person's handwriting, that witness could be qualified to testify regarding the handwriting.[20]

Ordinary witnesses who are drug users, or who are well acquainted with drugs or guns, could be held qualified by a trial court to testify about the identity of drugs[21] or guns and ammunition.[22] Where there was sufficient foundation to justify a deputy sheriff's opinion about the cause of a snowmobile accident, the judgment in the civil case of *Cline v. Durden,*[23] was affirmed in 1990.

The Federal Rules of Evidence provide that an ordinary witness may express an opinion that is "rationally based on the perception of the witness" (Rule 701). Under

Witnesses and Their Testimony

In order to qualify as a witness, a person
- Must have relevant information
- Must be competent
- Must declare that he or she will testify truthfully

To be competent, a witness
- Must be able to remember and tell what happened
- Must be able to distinguish fact from fantasy
- Must know that he or she must tell the truth

In evaluating a witness's testimony, the fact finder should consider
- Accuracy of perception
- Accuracy of memory and recall
- Accuracy of narration

Anglo-Saxon law seeks to keep witnesses honest by having them testify
- Under oath or affirmation
- In the presence of the fact finder and the accused
- Subject to cross-examination
- Subject to possible perjury charges for failure to tell the truth

Methods used to help forgetful witnesses include
- Jogging the memory by questions such as "What else happened at this point?"
- Handing reports, notes, files, and so on to the witness to refresh his or her memory
- Introducing the documents as evidence if refreshing memory does not work and documents exist.

---

this type of rule, ordinary witnesses expressed opinions concerning insanity,[24] intoxication,[25] drug impairment,[26] the speed of a vehicle,[27] the time of death testified to by a lieutenant in a fire department,[28] and the difficulty in interviewing a child witness by a police officer.[29]

When witnesses testify that the defendant was drunk, or looked surprised, or that the defendant "seemed like he was trying to break my neck," the witness is using a "shorthand way" of collecting facts and expressing opinions about what the witness saw or experienced. Trial courts have considerable discretion and generally will permit such opinions.[30]

For example, in the 2001 case of *United States v. Bogan* (267 F.3d 614 [7th cir. 2001]), the Seventh Circuit Court of Appeals permitted a lay witness to testify that based on his perception of the nature of an assault by defendants on the victim, he believed the defendants were trying to kill the victim. The defendants were convicted of assault with intent to commit serious bodily harm based on this and other evidence.

E DIRECT EXAMINATION OF WITNESSES

In criminal cases, the government has the burden of proving the charges made against the defendant beyond a reasonable doubt. The state also has the burden of coming forward first with evidence showing that the defendant committed the offenses with which he is charged. Therefore, the first witnesses to appear in criminal cases are government witnesses called by the prosecutor to support the state's case.

In most instances, the government's case is presented by testimony about the chronological order of events as they occurred. Usually an attempt is made to let the witness tell his or her story first with as few interruptions as possible, by using such questions as:

"Where were you on the night of June 23?"

"Will you tell the court and jury what you saw and heard at that time?"

The question-and-answer method must be used in American courtrooms so that the opposing lawyer may object to the question before the answer is in evidence. However, by the use of short general questions such as "What did you see?" "What did you do?" and "What happened next?" the witness is able to tell the story and at the same time is kept to the point. After the witness has presented a general account of the facts as known to the witness, the prosecutor may then go back and fill in or emphasize details with more specific questions.

Cross-Examination of Witnesses

After the **direct examination,** the witness may then be cross-examined by the opposing attorney. For centuries, cross-examination has been considered one of the essential safeguards of the accuracy and completeness of testimony given by a witness. The U.S. Supreme Court held in the 1974 case of *Davis v. Alaska*[31] that:

> Cross-examination is the principal means by which the believability of a witness and the truth of his testimony are tested. Subject always to the broad discretion of a trial judge to preclude repetitive and unduly harassing interrogation, the cross-examiner is not only permitted to delve into the witness' story to test the witness' perceptions and memory, but the cross-examiner has traditionally been allowed to impeach, i.e., discredit, the witness.

The most effective defense to cross-examination is for a witness to testify truthfully and simply in answering all questions, even though the answers may sometimes be embarrassing or harmful. The purposes of cross-examination are:

- To test the "believability of a witness and the truth of his testimony" (the U.S. Supreme Court in *Davis v. Alaska*)
- To bring out facts supporting the cross-examiner's case
- To impeach (discredit) the witness (which also is a means of testing the "believability of a witness and the truth of his testimony")

If a witness has not hurt the opposing party's case, there usually is no reason to cross-examine unless there is a possibility of bringing out facts that might help the case of the cross-examiner.

Cross-examination is often exploratory, and for that reason it is risky: Facts uncovered in cross-examination could hurt the cross-examiner's case. In the 1931 case of *Alford v. United States*,[32] the U.S. Supreme Court stated that:

> Counsel often cannot know in advance what pertinent facts may be elicited on cross-examination. For that reason it is necessarily exploratory; and the rule

An Example of Effective Cross-Examination

In 1984 former car maker John DeLorean was indicted for drug trafficking. In his California trial, which lasted five months, DeLorean did not take the witness stand in his own defense. It was through lengthy cross-examination of government witnesses that evidence supporting DeLorean's defense of entrapment was made part of the trial record. Through cross-examination, lawyers for DeLorean were able to show that potential evidence was destroyed, that investigative guidelines of the government agency were violated, and that government agents failed to keep a proper rein on their paid informant. When DeLorean backed out of the drug deal because of a lack of cash, it was government agents who called him back, suggesting the use of collateral. When the government's chief prosecutor and the drug agents had drinks together, the defense presented the meeting as a boozy celebration of DeLorean's imminent arrest. On cross-examination, government agents admitted that they speculated about whether they would make the cover of *Time* magazine.

With this evidence on the trial record as the result of cross-examination, the jury found DeLorean not guilty of all eight criminal charges after seven days of deliberation. The decision to not put DeLorean on the witness stand and subject him to lengthy cross-examination was probably not made until after the defense saw how successful their cross-examinations had been.

that the examiner must indicate the purpose of his inquiry does not, in general, apply. It is the essence of a fair trial that reasonable latitude be given the cross-examiner, even though he is unable to state to the court what facts a reasonable cross-examination might develop. Prejudice ensues from a denial of the opportunity to place the witness in his proper setting and put the weight of his testimony and his credibility to a test, without which the jury cannot fairly appraise them.

Impeachment is another aspect of cross-examination, and in criminal cases is probably the most effective cross-examination technique. By use of impeachment, "the cross-examiner intends to afford the jury a basis to infer that the witness' character is such that he would be less likely than the average trustworthy citizen to be truthful in his testimony."[33] Impeachment may be accomplished by cross-examination and also by the introduction of other evidence. The functions of impeachment may be classified as follows:

- To attack the witness's credibility and qualifications to testify truthfully because of prior criminal conviction (and in some jurisdictions and some instances, a showing of prior bad conduct). The Federal Rules of Evidence, Rule 609, limits evidence of prior criminal convictions to crimes with a penalty in excess of one year imprisonment, or crimes involving dishonesty or false statement, regardless of the punishment.

  EXAMPLE: Evidence of a witness's conviction of assault was admissible to attack the witness's credibility, where the punishment was more than one year in prison.[34]

  EXAMPLE: Evidence of a witness's conviction of a misdemeanor offense of receiving stolen property was not admissible, because the punishment was less than one year imprisonment, and the crime of receiving stolen property does not automatically involve dishonesty or false statement.[35]

- To attack the testimony given by the witness on direct examination by a showing of prior inconsistent statements.

  EXAMPLE: In a prosecution related to defendant's alleged spousal abuse, prior inconsistent statements made by the witness (defendant's wife) about the nature of the abuse were admissible on the witness's credibility.[36]

- To attack the witness's credibility by showing bias, prejudice, or ulterior motives of the witness.

Rule 611(a) of the Federal Rules of Evidence states that the "court shall exercise reasonable control over the mode and order of interrogating witnesses and presenting evidence so as to . . . (2) avoid needless consumption of time, and (3) protect witnesses from harassment or undue embarrassment."

In the 1988 case of *Olden v. Kentucky,*[37] the U.S. Supreme Court again pointed out that trial judges have "broad discretion . . . to preclude repetitive and unduly harassing interrogation." In the 1987 case of *Kentucky v. Stincer,*[38] the Supreme Court held that the "Confrontation Clause guarantees only 'an *opportunity* for effective cross-examination, not cross-examination that is effective in whatever way, and to whatever extent, the defense might wish.'"

Objections to Questions

Under the adversary system, **objections** to questions are the first line of defense against statements the opposing party seeks to use. It is the lawyers who must object, and not the judge. Failure to object, in most instances, waives the grounds for an appeal to a higher court.

The trial judge has considerable discretion in ruling upon objections and in determining what is relevant, material, and competent. The trial judge will not be overruled by a higher court unless there is an abuse of discretion or plain error.

Objections are classified as follows:

- *Objections to the substance of the question*   These objections concern the answer called for by the question. Usual objections in this area would be irrelevant, immaterial, incompetent, hearsay, and so on.

- *Objections to the form of the question*   These objections concern the manner in which the question is worded. In most instances, the question may be rephrased and asked again in a form in which both the question and answer will be admissible. Usual objections to the form of a question are that the question is leading, argumentative, calls for speculation, misstates a fact in evidence, and so on.

- *Objections to the answer*   If an attorney is slow in objecting, the attorney usually pays the penalty and is told to object faster. In this situation and others, a lawyer can object to an answer and ask that the answer be stricken from the record because: (1) The answer is unresponsive to the question. This most often occurs when the witness volunteers additional information beyond the scope of the

Objections to Questions

Objections to the Form of the Question

- Leading question (suggests the answer that is wanted)
- Calls for speculation
- Argumentative
- Misstates facts in evidence
- Assumes facts not in evidence
- Vague and ambiguous
- Repetitive or cumulative
- Misleading

Objections to the Substance of the Question

- Irrelevant
- Immaterial

- Incompetent
- Calls for hearsay
- Insufficient foundation
- Calls for inadmissible opinion answer
- Beyond the scope of the direct examination

Objections to the Answer

- Unresponsive
- Inadmissible opinion
- Inadmissible hearsay statement

question asked. (2) The answer contains an inadmissible opinion. (3) Inadmissible hearsay statements are included in the answer.

F THE REQUIREMENTS OF RELEVANCY, MATERIALITY, AND COMPETENCY

Criminal and civil trials would be much longer if there were no controls on the testimony and information allowed. Unrelated evidence would cause confusion and would clutter the fact-finding process. To minimize confusion and to make trials manageable, it is required that all evidence must be **relevant, material, and competent.** Therefore, to introduce facts, testimony, or a physical object as evidence, it must be shown that:

- The evidence must address a material fact.
- It must be relevant to that fact.
- It must be able to affect the probable truth or falsity of that fact by being competent.

A fact is *material* if it will affect the result of a trial. For example, a defendant is charged with a crime committed in a tavern at ten o'clock at night. State witnesses testifying that they saw the defendant in a tavern at that time would be relevant and material. Defense witnesses testifying that the defendant was at another place 5 miles away would also be relevant and material to the fact in issue.

Evidence is *relevant* if it has a tendency to make a material fact more or less probable. Testimony by a witness that he saw the defendant in the tavern at ten o'clock would be relevant evidence. However, testimony that the tavern was hit by lightning and burnt down a week later would not be relevant since the fire is not material to the case. The questions that must be asked are:

- Is the fact material to the dispute?
- If so, does the proposed evidence make the material evidence more or less probable (relevant)?

After our hypothetical witness has testified that the defendant was in the tavern at the time the crime was committed, the questioning might continue:

Q: "Were you in the tavern that night?"

A: "No, I wasn't."

Q: "How do you know the defendant was in the tavern?"

A: "John told me."

The testimony is relevant to the material issue in dispute but is not *competent,* because the personal knowledge foundation required by Rule 602 of the Federal Rules of Evidence has not been satisfied. However, changing the example slightly would make the testimony competent:

Q: "How do you know the defendant was in the tavern?"

A: "The defendant told me he was in the tavern."

Since the defendant is the opposing party in the criminal action, the matter about which the witness has personal knowledge is the defendant's incriminating admission. The testimony is now competent, relevant, and material. It is not forbidden by the hearsay rule.

Ⓖ REDIRECT EXAMINATION AND RECROSS-EXAMINATION

After the cross-examination, the lawyer who produced the witness may then conduct a **redirect examination** of the witness. Questions on redirect examination are generally limited to new matters drawn out during cross-examination and in refuting and explaining impeachment issues. The purposes of redirect examination can be defined as follows:

- To restore the credibility of a witness who has been impeached on cross-examination by explanations of matters on which the cross-examiner sought to impeach the witness. Questions such as the following may be asked: "Officer Smith, why did you . . . ?" and "Officer Smith, what did you mean when you stated . . . ?"
- To restore the credibility of a witness by pointing out prior consistent statements when the impeachment was made by means of prior inconsistent statements.

During the redirect examination, additional witnesses may be used to rebut the cross-examination and assist in rehabilitation. New evidence may also be presented if the cross-examiner has opened the door to new matters.

Recross-examination is the fourth and usually the last stage of the examination of the witness. With many witnesses, the questioning has been completed before reaching this stage. The recross-examination is usually confined to matters dealt with on the redirect examination.

Ⓗ THE ROLE OF THE TRIAL JUDGE

The trial judge manages the courtroom and the trial and rules on questions of law. The judge rules on motions and objections made by attorneys before and during a trial and gives instructions to the jury. The trial judge has an obligation to safeguard both the rights of an accused and the interests of the public in the efficient and effective administration of criminal and civil justice.

In the great majority of jurisdictions in the United States, the trial judge may not comment on the weight of the evidence. Juries are usually instructed on the manner in which they may determine the weight of the evidence—that is, the credibility of witnesses and the weight that they may give to physical evidence.

In only a very few jurisdictions in the United States may the trial judge comment on the weight of the evidence presented in a trial.

Federal Rule of Evidence 614(b) is followed by virtually all states. It states that the *court* (the term as used here refers to the trial judge) "may interrogate witnesses, whether called by itself or by a party." In a few states, jurors are permitted to question witnesses indirectly through the trial judge.

Because the trial judge must remain impartial, he or she must be careful in the use of leading questions in those jurisdictions that forbid the judge from commenting on the weight of the evidence. The improper use of leading questions could suggest to the jury that the judge believed that the witness was lying, which would violate the rule against commenting on the evidence. In the 1972 case of *Commonwealth v. Butler*,[39] the Supreme Court of Pennsylvania disapproved of a trial judge's practice of questioning only the witnesses he suspected of untruthfulness, while not questioning other witnesses. The court held:

> . . . If a judge followed the practice which this judge advocated here, a practice of questioning every witness whom the judge did not believe to be telling the truth, while questioning no other witnesses, it would be tantamount to telling the jury his views of which witnesses were to be believed. Credibility is solely for the jury. Just as a trial judge is not permitted to indicate to the jury his views on the verdict that they should reach in a criminal case, . . . similarly he is not permitted to indicate to a jury his views on whether particular witnesses are telling the truth.

Virtually all the federal courts permit jurors to ask questions of witnesses, by submitting the questions to the judge.[40] Many state courts also permit this practice,[41] and at least two states, Arizona and Florida, do so by statute.[42] As with questions posed

The Functions of the Trial Judge and the Jury

The Trial Judge Determines

- Whether a witness is qualified
- The competence of a witness
- Questions of law:
  Rules on motions
  Rules on objections by attorneys
  Instructs the jury
  Runs the courtroom and trial
  Safeguards both the rights of the accused and the interests of the public in the administration of criminal justice

As Fact Finders, the Jury Alone

- Determines the credibility of the testimony of all witnesses. The fact finders may believe one witness as against many

- Passes upon and resolves conflicts in the testimony of witnesses.
- Determines the weight to be given all evidence (statements of witnesses, physical evidence, and so on).
- Determines whether sufficient evidence exists to justify a verdict of guilty. (However, a guilty verdict is subject to review by the trial judge and appellate courts, who determine as a matter of law whether sufficient evidence exists to sustain the guilty verdict.)

by the judge, the parties may object to these questions on the same grounds as questions asked by one of the parties. However, the routine practice of allowing questions by jurors is generally discouraged. The court in *United States v. Collins,* 226 F3d 457 (6th Cir. 2000), suggested that juror questions be limited to cases where the trial is long and complicated, the parties are not properly questioning witnesses, or when a witness becomes difficult or confused.

❶ CAN A PERSON WHO HAS BEEN HYPNOTIZED TESTIFY AS A WITNESS?

Studies of **hypnosis** began over two hundred years ago, but to date there is no single explanation of the phenomenon that satisfies most scientists. Hundreds of cases involving hypnotized witnesses have come before American courts.[43] In the 1987 case of *Rock v. Arkansas,*[44] the U.S. Supreme Court identified the following three problems in the use of a witness whose testimony has been hypnotically refreshed:

> [T]he subject becomes "suggestible" and may try to please the hypnotist with answers the subject thinks will be met with approval; the subject is likely to "confabulate," that is, to fill in details from the imagination, in order to make an answer more coherent and complete; and, the subject experiences "memory

hardening," which gives him great confidence in both true and false memories, making effective cross-examination more difficult.

Because of these and other problems, some states will not permit the use of hypnotically refreshed testimony as evidence. Other states have established guidelines for the use of hypnotically refreshed testimony, such as those used in New Jersey[45] and New Mexico.[46] Such safeguards seek to ensure the accuracy and reliability of hypnotically refreshed testimony. The facts in the case of *Rock v. Arkansas* and the ruling of the U.S. Supreme Court follow:

Rock v. Arkansas
United States Supreme Court, 483 U.S. 44, 107 S.Ct. 2704 (1987)

The defendant was charged with manslaughter in the killing of her husband during an argument. Because she could not remember precise details of the shooting, her attorney suggested hypnosis in order to refresh her memory. After she underwent hypnosis to induce recollection, the trial court permitted her only to testify about what she had been able to remember before hypnosis.

After her conviction for manslaughter, she appealed to the U.S. Supreme Court on the issue that she had the constitutional right to testify in her own behalf. The Supreme Court vacated the conviction and ordered a new trial, stating:

> The more traditional means of assessing accuracy of testimony also remain applicable in the case of a previously hypnotized defendant. Certain information recalled as a result of hypnosis may be verified as highly accurate by corroborating evidence. Cross-examination, even in the face of a confident defendant, is an effective tool for revealing inconsistencies. Moreover, a jury can be educated to the risks of hypnosis through expert testimony and cautionary instructions. Indeed, it is probably to a defendant's advantage to establish carefully the extent of his memory prior to hypnosis, in order to minimize the decrease in credibility the procedure might introduce.
>
> . . . We are not now prepared to endorse without qualifications the use of hypnosis as an investigative tool; scientific understanding of the phenomenon and of the means to control the effects of hypnosis is still in its infancy. Arkansas, however, has not justified the exclusion of all of a defendant's testimony that the defendant is unable to prove to be the product of prehypnosis memory. A State's legitimate interest in barring unreliable evidence does not extend to per se exclusions that may be reliable in an individual case. Wholesale inadmissibility of a defendant's testimony is an arbitrary restriction on the right to testify in the absence of clear evidence by the State repudiating the validity of all posthypnosis recollections. The State would be well within its powers if it established guidelines to aid trial courts in the evaluation of posthypnosis testimony and it may be able to show that testimony in a particular case is so unreliable that exclusion is justified. But it has not shown that hypnotically enhanced testimony is always so untrustworthy and so immune to the traditional means of evaluating credibility that it should disable a defendant from presenting her version of the events for which she is on trial.

Another problem area commonly associated with hypnotically refreshed memory is that of "repressed memories." Accusations of sexual assaults that had occurred years prior to the accusation could be based upon a repressed memory that had been hypnotically or clinically refreshed.[47]

SUMMARY

To appear as a witness in a civil or criminal case, a person must have personal knowledge of an issue before the court. A witness must also be competent and declare (or swear) that he or she will testify truthfully.

Today, children as young as 3 may qualify to testify as witnesses. Because of the trauma that a child victim or witness may be subject to in appearing as a witness, all of the states and courts have statutes and procedures that attempt to help children who appear as witnesses.

Defendants have the right to compel the attendance of witnesses to testify for the defense. The Sixth Amendment right of a defendant to confront and cross-examine witnesses against the defendant is probably the most important tool of defense lawyers in defending their clients in criminal cases.

Witnesses are either ordinary witnesses or expert witnesses. Both ordinary and expert witnesses may testify as to opinions within the rules of evidence of your state. (See Appendix B for the Federal Opinion Evidence Rule 701, 703, 704, 705).

All witnesses testify under oath or affirmation and may be cross-examined by the opposing attorney. Witnesses may also be questioned on redirect and recross-examination.

PROBLEMS

AVAILABLE ANSWERS

a. Ordinary witnesses

b. Expert witnesses

c. Both of the above are correct

d. Neither of the above are correct

IN CRIMINAL TRIALS:

1. Most witnesses are

2. Law enforcement officers appear most often as

3. Medical doctors most often testify as

4. Children who appear would testify as

5. Would testify as to what they have seen

6. A witness testifying because of their special training and experience would be

7. Would have to take an oath or affirmation that they will testify truthfully

8. May testify as to an opinion within the rules of evidence

9. Are subject to cross-examination

10. Could be challenged by the opposing lawyer as not being competent

INFOTRAC COLLEGE EDITION EXERCISES

1. Go to InfoTrac College Edition and using the search term "expert witness" find the 2002 article in the *American Journal of Family Law* titled

"Presenting the Expert Witness in Child Physical and Sexual Abuse Cases," by Karen Steinhauser. This article discusses the kinds of experts available to testify in child sexual abuse cases, how to choose the right expert, how to prepare the expert for trial, and how to question the expert. Expert testimony is very important in child sexual abuse cases, and this article gives a good discussion on how experts are chosen and used in such cases.

2. Go to InfoTrac College Edition and using the search term "cross examination" find the 2002 article in *N.Y. Defenders Digest* titled "Under What Conditions Must a Trial Court Allow Defense Questioning Bearing upon a Witness's Motive to Fabricate?" Evidence used in cross-examining a witness must be relevant. This article and the cases it discusses considers when the defense may use information about a witness that is not necessarily relevant to the crime charge but may shed some light on the motive the witness has to testify, in particular, that the witness has a motive to fabricate his testimony. What are some situations where a witness might have such a motive?

NOTES

1. Most witnesses will cooperate in performing their civic duty, but unfortunately some witnesses will not. The following reasons are commonly given to explain why some witnesses are not cooperative: (a) *Threats against witnesses.* One experienced official estimated that half of all criminal cases dismissed are dropped because of witnesses' concerns for safety. (b) *Financial losses.* Most states pay up to $30 per day as witness fees, which means that many witnesses lose money or have to take vacation time from their job to appear as a witness. (c) *Too many court delays and adjournments.* The National Advisory Committee on Criminal Justice Standards and Goals recognized that "delays are an accepted defense practice for wearing down the witness. Not infrequently, the financial and emotional costs become too much for the victim, and [he or] she asks to withdraw." ("Report of the Task Force on Criminal Research and Development.")
2. See *United States v. Benn,* 476 F.2d 1127 (D.C. Cir., 1972); *State v. Manning,* 291 A.2d 750 (Conn., 1972).
3. 913 F.2d 782 (10th Cir., 1990).
4. 825 F.2d 538 (1st Cir., 1987).
5. See 24A Corpus Juris Secundum 1869.
6. 703 P.2d 448.
7. See Appendix A for the Sixth Amendment, which states in part that "In all criminal prosecutions, the accused shall enjoy the right . . . to be confronted with the witnesses against him; to have compulsory process for obtaining witnesses in his favor. . . ."

8. See 32A Corpus Juris Secundum, Evidence 1031, and the case of *Chapman v. State,* 230 N.W.2d 824 (Wis., 1975). In the *Chapman* case, a witness testified that the defendant stated that he participated in the crime charged and complained that he did not receive any of the proceeds of the joint criminal venture. The jury believed the testimony of the witness and convicted the defendant. The Wisconsin Supreme Court affirmed the conviction, holding: "This court will not upset a jury's determination of credibility . . . unless the fact relied upon is inherently or patently incredible. To be incredible as a matter of law, evidence must be . . . in conflict with the uniform course of nature or with fully established or conceded facts. . . . There is nothing inherently incredible about a participant in a crime telling others what he did. This is particularly so where his expressed complaint is that he received none of the proceeds of the joint criminal venture. The determination of this witness' credibility and the weight to be given his testimony was . . . properly a function of the trier of facts."
9. 201 F.2d 265 (2nd Cir., 1952).
10. 478 N.W. 2d 901, review denied, U.S. Sup. Ct. 112 S. Ct. 3015 (1991).
11. In the case of *Davis v. Alaska* (94 S.Ct. 1105), the defendant was convicted of burglary and grand larceny. A crucial witness for the prosecution (Richard Green) was a 16-year-old juvenile who was on probation for burglarizing two cabins. The state obtained a protective order forbidding the disclosure of Green's juvenile record

during his testimony in the trial of Davis. In reversing and remanding Davis's conviction for a new trial, the U.S. Supreme Court held that: "The State's policy interest in protecting the confidentiality of a juvenile offender's record cannot require yielding of so vital a constitutional right as the effective cross-examination for bias of an adverse witness. The State could have protected Green from exposure of his juvenile adjudication in these circumstances by refraining from using him to make out its case; the State cannot, consistent with the right of confrontation, require the petitioner to bear the full burden of vindicating the State's interest in the secrecy of juvenile criminal records. The judgment affirming petitioner's convictions of burglary and grand larceny is reversed and the case is remanded for further proceedings not inconsistent with this opinion."

12. 483 U.S. 44, 107 S.Ct. 2704.

13. In 1972 the case of *Brooks v. Tennessee* (406 U.S. 605, 92 S.Ct. 1891) was before the U.S. Supreme Court. In that case, the defendant wanted to testify in his own behalf but a Tennessee statute required a defendant "to testify before any other testimony for the defense is heard by the court trying the case." In holding that the defendant "was deprived of his constitutional rights when the trial court excluded him from the stand for failing to testify first," the Supreme Court stated that: "Although a defendant will usually have some idea of the strength of his evidence, he cannot be absolutely certain that his witnesses will testify as expected or that they will be effective on the stand. They may collapse under skillful and persistent cross-examination, and through no fault of their own they may fail to impress the jury as honest and reliable witnesses. In addition, a defendant is sometimes compelled to call a hostile prosecution witness as his own. Unless the State provides for discovery depositions of prosecution witnesses, which Tennessee apparently does not, the defendant is unlikely to know whether this testimony will prove entirely favorable."

14. U.S. Supreme Court in *McGautha v. California*, 91 S.Ct. 1454 (1971).

15. 113 S.Ct. 1111.

16. The term *perjury trap* was defined as follows in the case of *United States v. Chen*, 933 F.2d 793 (9th Cir., 1991): A "perjury trap is created when the government calls a witness before the grand jury for the primary purpose of obtaining testimony from him in order to prosecute him later for perjury. *United States v. Simone*, 627 F. Supp. 1264, 1268 (D.N.J.1986) (perjury trap involves 'the deliberate use of a judicial proceeding to secure perjured testimony, a concept in itself abhorrent'). It involves the government's use of its investigatory powers to secure a perjury indictment on matters which are neither material nor germane to a legitimate ongoing investigation of the grand jury."

Knowingly making a material false statement to a federal investigator can be charged as a crime under the federal False Statement Act. The U.S. Supreme Court affirmed a criminal conviction under this act in the 1998 case of *Brogan v. United States* (118 S.Ct. 805), when Brogan denied to federal investigators that he had received illegal cash or gifts in the incidents being investigated.

17. Rule 702 was amended in 2000 in response to the decisions of the U.S. Supreme Court in *Daubert v. Merrill Dow Pharmaceuticals Co.*, 509 U.S. 579 (1993), and *Kumho Tire Co. v. Carmichael*, 119 S.Ct. 1167 (1999). In those cases the Court established new standards for determining when a witness may be permitted to testify concerning scientific and technical knowledge. (*Daubert* and *Kumho,* and their influence on state court expert testimony rules, are discusses in more detail in Chapter 17 of this book).

Rule 702 and its counterparts in state evidence rules relate both to the qualification of a witness as an expert, and the nature of the testimony given by a witness, assuming he or she is an expert. As to the qualification aspect of Rule 702, a court usually will look at the witness's training, education, and experience to make the determination on the witness's qualification to be an expert. In the following cases courts considered the qualifications necessary to give expert testimony.

In the 2001 case of *United States v. Watson* (260 F.3d 301 [3rd Cir., 2001]), the Federal Third Circuit Court of Appeals held that narcotics officers with extensive experience in narcotics trafficking could give expert testimony about the meaning of behavior of persons involved in illegal narcotics possession or distribution. There, the narcotics expert testified that the presence of crack cocaine, together with several hundred small plastic baggies used by sellers of crack, was generally a sign that the holder of the crack was part of a distribution scheme, rather than holding the crack for personal use. The narcotics agent also testified, based on over two hundred arrests in bus interdictions, that bus trips between cities with brief layovers by persons in possession of crack and plastic bags was generally a sign of participation in a drug distribution system. The defendant, who was arrested on a bus trip to Philadelphia with a 4 hour layover, had in his possession small amounts of crack cocaine and several hundred plastic baggies of the type used in the sale of crack. He was convicted in the district court of possession with intent to distribute crack cocaine.

In the 2001 case of *United States v. Havvard* (260 F.3d 597 [7th Cir., 2001]), the Federal Seventh Circuit Court of Appeals held that an FBI agent who had studied the success rates of fingerprint comparisons in numerous national cases, and who had a detailed process that he used to establish such comparisons, could give expert testimony that the latent fingerprint found on a firearm matched the fingerprint of the defendant. The defendant was found guilty of illegal possession of a firearm.

The second aspect of Rule 702 goes to the reliability of the testimony of the expert, after the witness has been qualified as an expert. If the basis for the expert's opinion does not meet the Rule 702 and *Daubert* reliability tests, the expert may not testify. For example, in *United States v. Lea* (249 F.3d 632 [7th Cir. 2001]), a 2001 decision of the 7th Circuit Court of Appeals, the defense sought to introduce evidence from a polygraph test administered by a Food and Drug Administration agent to another person the defendant contended was the guilty party. While the agent was qualified as an expert on administering and interpreting polygraph tests, he was not permitted to testify because his opinion that the person taking the test was not telling the truth was unreliable. The FDA agent could not say exactly which question was answered untruthfully, and also had no statistical support for the accuracy of the testing methods used in the polygraph test administered. (The question of the reliability, and admissibility, of polygraph and voice spectography is discussed more fully in Chapter 11.)

It is the fact finger (jury or judge) who determines the weight and credibility to be given to the testimony of both expert and ordinary witnesses. To promote this, most states have a rule similar to Rule 704(b) of the Federal Rules of Evidence, which states that in a criminal case an expert may not give an opinion that the defendant had or not had the mental state constituting an element of the crime. That question must be decided by the jury. In *United States v. Watson,* discussed above, even though the narcotics agents were qualified as experts, the trial court erred in permitting the agents to give their opinion that Watson, the defendant, had the intent to distribute the cocaine in his possession. The agents could testify generally about common behavior observed by them in drug distribution activities, but the jury must decide if a given defendant exhibiting such behavior possesses the required intent to distribute. In *Watson,* the court of appeals reversed the defendant's conviction because of the expert's opinions on Watson's intent.

18. 15 N.E.2d 337 (Ill. App.).
19. 413 U.S. 15, 93 S.Ct. 2607, note 12.
20. *United States v. Tipton,* 964 F.2d 650 (7th Cir., 1992).
21. *United States v. Paiva,* 892 F.2d 148 (1st Cir., 1989).
22. *Waddell v. State,* 582 A.2d 260 (Md. App., 1990).
23. 803 P.2d 1077 (Mont.).
24. *United States v. Anthony,* 944 F.2d 780 (Okl., 1991).
25. *State v. Lamme,* 563 A.2d 1372 (Conn. App., 1989).
26. 1991 WL 263246.
27. *Commonwealth v. Cohen,* 605 A.2d 814 (Pa. Super., 1992).
28. *State v. Mallett,* 600 A.2d 273 (R.I., 1991).
29. *Kosbruk v. State,* 820 P.2d 1082 (Alaska App., 1991).
30. See the 1990 case of *Dysart v. State,* 581 So.2d 541 (Ala. Crim. App.).
31. 94 S.Ct. 1105.
32. 51 S.Ct. 218.
33. Idem.
34. *Loehr v. Walton,* 242 F.3d 834 (8th Cir., 2001).
35. *United States v. Foster,* 227 F.3d 1096 (9th Cir., 2000).
36. *Udemba v. Nicoli,* 237 F.3d 8 (1st Cir., 2001).

37. 488 U.S. 277, 109 S.Ct. 480.

38. 482 U.S. 730, 107 S.Ct. 2658.

39. 291 A.2d 9 (Pa.).

40. *United States v. Richardson,* 233 F.3d 1285, 1288 (11th Cir., 2000).

41. Idem.

42. Ariz. R. Ct. 39(b)(10); Fla. St. ch. 40.50(3).

43. Hypnosis has sometimes been used by law enforcement officers to assist an eyewitness in recalling a vehicle license plate, the description of a fleeing offender, or a person seen in the vicinity of serious crime. Hypnosis was instrumental in apprehending offenders in the case of *State v. Joubert,* 603 A.2d 861 (Maine, 1992), and in rescuing twenty-six children and their school bus driver in Chowchilla, California, when they were kidnapped in 1975. The school bus with all its occupants had been buried in the ground to prevent the escape of the children and the bus driver.

44. 483. U.S. 44, 107 S.Ct. 2704.

45. *State v. Hurd,* 432 A.2d 86 (1989).

46. *State v. Varela,* 817 P.2d 731 (1991).

47. More than one thousand families in the United States belong to an organization known as the False Memory Syndrome Foundation. (The problem of false memories first became known over one hundred years ago when Sigmund Freud began treating patients. Freud was amazed at the number of hypnotized women who told of being raped by their fathers. Years later, Freud concluded that most of these women were fantasizing and that their memories were false. The problem of false memory **syndrome** is commonly associated with hypnotic therapy.) Most of these families struggle with the problem of a family member who has made accusations of sexual assault against a family member, which they believe to be false. Such accusations, whether true or false, affect whole families. The purpose of the FMS Foundation is to assist such families. The FMS Foundation is located at 3401 Market Street, Philadelphia, PA 19104.

6

Judicial Notice and Privileges of Witnesses

Ⓐ JUDICIAL NOTICE IN GENERAL

If parties to criminal and civil trials had to prove every fact of common knowledge and define every term used, trials would be unreasonably long. Court calendars would back up and delays in getting a case to trial would increase considerably.

To avoid many unnecessary delays, courts have developed the commonsense doctrine of **judicial notice.** This notice relieves parties in criminal and civil trials from the duty of introducing additional witnesses, documents, and other evidence to prove uncontroverted facts. For example, in 1919 the California Supreme Court held that "Judicial notice is a judicial short cut, a doing away . . . with formal necessity of evidence because there is no real necessity for it."[1]

All states have statutes or court rules authorizing the use of a judicial notice doctrine. Many state statutes permitting this use are similar to the Federal Rules of Evidence, Rule 201, found in Appendix B of this text.

Judicial Notice of Matters of General Knowledge

Judicial notice of matters generally known within the community or state is probably the oldest application of the doctrine of judicial notice.[2] The doctrine permits judges and jurors to recognize facts commonly known to them without the formal necessity of evidence proving those facts. In this way, judicial notice shortens and simplifies trials. The Supreme Court of California gave the following explanation of the "general knowledge" rule in a 1970 case:

> Judicial notice may not be taken of any matter unless authorized or required by law (Evid. Code, § 452). This court is compelled to take judicial notice only of facts and propositions of generalized knowledge that are so universally known that they cannot reasonably be the subject of dispute (Evid.Code, § 451). If there is any doubt whatever either as to the fact itself or as to its being a matter of common knowledge, evidence should be required.[3]

Some of the more common examples of the use of judicial notice to prove matters of general knowledge include:

- Establishing the meaning of words, phrases, or abbreviations commonly used "on the street." The street terms *fix* in drug cases and *turning a trick* in prostitution cases might be established by judicial notice. This can also be done by asking the law enforcement witness to define the term.

- Establishing the sex of a witness or defendant. For example, the Supreme Court of Indiana held that "The sex of a human being is generally its most obvious characteristic. We can look at another human being and, with a very high degree of certainty, ascertain his or her sex. Therefore, why couldn't a presiding judge take judicial notice of a defendant's sex? We believe he can and should."[4]

- Establishing the location of well-known sections of a city or well-known streets and buildings. Or determining the distances to other well-known cities, and the interstates or highways used to drive to those cities.

- Establishing well-known habits. For example, in the 1991 case of *State v. Mundell*,[5] the Court of Appeals of Hawaii held that "We take judicial notice that drug dealers and traffickers rarely carry 'large' amounts of drugs on their person. Their supplies are generally secreted in their homes, in their luggage, or in other such places where they may be accessible for sale. Drug dealers often use other people to transport large quantities of drugs for them."

However, a court may not take judicial notice of a fact solely because the fact is well known to the trial judge. For example, in the 2002 case of *United States v. Mariscal*, the 9th Circuit Court of Appeals held that a trial judge could not take judicial notice of traffic conditions at a local intersection, when knowledge of those conditions arose only from the judge's personal driving experience. Narcotic agents made an investigative stop of a vehicle in which the defendant was present, and the prosecution attempted to justify the stop by evidence the driver of the vehicle made an unsignaled right turn. This court ruled that an unsignaled turn is illegal only if traffic is present at the intersection where the turn occurred. The prosecution failed to offer evidence of such traffic, but the trial court filed that gap by taking judicial notice that the intersection was one of the busiest in the city. The court of appeals found the investigative stop unlawful because the agents had no reasonable belief that a law had been broken.

Judicial Notice of Facts Obtained from Sources Such as Records, Books, and Newspapers

A court may properly take judicial notice of facts contained in recognized reports, learned treatises or dictionaries, or simple data printed in newspapers, such as dates or temperatures. Such facts are not in controversy but may be very important to one of the parties in the trial.

Examples of the use of judicial notice in this area include the following:

- In 1921, the U.S. Supreme Court held that judicial notice could be taken of the date on which a state ratified a proposed constitutional amendment, as this information could be easily obtained from records or books.[6]

- Courts could take judicial notice of dates, days, or time since this information is readily available in almanacs, newspapers, and the like (such as, that the Fourth of July falls on a Friday in the year 2003; at what hour daylight ended on a given day; or whether it rained or snowed on a given day).

- Courts may take notice of statutes of other states, court records of your state or other states, and ordinances of counties and cities within your state. In the 1992 case of *People v. Hardy*,[7] the Supreme Court of California pointed out that California Evidence Code, Section 452, provides that "Judicial notice may be taken . . . (of the) records of . . . any court of record of the United States." As an example of when this may be used, in the 1991 case of *In the Matter of Breedlove*,[8] the West Virginia Supreme Court held that it was proper to take judicial notice of a previous drunk-driving conviction in ordering a ten-year revocation of the driver's license.

Scientific and Technological Facts
Recognized by Judicial Notice

- Judicial notice can be taken of a court ruling that a scientific technique was reliable. For example, once a state or federal court establishes that DNA fingerprinting is a reliable scientific technique, there is no need to bring in expert witnesses again and again in every case to prove in each case that DNA fingerprinting is reliable and accurate. In the 1993 case of *United States v. Jacobetz,*[9] DNA fingerprinting was used to identify the defendant as the man who abducted a woman in Vermont, repeatedly raped her, and released her in New York. The court held that "in future cases with a similar evidentiary issue, a court could properly take judicial notice of the general acceptability of the general theory and the use of these specific techniques."

- An Ohio court of appeals held in the 1973 case of *State v. Brock,*[10] that "courts may take judicial notice of any scientific fact which may be ascertained by reference to a standard dictionary or is of such general knowledge that it is known by any judicial officer. In the instant case, the trial court was correct in taking judicial notice of the fact that heroin is a narcotic drug and is habit forming."

Ⓑ THE PRIVILEGE AGAINST SELF-INCRIMINATION

In tracing the origins and roots of the Fifth Amendment's right to remain silent, the U.S. Supreme Court pointed out in the case of *Miranda v. Arizona* that the privilege's "roots go back into ancient times" and probably has origins in the Bible.[11]

The Fifth Amendment **privilege against self-incrimination** is the only privilege that has been incorporated into the U.S. Constitution and the constitutions of many states. All other privileges exist only in statutory or common law. The Fifth Amendment of the U.S. Constitution provides that: "No person . . . shall be compelled in any criminal case to be a witness against himself. . . ."

This privilege "protects a person . . . against being incriminated by his own compelled testimonial communications."[12] Because statements made by a person in any civil hearing or questioning might later be used against that person in a criminal proceeding, the U.S. Supreme Court has repeatedly held that the privilege "can be asserted in any proceeding, civil or criminal, administrative or judicial, investigatory or adjudicatory."[13] The privilege has thus been invoked, for example, in divorce and tax cases as well as in criminal cases and questioning by law enforcement officers.[14]

The U.S. Supreme Court has held that the privilege against self-incrimination "reflects many of our fundamental values and noble aspirations."[15] Because it is "the essential mainstay of our adversary system," the U.S. Constitution requires "that the government seeking to punish an individual produce the evidence against him by its own independent labor rather than by the cruel, simple expedient of compelling it from his own mouth."[16]

Areas Where the Fifth Amendment Privilege Against Self-Incrimination Does Not Apply

The Fifth Amendment privilege against self-incrimination applies only to evidence of a communicative or testimonial nature. It does not apply when only physical evidence is sought and obtained. Seizure of physical evidence is controlled by the Fourth Amendment to the U.S. Constitution. Thus, the privilege against self-incrimination does not apply in the following circumstances:

- The withdrawal of blood and the use of the blood as evidence to show that the defendant was driving a vehicle while intoxicated (*Schmerber v. California*).[17]

- The use of a handwriting exemplar, or sample, was held to be controlled by the Fourth Amendment (*Gilbert v. California*).[18]

- Compelling the accused to exhibit his person for observation, as in a lineup or showup (*United States v. Wade*).[19]

- To make a voice exemplar, or sample (*United States v. Dionisio*).[20]

- Federal Courts of Appeal have held that no Fifth Amendment violation occurred when for identification purposes the defendant was compelled to wear a false goatee (*United States v. Hammond*);[21] to wear a wig (*United States v. Murray*);[22] to shave for identification purposes (*United States v. Valenzuela*);[23] to put on a stocking mask at trial to permit a witness to testify as to similarity to the masked robber (*United States v. Roberts*);[24] or to dye her or his hair to the color it was at the time of the offense (*United States v. Brown*);[25]

- A witness could testify that the defendant was compelled to put on a shirt and it fit him (*Holt v. United States*).[26] (Would also apply to any clothing or hat.)

- Where immunity has been granted and the person is compelled to testify or agrees to testify as part of a plea agreement. An example of a person agreeing to the grant of immunity is Monica Lewinsky, who received immunity as part of a plea agreement. In the Iran-Contra scandal, Colonel Oliver North (a presidential advisor) and Admiral John Poindexter (North's boss) were both granted limited immunity to compel them to answer questions before congressional committees in 1986.[27]

- The U.S. Supreme Court has repeatedly ruled that the Fifth Amendment privilege applies only to people and does not apply to corporations, labor unions, and other organizations. Corporations and unincorporated unions and other organizations cannot claim the privilege against self-incrimination.[28]

- Where the incrimination is of others and is not self-incrimination.[29]

- Where the public interest in protecting children from abuse outweighs Fifth Amendment privilege. After a small child had received numerous physical injuries and the child's mother was seen abusing the child, the mother was ordered to disclose the location of the child. The mother was jailed on contempt when she would not do so. The U.S. Supreme Court affirmed the contempt sentence in the 1990 case of *Baltimore Department of Social Services v. Bouknight*.[30]

- U.S. military personnel and law enforcement officers are obligated to report illegal conduct of their fellow officers and military associates. The U.S. Supreme Court upheld this service requirement as not being in violation of the Fifth Amendment privilege. It was held that the defense of fear of retaliation could not be used against the offense of failure to report the illegal conduct of others.[31] However, the Fifth Amendment privilege would apply if the military service person or law enforcement officer had also been a party to the crime such as drug use.[32]

- Where there has been a voluntary, intelligent waiver of the privilege.

Recent Examples Where the Fifth Amendment Privilege Against Self-Incrimination Does Apply

- A witness may raise the Fifth Amendment privilege even where the witness insists she is innocent of any crime. In *Ohio v. Reiner*,[33] the U.S. Supreme Court held that a babysitter called to testify in the prosecution of a father for the death of his infant son could assert the privilege, even though she professed her complete innocence of any relation to the crime.

- A taxpayer may invoke the privilege to refuse to answer specific questions on a tax return but may not refuse to file a return altogether (*United States v. Sabino*).[34]

- The privilege is available when a person is questioned by a probation officer, so long as the officer makes it clear that answers to the question are mandatory, not optional. Answers could lead to violations of probation, which is a form of incrimination (*United States v. Davis*).[35]

- Where a defendant remains silent under questioning the Fifth Amendment prohibits the prosecution from introducing evidence of that silence at trial. The fact that the defendant remained silent may lead one to conclude the defendant admitted the accuracy of the questions, and the silence is thus incriminatory. (*United States v. Velarde-Gomez*).[36]

ⓒ THE ATTORNEY–CLIENT PRIVILEGE

As the U.S. Supreme Court pointed out in the 1981 case of *Upjohn Company et al. v. United States et al.*, "the attorney–client privilege is the oldest of the privileges for confidential communications known to the common law."[37] In that case the Supreme Court held that communications by Upjohn employees to corporate lawyers about illegal payments made to foreign government officials were covered by the **attorney–client privilege.** The Court stated that the purpose of the privilege was

> to encourage full and frank communication between attorneys and their clients and thereby promote broader public interests in the observance of law and administration of justice. The privilege recognizes that sound legal advice or advocacy serves public ends and that such advice or advocacy depends upon the lawyer being fully informed by the client. As we stated last Term in *Trammel v. United States*, 445 U.S. 40, 51 (1980), "The attorney–client privilege rests on the need for the advocate and counselor to know all that relates to the client's reasons for seeking representation if the professional mission is to be

carried out." . . . Admittedly complications in the application of the privilege arise when the client is a corporation, which in theory is an artificial creature of the law, and not an individual; but this Court has assumed that the privilege applies when the client is a corporation, and the Government does not contest the general proposition.

Many states have statutes regulating the attorney-client privilege. Others states, like the federal government, use the *principles of common law.* For example, Rule 501 of the Federal Rules of Evidence (see Appendix B) provides that the "common law as . . . interpreted by the courts of the United States in light of reason and experience" is to be used for all of the communicative privileges.

Requirements of the Attorney–Client Privilege

For the attorney–client privilege to exist, both state and federal governments require that certain conditions be met. The client must seek the professional legal services of an attorney and have the intention of establishing an attorney–client relationship. Consulting with an attorney for nonlegal services has been held not to fall within the privilege. Situations in which one informally seeks free legal advice from an attorney, such as at a chance meeting with the attorney, do not create the privilege. Additionally, it is generally held that the privilege applies only to confidential communications made within the attorney–client relationship. Talking about legal matters with an attorney at a social function, for example, would probably not fall within the privilege.

However, the necessary presence of the attorney's secretary, law clerk, or other employee during a conference in the attorney's office would not cause a court to hold that the communications were not privileged. The privilege would also probably hold for most situations in which the client brought another person with him to the attorney's office for a conference. The presence of a parent or spouse in a conference just before a trial or hearing is not uncommon, and there is every reason to believe that the privilege would apply to such communications.

Limits of the Attorney–Client Privilege

The U.S. Supreme Court pointed out in the 1989 case of *United States v. Zolin*[38] that since "the privilege has the effect of withholding relevant information from the fact finder, it applies only where necessary to achieve its purpose." There are therefore limits to the attorney–client privilege and it does not apply to the following:

- The privilege applies when a client discloses past wrongdoing to the attorney, but the privilege does not protect disclosures about future wrongdoing. An attorney becomes part of a criminal conspiracy when the attorney advises a client on how to best commit a crime or fraud. Quoting a lower court, the Supreme Court ruled in the *Zoline* case that:

  It is the purpose of the crime-fraud exception to assure that "the seal of secrecy" between lawyer and client does not extend to communications "made for the purpose of getting advice for commission of a fraud" or crime.

- Most courts hold that an attorney has a legal and ethical obligation to deliver physical evidence of a crime to the police. The highest court of Maryland reviewed cases addressing this question in the 1992 case of *Rubin v. State,*[39] stating that:

  . . . ("[D]efense counsel may not retain physical evidence pertaining to the crime charged."); Commonwealth v. Stenhach, 356 Pa.Super. 5, 16, 514 A.2d 114, 119 (1986), appeal denied. 517 Pa. 589, 534 A.2d 769 (1987) ("[T]he overwhelming majority of states . . . hold that physical evidence of crime in the possession of a criminal defense attorney is not subject to a privilege but must be delivered to the prosecution.") . . .

- The general rule is that the attorney–client privilege does not protect the name and identity of a client and the amount of the attorney fee.[40] This rule was stated as follows by the 4th Federal Court of Appeals:

  . . . the identity of a client is a matter not normally within the privilege . . . nor are matters involving the receipt of fees from a client usually privileged. *United States v. (Under Seal),* 774 F.2d 624, 628 (4th Cir. 1985), review denied 475 U.S. 1108, 106 S.Ct. 1514 (1986).

D THE HUSBAND–WIFE PRIVILEGE

To foster marital harmony and to encourage a bond of confidentiality between wife and husband, English courts began in the early 1600s to use the rule that a spouse could not be forced to testify against the other spouse. Today, all states and the federal government use the **husband–wife privilege** (also known as the *marital privilege*), which has its origins in the years before the creation of the United States as a nation.

The U.S. Supreme Court pointed out in the 1980 case of *Trammel v. United States,*[41] that when the husband–wife privilege came into use, women were "regarded as chattel or demeaned by denial of a separate legal identity and dignity associated with recognition as a whole human being." The Supreme Court stated that because the "ancient foundations for so sweeping a privilege have long since disappeared," many changes have been made in the laws of states regarding the privilege. Today, the husband–wife privilege varies somewhat from state to state. The requirements that must exist to use the privilege in federal courts are stated as follows in the 1992 case of *United States v. Evans:*[42]

1. . . . The marital confidential communications privilege prohibits testimony regarding private intra-spousal communications. . . . The privilege extends only to words or acts that are intended as a communication to the other spouse.

2. . . . The communication must also occur during a time when the marriage is valid under state law and the couple is not permanently separated.[43]

3. . . . Finally, the communication must be made in confidence; in other words, it cannot be made in the presence of a third party, and the communicating spouse cannot intend for it to be passed on to others. . . . Once these three prerequisites are met, a defendant may invoke the privilege to prevent his spouse from testifying as to the content of the protected communication. See 2 Weinstein's Evidence § 505[04] (1991). This privilege continues even after the marriage has ended.

Partnership-in-Crime Exception to the Husband–Wife Privilege

The husband–wife privilege does not extend to situations where the wife and the husband are committing a crime (or crimes) together. Examples of the *partnership-in-crime,* or the *joint-criminal-participation, exception* to the husband–wife privilege are:

- Both the wife and husband were involved in growing marijuana. In holding that the marital privilege did not apply, the Federal Court of Appeals held that "the interests of justice outweighs the goal of fostering marital harmony."[44]

- The husband–wife privilege was held not to apply where both spouses were involved in trafficking cocaine.[45]

- When the husband ran off with his secretary, the angry wife provided the Internal Revenue Service with information of criminal tax evasion. The husband argued the marital privilege when the wife appeared as a prosecution witness against him at his criminal trial. The court held that the privilege would ordinarily be available to prevent the wife's testimony, but that in this case the wife was also guilty of the criminal conduct and that the partnership-in-crime exception applied. It did not matter, the court held, that the wife was not prosecuted in return for her cooperation. The husband's conviction based upon the testimony of his ex-wife was affirmed.

When One Spouse Commits Crimes Against the Other Spouse or Children

If a husband were able to beat his wife or children and his wife could not testify against him in a criminal or divorce court because of the husband–wife privilege, the law would not make sense.

"Privileges apply only to prevent the use of testimony in a judicial proceeding (in-court)" [*United States v. Kaprelian,* 768 F.2d 893 (7th Cir., 1985), cert. denied 474 U.S. 1008, 106 S.Ct. 533 (1985)].

Therefore, law officers can talk to and question spouses, children, and other persons. Whether a willing spouse could testify in a courtroom against the spouse in a criminal trial would depend on the privilege law in your state.

The case of *People v. Ward* [604 N.Y.S.2d 320 (A.D., 1993)] illustrates. The defendant (Ward) confessed to a clergyman that he had committed a murder. The clergyman called the police, and the defendant then confessed to the police. The New York clergy–penitent privilege did not apply to this situation as privileges are evidentiary rules having to do with testimony in a courtroom. Ward's conviction for murder was affirmed because the police had probable cause to arrest him after his confession.

Spouses can testify in criminal courts and divorce courts of beating and other violence either against the spouse or children. The husband–wife privilege does not forbid the testimony in such cases of the victim spouse against the offending spouse.[46]

However, some states limit this exception to personal violence committed against the victim spouse. In the 1992 case of *State v. Webb,*[47] the husband destroyed property of the wife, and the wife could not testify against her husband because the crime was not a crime of personal violence against her. But in the 1992 case of *State v. Delaney,*[48] the defendant's ex-wife could testify about the husband's sexual assaults against their child and the wife's two younger sisters, which occurred during the marriage.

Ⓔ THE PHYSICIAN–PATIENT PRIVILEGE

The **physician–patient privilege** did not exist at common law and therefore exists only in states that have created such a privilege by statutes. The state statutes define the extent and the limitations of the privilege. In the absence of a statute, there would be no privilege to information obtained by a nurse, a dentist, a druggist, an orthopedist, a chiropractor, a Christian Science practitioner, or a veterinary surgeon. All these professions, however, have codes of ethics and would ordinarily be reluctant to reveal information obtained in a professional relationship unless compelled to do so.[49]

Because state statutes control the privilege if it does exist, physicians have to comply with the statutory requirements of their state. If the statutes of the state require the reporting of the treatment of persons treated for gunshot wounds, physicians would have to comply with this requirement. If the statutes required the reporting of persons treated for venereal disease, this requirement would have to be complied with.

The physician–patient privilege is considered to be a very limited privilege subjected to the interpretation of the statutes of each state. The privilege, where it does exist, is for the protection of the patient, not the physician. Where the privilege does exist, it may be waived by the patient, or a representative of the patient. Whether the privilege exists after the death of the patient would depend upon the laws and court rulings of the state. However, the attending physician must file a death certificate, and all states have laws that permit the ordering of autopsies and the use of coroner's inquests by public officials who have such statutory authority.

The Requirement of the Physician–Patient Relationship

For the privilege to exist, the patient must have consulted the physician for treatment or diagnosis for possible treatment. Where such conditions exist, it is immaterial by whom the physician is employed or paid. If the physician under these circumstances calls in other medical doctors to aid in the treatment or diagnosis, any disclosures made to any of the physicians are also privileged.

The general rule is that a physician–patient privilege does not exist when a suspect or a defendant is being examined at the request of a court, a law enforcement agency, or a prosecutor. Such examinations could be requested or ordered when a court or prosecutor want to determine whether a defendant is competent to stand trial or whether commitment proceedings should be commenced instead of filing criminal charges. When probable cause exists to believe a person has been driving a vehicle under the influence, a law enforcement agency might request medical testing be done to determine whether a crime has been committed.

Ⓕ THE PSYCHOTHERAPIST–PATIENT PRIVILEGE

Although no **psychotherapist–patient privilege** existed at common law, many states have created this privilege by statute. For a patient to qualify for this privilege, the patient would have to seek the treatment or diagnosis of a licensed psychotherapist for treatment of mental or emotional conditions, including drug addiction. The definition of a psychotherapist ordinarily includes licensed physicians and psychologists, or persons reasonably believed by the patient to be so licensed. The conditions and limitations of this privilege are ordinarily similar to the physician–patient privilege.

Under Rule 501 of the Federal Rules of Evidence, the United States courts are responsible for formulating privileges. The federal courts have generally recognized those privileges available in state courts. In *Jaffee v. Redmond*, 518 U.S. 1, 15 (1996), the Supreme Court recognized the psychotherapist–patient privilege: "confidential communications between a licensed psychotherapist and his or her patients in the course of diagnosis and treatment are protected from compelled disclosure under Rule 501 of the Federal Rules of Evidence." The Jaffee court observed that all fifty states had enacted some form of psychotherapist privilege.

The psychotherapist privilege can be avoided in some kinds of cases. For example, in *United States v. Butrum*,[50] the court held the privilege was not available where the patient was charged with child sexual abuse. The court permitted evidence of communications and records of psychiatric treatment received by the defendant following the sexual abuse incidents.

The "Dangerous Patient" Exception to the Psychotherapist–Patient Privilege

Beginning with the 1976 case of *Tarasoff v. Regents of the University of California*,[51] states begin adopting a "duty to protect" rule. Under this rule, once a psychotherapist discovers that a patient poses a serious threat to a third person, the psychotherapist must exercise reasonable efforts to protect that person. Many states have codified this duty. (See, for example, Tenn. Code Ann. 33-10-302.) California has adopted as part of its Evidence Code an exception to the psychotherapist–patient privilege that communications by a dangerous patient are not privileged. (See West's Cal. Evid. Code 1024.)

One federal court has adopted a "dangerous patient" exception to the psychotherapist privilege. In *United States v. Glass*,[52] the court held that a psychotherapist could testify in a criminal case about otherwise privileged communications only if no other alternative to disclosure of threats made by the patient against a third party existed to avert harm to that person. The defendant was charged with threats to kill the president of the United States, a federal crime. Testimony of the psychotherapist to whom the threats were made was the only evidence of the threats, upon which the defendant's conditional guilty plea was based. While the *Glass* court found the evidence did not support the government's position that disclosure by the psychotherapist was the only way to protect the president, and therefore vacated the guilty plea, it found that under the proper circumstances the privilege could be lost. The *Glass* court based its decision on a footnote in *Jaffee* where the Supreme Court said: "[W]e do not doubt that there are situations in which the privilege must give way, for example, if a serious threat of harm to the patient or to others can be averted only by means of a disclosure by a therapist" (518 U.S. 1, 18).

One other federal court has refused to adopt the "dangerous patient" exception. In *United States v. Hayes*,[53] the court held that grafting such an exception on the psychotherapist privilege would have a serious chilling effect on patients' willingness to seek treatment. It concluded that while the "duty to protect" might permit a psychotherapist to inform authorities about a patient's threats, that duty did not require that the psychotherapist be compelled or permitted over the patient's objection to testify at a criminal trial based on those threats.

ⓖ THE SEXUAL ASSAULT COUNSELORS' PRIVILEGE AND PRIVILEGES COVERING OTHER COUNSELORS

Victims of sexual assaults and other crimes of violence often need and are provided with counseling. Drug rehabilitation and alcohol rehabilitation counseling is also available in all states. Counselors are found and are available in schools at all levels of education. Families under stress often receive counseling.

States often have statutes protecting private communications of persons receiving counseling. In the 1992 case of *Commonwealth v. Wilson*,[54] which was before the Supreme Court of Pennsylvania, the court held that the Pennsylvania sexual assault privilege statute provided an absolute privilege protecting not only testimony but also the production of documents covering the history of persons protected by the privilege. The defendants in this case were charged with sex crimes and sought records of their victims in the files of the **sexual assault counselor** to use in their defense. The court held the privilege prevented the production of the counselor's files.

Ⓗ THE CLERGY–PENITENT PRIVILEGE

About two-thirds of the states have statutes defining the **clergy–penitent privilege,** with a few other states recognizing the privilege by court decisions. No clear-cut privilege emerged from the old common law protecting confidential communications with clergy.

Statutes ordinarily define clergy as a minister, priest, rabbi, or other similar functionary of a religious organization, or a person reasonably believed to be so by the penitent consulting him or her. A clergyperson would not have to be engaged full time in the profession, but the definitions are not so broad to include all self-denominated "ministers."

Because of moral and ethical reasons, ministers, priests, and rabbis would not ordinarily reveal confessions and confidential disclosures made to them. The privilege establishes a legal protection against being forced to testify on a witness stand as to confidential disclosures made to them.

Ⓘ DO NEWS REPORTERS HAVE A PRIVILEGE IN YOUR STATE?

The Privilege Not to Reveal the Source of Information

We have all read stories about the newsperson who is sent to jail for contempt of court for refusal to disclose the source of a story or article. The newsperson usually contends that the **news reporter's privilege,** based on the First Amendment provides a privilege against such disclosure. Does such a right exist? In the 1972 case of *Branzburg v. Hayes,*[55] the Supreme Court held it did not.

> . . . [T]he great weight of authority is that newsmen are not exempt from the normal duty of appearing before a grand jury and answering questions relevant to a criminal investigation. At common law, courts consistently refused to recognize the existence of any privilege authorizing a newsman to refuse to reveal confidential information to a grand jury.

There was no generally recognized journalist privilege at common law, but most states have enacted such a privilege by statute. For example, the Nebraska statute states that

> No person engaged in procuring, gathering, writing, editing, or disseminating news or other information to the public shall be required to disclose in any federal or state proceeding: (1) The source of any . . . [information] . . . for any medium of communication to the public.[56]

Unless a state has a statute of this type, news reporters have no general First Amendment privilege and right not to reveal sources of news articles when ordered by a court.[57]

J IS THERE A PARENT–CHILD PRIVILEGE?

Can a parent be compelled to testify against a child? Could a child be compelled to testify against a parent? Or could either voluntarily testify in a criminal case against the other?

The question of whether a privilege exists based solely on the parent-child relationship has come before many courts in recent years. The 7th Circuit Court of Appeals reviewed these cases in the following case and found that only one federal trial court and only one state appellate court have recognized some type of parent–child privilege.[58] Most courts have refused to recognize a parent–child privilege.

In rejecting the rulings of the two courts that recognized a parent–child privilege, the Federal Court of Appeals in the following case refused to recognize such a privilege.

United States v. Davies and Kaprelian
U.S. Court of Appeals, Seventh Circuit (1985) 768 F.2d 893,
review denied 474 U.S. 1008, 106 S.Ct. 533, 38 CrL 4105

While a jewelry salesman was paying for gasoline at a self-service station, another man got into his Cadillac and drove away with the car and sample cases filled with jewelry. The Cadillac was driven to another state, where a witness and other information led the FBI to believe that a man named Kaprelian was involved in the theft. While FBI agents had Kaprelian's house under surveillance, Kaprelian's teenaged daughter left the house. FBI agents questioned Kaprelian's daughter and learned that Kaprelian was living with a Ms. Davies. FBI agents obtained Davies telephone number from Kaprelian's daughter and were able to arrest Davies as she was transporting the jewelry in a tote bag. In rejecting Kaprelian's claim of parent–child privilege, the court held:

> Even were there some substantial support for the defendant's proposition that there is a parent–child privilege this case would not be one in which it could be applied. Privileges apply only to prevent the use of testimony in a judicial proceeding. Kaprelian's daughter gave the F.B.I. agent his telephone number during the F.B.I.'s investigation of the jewel robbery. As the Supreme Court has noted, "... [neither the husband–wife privilege] nor any other privilege, prevents the Government from enlisting one spouse to give information concerning the other to aid in the other's apprehension." Trammel, 445 U.S. at 52 n. 12, 100 S.Ct. at 913 n. 12. Kaprelian makes no assertion that the government ever intended to call his daughter at the trial; his assertions of privilege are based solely on her questioning during the investigation.

Thus neither this phone number nor any other evidence obtained through this critical investigative lead are subject to suppression by the district court.

We thus reject Kaprelian's claim that there exists a privilege for communications between parents and their children in criminal cases and find no error in the admission of evidence developed as a result of obtaining Kaprelian's telephone number from his daughter.

Ⓚ THE GOVERNMENT'S PRIVILEGE NOT TO REVEAL GOVERNMENT SECRETS[59]

The Privilege Concerning the Identity of Informants

Law enforcement agencies and government have always realized that information from private citizens and paid informers is needed for effective law enforcement. When a major crime occurs, law enforcement agencies often need information to head their investigations in the right direction. Most information that law officers receive from private citizens and informers is of little value in solving major crimes, but some information identifies wrongdoers or provides important information regarding crimes.

To encourage people to provide information, governments must be able to assure those people providing the information that their identity will not be disclosed, whether it is a private citizen voluntarily providing the information or a person providing information for money or other consideration.

The common law has always recognized the **informant's privilege** as an essential aid to law enforcement. Today, many states have enacted statutes defining the privilege, while other states and the federal government use the privilege in its common-law form.

In the 1957 case of *Roviaro v. United States,*[60] the U.S. Supreme Court commented as follows regarding the informer's privilege:

What is usually referred to as the informer's privilege is in reality the Government's privilege to withhold from disclosure the identity of persons who furnish information of violations of law to officers charged with the enforcement of that law. . . . The purpose of the privilege is the furtherance and protection of the public interest in effective law enforcement.

THE LIMITS TO THE INFORMANT'S PRIVILEGE The informant's privilege is not an absolute privilege and must give way when there is a compelling need to protect the rights of the accused. In the *Roviaro* case, the Supreme Court held that the limits of the privilege arises from

. . . fundamental requirements of fairness. Where the disclosure of an informer's identity, or of the contents of his communication, is relevant and helpful to the defense of the accused, or is essential to the fair determination of a cause, the privilege must give way. In these situations the trial court may require disclosure. 353 U.S. at 60, 77 S.Ct. at 628.

Defendants in criminal trials have the right to know the names of people who were at the scene of the alleged crime, or persons who were participants in the crime that is alleged. These people could be important material witnesses for the defense, and their testimony could be very relevant. The courts have held that defense lawyers should have access to these people as potential witnesses. If the informant was at the scene of the crime or participated in the crime, courts hold that the informant's identity must be disclosed to the defense lawyer.

It is unlikely that a court will order the disclosure of the identity of an informant unless the informant was present at the scene of the crime charged, participated in the crime charged, or was at the scene of the arrest. As the informant could be an undercover police officer, informants should be kept away from the scene of a crime or of an arrest, if possible.

The question of an informant's identity is frequently raised in drug prosecutions. Search warrants used to search for illegal drugs are often based on "tips" by confidential informants. When drugs are found and the defendants charged, they may demand the name of the informant to judge the accuracy of the search warrant. Since the informant does not testify at the trial, and has no direct evidence of the crime, his identity is not "material to the determination of the case," and the privilege applies.[61]

When there are multiple drug transactions for which a suspect could be charged, prosecutors can avoid problems by not charging crimes where an informant was present at the scene of the crime or participated in the crime. If the identity of an informant is ordered by a court, the following options are available:

1. Drop the criminal charge against the defendant, which means that the defense has won their case because this is what the defense lawyer seeks.

2. Disclose the identity of the informant if this is practical and go to trial, possibly using the informant as a witness.

The Privilege Not to Disclose Military or Diplomatic Secrets Vital to National Security

The U.S. Congress enacted the Classified Information Procedures Act (18 U.S.C.A. App. 1), which recognizes the power of the executive branch of the federal government to determine whether classified information should be disclosed in criminal or civil trials.

The use of this privilege was before the U.S. Supreme Court in the 1953 case of *United States v. Reynolds.*[62] Widows of civilians killed in the crash of a U.S. Air Force plane attempted to obtain the accident report of the crash for use in their civil lawsuit. The Secretary of the Air Force wrote to the trial judge stating that the report contained information on secret electronic devices, so it was against public interest to make the accident report public. In holding that the **government** had a **privilege** not to reveal such information, the Supreme Court held that

> In the instant case we cannot escape judicial notice that this is a time of vigorous preparation for national defense. Experience in the past war has made it common knowledge that air power is one of the most potent weapons in our

scheme of defense, and that newly developing electronic devices have greatly enhanced the effective use of air power. It is equally apparent that these electronic devices must be kept secret if their full military advantage is to be exploited in the national interests. On the record before the trial court it appeared that this accident occurred to a military plane which had gone aloft to test secret electronic equipment. Certainly there was a reasonable danger that the accident investigation report would contain references to the secret electronic equipment which was the primary concern of the mission.

[W]hen the formal claim of privilege was filed by the Secretary of the Air Force, under circumstances indicating a reasonable possibility that military secrets were involved, there was certainly a sufficient showing of privilege to cut off further demand for the document on the showing of necessity for its compulsion that had then been made.

The President's Privilege of Confidentiality

In holding that the president of the United States has a privilege of confidentiality of his conversations and correspondence, the U.S. Supreme Court held in the 1974 case of *United States v. Nixon*,[63] that

There is nothing novel about governmental confidentiality. The meetings of the Constitutional Convention in 1787 were conducted in complete privacy. . . . Moreover, all records of those meetings were sealed for more than 30 years after the Convention. . . . Most of the Framers acknowledge that without secrecy no constitution of the kind that was developed could have been written. 418 U.S. at 705, 94 S.Ct. at 3106, n.15.

The Supreme Court gave these reasons for the privilege that protects confidential communications between the president and the president's immediate advisors:

A President and those who assist him must be free to explore alternatives in the process of shaping policies and making decisions and to do so in a way many would be unwilling to express except privately. These are the considerations justifying a presumptive privilege for Presidential communications. The privilege is fundamental to the operation of Government and inextricably rooted in the separation of powers under the Constitution. 418 U.S. at 708, 94 S.Ct. at 3107.

The Court held, however, that the privilege is a qualified privilege and would give way should a party to a legal action show a great need for relevant evidence that is protected by the privilege.

The Secrecy of Grand Jury Proceedings as a Privilege

The federal government and some states use grand juries to criminally indict, or charge, persons. Probably all states and the federal government also use grand juries to investigate situations where criminal activities may be occurring.

The use of grand juries goes back in English history more than one hundred years before the American Revolution. The Framers of the Constitution included in the Fifth

Amendment the requirement that the federal government use a grand jury of private citizens for indicting persons with federal felonies (see Appendix A). States do not have to follow this requirement.

Citizens serving on a grand jury are required to take an ancient oath, which binds them to keep secret "the King's counsel, your fellows' and your own." The Federal Rules of Criminal Procedure forbids disclosure of "matters occurring before . . . [a] grand jury" and provides that violations can be punished as contempt of court [Rule 6(e)].

According to the **grand jury secrecy requirements,** those serving on a grand jury, therefore, cannot disclose proceedings and deliberations by that body. They have a privilege not to answer questions requiring disclosure of such matters unless they fall within exceptions listed in the Federal Rules of Criminal Procedure 6(e).

Some of the reasons given for the historic use of secrecy regarding deliberations and evidence considered by grand juries are to encourage and protect the independence and freedom of deliberations of grand juries; to protect the reputations of people who are not indicted for criminal offenses but were considered; to prevent people who are to be indicted from fleeing because they had information of the coming criminal charges; to encourage witnesses to testify freely; and to encourage members of the grand jury to deliberate freely knowing that what was said will not be made public.

SUMMARY

Judicial notice statues in every state make it possible to avoid unnecessary delays in courts. Trial judges may take judicial notice of facts known to the community that are not subject to reasonable disputes and to other information listed in the statues of the state. This saves time and much effort in helping to move both criminal and civil cases along.

Testimonial privileges are rules of evidence that have been created for different reasons. The privilege against self-incrimination is a constitutional requirement that protects suspects from becoming witnesses against themselves unless this privilege is voluntarily waived.

Other testimonial privileges were created to protect relationships and interests such as husband–wife, attorney–client, and physician–patient. These relationships have been determined to be of sufficient importance so a to justify sacrificing what might be very reliable evidence from being used in criminal and civil trials.

Privileges apply only to prevent the use of testimony in criminal trials and other judicial proceedings. In investigating criminal matters, law officers may talk to spouses, children, and others who will cooperate. Whether a spouse can testify against the other spouse would depend upon whether the evidence falls within the spousal privilege and whether the privilege is asserted by the other spouse.

PROBLEMS

AVAILABLE ANSWERS

a. Privilege against self-incrimination

b. Husband–wife privilege

c. Lawyer–client privilege

d. Physician–patient privilege

e. All of the above are correct

1. Is the only privilege protected by the U.S. Constitution

2. May be waived by the person who has the privilege

3. Use of the privilege could prevent the use of important evidence in a criminal case

4. Is the oldest of the privileges other than #1

5. Unless there is a valid marriage, _____ would not apply

6. The "crime-fraud" exception applies to

7. The "partnership-in-crime" exception applies to

8. This privilege is found in the statutes or case law of your state

9. Prevents a prosecutor from forcing your doctor to take the witness stand to testify against you as to confidential communications

10. Prevents a prosecutor from forcing your lawyer to take the witness stand to testify against you as to confidential communications

TRUE OR FALSE

11. The informant's privilege permits the government or an authorized law officer to assure a private citizen that his or her identity will be kept secret when he or she provides information.

12. Only the informant or the person providing information can waive this privilege as the privilege belongs to the informant.

13. The informant privilege is really the government's privilege, and it is the government who may waive the privilege and disclose the information.

14. The lawyer–client privilege may only be waived by the lawyer as it is a lawyer privilege.

15. The physician–patient privilege may only be waived by the medical doctor as it is the doctor's privilege.

INFOTRAC COLLEGE EDITION EXERCISES

1. Go to InfoTrac College Edition and using the search term "confidential communications" and the "attorney" subdivision find the 2002 *Cornell Law Review* article titled, "A Rule unfit for All Seasons: Monitoring Attorney–client Communications Violates Privilege and the Sixth Amendment," by Avidon Cover. The Anti-Terrorism and Effective Death Penalty Act of 1996 gives the government authority, under certain conditions, to monitor conversations between prisoners and their attorneys. What are the problems this author sees with that practice? Given the events of 9/11 and their aftermath, do you agree with the author's analysis?

2. Go to InfoTrac College Edition and using the search term "psychotherapist–patient privilege" find the 2001 article in the *Journal of Law, Medicine, & Ethics* titled "Evidence: Expanding the Psychotherapist–Patient Privilege to Include Unlicensed Counselors," by Taruna Garg. This article discusses the extension of the privilege by the 9th Circuit Court of Appeals, based on language from the *Jaffee v. Redmond* case discussed in Chapter 6, section F. Do you see any problems with adopting an extension like that discussed by the author? What problems?

3. Go to InfoTrac College Edition and using the search term "psychotherapist–patient privilege" find the 2001 article in *Army Lawyer* titled "The Military's Psychotherapist–Patient Privilege: Benefit or Bane for Military Accused?" by R. Peter Masterson. Military courts have their own evidentiary rules and their own common law history. This article looks at that history for this privilege, how the privilege works in military cases, and its defects.

4. Go to InfoTrac College Edition and using the search term "self-incrimination" and the subdivision "cases" find the article in the 2000 *Corrections Caselaw Quarterly* titled "U.S. Appeals

Court: Programs Self-Incrimination." Should a state prison inmate be compelled to provide potentially incriminating evidence of past sexual criminal activity as a condition of participating in a sexual abuse treatment program? What factors seem relevant to this question? What exactly does "compelled" mean in this context?"

NOTES

1. *Varcoe v. Lee,* 181 pp. 223, 226.
2. Either party to a civil or criminal action may challenge a ruling by a judge who takes judicial notice of a fact. Many states have statutes similar to Federal Rule of Evidence 201(b), which provides that a "judicially noticed fact must be one not subject to reasonable dispute. . . ." In the case of *Palmer v. Mitchell,* 206 N.E. 2d 776 (Ill. App., 1965), a finding of judicial notice was reversed because the information was within the personal knowledge of the judge but was not a matter of common and general knowledge of the community.
3. *Barreiro v. State Bar of California,* 88 Cal.Rptr. 192, 471 P.2d 992 (1970).
4. *Sumpter v. State,* 306 N.E. 2d 95 (1974).
5. 822 P.2d 23.
6. *Dillon v. Gloss,* 256 U.S. 368, 41 S.Ct. 510.
7. 825 P.2d 781.
8. 412 S.E. 2d 473.
9. 955 F. 2d. 799 (2nd Cir.).
10. 296 N.E.2d 837.
11. Footnote 27 of the *Miranda* decision, 384 U.S. at 458, 86 S.Ct. 1619, states: "Thirteenth century commentators found an analogue to the privilege grounded in the Bible. 'To sum up the matter, the principle that no man is to be declared guilty on his own admission is a divine decree.' Maimonides, Mishneh Torah (Code of Jewish Law), Book of Judges, Laws of the Sanhedrin, c. 18, ¶ 6. III Yale Judaica Series 52–53. See also Lamm, The Fifth Amendment and Its Equivalent in the Halakhah, 5 *Judaism 53* (Winter 1956).
12. *Fisher v. United States,* 425 U.S. 391, 409, 96 S.Ct. 1569, 1580 (1976).
13. *Kastigar v. United States,* 406 U.S. 441, 444, 92 S.Ct. 1653, 1656 (1972).
14. The problem of determining whether a person is properly using the privilege against self-incrimination and whether the person's answer will subject the person to criminal prosecution is complex. The U.S. Supreme Court stated in the 1953 case of *United States v. Reynolds,* 73 S. Ct.528 that:

. . . Too much judicial inquiry into the claim of privilege would force disclosure of the thing the privilege was meant to protect, while a complete abandonment of judicial control would lead to intolerable abuses. Indeed, in the earlier stages of judicial experience with the problem, both extremes were advocated, some saying that the bare assertion by the witness must be taken as conclusive, and others saying that the witness should be required to reveal the matter behind his claim of privilege to the judge for verification. Neither extreme prevailed, and a sound formula of compromise was developed. This formula received authoritative expression in this country as early as the Burr trial. There are differences in phraseology, but in substance it is agreed that the court must be satisfied from all the evidence and circumstances, and "from the implications of the question, in the setting in which it is asked, that a responsive answer to the question or an explanation of why it cannot be answered might be dangerous because injurious exposure could result." *Hoffman v. United States,* 341 U.S. 479, 486–487, 71 S.Ct. 814, 818 (1951). If the court is so satisfied, the claim of the privilege will be accepted without requiring further disclosure. . . .

15. *Murphy v. Waterfront Comm.,* 378 U.S. 52, 55, 84 S.Ct. 1594, 1596 (1964).
16. *Miranda v. Arizona,* 384 U.S. 436, 460, 86 S.Ct. 1602, 1620 (1966).
17. *Schmerber v. California,* 384 U.S. 757, 86 S.Ct. 1826 (1966).
18. *Gilbert v. California,* 388 U.S. 263, 87 S.Ct. 1951 (1967).
19. *United States v. Wade,* 388 U.S. 218, 87 S.Ct 1926 (1967).
20. *United States v. Dionisio,* 410 U.S. 1, 93 S.Ct. 764 (1973).

21. *United States v. Hammond,* 419 F.2d 166, 168 (4th Cir., 1969), cert. denied, 397 U.S. 1068, 90 S.Ct. 1508 (1970).

22. *United States v. Murray,* 523 F.2d 489, 492 (8th Cir., 1975).

23. *United States v. Valenzuela,* 722 F.2d 1431, 1433 (9th Cir., 1983).

24. *United States v. Roberts,* 481 F.2d 892 (5th Cir., 1973).

25. *United States v. Brown,* 920 F.2d 1212 (5th Cir., 1991).

26. *Holt v. United States,* 218 U.S. 245, 31 S.Ct. 2 (1910).

27. Granting immunity has always been a means used by states and the federal government for obtaining information. Immunity can either be complete or limited. *Use and fruits* is a limited immunity; it differs from *transactional immunity,* which is referred to as an *immunity bath.* The Fourth Federal Court of Appeals defined each in the 1992 case of *United States v. Harris,* 973 F.2d 333, 336, as follows: "The Supreme Court in *Kastigar v. United States,* 406 U.S. 441, 92 S.Ct. 1653, 32 L.Ed.2d 212 (1972), approved the government's grant of 'use' immunity under 18 U.S.C. § 6002 to compel a witness' self-incriminating testimony. Because the government, under the statute, cannot use the immunized testimony or any evidence derived from it either directly or indirectly, the Court held that use immunity is 'coextensive with the scope of the privilege against self-incrimination, and therefore is sufficient to compel testimony over a claim of the privilege.' Id. at 453, 92 S.Ct. at 1661. The Court in *Kastigar* distinguished between use and the broader concept of transactional immunity. Transactional immunity protects an individual against prosecution for anything concerning the substance of compelled testimony. Use immunity, on the other hand, only protects against the government's use of compulsory testimony as a source of evidence, leaving the government free to use any other evidence to prosecute."

28. *George Campbell Painting Corp. v. Reid,* 392 U.S. 286, 88 S.Ct. 1978 (1968); *United States v. Doe,* 465 U.S. 605, 104 S.Ct. 1237 (1984); *United States v. White,* 322 U.S. 694, 64 S.Ct. 1248 (1944).

29. *Bursey v. United States,* 466 F.2d 1059 (9th Cir., 1972).

30. The U.S. Supreme Court held in the *Bouknight* case that: "In *New York v. Quarles,* 467 US 649 . . . (1984), we recognized a public safety exception to the usual Fifth Amendment rights afforded by *Miranda v. Arizona,* 384 US 436 . . . (1966), so that police could recover a firearm which otherwise would have remained in a public area. In the present case, a citation for civil contempt in order to obtain the production of a child such as Maurice M., or knowledge about his whereabouts, is not essentially criminal in nature and aims primarily to securing the safety of the child. Protecting infants from child abuse seems to me to rank in order of social importance with the regulation and prevention of traffic accidents."

31. *United States v. Medley,* 33 M.J. 75 (1991), review denied U.S. Supreme Court, U.S. 112 S.Ct. 1473, 50 CrL 3199 (1992).

32. *United States v. Heyward,* 22 M.J. 35 (C.M.A., 1986).

33. 532 U.S. 17 (2001).

34. 274 F.3d 1053 (6th Cir., 2001).

35. 242 F.3d 49 (1st Cir., 2001).

36. 269 F.3d 1023 (9th Cir., 2001).

37. The "work–product" doctrine is closely related to the attorney–client privilege. The U.S. Supreme Court stated in *Upjohn Co. v. United States,* 449 U.S. 383, 101 S.Ct. 677 (1981), that: "This doctrine was announced by the Court over 30 years ago in *Hickman v. Taylor,* 329 U.S. 495 (1947). In that case the Court rejected 'an attempt, without purported necessity or justification, to secure written statements, private memoranda, and personal recollections prepared or formed by an adverse party's counsel in the course of his legal duties.' Id., at 510. The Court noted that 'it is essential that a lawyer work with a certain degree of privacy' and reasoned that if discovery of the material sought were permitted, 'much of what is now put down in writing would remain unwritten. An attorney's thoughts, heretofore inviolate, would not be his own. Inefficiency, unfairness and sharp practices would inevitably develop in the giving of legal advice and in the preparation of cases for trial. The effect on the legal profession would be demoralizing. And the interests of the clients and the cause of justice would be poorly served.'" Id., at 511.

38. 109 S.Ct. 2619.

39. 602 A.2d 677.

40. Many courts have adopted what is called the *last link doctrine* or *legal advice rule,* where a

client goes to an attorney for legal advice and where revealing the client's identity would be the last link in information needed to convict the client of a crime, the client's name is privileged. Examples of such rare situations where the last link doctrine would apply include: (a) In 1960 the Internal Revenue Service received a letter from an attorney stating that a check enclosed of $12,706.85 was forwarded for additional taxes owed by undisclosed taxpayers. The attorney refused to disclose any names citing the attorney–client privilege. When the matter was appealed, the Federal Court of Appeals, applying California law, upheld the privilege holding that disclosing the clients' names would amount to an acknowledgement of guilt by the clients of the very matter for which legal advice was sought [*Baird v. Koerner,* 279 F.2d 623 (9th Cir., 1960)]. (b) In a federal drug conspiracy prosecution, prosecutors sought to compel the defense lawyer to disclose the name of the unknown person who paid the defense lawyer's fees. Claiming his client was also involved in the drug conspiracy and that disclosing his client's name would disclose a confidential communication, the defense lawyer was successful in asserting the attorney–client privilege [*Matter of Grand Jury Proceeding,* 898 F.2d 565 (7th Cir., 1990)].

The last link or legal advice rule is not applicable if a lawyer is hired to further illegal activity. For example, this could occur where legal advice is sought for the operation of an illegal drug operation or to provide tax advice for illegal activities. See *In re Grand Jury Investigation,* 723 F.2d 447 (6th Cir., 1983), review denied U.S. Supreme Court, 467 U.S. 1246, 104 S.Ct. 3524 (1984).

41. 445 U.S. 40, 100 S.Ct. 906.

42. 966 F.2d 398 (8th Cir.).

43. See 260 F.3d 1295 (11th Cir., 2001). Probably no state extends the husband–wife privilege to people living together but not married. See the 1991 case of *Montanez v. State,* 592 So.2d 650 (Ala. Crim. App.) where the court held that defendant's communications with his "paramour" were not protected by the marital communications privilege. In that case, the woman was granted use immunity and testified against the defendant. In addition, she was a joint participant in the drug trafficking and came under the partners-in-crime exception.

Most states have abolished common-law marriages but the husband–wife privilege may generally be invoked not only in states recognizing common-law marriages but also in other states where common-law married couples have moved. See the 1998 case of *People v. Schmidt,* 1998 WL 101837, where Michigan extended the privilege to a couple who had entered into a valid common-law marriage in Alabama and then moved to Michigan.

44. *United States v. Evans,* 966 F.2d 398 (8th Cir., 1992).

45. *United States v. Hill,* 967 F.2d 902 (3rd Cir., 1992).

46. *United States v. Marashi,* 913 F.2d 724 (9th Cir., 1990).

47. 824 P. 1257 (Wash. App.).

48. 417 S.E. 2d 903 (W. Va.).

49. For an extensive discussion of the physician–patient relationship, see Chapter 12 of the *McCormick on Evidence,* 4th ed. (St. Paul: West Publishing, 1992).

50. 17 F.3d 1299 (10th Cir., 1993) review denied 513 U.S.863.

51. 551 P.2d 334 (CAL. 1976).

52. 133 F.3d 1356 (10th Cir., 1998).

53. 227 F.3d 578 (6th Cir., 2000).

54. 602 A.2d 1290.

55. 408 U.S. 665, 92 S.Ct. 2646.

56. Nebraska Rev. Stat. 20–146 (Reissue 1991).

57. If the general public is excluded from a crime scene or an area where a disaster has occurred, do newspersons have rights and privileges that the general public does not have? The U.S. Supreme Court addressed this question in the 1972 case of *Branzburg v. Hayes* (92 S.Ct. 2646) stating: "Newsmen have no constitutional right of access to the scenes of crime or disaster when the general public is excluded, and they may be prohibited from attending or publishing information about trials if such restrictions are necessary to assure a defendant a fair trial before an impartial tribunal. . . ."

In 1989 a Milwaukee news reporter refused to leave the scene of the crash of a commercial airline. The site was sealed off so that emergency equipment and personnel could assist the injured and dying. The newsman was arrested because he insisted that he had a right to photograph and view the scene. The Wisconsin Supreme

Court affirmed his conviction for disorderly conduct in *City of Oak Creek v. King,* 436 N.W.2d 285.

58. The courts and cases holding a parent–child privilege exist are: *In re Agosto,* 553 F.Supp. 1298 (D. Nev., 1983) and *In re Application of A & M,* 403 N.Y.S.2d 375 (App. Div., 1975).

59. Since 1981, courts have held that the government has a privilege not to reveal the location of surveillance sites and the type of equipment that was used in lawful electronic surveillance unless a defendant shows a sufficient need for that information. Such disclosures could also educate people on how to use such methods themselves, which might be done in violation of federal or state laws. The courts held, however, that the privilege would have to give way if a defendant could show that such information was necessary for the defense, such as a strong likelihood of voice identification. See *United States v. Green,* 670 F.2d 1148 (D.C. Cir., 1981).

60. 353 U.S. 53, 77 S.Ct. 623.

61. See *United States v. Hollis,* 245 F.3d 671 (8th Cir., 2001).

62. 345 U.S. 1, 73 S.Ct. 528.

63. 418 U.S. 683, 94 S.Ct. 3090.

7

The Use of Hearsay in the Courtroom

Ⓐ WITNESSES AND THE HEARSAY RULE

Central to the nature of criminal prosecutions in the United States is the role of witnesses. It is through the testimony of witnesses that the facts are presented to the jury upon which the guilt or innocence of the accused is determined.

When witnesses give their testimony, the subject matter is typically some event observed in some manner by them, which observation is subsequently recollected in the courtroom. This testimony is generally seen as presenting four risks relating to its truthfulness: the accuracy of the witnesses' perception, the memory of the witnesses, the meaning of the testimony, and the sincerity of the witness.

The principal means used by courts to guard against these risks are the requirements that the witness testify under oath, which helps ensure sincerity, and that the witness be available for cross-examination, which can be used to test recollection, narration, and perception.

Imagine a witness in an arson trial gives the following testimony: "I saw the defendant throw something through the window of the building, and then the building caught fire." The truth of this statement carries the risks identified above: Is the witness sincere? Is his memory of the event clear? Were his perceptions of the event accurate? Did the event mean what he said it meant?

These risks can be tested by cross-examination since the witness is available to explain his perceptions or to demonstrate the clarity of his memory. Questions about the witnesses' eyesight, the time of day or night, his distance from the defendant, and so forth can judge the accuracy of his perceptions. Similar questions can judge his memory and narration of the event.

But what if the witness testifies that "Fred told me he saw the defendant throw something through the window of the building, and then the building caught fire?" It is possible, but very unlikely, that the witness may have questioned Fred to determine the accuracy of this statement. If not, the defendant will not be able to do so, since Fred is not at the trial.

The witness's statement about what Fred said is of course hearsay and in most federal and state criminal proceedings would be inadmissible under the relevant hearsay rule. Unfortunately, identifying what is and is not "hearsay" is considerably more complex than this simple example. Moreover, even if something is hearsay, the rule excluding its admissibility is subject to numerous exceptions: The hearsay rule in the Federal Rules of Evidence has two exemptions and twenty-eight exceptions. Finally, in criminal trials, the Confrontation Clause of the Sixth Amendment to the United States Constitution imposes a constitutional restriction on out-of-court testimony by witnesses.

In this chapter we explore the basic elements of hearsay evidence, giving examples of what is and is not hearsay. In Chapter 8 we discuss the Confrontation Clause and the exceptions to the hearsay rule.

Ⓑ THE HISTORY OF THE HEARSAY RULE

As we observed in Chapter 1, as far back as the thirteenth century hearsay evidence was regarded as unreliable. Yet, between the thirteenth and seventeenth centuries, English criminal courts continued to convict defendants based on "anonymous accusers and absentee witnesses."[1]

This practice was particularly prevalent in the infamous Star Chamber trials of the Elizabethan period in England, during the reign of Queen Elizabeth I (1558–1603) and her successor, King James I (1603–1625). The Star Chamber, consisting of royal officers, was used by the monarch to control political enemies. Such persons were often charged with treason and tried in the Star Chamber rather than the usual courts. In such trials the evidence was frequently the "confession" of a single "conspirator," who was not available for cross-examination by the accused and who did not repeat his "confession" under oath at the trial.

These abuses were condemned by many of Elizabeth's subjects, among them William Shakespeare. In his play *King Richard II,* written in 1595, Shakespeare has his fictional king set the following procedure for trial, as compared with the standard the actual sovereign, Queen Elizabeth, was using: "Then call them into our presence—face to face, and frowning brow to brow, ourselves will hear the accuser and the accused freely speak . . ." (*Richard II,* Act I, Scene I).

The 1603 Trial of Sir Walter Raleigh

The trial of Sir Walter Raleigh in 1603 illustrates the abuses that were occurring before hearsay rules were used. As a soldier and explorer, Sir Walter Raleigh was a colorful member of the English Court of Queen Elizabeth.[2] Raleigh enjoyed the patronage and protection of Queen Elizabeth during her lifetime but had powerful enemies in the English Court.

Upon Queen Elizabeth's death in 1603, the new king, James I, feared Raleigh and had him seized and thrown into the Tower of London in July 1603. In November 1603, Raleigh was tried for treason against the king. He was convicted based upon the confession of a single conspirator, who did not appear as a witness at the trial. The confession was probably obtained by torture and was denied by the man before Raleigh's trial.

In the years following the trial of Sir Walter Raleigh, the English courts began developing hearsay rules and by 1690, it is reported that English courts were using hearsay rules to prevent abuses that are recorded in the history of that period.

After the 1670 trial of William Penn (see Chapter 5), the historic development of the concept of an impartial jury continued along with the development of the hearsay rule. Wigmore (5 Wigmore, Evidence Sec. 1364) called the hearsay rule "the greatest contribution of the [English] legal system . . . next to the jury trial."

Hearsay Rules and the Use of Independent Juries in the American Colonies/States

The concepts of impartial, independent juries and hearsay rules were brought to the American Colonies by English settlers as part of the English common law system.

After the American Revolutionary War, both the right to an impartial jury and the use of hearsay rules were made part of the American legal system. The Sixth Amendment Confrontation Clause was made part of the American Bill of Rights in 1791: "In all criminal prosecutions, the accused shall enjoy the right . . . to be confronted with witnesses against him . . . ."[3]

The U.S. Supreme Court observed that the rule against hearsay is closely related to the constitutional right of confrontation as both "stem from the same roots" and that ". . . hearsay rules and the Confrontation Clause are generally designed to protect similar values. . . ."[4]

WHAT IS HEARSAY

Rule 801(c) of the Federal Rules of Evidence defines **hearsay** as follows: "'Hearsay' is a statement, other than one made by the declarant while testifying at the trial or hearing, offered in evidence to prove the truth of the matter asserted." The **declarant** is the person who made the statement. That statement is *offered* into evidence by some other person, usually one to whom the declarant made the statement or who overheard (or observed[5]) the statement.

What Is an Assertive Statement?[6]

To fall within the hearsay rule, the declarant's statement must be an **assertive statement** offered as proof that the subject matter of the statement is true. An assertive statement is one in which the declarant intends to communicate his thoughts or beliefs.

EXAMPLES:

- Witness W testifies: "My brother (X) told me that he shot my dad because he thought my dad was planning to kill him." This is hearsay and not admissible, as this is an assertive statement. There is no opportunity to test the accuracy of this statement by cross-examination unless the brother is brought into court. However, if the brother is the defendant in this trial, this would be an incriminating statement that would be admissible under Federal rule 807(d) (2) (see Appendix B).
- Witness W testifies: "I heard my brother (X) mutter 'I killed my dad' in his sleep." This is not hearsay because X, while sleeping, did not intend to communicate.[7] It is not hearsay if X is a defendant in this action charged with killing his dad. See Rule 807(d) (2).

Nonverbal Communications Can Be Assertive

Nonverbal acts can be used to communicate. If the purpose of the nonverbal act is to communicate and the communication is assertive, it is then hearsay.

EXAMPLES:

- The witness testifies that when she asked X where his drug dealer lived, X pointed to the defendant's house. This is hearsay because it is an assertion that cannot be tested by cross-examination. X should be brought in as a witness if he is available.
- The witness testifies that she requested the victim of a mugging to draw a sketch of the mugger. This is hearsay because it is assertive conduct that cannot be tested by cross-examination. The victim has to be brought in as a witness.

Conduct that Is Not Meant to Communicate

If a person is engaging in conduct that is not meant to communicate, this would generally not be treated as hearsay as there is no attempt to be assertive.[8]

EXAMPLE: A police officer testifies: "I showed Ms. _____ (rape victim) a display of seven photographs. When she saw the picture of X (the defendant), she gasped and began to cry." This is not hearsay because the rape victim's conduct is not meant as a communication even though it creates the indirect inference that she believes the defendant was the person who raped her.[9]

The Hearsay Rule Forbids Only Statements Offered to Prove the Truth of that Statement

If an attorney can convince a judge that a statement offered for use in evidence is meant to prove something other than the truth of that statement, the judge will rule that it is admissible for evidence.

The hearsay rule forbids only statements offered to prove the **truth of the matter asserted.** The hearsay rule does not forbid something other than the truth of that statement.

McCormick on Evidence,[10] second edition, points out there are "an almost infinite variety of other purposes" to take a statement out of the hearsay rule and permit the statement to be used as evidence. The following examples illustrate only a few of the numerous other purposes that would take an out-of-court statement out of the hearsay classification:

- *Knowledge.* William Witness testifies that Fred Firebug told him that a can of gasoline was in the attic of the house the day before the fire occurred. Witness's testimony would *not* be admissible to prove that there was gasoline in the attic the day before the fire. It would be admissible to show that Firebug *knew* that there was gasoline in the attic before the fire.

- *Feelings or state of mind.* William Witness testifies that Fred Firebug had said "Bobby Burnout took my money, stole my girl, and wrecked my car on the night of the senior prom." This testimony would not be admissible to show that Burnout had taken Firebug's money, or stolen his girlfriend, or wrecked his car. It would be admissible to show Firebug's feelings or state of mind about Burnout.

- *Insanity.* William Witness testifies that Charles Crazy had said, "I am Napoleon Bonaparte, Emperor of All France." Witness's testimony would not be admissible to show that Crazy was in fact a person named Napoleon Bonaparte. It would, however, be admissible to show circumstantially that Crazy was insane.

- *Effect on hearer.* William Witness testifies that he heard Bill Bully say to Tom Timid, "No one better mess with me. I am carrying a loaded .38." The testimony would not be admissible to show that Bully was carrying a gun. It would be admissible to show the effect on Timid's state of mind.

The trial judge should instruct the jury that it is to consider the evidence only for the allowable purpose. This would work well in the above Charles Crazy example. The jury would view the statement as bearing on Crazy's state of mind and would not conclude that Crazy might indeed be Napoleon Bonaparte.

But as Professor McCormick points out, "such . . . instructions may not always be effective," and there are situations in which juries misuse the evidence, or become unduly confused by the judge's instructions.

Ⓓ WHAT IS NOT HEARSAY? FEDERAL RULES OF EVIDENCE 801(D)(1), (2), AND (2E)

Besides being limited to assertions offered to establish proof of the assertion, the hearsay rule also does not apply to various out-of-court statements that would otherwise literally fall within the definition of hearsay. Under the Federal Rules of Evidence, these statements are contained in Rule 801(d)(1) and (2).

Prior Statement by a Witness

If a witness testifies at a trial, and is cross-examined concerning an earlier statement made by the witness, the statement is not hearsay if: (a) The statement is inconsistent and was given under oath at a previous trial, hearing, or deposition.

> **EXAMPLE:** At D's murder trial, W testifies he saw D in the victim's car on the night the victim was killed. In a deposition taken prior to trial, where D's attorney was present and able to cross-exam W, W stated D was not in the victim's car. W's earlier statement is not hearsay.

(b) The statement is consistent and is offered to rebut a charge that the witness's present testimony is a recent fabrication or stems from an improper motive.

> **EXAMPLE:** The witness, who is the defendant's employee, testifies that he saw the defendant in Cleveland on the date a robbery occurred in Denver. On cross-examination, the prosecutor suggests the witness's motive is to protect his employer. A similar, consistent statement made by the witness to a police officer investigating the robbery, made before the witness was employed by the defendant, is not hearsay.

Admission by Party-Opponent

Where the statement sought to be admitted is an out-of-court statement made by the defendant (a "party" in the trial) or someone acting on his or her behalf, Rule 801(d)(2) provides that the statement is not hearsay.[11]

Different reasons are given as the basis for the rule, but as Professor McCormick points out, the hearsay rule never forbids admissions by a **party-opponent** (the defendant in a criminal case).

> **EXAMPLE:** The witness, W, testifies in D's trial for possession of stolen property that shortly after a burglary D stated "I have the jewels stolen from the Johnson house." The statement is not hearsay.

> **EXAMPLE:** The witness, W, testifies at D's trial for assault against V that, in the presence of D, V stated "last night after work D beat me up," and D said nothing. D's silence can be seen as adoption or belief in the statement and prevents the statement from being hearsay.

> **EXAMPLE:** The witness, W, testifies at D's trial for illegal bookmaking that E, a person who worked for D by picking up betting slips, stated "these are markers in D's sports book." The statement is not hearsay.

The Co-Conspirator Rule

Rule 801(d)(2)(E) provides that statements by a co-conspirator made during and in furtherance of the conspiracy are not hearsay.[12] The justification for this rule is that parties in a **conspiracy** are essentially partners, and an admission by one partner is fairly attributable to the other partners. The U.S. Supreme Court has said statements by a co-conspirator "provide evidence of the conspiracy's context that cannot be replicated, even if the [co-conspirator] testifies to the same matters in court." The Court also noted that "simply calling the [co-conspirator] in hopes of having him repeat his prior out-of-court statements is a poor substitute for the full . . . significance that flow[s] from statements made when the conspiracy is operating in full force[11] (**co-conspirator rule**).

> **EXAMPLE:** A and B are engaged in a conspiracy to import and sell illegal drugs. While acting in furtherance of the conspiracy, A states to B, "C sold the cocaine from the last shipment." A's statement is not hearsay as an admission of a coconspirator and is admissible in C's prosecution.

SUMMARY

It is reported that the word *hearsay* is a contraction of the old English phrase, "I heard it said."

When a witness at a criminal trial is asked to repeat in court a statement made out of court, the following questions should be asked to determine if that testimony is inadmissible hearsay:

1. Is the statement (verbal or nonverbal conduct) an *assertion*?
2. Is the statement offered to prove the truth of the assertion?
3. Was the statement made under oath and subject to cross-examination at a prior trial, hearing, or deposition?
4. Was the admission (or statement) made by a party-opponent in a civil case, or the defendant in a criminal case?

Even if a statement ends up being hearsay, under many circumstances hearsay testimony is admissible under one of many exceptions to the hearsay rule. Many of these exceptions, and their relationship to the Confrontation Clause, are considered in Chapter 8.

PROBLEMS

1. A series of robberies and murders were occurring in a city. In three of these robberies, the robber staked out small businesses and after obtaining cash, shot the owner. There were no live witnesses to the crimes, no videos of the crime, no fingerprints or DNA evidence.

In a fourth robbery, the owner of a small grocery store was critically wounded but was alive and conscious enough to give an excellent description of the perpetrator. He then clearly identified the man from a photo array. Because of the critical condition of the victim, an immediate preliminary hearing was scheduled after the suspect was arrested and charged.

The judge, the defense lawyer, and the prosecutor (with other court attendants) conducted the preliminary hearing in the hospital room of the victim in the presence of the defendant. Pain medication was withheld for a day from the victim at his request. The victim again clearly identified the defendant as the robber and responded to cross-examination by the defense lawyer. An early trial date was set, but the victim died before the trial.

Neither the shooting weapon nor the murder weapons were recovered and with no other evidence other than the testimony of the victim, the trial began. Can the testimony of the deceased victim be used as evidence? Why?

The series of robberies and murders stopped with the arrest of the defendant. Can this be used as evidence? (Check the Index under "signature crime" for this answer.)

"Ballistic fingerprints" were available, but no murder weapons were found that they could be matched up to. Can the defendant be convicted of the other robberies and murders on the evidence available?

2. The defendant ("J") bragged in a tavern to another man how he would pick up prostitutes, pay them for sex, and then later kill them, after taking their money before burying the bodies. The man reported J's statements to a police officer and agreed to cooperate with the police.

Three bodies and other evidence were obtained to corroborate J's statements. J was arrested and charged with three murders, kidnappings, and robberies. Can the State of California's witness testify as to J's statements in the tavern? Why? See the case of *People v. Jennings*, 807 P.2d 1009 (Sup. Ct. Calif., 1991) in the Table of Cases in this text.

3. When the State of California's witness in problem 2 testifies about Jennings' statements made in the tavern, it will be the defense lawyer's job to try to impeach this witness. As Jennings faces the death penalty, the defense lawyer has to make every effort to challenge the credibility of the witness.

What does "impeaching" a witness mean? How would a good lawyer go about impeaching this witness? Who will be the final judge as to the credibility of the witness and the weight that should be given to the testimony of the witness?

INFOTRAC COLLEGE EDITION EXERCISES

1. Go to InfoTrac College Edition and using the search term "hearsay" find the 2002 *New Jersey Law Journal* article titled "Criminal Practice-Hearsay-Homicide-Res Gestae (Supreme Court)," by P. R. Chenoweth. Assume that W is called as a witness in the murder trial of D, who is accused of killing V. W is prepared to testify that D stated to her on June 1 that V died on May 30 after falling down some stairs. In fact, V died on June 3 after falling down some stairs on June 2. Is W's testimony hearsay? Why or why not? Would it matter if W is prepared to testify that X told her that D stated V died on May 30 after falling down some stairs? Would W's testimony be hearsay in that case? This article discusses a case with similar facts and provides the answer to the questions just posed. It also discusses an exception to the hearsay rule called the "res gestae."

2. Go to InfoTrac College Edition and using the search term "hearsay" find the 2001 article in the *William and Mary Law Review* titled "Meaning, Intention and the Hearsay Rule," by Paul Kirgis. This article helps to explain what is meant by the question "When is a statement offered to prove the truth of that statement, and when not?" One way to approach the question is to identify the facts contained in the statement and ask if those facts are the ones some party is attempting to prove. Thus, in the previous exercise, the statement made by D to W is not hearsay, because it was not offered to prove the facts in the statement, namely, that V died on May 30. The only fact in the statement that is offered for proof purposes is that D made the statement. On that question, W has direct knowledge and can therefore testify that D made it.

NOTES

1. See Chapter 8 (p. 143)—*White v. Illinois,* 502 U.S. 346 (1992)—for a discussion of the development of Confrontation Clause law.

2. Sir Walter Raleigh established a reputation as a ruthless fighter and is said to have come to the attention of Queen Elizabeth by spreading his coat over a large mud puddle so that the Queen could walk on his coat. With the death of Elizabeth, the new king, James I, distrusted and feared Raleigh. The conviction for treason put Raleigh in the Tower of London for twelve years where he lived comfortably with his family and servants. Upon his release, he violated the king's order not to invade Spanish territory in South America and was sentenced to death for disobeying.

3. Justices Thomas and Scalia state in the 1992 case of *White v. Illinois,* 502 U.S. 346, 112 S.Ct. 736, 744, 50 CrL 2036, that there "is virtually no evidence of what the drafters of the Confrontation Clause intended it to mean." They quote Justice Harlan's concurring opinion in the 1970 case of *Dutton v. Evans,* 400 U.S. 74, 94, 91 S.Ct. 210, 222, that "From the scant information available it may tentatively be concluded that the Confrontation Clause was meant to constitutionalize a barrier against flagrant abuses, trials by anonymous accusers, and absentee witnesses."

The famous English Judge, Sir James Stephens, stated in his 1883 book, *A History of the Criminal Law of England* (Macmillan, 1883) that early English judges would question the prisoner, accomplices, and others prior to criminal trials and that the "prisoner had no right to be, and probably never was, present." At the trial itself, "proof was usually given by reading depositions, confession of accomplices, letters, and the like; and this occasioned frequent demands by the prisoner to have his 'accusers,' i.e., the witnesses against him, brought before him face to face" (vol. 1, p. 326, *A History of the Criminal Law of England*).

4. *Dutton v. Evans,* 400 U.S. 74, 86, 91 S.Ct. 210, 218 (1970).

5. A statement need not be verbal. It could be in writing, or it could be a nonverbal act intended as an assertion. See Federal Rule of Evidence 801(a).

6. See *Martinez v. McCaughtry,* 951 F.2d 130 (7th Cir., 1991). Statements by declarant that "you're a dead man" made to accused are not hearsay because they are not assertions. Many courts use the kind of sentence made by the declarant as a guide to whether the statement is assertive. Sentences that are questions (interrogative) or commands (imperative) are not assertions. Only indicative or declaratory sentences can be assertions. See, e.g., *Holland v. State,* 713 A.2d 364 (Md. App., 1998).

7. See, e.g., *State v. Tate,* 817 S.W.2d 578 (Mo. App., 1991).

8. The Advisory Committee on Rules of Evidence, which drafted Rule 801 of the federal rules, made this comment about nonassertive conduct: "Subdivision (a). The definition of 'statement' assumes importance because the term is used in the definition of hearsay in subdivision (c). The effect of the definition of 'statement' is to exclude from the operation of the hearsay rule all evidence of conduct, verbal or nonverbal, not intended as an assertion. The key to the definition is that nothing is an assertion unless intended to be one." Cited in *People v. Jones,* 579 N.W.2d 82, 92 (Mich. App., 1998).

9. Federal Rule of Evidence 801(d)(1)(C) also permits prior out-of-court identifications by a witness available for cross-examination at the trial. See *Gilbert v. California,* 388 U.S. 263 (1967).

10. *McCormick on Evidence,* 4th ed. (West, 1992).

11. However, under the *Bruton* rule (see Chapter 12), the confession of an accomplice may not ordinarily be introduced at a joint trial of persons committing a crime together if the confession incriminates the other defendant or defendants. Such a confession could be admissible, however, (a) if the person making the confession takes the witness stand, (b) if the confession does not incriminate other defendants, or (c) all defendants confess and the reliability of the confessions are significantly interlocking to rebut the presumption of unreliability.

12. Rule 801(d)(2) provides that the co-conspirator's statement, while relevant to the question, cannot alone establish that the person against whom the statement is offered was a party to the conspiracy. Most courts require some independent proof of that fact, and if such proof is not available the co-conspirator's statement is inadmissible. See *United States v. Tellier,* 83 F.3d 578 (2d Cir., 1996), cert. denied 117 S.Ct. 373 (1996).

8

Exceptions to the Hearsay Rule

Ⓐ HEARSAY AND THE CONFRONTATION CLAUSE

In criminal trials, the admission of out-of-court statements presents not only issues under relevant hearsay rules but also potential conflict with the Sixth Amendment's **Confrontation Clause.** That clause states "In all criminal prosecutions, the accused shall enjoy the right . . . to be confronted with the witnesses against him. . . ." The implications of hearsay evidence for the Confrontation Clause are clear: If an out-of-court statement is admitted as evidence against the accused, the person making that statement is a "witness"[1] who is not "confronting" the accused.

Prior to 1965 there were few cases discussing the relationship between the hearsay rule, hearsay exceptions, and the Confrontation Clause. This was because the Confrontation Clause had not been extended to state criminal cases and applied only to federal criminal trials. In those trials, admissibility tended to be determined by reference only to federal evidentiary rules.[2]

In the 1965 case of *Pointer v. Texas,*[3] the U.S. Supreme Court held that the Fourteenth Amendment Due Process Clause made the Confrontation Clause binding in state criminal trials. Because state evidentiary rules differed widely from federal evidence rules and from each other, the Supreme Court was forced to consider admissibility of hearsay evidence as a Confrontation Clause problem. A state might, for example, have an evidentiary rule that permits admissibility of hearsay evidence in criminal cases for reasons unique to that state's evidentiary system. In such a case, the state's justification for admission of the hearsay evidence must pass the Confrontation Clause test.

In the early cases decided after *Pointer v. Texas,* the Supreme Court noted that "hearsay rules and the Confrontation Clause are generally designed to protect similar values."[4] They both recognize the importance of face-to-face contact between witness and accused, and the crucial role of cross-examination, "the greatest legal engine ever invented for the discovery of truth."[5] However, the Court was careful not to equate the Confrontation Clause with the hearsay rule.[6]

The "Indicia of Reliability" Requirement

Hearsay ("I heard it said") is not admissible as evidence unless there is a showing of substantial reliability for the statement. The major exceptions to the hearsay rule are presented in this chapter. Each exception has conditions and circumstances that the courts and legislative bodies have determined create sufficient reliability and trustworthiness to allow the hearsay statements to be used as evidence. The showing of reliability and trustworthiness necessary to use the statements as evidence is known as "indicia of reliability."

State and federal law provide that several exceptions to the hearsay rule involve a showing that the declarant (the speaker) be unavailable as a witness at the trial. If the state or federal law requires a showing of "unavailability" for an exception, then this burden must be carried before the statement (or statements) can be used as evidence.

Most states and the federal government provide that a showing of "unavailability" is not required for the hearsay exceptions listed under Federal Rule 803. Federal Rule 804 defines "unavailability" and then lists the hearsay exceptions not excluded if the declarant is unavailable as a witness.

The following U.S. Supreme Court cases illustrate the "indicia of reliability" requirement and deal with the question of whether the prosecutor had a burden to show "unavailability" for a declarant before that person's statements could be used as evidence:

Ohio v. Roberts
United States Supreme Court, 448 U.S. 56 (1980)

Roberts was arrested and charged with forgery and receiving stolen property. At his preliminary hearing, the owner of the stolen checks and credit cards testified, and the daughter of the owner also testified, denying that she had given Roberts permission to use the credit cards or the checks. Roberts was subsequently indicted for forgery and credit card theft. At his trial, Roberts testified the daughter had given him permission to use her parents' checkbook and credit cards. The daughter was unavailable to testify, and the prosecutor introduced the preliminary hearing testimony given by the daughter to rebut Roberts' testimony. Roberts was convicted and appealed on the grounds that there was no showing by the prosecutor that the witness was "unavailable" as is required and that the hearsay evidence did not have adequate and sufficient "indicia of reliability."

The U.S. Supreme Court affirmed Robert's conviction, holding:

1. That the prosecutor did show that the daughter was "constitutionally unavailable"[7] as five subpoenas for four different trial dates were issued to the daughter at her parent's Ohio residence. The daughter had left for Arizona soon after the preliminary hearing and did not contact her parents or other persons in Ohio for months until she was in California. About seven or eight months before the trial, she telephoned her parents to say that she "was traveling." Her parents did not know where she was and her mother stated she had no way to reach her daughter in case of an emergency.

2. That the defense attorney did test the daughter's testimony with "significant cross-examination." The defense lawyer used leading questions and challenged the daughter's veracity. The U.S. Supreme Court held the cross-examination was in "substantial compliance with the purposes behind the confrontation requirement" and therefore had adequate "indicia of reliability."

United States v. Inadi
United States Supreme Court, 475 U.S. 387 (1985)

Inadi was convicted of conspiracy to manufacture and distribute methamphetamine. At his trial, several taped conversations between co-conspirators were admitted into evidence under Federal Rule of Evidence (FRE) 801(d)(2)(E). Inadi objected to their admission, contending his Confrontation Clause rights were violated because the prosecution did not show the co-conspirators were unavailable.

The Third Circuit Court of Appeals reversed Inadi's conviction, holding that the government must show, as a condition of admission of *any* out-of-court statement, that the declarant was unavailable.

The U.S. Supreme Court reversed. It held that the Confrontation Clause has no general requirement that the declarant be unavailable. Unavailability was important in *Roberts*, the Court said, because prior testimony is a kind of out-of-court statement that is admissible not because it is reliable, but because it is necessary where the declarant is now unavailable. If the declarant is available for live testimony, the prior testimony is a "weak substitute" and cannot be used:

> Those same principles do not apply to coconspirator statements. Because they are made while the conspiracy is in progress, such statements provide evidence of the conspiracy's context that cannot be replicated, even if the declarant testifies to the same matters in court. When the Government—as here—offers the statement of one drug dealer to another in furtherance of an illegal conspiracy, the statement often will derive its significance from the circumstances in which it was made.[8]

White V. Illinois
United States Supreme Court, 502 U.S. 346 (1992)

White was convicted after a jury trial for sexual assault upon a 4-year-old girl. The little girl was in the courtroom during the trial but did not testify. Testimony as to statements the little girl made immediately after the crime were presented to the jury as evidence by the little girl's babysitter, her mother, an investigating officer, an emergency room nurse, and a doctor. The statements were admitted under the Illinois hearsay exceptions for spontaneous declarations and for statements made in the course of securing medical treatment.[9] No attempt was made to declare the victim unavailable, and the testimonies of the witnesses were admitted over White's objections.

The U.S. Supreme Court affirmed White's conviction holding:

> We therefore think it clear that the out-of-court statements admitted in this case had substantial probative value, value that could not be duplicated simply by the declarant later testifying in court. To exclude such probative statements under the strictures of the Confrontation Clause would be the height of wrongheadedness, given that the Confrontation Clause has as a basic purpose the promotion of the "integrity of the factfinding process." And as we have also noted, a statement that qualifies for admission under a "firmly rooted" hearsay exception is so trustworthy that adversarial testing can be expected to add little to its reliability. Given the evidentiary value of such statements, their reliability, and that establishing a generally applicable unavailability rule would have few practical benefits while imposing pointless litigation costs, we see no reason to treat the out-of-court statements in this case differently from those we found admissible in *Inadi*. A contrary rule would result in exactly the kind of "wholesale revision" of the laws of evidence that we expressly disavowed in *Inadi*. We therefore see no basis in *Roberts* or *Inadi* for excluding from trial, under the aegis of the Confrontation Clause, evidence embraced within such exceptions to the hearsay rule as those for spontaneous declarations and statements made for medical treatment. . . .[10]

Lilly v. Virginia
United States Supreme Court (1999) 527 U.S. 116, 119 S. Ct. 1887

Two brothers, Mark and Gary Lilly, and Gary Barker were arrested after a two-day crime spree, which ended in the kidnapping and later shooting and killing of a man. Under police questioning, Mark admitted the other crimes but claimed that his brother and Gary Barker stole guns and that his brother shot the deceased victim.

At the murder trial, Mark was called as a witness but invoked his Fifth Amendment privilege against self-incrimination.[11] The trial court then admitted Mark's statements to the police as declarations of an unavailable witness against penal interest. The Viriginia Supreme Court affirmed the convictions as Mark incriminated himself for the other crimes committed. The murder conviction was appealed to the U.S. Supreme Court.

The U.S. Supreme Court reversed and remanded the case, holding:

> It is abundantly clear that neither the words that Mark spoke nor the setting in which he was questioned provides any basis for concluding that his comments regarding petitioner's guilt were so reliable that there was no need to subject them to adversarial testing in a trial setting. Mark was in custody for his involvement in, and knowledge of, serious crimes and made his statements under the supervision of governmental authorities. He was primarily responding to the officers' leading questions, which were asked without any contemporaneous cross-examination by adverse parties. Thus, Mark had a natural motive to attempt to exculpate himself as much as possible. . . . Mark also was obviously still under the influence of alcohol. Each of these factors militates against finding that his statements were so inherently reliable that cross-examination would have been superfluous.
>
> The admission of the untested confession of Mark Lilly violated petitioner's Confrontation Clause rights.

B FIRMLY ROOTED EXCEPTIONS TO THE HEARSAY RULE[12]

Hearsay rules and the right of a defendant to view and confront witnesses against him were "designed to protect similar values."[13] The U.S. Supreme Court points out that they have been "careful not to equate the Confrontation Clause's prohibitions with the general rule prohibiting the admission of hearsay statements."[14]

The Supreme Court has refused many times the requests of defense lawyers to interpret the Sixth Amendment Confrontation Clause so strictly that it would eliminate virtually every hearsay exception. The Supreme Court has stated that this is "a result long rejected as unintended and too extreme."[15]

The Court recognizes that the Sixth Amendment Confrontation Clause "reflects a preference for face-to-face confrontation at trial." It also recognizes that cross-examination is a right of criminal defendants and refers to cross-examination as the "greatest legal engine ever invented for the discovery of truth."[16]

The hearsay rule and its exceptions developed over a three-hundred-year history in English and American law. The rule developed by English and American courts has now been made a part of federal and state law. The present Federal Rules of Evidence, which are followed by most states, list twenty-eight specific, firmly rooted exceptions. In enacting these exceptions into statutory law, the U.S. Congress and state legislatures have concluded that these exceptions have sufficient guarantees of reliability to be classified as firmly rooted hearsay exceptions. Some of the most widely used exceptions, which are part of federal law and the law of most states, are described in the remaining sections of this chapter.

Excited Utterance Exception[17]

Federal Rule of Evidence 803(2), **Excited utterance:** "A statement relating to a startling event or condition made while the declarant was under the stress of excitement caused by the event or condition."

REASON FOR THE EXCEPTION Many crimes are "startling events" that cause victims and witnesses to make excited statements during or immediately after the event. If such statements are in response to the startling event, the trustworthiness of such statements comes from the fact that the victim or witness had no time to reflect and possibly fabricate the statements.

EXAMPLES

- Statements by witnesses and victims during or immediately after shootings, stabbings, or robberies are almost always made "under the stress of excitement" caused by the startling event of the crime of violence.[18]

- Statements of rape victims immediately after the crime.[19]

- Recorded 911 calls and other telephone calls where courts held the caller was speaking under the stress of excitement and permitted the recording to be used as evidence.[20]

- Many courts hold that there can be more of a time lapse between the startling event and statements when crimes such as sex crimes are reported by children or mentally retarded persons.[21]

Then Existing Mental, Emotional, or Physical Condition Exception

Federal Rule of Evidence 803(3), **Then existing mental, emotional, or physical condition:** "A statement of the declarant's then existing state of mind, emotion, sensation, or physical condition (such as intent, plan, motive, design, mental feeling, pain, and bodily health). . . ."

REASON FOR THE EXCEPTION Hearsay is defined by statute as a statement "offered in evidence to prove the truth of the matter asserted." If a statement is not offered to prove the truth of the matter asserted, courts almost always hold that such statements are not hearsay and are admissible as evidence.

- *Motive* of the offender can be shown. Prior to death, murder victims sometimes make statements to other persons about why they are afraid of the killer. The statement is not offered to show that the defendant committed the murder but is offered to show motive or state of mind. In the 1990 case of *State v. Alvarez*,[22] the victim owed defendant money for cocaine; in the 1992 case of *Parker v. State*,[23] a woman victim was afraid of defendant because she had been with another man.

- *Intent* can be shown. In a murder case, the victim had stated to a friend that she was going to visit the defendant (her boyfriend) and then go skating. The victim was then found strangled and beaten to death. The state-of-mind statement was allowed in evidence to show the victim's present purpose and intent at the time the statements were made. [24]

- *Insanity or mental illness* can be shown. Witness A testifies that X repeatedly said that he heard voices and that he believed he was Napoleon. The testimony is not being offered to prove that X was Napoleon but to prove X had serious mental problems.

- *State of mind* can be shown. In 1962 a bigamy case, *People v. Marsh*,[25] came before the Supreme Court of California. The defendant was charged with being married to two women at the same time. It was held that statements supporting the defendant's defense of his reasonable belief that he was free to remarry were admissible to prove his state of mind at that time.

Statements for the Purposes of Medical Diagnosis or Treatment Exception

Federal Rule of Evidence 803(4), "**Statements for purposes of medical diagnosis or treatment....**"

USE OF THE EXCEPTION IN CRIMINAL TRIALS Because the physician–patient privilege forbids medical doctors from disclosing information regarding their patients, there are few cases regarding adult defendants. Most of the cases concern child victims of sexual abuse. If the child reasonably understands the need to be truthful to their physician and the identification of their assailant is reasonably necessary to their medical diagnosis and treatment, the exception would apply and the physician could testify about statements the child made under such circumstances.

> **EXAMPLE:** In the 1992 case of *White v. Illinois*,[26] the U.S. Supreme Court held that testimony of an emergency room nurse and a medical doctor about statements made to them by a four-year-old child concerning sexual abuse by the defendant were admissible under the Illinois medical-treatment hearsay exception and did not violate the Sixth Amendment's Confrontation Clause. At the criminal trial, the state attempted on two occasions to call the child as a witness, but in both instances the child left without testifying because of emotional difficulty. The defense made no attempt to call the child as a witness. The defendant's convictions were affirmed.[27]

Regularly Kept Records Exception

Regularly kept business records, public records, records of religious organizations, and family records are admissible under certain federal rules (**regularly kept records exception**).

Federal Rule of Evidence 803

- 803(6)   Records of regularly conducted (business) activity
- 803(8)   Public records and reports
- 803(9)   Records of vital statistics
- 803(11) Records of religious organizations (marriage, baptism, and so on)
- 803(13) Family records (personal and family history)
- 803(16) Statements in ancient documents (over twenty years old)
- 803(18) Learned treatises (history, medicine, or other science established as a reliable authority)

REASON FOR THE EXCEPTION Regularly kept records exception (shop books) go back in history to the 1600s in England and were adopted by the American states. These usually accurate records can be attacked by the opposing party. The fact finder (jury or judge) always determines the credibility and weight to be given to such evidence.

Dying Declaration Exception[28]

Federal Rule of Evidence 804(2), statement under belief of impending death (**dying declaration**). "In a prosecution for homicide or in a civil action or proceeding, a statement made by a declarant while believing that the declarant's death was imminent, concerning the cause or circumstances of what the declarant believed to be impending death."

REASON FOR THE EXCEPTION The use of dying declarations as evidence goes back to the 1500s in early England. The practice became an exception to the hearsay rules by the 1700s. In the 1789 King's Bench case of *Rex v. Woodcock*,[29] the English court stated the reason for the exception as follows:

> they are declarations made in extremity, when the party is at the point of death, and when every hope of this world is gone, when every motive to falsehood is silenced, and the mind is induced by the most powerful considerations to speak the truth. A situation so solemn and so awful is considered by the law as creating an obligation equal to that which is imposed by an oath administered in court. Woodcock's case, I Leach, 502.

In the 1990 case of *State v. Weir*,[30] it was held by the Florida Appellate Court that:

> Admission of dying declarations is justified on the grounds of public necessity, manifest justice and the sense that impending death makes a false statement by the decedent improbable. Section 90.804, Law Revision Council Note–1976.

EXAMPLES: To use a dying declaration as evidence, the person must have died, or otherwise become unavailable (lack of memory, in a coma, etc.). The Supreme Court of Minnesota stated the requirement for use of the exception as follows in the 1990 case of *State v. Bergeron*:[31]

To make a dying declaration admissible, something more is required than that declarant realize the seriousness of his condition and the possibility of death. The testimony offered as a dying declaration . . . must have been spoken without hope of recovery and in the shadow of impending death. This state of mind must be exhibited in the evidence and not left to conjecture.

The Supreme Court of Florida held in the 1991 case of *Henry v. State*[32] that:

It is not required that the declarant make "express utterances . . . that he knew he was going to die, or could not live, or would never recover." *Lester v. State,* 37 Fla. 382, 385, 20 So. 232, 233 (1896). Rather, the court should satisfy itself, on the totality of the circumstances, "that the deceased knew and appreciated his condition as being that of an approach to certain and immediate death." *Id.,* 20 So. at 233.

Because killings are startling events, statements made immediately after a fatal shooting or knifing could be found to be admissible under both the excited utterance exception and also the dying declaration exception to the hearsay rule. Examples of cases where statements were admissible under both exceptions are *Lyons v. United States*[33] and *State v. Griffin*.[34]

Statement Against-Penal-Interest Exception

Federal Rule of Evidence 804(3), **Statement against-penal-interest:** "A statement that was at the time of its making so far contrary to the declarant's pecuniary or proprietary interest or so far tended to subject the declarant to civil or criminal liability . . . that a reasonable person in the declarant's position would not have made the statement unless believing it to be true. . . ."

REASON FOR THE EXCEPTION Persons who admit they have committed a crime or were involved in criminal activity are making a statement against penal interest. Such incriminating admissions or confessions ordinarily are considered to have a reliable basis. The U.S. Supreme Court pointed out in the 1971 case of *United States v. Harris*[35] that "People do not lightly admit a crime and place critical evidence in the hands of the police in the form of their own admissions."

In the *Harris* case, the statement against penal interest was made by a known informant. The Supreme Court held that the statement against penal interest plus other evidence established the trustworthiness of the informant's statement.

EXAMPLES: In the 1973 U.S. Supreme Court case of *Chambers v. Mississippi,*[36] the defendant was charged with a murder to which another person had admitted committing and had signed a number of confessions. But Mississippi's hearsay rules prevented Chambers from introducing any of the confessions or statements into evidence in his defense. The Supreme Court held that a state

When the state has a strong case against a defendant, the defense that someone else committed the crime is sometimes offered as evidence, usually with a confession of another person. This defense is admissible as evidence for the defense of an accused if it can be shown that "corroborating circumstances clearly indicate the trustworthiness of the [defense]." [FRE 804(3)].

EXAMPLE: As of the writing of this material, Scott Peterson is preparing to go to trial in California for the murder of his wife and unborn son. His defense lawyer has suggested to the press that a "satanic cult" committed the crimes. This is viewed by many as "farming the jury pool" (that is, seeking to sow seeds of doubt in the minds of potential jurors).

Should the defense seriously seek to use this defense in Peterson's murder trial, a pretrial hearing would have to be scheduled before the trial judge. At the hearing, the defense would have to satisfy the requirements of the California version of Federal Rule 804 (3). They would have to show that the defense had corroborating trustworthy evidence that someone else committed the crime. Failure to carry this burden of proof would mean that the defense could not use evidence of this defense in the Peterson murder trial.

may not use the hearsay rule to deprive defendants in criminal cases of reliable and important evidence.

In the *Chambers* case, there was sufficient corroborating evidence that "clearly" supported the "trustworthiness of the statement [confession]." For cases where trial courts held there was insufficient evidence to support the trustworthiness of confessions, see *State v. Rosado*[37] and *Lee v. McCaughtry*.[38]

In these cases, the defendants were convicted (one of murder and the other of drug trafficking) when evidence that other people had confessed to the crimes was not allowed because of a lack of supporting evidence.[39]

C THE FRESH COMPLAINT AND THE OUTCRY RULE

Hundreds of years ago, the victim of a crime was expected to raise an immediate *hue and cry*, or *outcry*. The failure to do so frequently resulted in the victim losing the right to charge the perpetrator with the crime in a later trial. The requirement of raising the outcry was imposed as a method of marshaling the neighborhood defenses to catch the assailant. It also served to negate the inference that the victim somehow was in complicity with the defendant. The requirement that one make an outcry was dropped from the law many years ago, but a vestige of the requirement survives in the **fresh complaint and outcry rule.**

In the nineteenth century and well into the twentieth century, the common law assumed that only those victims who immediately complained of rape were actually raped, whereas those persons who remained silent somehow consented to the sexual assault.

Today, modern courts reject the concept that if there were no immediate, or fresh, complaint, there was no rape. However, a long delay in reporting a sexual assault could be a factor considered by a jury in determining whether there was consent to the sexual act. Delay could also cause the loss of important physical evidence of the crime of sexual assault.

Some states continue to use the old common-law exception to the hearsay rule known as the fresh complaint exception. In 1990 the Maryland Court of Special Appeals pointed out that a victim's timely complaint of a sexual assault is admissible as follows:

> In prosecution for sex offenses, evidence of the victim's complaint, coupled with the circumstances of the complaint is admissible as part of the prosecution's case if the complaint was made in a recent period of time after the complaint. *Cole v. State,* 574 A.2d 326, 330 (Md. App., 1990)

Among the states that use the fresh complaint rule are California,[40] New Jersey,[41] Oregon,[42] Maryland,[43] Massachusetts,[44] and Florida.[45] The outcry rule is used by Texas.[46]

In other states, the excited reporting of a rape or other crimes, which are startling events, while under the stress of excitement could be admissible under the excited utterance exception to the hearsay rule.

Ⓓ MODERN HEARSAY EXCEPTIONS IN CHILD SEXUAL ABUSE CASES

Statements by children reporting crimes are often admitted as evidence under the excited utterance hearsay exception. Statements children make to physicians and nurses often qualify as evidence under the medical diagnosis and treatment exception of the hearsay rule. These exceptions and other exceptions have been relaxed for children so that juries and judges may determine the reliability and weight that should be given to such evidence in child sexual abuse cases.

Not only have existing hearsay rules been relaxed for children in response to the increasing number of child sexual abuse cases reported in every city throughout the United States, but new state laws have also been enacted in more than thirty states. The new child hearsay statutes permit more out-of-court statements by children to be used as evidence in child sexual abuse cases.

Because these new state hearsay exceptions are not firmly rooted hearsay exceptions that go back hundreds of years in the law, the reliability of such statements cannot be inferred. Therefore, prosecutors must show that statements by children have "particularized guarantees of trustworthiness."

The U.S. Supreme Court held in the 1990 case of *Idaho v. Wright,*[47] that for a child's out-of-court statement to be admissible, the child's truthfulness must be "so clear from the surrounding circumstances that the test of cross-examination would be of marginal utility." The Supreme Court listed the following factors that it thought "properly relate to whether hearsay statements made by a child witness in child sexual abuse cases are reliable:"[48]

1. "spontaneity and consistent repetition"[49]
2. "mental state of the declarant [child]"[50]

3. "use of terminology unexpected of a child of similar age"[51]

4. "lack of motive to fabricate"[52]

The U.S. Supreme Court added that these "factors are . . . not exclusive, and courts have considerable leeway in their consideration of appropriate factors."[53]

Have Innocent People Been Charged or Convicted in Child Sexual Abuse Cases?

Sexual abuse of children does occur in the United States. The frequency of child sexual abuse is shocking. Courts have responded to the problems of very young children as victims by relaxing hearsay rules so that more adults could testify about out-of-court statements made by children.

The new state child hearsay statutes permit additional use of out-of-court statements by children as evidence in criminal trials. Such statements could be used to corroborate the testimony of children concerning sexual abuse or might be sufficient to present a case without the child testifying where it is shown that the child has been traumatized or otherwise unable to testify, due to loss of memory, for example.

However, after years of prosecutions in the 1980s and 1990s and thousands of cases where accusations of child sexual abuse were made against child-care workers, babysitters, family members, and others, it has become clear, as illustrated by the following examples, that many problems exist.

Child Day-Care Cases That Received National Attention

- In 1990 the California *McMartin* trial ended without any criminal convictions against a 62-year-old woman and her 30-year-old son who ran a child day-care center. The two were charged with 321 criminal counts of child molestation. The trial was the longest and probably the most expensive criminal trial in the United States, with more than $13 million in costs. The son spent over five years in jail because bail was set high.[54]

- In 1993 the Supreme Court of Nevada threw out numerous sexual assault convictions against day-care workers in the case of *Felix v. State,* holding that "most of the claims of sexual assault could not have occurred as described by these girls."[55]

- In 1993 the Superior Court of New Jersey reversed the convictions of a nursery school teacher of 115 counts of sexual offenses alleged to have been committed on very young children in the case of *State v. Michaels.*[56]

SUMMARY

The hearsay rules that we use today have been developed over more than three hundred years. If all hearsay was inadmissible as evidence, important relevant evidence would not be heard by juries and judges. If all hearsay was admitted as evidence, criminal and civil trials would be cluttered with unreliable evidence.

An accused in a criminal case has a Sixth Amendment right ". . . to be confronted with the witnesses against him . . ." To qualify as an exception to the hearsay rule, the statement (or statements) must have sufficient reliability and trustworthiness to allow the evidence to be admitted for use in a civil or criminal trial.

Some of the firmly rooted exceptions developed many years ago are the excited utterance exception, the then existing mental, emotional, or physical condition exception, statements for the purposes of medical diagnosis or treatment exception, regularly kept records exception, dying declaration exception, and statements against-penal-interest exception.

PROBLEMS

AVAILABLE ANSWERS

a. Is *not* hearsay and if otherwise qualified would be held admissible as evidence

b. Is hearsay and is not admissible as evidence

c. Is hearsay but is admissible as evidence under the rules of evidence of your state (or federal or military rules)

1. A confession or incriminating statement by a defendant in a criminal trial.

2. A confession by the defendant's brother that he committed the crime charged, but there is no evidence to corroborate the confession.

3. Hospital records showing the victim was admitted for treatment at 1:05 A.M. on April 16, 2002.

4. A witness testifies she heard the victim scream, "Don't shoot me, Joe!"

5. The dying victim tells the women, "Joe shot and killed me."

6. The victim lives long enough to testify at a preliminary hearing that Joe shot him. The victim dies before the trial, and the state seeks to use his statement at the murder trial.

7. An emergency room nurse testifies as to statements made to her by a 5-year-old girl who had been sexually assaulted.

8. A police officer hears two prisoners arguing. They both made incriminating statements about a crime they both are charged with committing.

9. One of two women charged with a felony testifies as to statements each made while they were committing the crime.

10. A child testifies that he saw his mother's boyfriend beat the woman.

INFOTRAC COLLEGE EDITION EXERCISES

1. Go to InfoTrac College Edition and using the search term "evidence, hearsay" and the "periodical references" view, find the winter 2002 article *Law and Contemporary Problems* titled "The Maturation and Disintegration of the Hearsay Exception for Statements for Medical Examination in Child Sexual Abuse Cases," by Robert Mosteller. This exception permits a doctor or nurse to testify about what a child said concerning sexual abuse, if the child's answers are given to questions about the child's medical conditions. What does the author see as the problem with the use of that exception?

2. Go to InfoTrac College Edition and using the search term "hearsay" find the 2002 *Daily Business Review* (Miami, Florida) article discussing the admissibility of emergency 911 tapes made by 911 operators. What is the difference between the "excited utterance" exception to the hearsay rule, and the "present sense impression" exception? How do these exceptions apply when a defendant wishes to introduce a 911 tape of her call to the 911 operator, in order to corroborate her version of a crime? Which of these exceptions seems more reliable?

NOTES

1. Some have contended that the term *witness* in the Confrontation Clause was originally intended to refer only to out-of-court statements directed solely at inculpating the defendant, such as affidavits, depositions, and confessions. Those were "particular abuses common in 16th and 17th century England: prosecuting a defendant through the presentation of ex parte affidavits without the affiants ever being produced at trial" [*White v. Illinois,* 502 U.S. 346, 352 (1992)]. The federal government—and Justice Thomas, concurring in *White v. Illinois*—argued that the Confrontation Clause "extends to any witness who actually testifies at trial, but the Confrontation Clause is implicated by extrajudicial statements only insofar as they are contained in formalized testimonial materials, such as affidavits, depositions, prior testimony, or confessions" [*White,* 502 U.S. 365 (J. Thomas, concurring) (1992)].

The majority in *White* rejected this argument: "We think that the argument presented by the Government comes too late in the day to warrant reexamination of this approach" [*White,* 502 U.S. 353]. In *Lilly v. Virginia,* 527 U.S. 116 (1999), the Court again rejected this argument. See 119 S.Ct. at 1894.

2. See Friedman, *Confrontation: The Search for Basic Principles,* 86 GEO. L.J. 1011,1014 (1998).
3. 380 U.S. 400.
4. *California v. Green,* 399 U.S. 149, 155 (1970).
5. 399 U.S. at 158.
6. *Idaho v. Wright,* 497 U.S. 805 (1990).
7. *Ohio v. Roberts,* 448 U.S. 56, 66 (1980).
8. 475 U.S. 387, 395.
9. The babysitter's and mother's testimony, though clearly hearsay, was admitted under Illinois's "spontaneous declaration" exception to the hearsay rule. See FRE 803(2), discussed *infra.* The medical doctor's testimony was admitted under the medical treatment exception. See FRE 803(4).
10. 502 U.S. at 356–357.
11. This made Mark "unavailable" as a witness under Virginia hearsay rules. See FRE 804(a)(1).
12. Almost by definition, the hearsay exceptions in FRE 803 and 804 are firmly rooted because most of them stem from federal common law or English law.

Even if a hearsay exception is not of the firmly rooted variety, *Ohio v. Roberts* held that the evidence may still be admissible if there exist "particularized guarantees of trustworthiness." The Supreme Court in *Lilly* found that those guarantees did not exist in the case of Mark's statements (*Lilly,* 119 S.Ct. 1900).
13. *California v. Green,* 399 U.S. 155, 90 S.Ct. 1933 (1972).
14. *White v. Illinois,* 502 U.S. 346, 112 S.Ct. 741.
15. *Ohio v. Roberts,* 448 U.S. 56, 63, 100 S.Ct. 2531 (1980).
16. Idem.
17. The excited utterance exception is one of the exceptions that many years ago was lumped with other exceptions under a broad exception known as the *res gestae exception* to the hearsay rule. A few states continue to use the res gestae exception.

FRE 803(1) states the hearsay exception called *present sense impression,* which in some states is called the *spontaneous statement exception.* The unexcited statement exception of present sense impressions is made part of the laws of many states. Rule 803(1): *Present sense impression:* A statement describing or explaining an event or condition made while the declarant was perceiving the event or condition, or immediately thereafter.
18. *Webb v. Lane,* 922 F.2d 390 (7th Cir., 1991); *State v. Farmer,* 408 S.E.2d 458 (W.Va., 1991); *State v. Anaya,* 799 P.2d 876 (1990); *State v. Baker,* 582 So.2d 1320 (La. App., 1991); *State v. Gibson,* 413 S.E.2d 120 (W.Va., 1991); *Russell v. State,* 815 S.W.2d 929 (Ark., 1991); *Royal v. Commonwealth,* 407 S.E.2d 346 (W.Va., 1991).
19. *State v. Reaves,* 596 So.2d 650 (La. App., 1990); *State v. Ferguson* 540 So.2d 1116 (La. App., 1989); *Cole v. State* 818 S.W.2d 573 (Ark., 1991).
20. *Ware v. State,* 596 So.2d 1200 (Fla. App., 1992); *State v. Edwards,* 485 N.W.2d 911 (Minn., 1992); *State v. Guizzotti,* 1991 WL 4995 (Wash. App., 1991).
21. *State v. Fox,* 585 N.E.2d 561 (Ohio, 1990); *People v. Garcia,* 826 P.2d 1259 (Colo., 1992); *People v. Houghteling,* 455 N.W.2d 440 (Mich. App., 1990); *Cole v. State,* 818 S.W.2d 573 (Ark., 1991); *State v. Hy,* 458 N.W.2d 609 (Iowa, 1990); *State v. Murphy,* 462 N.W.2d 715 (Iowa App., 1990); *Commonwealth v. Sanford,* 580 A.2d 784 (Pa. Super.,

1990); *State v. Bryant*, 828 p.2d 1121 (Wash. App., 1992); *People v. Enoch*, 545 N.E.2d 429, 45 CrL 1059 (Ill., 1989).

22. 579 A.2d 515 (Conn.).

23. 606 So.2d 1132 (Miss.).

24. *State v. MacDonald*, 598 A.2d 1134 (Del. Super., 1991).

25. 376 P.2d. 300.

26. 502 U.S. 346, 112 S.Ct. 736.

27. Other cases where it was held that physcans and other medical personnel could testify as to statements made by children while receiving medical treatment include statements that a 5-year-old made to the examining physician, *State v. Alvarez*, 822 P.2d 1207 (Or. App., 1991); a 6-year-old child, *People v. Meeboer*, 1992 WL 113254 (Mich., 1992); a 5-year-old daughter, *State v. Olesen*, 443 N.W.2d 8 (S.D., 1989); an 8-year-old child's statements to pediatrician, psychologist, and social worker as to medical history and sexual abuse were admissible, *United States v. Balfany*, 965 F.2d 575 (8th Cir., 1992); a 4-year-old child's statements to pediatrician and mental health therapist as to sexual abuse were admissible hearsay, *Fleming v. State*, 819 S.W.2d 237 (Tex. App., 1991).

28. The U.S. Supreme Court has held that the use of a dying declaration as evidence does not violate a defendant's Sixth Amendment right to confrontation and cross-examination in the following cases: *Mattox v. United States*, 146 U.S. 140, 13 S. Ct. 50 (1892); *Mattox v. United States*, 156 U.S. 237, 15 S. Ct. 337 (1895); and *Pointer v. Texas*, 380 U.S. 400, 85 S. Ct. 1065 (1965).

29. 168 Eng. Rep. 352.

30. 569 So.2d 897.

31. 452 N.W.2d 918, 922.

32. 586 So.2d 1033.

33. 606 A.2d 1354 (D.C. App., 1992).

34. 540 So.2d 1144 (La. App., 1989).

35. 403 U.S. 573, 91 S.Ct. 2075.

36. 410 U.S. 284, 93 S.Ct. 1038.

37. 588 A.2d 1066 (Conn., 1991).

38. 933 F.2d 536 (7th Cir., 1991).

39. There is some disagreement as to the amount of corroboration needed for the admissibility of statements by people who assert they committed the crime being charged. More corroboration seems to be required for out-of-court confessions than for in-court confessions. For a discussion of some of the cases, see *McCormick on Evidence*,

4th ed. (West Publishing Co., 1992), vol. 2, pp. 340–43.

40. *People v. Burton*, 359 P.2d 433 (1961).

41. *State v. Hill*, 578 A.2d 370 (1990).

42. *State v. Campbell*, 705 P.2d 694 (1985).

43. *Cole v. State*, 574 A.2d 326 (App., 1990).

44. *Commonwealth v. Licata*, 591 N.E. 2d 672 (1992).

45. *McDonald v. State*, 578 So.2d 371 (1991).

46. *Anderson v. State*, 831 S.W.2d 50 (App., 1992).

47. 497 U.S. 805, 806, 110 S.Ct. 3139, 3142.

48. 497 U.S. 821, 110 S.Ct. 3150.

49. *State v. Robinson*, 735 P.2d 801 (Ariz., 1987).

50. *Morgan v. Foretich*, 846 F.2d 941 (4th Cir., 1988).

51. *State v. Sorenson*, 421 N.W.2d 77 (Wis., 1988).

52. *State v. Kuone*, 757 P.2d 289 (Kans., 1988).

53. 497 U.S. 822, 110 S.Ct. 3150.

54. The criminal proceedings in the *McMartin* case went on more than five years with the preliminary hearing alone lasting a year and a half. The trial and proceedings received national attention with all of the national talk shows covering the trial in which there were many criminal charges of bizarre sex acts and naked children. Civil lawsuits by former defendants are discussed in *Satz v. Supreme Court* (*McMartin*), 275 Cal.Rptr. 710 (1990) and *McMartin v. Children's Institute International*, 261 Cal.Rptr. 437 (1989), review denied 494 U.S. 1057, 110 S.Ct. 1526 (1990).

55. The Supreme Court of Nevada noted that the *Felix* (849 P.2d 220) case was "the most extensive and costly criminal investigation and prosecution in Carson City [Nevada] history." It was alleged that as many as nineteen children had been sexually assaulted.

56. In the *Michaels* (625 A.2d 489) case, parents of very young children were permitted to testify as to out-of-court statements of their very young children under the New Jersey Child Hearsay law without any showing that the hearsay "was probably trustworthy" as required by New Jersey statutes and also the U.S. Supreme Court (625 A.2d 517).

The New Jersey court also cited an unpublished Hawaii opinion that "each child had been subjected to layers and layers of interviews, questions, examinations, etc., which were fraught with textbook examples of poor interview techniques" [*State v. McKellar*, No. 85-0553 (Haw. Cir. Ct. Jan. 15, 1983)].

III

When Evidence Cannot Be Used Because of Police Mistakes or Misconduct

9

The Exclusionary Rule

A THE EXCLUSIONARY RULE (OR THE RULE OF THE EXCLUSION OF EVIDENCE)

There are over 17,000 police and sheriff departments in the United States, employing over 600,000 full-time officers with general arrest powers. Although these officers are charged with the responsibility of performing their duties within the limitations set by statutes, state constitutions, and the U.S. Constitution, they do not always do so. When that happens, the criminal justice system "polices the police."[1]

Just as football teams are penalized 5 or 10 yards for a rule violation by an individual player, the **exclusionary rule** excludes (keeps out) evidence that was improperly or illegally obtained (Figure 9.1). Like a football penalty, the exclusionary rule seeks to discourage improper or illegal investigative procedures by law enforcement officers.

Investigative conduct by law enforcement officers (both state and federal officers) can be improper for many reasons. Conduct might violate a police department rule, an FBI procedures handbook, or even a police union rule. These violations, which may have no real impact on a defendant, can be dealt with by internal police procedures.

Some law enforcement conduct is improper because it does adversely affect a criminal defendant's statutory or constitutional rights.[2] The principal U.S. constitutional rights threatened by police misconduct are the Fifth Amendment's privilege against self-incrimination[3] and the Fourth Amendment's protection against unreasonable searches and seizures. Other constitutional protections are secured for both federal and state defendants under the Due Process Clauses of the Fifth and Fourteenth Amendments.[4]

For much of U.S. history, relevant and reliable evidence was admissible in criminal prosecutions even if obtained illegally. Beginning in 1914 in federal cases[5] and 1961 in state cases,[6] the U.S. Supreme Court required courts to exclude such evidence—that is, declare the evidence inadmissible to help prove the prosecution's case.

The U.S. Supreme Court has also used the exclusionary rule for violations of court-fashioned rules, like the famous *Miranda*[7] rule. In the *Miranda* case, the Supreme Court

FIGURE 9.1 *The Function of the Exclusionary Rule*

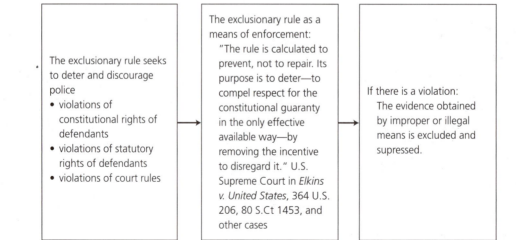

The exclusionary rule seeks to deter and discourage police	The exclusionary rule as a means of enforcement: "The rule is calculated to prevent, not to repair. Its purpose is to deter—to compel respect for the constitutional guaranty in the only effective available way—by removing the incentive to disregard it." U.S. Supreme Court in *Elkins v. United States*, 364 U.S. 206, 80 S.Ct 1453, and other cases	If there is a violation: The evidence obtained by improper or illegal means is excluded and supressed.
• violations of constitutional rights of defendants • violations of statutory rights of defendants • violations of court rules		

adopted a court rule[8] for determining the minimum safeguards that must be used by police before obtaining a confession or other incriminating statements. If these safeguards are not met, any resulting confession or incriminating statement is inadmissible.

The use of exclusionary rules to suppress otherwise reliable, relevant evidence has a cost to society, since some clearly guilty defendants may go free if vital evidence is excluded from their trials. Exclusionary rules are usually defended by arguments that such rules are necessary to deter official police misconduct and are the only practical alternatives available to achieve that deterrence.

Ⓑ THE "FRUIT OF THE POISONOUS TREE" DOCTRINE (OR THE DERIVATIVE EVIDENCE RULE)

The exclusionary rule applies not only to evidence obtained directly as a result of improper police conduct but also to evidence obtained indirectly from that improper conduct. Evidence derived from initial improper conduct is usually called **fruit of the poisonous tree.** For example, if the police wrongfully enter a house and find a key to a storage locker, the key is a direct result of the wrongful entry and inadmissible. If the police then use the key to unlock the storage locker and find illegal drugs, the drugs are excluded as fruit of the initial wrongful entry.

> **EXAMPLE:** Assume that the police officers either do not comply with the *Miranda* requirements or they beat a suspect until he confesses to a murder. In either example, the confession is a direct product of improper police conduct and cannot be used as evidence in an American criminal court.
>
> Assume also that in his confession, the suspect told the police where the murder weapon is hidden. Even if the police obtain the weapon by lawful means, the weapon cannot be used as evidence to link the suspect to the crime under the fruit of the poisonous tree doctrine. The weapon is the indirect product of improper police conduct; that improper conduct is the "poisoned tree," and any evidence derived solely from that improper conduct is the "fruit."[9]

Not only would the weapon in the example be suppressed ("thrown out"), but any evidence obtained from the weapon, such as fingerprints and ballistic tests, also would be excluded under the derivative evidence rule.

The "fruit of the poisonous tree" doctrine is applicable if improperly or illegally obtained evidence is the basis for the discovery of:

- Other evidence that otherwise would not have been found
- A witness who otherwise might not have been found
- A confession or incriminating admission that would not have been made if the suspect or defendant had not been confronted with the tainted (soiled) evidence

The following U.S. Supreme Court case further illustrates the derivative evidence rule (fruit of the poisonous tree doctrine):

Fahy v. Connecticut
Supreme Court of the United States (1963) 375 U.S. 85, 84 S.Ct. 229

A police officer saw a car driving slowly in downtown Norwalk, Connecticut, at about 4:40 in the morning. The police officer lawfully stopped the car and questioned the two men in the car. In checking the car for weapons, the officer found a can of black paint and a paint brush under the front seat. Fahy (the driver of the car) then drove his car home. A short time later, the police officer found that someone had painted swastikas on a synagogue a short distance from where he had stopped Fahy's car.

The officer went to Fahy's home and, without a search warrant or consent from Fahy, entered Fahy's garage and removed the paint and brush from Fahy's car. After determining that the paint and brush fit the markings on the Jewish synagogue, the officer obtained an arrest warrant. When arrested, Fahy made incriminating statements; and later, at the police station, Fahy made a full confession. All the evidence was used in obtaining a conviction of Fahy and his companion. In reversing, the U.S. Supreme Court held that:

> . . . petitioner (Fahy) should have had a chance to show that his admissions were induced by being confronted with the illegally seized evidence.
>
> Nor can we ignore the cumulative prejudicial effect of this evidence upon the conduct of the defense at trial. It was only after admission of the paint and brush and only after their subsequent use to corroborate other state's evidence and only after introduction of the confession that the defendants took the stand, admitted their acts, and tried to establish that the nature of those acts was not within the scope of the felony statute under which the defendants had been charged. We do not mean to suggest that petitioner has presented any valid claim based on the privilege against self-incrimination. We merely note this course of events as another indication of the prejudicial effect of erroneously admitted evidence.

C EXCEPTIONS TO THE "FRUIT OF THE POISONOUS TREE" DOCTRINE

The *derivative evidence rule* as the name suggests, applies only if the challenged evidence is directly and exclusively derived from the improper police conduct. The U.S. Supreme Court has developed three exceptions to the doctrine in those situations where the police misconduct has not "tainted" the challenged evidence.

The Independent Source Doctrine

Improper police conduct may lead to the discovery of evidence, while at the same time another, proper source may lead to the same evidence. If the second, proper source of the evidence is **independent**—that is, not tainted by the improper conduct—the evidence is admissible.[10]

Murray v. United States
United States Supreme Court, 487 U.S. 533 (1988)

Federal agents made an unlawful entry into a warehouse where they saw bales of marijuana. The federal agents later applied for a search warrant without making reference to the unlawful entry. The U.S. Supreme Court sent the case back to the trial court "for determination whether the [search authorized by the warrant] was an independent source of the challenged evidence . . ." stating:

> . . . Knowledge that the marijuana was in the warehouse was assuredly acquired at the time of the unlawful entry. But it was also acquired at the time of entry pursuant to the warrant, and if that later acquisition was not the result of the earlier entry there is no reason why the independent source doctrine should not apply. Invoking the exclusionary rule would put the police (and society) not in the same position they would have occupied if no violation occurred, but in a *worse* one. . . .

The Inevitable Discovery Rule

If police error or police misconduct has tainted some evidence, that evidence and also derivative evidence will be suppressed and cannot be used in a criminal trial.

However, if it can be shown that the challenged derivative evidence would have certainly been discovered by legitimate police efforts, it would be admissible under the **inevitable discovery rule.** The U.S. Supreme Court adopted the inevitable discovery rule in the following case and explains its relationship to the independent source test:

Nix v. Williams
United States Supreme Court, 467 U.S. 431 (1984)

A 10-year-old Iowa girl was reported missing, and a massive search involving hundreds of police officers and volunteers was organized. During the search, Williams was arrested, based upon reports he had been seen carrying a small girl near the place and at the time she was reported missing. During questioning, the police violated the Massiah[11] rule by questioning Williams about the location of the girl's body without the consent or presence of his attorney. Based on Williams's statements, the girl's body was found and the search suspended.

Williams's statements to police were declared inadmissible, but the prosecution sought to introduce evidence of the condition of the body, articles of clothing found, and results of medical tests on the body. The defense contended that this evidence was the "fruit" of the "poisoned" questioning.

In upholding the admissibility of this evidence, the Supreme Court concluded that the "inevitable discovery" rule has the same justification as the "independent source" rule:

[The] core rationale consistently advanced by this Court for extending the Exclusionary Rule to evidence that is the fruit of unlawful police conduct has been that this admittedly drastic and socially costly course is needed to deter police from violations of constitutional and statutory protections. [On] this rationale, the prosecution is not to be put in a better position than it would have been in if no illegality had transpired.

By contrast, the derivative evidence analysis ensures that the prosecution is not put in a worse position simply because of some earlier police error or misconduct. The independent source doctrine allows admission of evidence that has been discovered by means wholly independent of any constitutional violation. That doctrine, although closely related to the inevitable discovery doctrine, does not apply here: Williams' statements to Learning [police officer] indeed led police to the child's body, but that is not the whole story. The independent source doctrine teaches us that the interest of society in deterring unlawful police conduct and the public interest in having juries receive all probative evidence of a crime are properly balanced by putting the police in the same, not a worse, position than they would have been in if no police error or misconduct had occurred. When the challenged evidence has an independent source, exclusion of such evidence would put the police in a worse position than they would have been in absent any error or violation. There is a functional similarity between these two doctrines in that exclusion of evidence that would inevitably have been discovered would also put the government in a worse position, because the police would have obtained that evidence if no misconduct had taken place. Thus, while the independent source exception would not justify admission of evidence in this case, its rationale is wholly consistent with and justifies our adoption of the ultimate or inevitable discovery exception to the Exclusionary Rule. . . .

The U.S. Supreme Court concluded that the search parties, which were systematically searching the area where the body was found, would have found the body in a short time without Williams's directions, and thus the evidence found on or near the body would have been found at the same time.

The Attenuation, or Passage of Time, Rule

Where improper police conduct occurs and shortly thereafter that conduct leads to the discovery of other evidence, the poisonous tree doctrine reasonably concludes a connection exists between the improper conduct and the other evidence. Where, however, a significant period of time goes by between the improper conduct and the new evidence, the U.S. Supreme Court has long held that the "taint" from the improper conduct can be dissipated. This is termed the **passage of time rule** or **attenuation.**

Additional Recent "Fruit of the Poisonous Tree" Cases

In the July, 2003 Wisconsin case ot *State v. Knapp*, 203 WL 21704408, a suspect in a murder case permitted a police officer into his home to wait while the defendant got dressed to go down to the police station and answer questions. The defendant thought he was simply being asked to cooperate with the police in the investigation. The officer

Types of Evidence Controlled by the Exclusionary Rule

Type of Evidence	U.S. Constitutional Amendment that Controls the Evidence	Test of Admissibility for Use of Evidence
Physical evidence (drugs, weapons, contraband, clothing, fingerprints, etc.)	*Fourth Amendment:* "The right of the people to be secure . . . against unreasonable searches and seizures shall not be violated . . ."	The Fourth Amendment requires a search warrant if a right of privacy is involved. If a warrant is not used, the burden is on the officer to show that the search was authorized by one of the well-recognized exceptions to the requirement of a search warrant. (See Chapters 14–15.)
Confessions, incriminating admissions, and statements	*Fifth Amendment:* "No person . . . shall be compelled . . . to be a witness against himself . . ." *Sixth Amendment:* "In all criminal prosecutions, the accused shall enjoy the right . . . to have the assistance of counsel for his defense."	The voluntariness test is used for the use of all statements as evidence. The following test may be applicable depending upon the circumstances: *Miranda* requirements and test; *Massiah* test; *Bruton* requirements (see Chapter 12).
Eyewitness and voice identification	*Fifth and Fourteenth Amendments:* "No person shall be . . . deprived of life, liberty, or property, without due process of law . . ." *Sixth Amendment:* "In all criminal prosecutions, the accused shall enjoy the right . . . to have the assistance of counsel for his defense."	Were the procedures used so unnecessarily suggestive and conducive to irreparable mistaken identification as to be a denial of due process of law? (See Chapter 13.) Was the accused denied the assistance of counsel at an important and critical stage of the criminal proceedings? [See *Kirby v. Illinois,* 406 U.S. 682, 92 S.Ct. 1877 (1972).]
Evidence obtained as a result of wiretapping and electronic surveillance	Wiretapping and electronic surveillances are searches controlled by the Fourth Amendment. Wiretapping is also controlled by Title III, Federal Omnibus Crime Control and Safe Streets Act, and applicable statutes in every state.	Was the evidence obtained in conformity with the applicable statute (or statutes)? (See Chapter 15.)

> ### Wong Sun v. United States
> #### United States Supreme Court, 371 U.S. 471 (1963)
>
> Federal narcotics agents illegally broke into a suspect's laundry and pressured him to make statements that led to the arrest of Wong Sun on narcotics charges. After his arrest, Wong Sun was arraigned and released on his own recognizance. Several days later, Wong Sun voluntarily appeared at the San Francisco Narcotics Bureau and confessed to the illegal transportation and concealment of heroin.
>
> At his trial, Wong Sun sought to exclude his confession as the fruit of the illegal entry. The Supreme Court found the evidence admissible because the connection between Wong Sun's illegal arrest and his confession "had became so attenuated as to dissipate the taint."

asked the defendant, while he was getting dressed, what the defendant had worn the night before, which was the night of the murder. The defendant pointed to a sweat-shirt, and the police officer seized it. No *Miranda* warning was given to Knapp.

Subsequent DNA tests established the presence of the victim's blood on the sweatshirt. Based on that and other evidence, the defendant was charged with murder. He moved to suppress both his pre-*Miranda* warning statements made to the officer, and also the physical evidence (the sweatshirt) seized as a result of those statements. The Prosecution conceded the statements must be excluded, but argued the physical evidence was admissible.

The Wisconsin Supreme Court held that the physical evidence must be excluded as the "fruit of a poisonous tree." The "poisonous tree" was the intentional failure to give the defendant *Miranda* warnings. Since the violation was intentional, the Court concluded the deterrent effect of the exclusionary rule required suppression of the evidence.

Other courts have decided this issue differently. For example, in *United States v. Sterling*, 283 F.3d 216 (4th Cir. 2002), *cert, denied*, 536 U.S. 931 (2002) the Court of Appeals upheld the admission of a gun found as a result of statements made by the defendant without a *Miranda* warning. That court concluded, that so long as the statement was voluntary, physical evidence can never be the "fruit of the poisonous tree."

In the case of *United States v. Patane*, 304 F. 3d 1013 (10th cir. 2002), the court went further than the Wisconsin *Knapp* case and held that physical evidence obtained by the police as a result of a negligent failure to give a defendant his *Miranda* warnings must be suppressed. The United States Supreme Court granted certiorari, 123 S. Ct. 1788 (2003) and will likely decide this issue in the 2003–2004 term.

Ⓓ MANY STATES NOW HAVE TWO SETS OF EXCLUSIONARY RULES

The federal exclusionary rule has become very complex since the 1961 *Mapp v. Ohio* case.[12] All states must follow the federal *Mapp* rule in determining the admissibility of evidence. However, it is not uncommon for state courts to impose additional requirements in interpreting the constitution or statutes of that state. State statutes, by themselves, could also alter the federal *Mapp* rule and impose a stricter standard in a given area of the law.

Therefore, two sets of exclusionary rules exist in many states. The federal rule is defined by the U.S. Supreme Court and other federal courts while the state exclusionary rule is defined and required by the state supreme court (and sometimes by state statutes). State law enforcement officers would be required to comply with the state requirements, which could be more stringent than those required by the federal *Mapp* rule. However, evidence to be used in criminal cases in federal courts in all states would be judged by the federal *Mapp* rule. Because most crimes are violations of state criminal codes, most criminal cases go into state criminal courts.

Some states have simplified this situation by eliminating, to a large extent, their state exclusionary rule. California and Florida are among the states that have enacted sections to their state constitutions requiring state courts in that state to determine the admissibility of evidence "in conformity with the 4th Amendment . . . as interpreted by the U.S. Supreme Court," Florida Constitution. [For the California change, see *In re Lance W.*, 210 Cal.Rptr. 631, 694 P.2d 744 (1985).]

SUMMARY

Prior to 1914, practically all relevant and material evidence was admitted for use at criminal trials regardless of how law enforcement officers obtained the evidence.

A federal exclusionary rule was established in 1914 by the case of *United States v. Weeks.* In the *Weeks* case, federal agents had violated the privacy of Week's home in violation of the Fourth Amendment. In the years that followed, some states established exclusionary rules to be used within that state.

The exclusionary rule or the rule of the exclusion of evidence suppresses (throws out) evidence that has been obtained by a law enforcement officer in violation of the constitutional or statutory rights of a defendant.

In the 1961 case of *Mapp v. Ohio,* the U.S. Supreme Court mandated and imposed upon all states the standards established by the federal *Weeks* rule. Not only must law enforcement officers observe the federal constitutional limitations on obtaining evidence, but many states have imposed additional state limitations that must be complied with within that state.

The three exceptions to the "fruit of the poisonous tree" doctrine (or the derivative evidence rule) are:

1. The independent source doctrine; 2. The inevitable discovery rule; 3. The attenuation, or passage of time, rule

In an attempt to make the exclusionary rule practical and workable, the rule of the exclusion of evidence is not applied in the areas pointed out in Chapter 10.

PROBLEMS

All of the following cases were before the U.S. Supreme Court.

1. Two officers of a lumber company were arrested in their homes early one morning. While they were being held, federal agents "without a shadow of authority went to the office of their company and made a clean sweep of all the books, papers and documents found there." Photographs and copies of material papers were made. The original documents were returned to the defendant, but a criminal charge (an indictment) "was framed based upon the knowledge thus obtained."

Can the indictment stand, and can the evidence be used in criminal proceedings against the defendant corporation? *Silverthorne Lumber Company et al. v. United States,* 251 U.S. 385, 40 S.Ct. 182 (1920).

2. A police officer was killing time talking to a woman employee of a flower shop. While the woman was busy with a customer, the officer saw an envelope on the cash register. The officer opened the envelope and saw evidence of illegal gambling. The officer returned the envelope and its contents but reported the discovery to his superiors, which led them to question the clerk in the shop. The clerk agreed to testify against Ceccolini, the shop's owner and defendant. Ceccolini was summoned before a federal grand jury, where he testified that he had never taken gambling bets. The defendant was later indicted and convicted of perjury for that statement.

Could the police officer testify about what he saw in the envelope? Can the clerk testify about the gambling activities of the defendant? Should the conviction be affirmed by the U.S. Supreme Court? *United States v. Ceccolini,* 435 U.S. 268, 98 S. Ct. 1054 (1978).

3. A young man robbed a woman in a woman's restroom at the Washington National Monument. During the robbery, the woman had a good opportunity to see the young man. The woman immediately reported the robbery and described the young man who robbed her. Three days later, a young man (Crews) was improperly and illegally detained. Photographs were taken of the young man and a photographic display (array) was shown to the woman. She immediately identified Crews as the man who robbed her at gunpoint. In a lineup, the woman again identified Crews as the robber. At Crews's trial for armed robbery, the woman appeared as a witness and identified the defendant as the robber. Crews was convicted and appealed, arguing that the in-court identification was the "fruit of the poisonous tree" and should not be used as evidence.

Should the U.S. Supreme Court affirm Crews's conviction, and should the woman's in-court identification be allowed as evidence? Why? *United States v. Crews,* 445 U.S. 463, 100 S. Ct. 1244 (1980).

4. California police officers improperly arrested Williams in his apartment. Before taking Williams to the police station, arrangements had to be made for the care of Williams's cat and dog. In an attempt to provide for the care of these animals, the officers went to the apartment of a neighbor (Mrs. Lopez) to inquire if she would take care of the animals. Mrs. Lopez told the officers that they should investigate Williams for a recent bank robbery in which the robber had presented his demand in a note threatening that he had nitroglycerin on his person. Mrs. Lopez stated that she was in Williams's apartment on the morning of the robbery and that he was writing a note and had asked her how to spell *nitroglycerin.* The officers had not suspected Williams of the robbery, but the investigation that followed produced sufficient evidence to convict Williams of the bank robbery. An appeal was taken from the conviction, arguing among other issues the defense position that the fruit of the poisonous tree doctrine required suppression of the evidenced used to convict Williams.

Should the evidence be suppressed, or should it be admissible in Williams's trial for armed robbery? Explain. *United States v. Williams,* 436 F.2d 1166 (9th Cir., 1970), review denied 402 U.S. 912, 91 S.Ct. 1392 (1971).

INFOTRAC COLLEGE EDITION EXERCISES

1. Go to InfoTrac College Edition and using the search term "Fourth Amendment" find the 2002 article in *Mother Jones* titled "Big Brother and the Bookie . . ." by George Anastasia. Is it a search to monitor your keystrokes on your PC in order to discover the password you used to hide records of illegal activities? Can the government use secret high-tech methods to conduct the search, and then use national security as a basis for avoiding disclosing how the search proceeded?

2. Go to InfoTrac College Edtion and using the search term "Fourth Amendment" find the 2000 article in the *Michigan Law Review* titled "Establishing Inevitability Without Active Pursuit," by Stephen Hessler. Does the "inevitable discovery" exception to the exclusionary rule in *Nix v. Williams,* discussed in section C of this chapter, require that the police be engaged in the "active pursuit" of an alternative, legal investigation at the same time the illegal investigation produces the evidence sought to be excluded under the Fourth Amendment? Why or why not?

NOTES

1. The former chief justice of the U.S. Supreme Court, Warren Burger, raised the question in his 1964 article, "Who Will Watch the Watchman?" 14 Amer.U.L.R. 1, before he was appointed to the U.S. Supreme Court.
2. See Chapter 12 for material on Fifth Amendment rights.
3. See Chapter 14 for material on Fourth Amendment rights.
4. Early Supreme Court cases seem to have tied inadmissibility of involuntary confessions to the Fifth Amendment's privilege against self-incrimination. See *Bram v. U.S.,* 168 U.S. 532 (1897). Since *Brown v. Mississippi,* 297 U.S. 278 (1936), the Due Process Clause has been regarded as the basis for the requirement that confession be voluntary.
5. The federal *Weeks* rule is named after the 1914 case of *Weeks v. United States,* 34 S.Ct. 341, in which federal agents entered Weeks's home without consent and without a search warrant or any other authority. The agents seized evidence in Week's home, which was used to obtain Weeks's criminal conviction.
6. *Mapp v. Ohio,* 81 S.Ct. 1684 (1961), in which police officers forced their way into Ms. Mapp's home without probable cause, without consent, without a search warrant, or any other authority. The officers suspected that a fugitive was hiding in the house. When they did not find a fugitive, they went into drawers and boxes until they found evidence of pornography, which they used to convict Ms. Mapp of the crime of possession of pornography.

7. *Miranda v. Arizona,* 384 U.S. 436 (1966). The *Miranda* rule is discussed more fully in Chapter 12.
8. The *Miranda* warnings are (1) the right to remain silent, (2) any statements made can be used against the suspect, (3) the right to have an attorney present, and (4) an attorney will be appointed if the suspect cannot afford one.
9. It is clear that the murder weapon would be excluded if the police beat the confession out of the suspect. However, if the police "merely" failed to give the *Miranda* warning and the suspect's inadmissible statements lead to discovery of physical evidence, the poisonous tree doctrine may not apply. See *Oregon v. Elstad,* 470 U.S. 298 (1985). While *Elstad* is not explicit on this issue, lower federal and state courts seem to be admitting such physical violence. See Wollin, *Policing the Police: Should Miranda Violations Bear Fruit?* 53 Ohio St. L.J. 805, 835–36 (1992): "[F]ollowing *Elstad,* federal and state courts have almost uniformly ruled that the prosecution can introduce nontestimonial fruits of a *Miranda* violation in a criminal trial."
10. See *Silverthorne Lumber Co. v. United States,* 251 U.S. 385 (1920) and *Nardone v. United States,* 308 U.S. 338 (1939). *Nardone* was the first case to use the fruit of the poisonous tree analogy.
11. *Massiah v. United States,* 377 U.S. 201 (1964), discussed in Chapter 12. The rescue exception or the public safety exception to the *Miranda* rule might reasonably be applied to the *Massiah* doctrine in cases like *Williams.*
12. See note 6 for a summary of the case of *Mapp v. Ohio.*

10

Where the Exclusionary Rule Does Not Apply

The exclusionary rule and its applications (discussed in Chapter 9) have been the subject of extensive criticism. The principal argument against the rule is that society pays a high cost to secure the rule's benefits. The goal of the exclusionary rule is to deter improper police conduct, which in theory benefits all citizens, but in most cases the direct beneficiary of the rule is one who would be convicted if the evidence was not excluded. The rule can thus result in dangerous criminals going free.

Mindful of this cost, the U.S. Supreme Court has repeatedly held that "the [exclusionary] rule has been [and is] restricted to those areas where its remedial objectives are thought most efficaciously served."

In this chapter we define the scope and extent of the exclusionary rule by examining the borders of the rule. In what areas of conduct, even improper or illegal conduct, should the exclusionary rule be inapplicable?

Ⓐ THE EXCLUSIONARY RULE DOES NOT APPLY TO EVIDENCE OBTAINED IN A PRIVATE SEARCH BY A PRIVATE PERSON

The Fourth Amendment to the U.S. Constitution prohibits unreasonable search and seizures. Evidence obtained in violation of the Fourth Amendment is inadmissible under the exclusionary rule.[1] This prohibition applies to mistakes or misconduct by the police and other officials in the executive branch of government. The exclusionary rule does not apply to private persons. Evidence obtained by private persons, even if the result of illegal conduct, is not subject to the exclusionary rule, as the Supreme Court held in the following case.

Burdeau v. McDowell
United States Supreme Court, 256 U.S. 465 (1921)

An unknown person or persons burglarized the defendent's office, breaking into his desk and private safe. Files and papers that implicated the defendant in criminal activity were taken by the burglars. These papers and files ended up in the possession of federal prosecutors, who showed "clean hands" and then used them in the indictment and conviction of the defendant.

The defendant argued that the evidence should have been excluded because it was obtained by an unlawful search and seizure. The Supreme Court rejected that argument, holding "the record clearly shows that no official of the federal government had anything to do with the wrongful seizure of the petitioner's property, or had any knowledge thereof until several months after the property had been taken from him."

In refusing to make the Fourth Amendment applicable to purely private conduct, the Supreme Court observed that the origin and history of that amendment "clearly shows that it was intended as a restraint upon the activities of sovereign authority and was not intended to be a limitation upon other than government agencies."[2]

If a search is **private** (solely by a private person), the exclusionary rule does not apply. Courts have adopted the following requirements for a search to be purely private:

	Held Not Private	Held Private
The evidence was obtained by a private person acting in a private capacity.[a]	*State v. Woods,* 790 S.W.2d 253 (Mo. App., 1990): Off-duty officer working as caretaker searched cabin for drugs.	*State v. Castillo,* 697 P.2d 1219 (Idaho, 1985): Off-duty police officer inadvertently opened a letter to brother-in-law and found drugs.
The idea or initiative to obtain the evidence originated with the private person.	*United States v. Knoll,* 16 F.3d 1313 (2d Cir., 1994): Prosecutor knew the private person who burglarized the defendant's office, and expressed the need for more information, which private party then inspected stolen papers to find.	*United States v. Jacobson,* 466 U.S. 109 (1984): FedEx employee opened a package, found drugs, and called police, who then reopened the package. The Court held that the search did not go beyond the initial private search.
The police or governmental agent did not participate in obtaining the evidence.	*People v. Aguilar,* 897 P.2d 84 (Colo., 1995): Police and tow truck operator acted together to see if an impounded vehicle held "anything suspicious."	*State v. Patch,* 702 A.2d 1278 (N.H., 1997): When police ordered a woman to leave the defendant's apartment, they had no duty to prevent the woman from taking the defendant's drugs with her and handing it over to police.

[a]State courts differ as to whether an off-duty police officer is a private person. The different rulings of the Missouri and Idaho courts illustrate the different rulings.

B THE EXCLUSIONARY RULE APPLIES ONLY IN CRIMINAL CASES

The exclusionary rule forbids the use of evidence tainted or soiled by improper or illegal police conduct in criminal cases. Such evidence, however, can be used in civil cases. For example, after O. J. Simpson was found not guilty of murder charges in 1995, a civil lawsuit was brought against him by the estates of the two homicide victims. Evidence that had been suppressed in the Simpson murder case was used against him in the civil lawsuit which resulted in jury awards of more than $34 million against Simpson.

In the 1976 case of *United States v. Janis,*[3] evidence that had been suppressed in a criminal action against Janis for illegal wagering was turned over to the IRS. The evidence was used against him to obtain a civil judgment of tax fraud. The U.S. Supreme Court affirmed the judgment against Janis, holding that:

Jurists and scholars uniformly have recognized that the exclusionary rule imposes a substantial cost on the societal interest in law enforcement by its proscription of what concededly is relevant evidence. . . . And alternatives that would be less costly to societal interests have been the subject of extensive discussion and exploration. . . .

. . . We conclude that exclusion from federal civil proceedings of evidence unlawfully seized by a state criminal enforcement officer has not been shown to have a sufficient likelihood of deterring the conduct of the state police so that it outweighs the societal costs imposed by the exclusion. This Court, therefore, is not justified in so extending the exclusionary rule.

C THE EXCLUSIONARY RULE DOES NOT APPLY IF A DEFENDANT DOES NOT HAVE STANDING OR IF NO RIGHT OF PRIVACY OF THE DEFENDANT HAS BEEN VIOLATED

Evidence is excluded under the exclusionary rule by the defendant making a motion to suppress that evidence. However, to succeed in this motion, the defendant must show his or her rights were violated, not the rights of some other person. This concept is called **standing,** meaning the defendant is the proper person to challenge the police conduct because it violated the defendant's rights.

In the following cases, defendants argued that the police violated their Fourth Amendment rights. In Fourth Amendment cases, the right violated is often characterized as a "sufficient expectation of privacy." Those with such an expectation have standing; those without do not.

Alleged Improper or Illegal Police Conduct	Ruling	Case
The defendant placed a large amount of illegal drugs in the purse of a woman friend for safekeeping. When the police searched the woman's purse, the defendant admitted ownership of the drugs.	The defendant did not have standing to "challenge the legality of the search of [the woman's] purse . . . as he had no legitimate expectation of privacy in [the] purse at the time of the search."	*Rawlings v. Kentucky,* U.S. Supreme Court, 448 U.S. 98, 100 S.Ct. 2556 (1980)

(continued on next page)

Alleged Improper or Illegal Police Conduct	Ruling	Case
The defendants were convicted of armed robbery and challenged the police search of the trunk of the car in which they were passengers. The owner of the car was driving the car at the time of the lawful stop of the car by the police.	The defendants "made no showing that they had any legitimate expectation of privacy in the glove compartment [or trunk] or area under the seat of the car in which they were merely passengers . . . a passenger would not normally have a legitimate expectation of privacy." Mere lawful presence in a car is only a fact which a court will consider in determining the existence of a legitimate expectation of privacy.	*Rakas v. Illinois,* U.S. Supreme Court, 439 U.S. 128, 99 S.Ct. 421 (1978)
Evidence obtained from a home where the defendant was an overnight guest was used to charge and convict the defendant.	It was held that the overnight guest had a sufficient expectation of privacy in the home of the host to claim Fourth Amendment protection against unreasonable searches and seizures.	*Minnesota v. Olson,* U.S. Supreme Court 495 U.S. 91 (1990)
Police looked through a window of an apartment after an informant stated that white powder was being packaged in small bags in the apartment. When two men left the apartment, police stopped their car. The men were arrested when a handgun was seen in the car. Cocaine was found in the car in the search incident to the arrest, and a search warrant was then obtained to search the apartment.	It was held that the defendants did not have a sufficient expectation of privacy in the apartment because (1) they were not overnight guests, (2) they were essentially in the apartment for a business transaction, and (3) they were only in the apartment for a few hours. The U.S. Supreme Court held that the men had no standing to challenge the evidence used for the car stop. The Court did not decide if looking through the apartment window was a search, since the defendants had no expectation of privacy while in the apartment.	*Minnesota v. Carter,* U.S. Supreme Court 525 U.S. 83 (1998)

Alleged Improper or Illegal Police Conduct	Ruling	Case
After a murder, the defendant hid the murder weapon in his cousin's house. Police seized the weapon when they searched the cousin's house. Evidence against the defendant was obtained in a search of the hotel room in which the defendant was sleeping.	The defendant lacked a standing to challenge the police search of his cousin's house, and the defendant's conviction and death penalty were affirmed. Because the room was not registered in the defendant's name and it was three hours after checkout time, it was held that the defendant did not meet the burden of showing a legitimate right of privacy in a hotel room.	*People v. McPeters,* Supreme Court of California 832 P.2d 146 (1992) *State v. Rhodes,* Wisconsin Court of Appeals 149 Wis.2d 722 439 N.W.2d 630 (1989)
Police gained entrance into an apartment building and obtained evidence against the defendant in the common hallway.	Courts held that there may be an "expectation of security" but there "can be no expectation of privacy in the [locked] common hallway."	*United States v. Eisler,* 567 F.2d 814 (8th Cir., 1977)
Police stopped the defendant as he was driving a stolen vehicle. Evidence against the defendant was obtained in a search of the vehicle.	A defendant lacks standing to assert a Fourth Amendment right of privacy in stolen property. But in a traffic stop, defendants can challenge the seizure (stop) of their person.	*Nelson v. State,* Supreme Court of Florida 578 So.2d 694 (1991)
Police stopped the defendant as he was driving a vehicle that he said that he had borrowed from his uncle.	Because the defendant was driving the vehicle with the owner's consent, he had a right of privacy in vehicle and standing to challenge the police search of the car.	*United States v. Soto,* 988 F.2d 1548 (10th Cir., 1993)

Ⓓ EVIDENCE OBTAINED FROM ABANDONED PROPERTY WILL NOT BE SUPPRESSED

If by conduct or words the defendant shows that he or she has relinquished the expectation privacy in property, the object may be used as evidence. This legal concept of abandonment was defined in the 1989 case of *United States v. Thomas,*[4] as follows:

Privacy Defined

The Fourth Amendment protects the right of privacy of persons. The U.S. Supreme Court held in the case of *Katz v. United States,* 88 S.Ct. 507 (19667) that:

> The Fourth Amendment protects people, not places. What a person knowingly exposes to the public, even in his own home or office, is not a subject of Fourth Amendment protection. . . . But what he seeks to preserve as private, may be constitutionally protected.

A reasonable expectation of privacy exists *only* if:

- An individual actually expects privacy
- His (or her) expectation is reasonable

Therefore, a person who beats his spouse in the front room of their home and can be seen by police and other persons standing on a public sidewalk does not have a reasonable expectation of privacy.

A police search is an intrusion into a right of privacy. The U.S. Supreme Court stated in *United States v. Jacobson,* 104 S.Ct. 1654 (1984), that "a search occurs when a expectation of privacy that society is prepared to consider reasonable is infringed." If the officer can show authority to make the search, the intrusion into privacy is lawful.

The test for abandonment in the search and seizure context is distinct from the property notion of abandonment: it is possible for a person to retain a property interest in an item, but nonetheless to relinquish his or her reasonable expectation of privacy in the object.

The following sections present the different forms of abandonment.

Throwaway as a Type of Abandonment

Persons fleeing the police with illegal drugs or other contraband on their person will often throw away what can be very incriminating evidence. If the throwaway is a voluntary abandonment of the object, courts will allow the object to be used as evidence against the person. But if the throwaway is the direct or indirect product of an illegal police stop or other improper police conduct, courts will generally forbid the use of the throwaway item as evidence. The following U.S. Supreme Court cases are examples of this type of abandonment.

Michigan v. Chesternut
United States Supreme Court, 486 U.S. 567, 108 S.Ct. 1975 (1988)

Chesternut was standing on a street corner in Detroit, and when he saw a police car approaching the corner, he began to run. The police, on routine patrol, followed Chesternut in their car "to see where he was going." As he ran, Chesternut began throwing objects away. A police officer picked up the packets and found they contained pills. Based on the officer's experience as a paramedic, he believed that the pills contained codeine. Chesternut was arrested, and in the search incident to the arrest, heroin and a hypodermic needle were found. The Supreme Court held that the defendant "was not unlawfully seized during the initial police pursuit" and affirmed the use of the pills, heroin, and needle as evidence, holding that:

> . . . the police conduct here—a brief acceleration to catch up with respondent, followed by a short drive alongside him—was not "so intimidating" that respondent could reasonably have believed that he was not free to disregard the police presence and go about his business. The police therefore were not required to have "a particularized and objective basis for suspecting [respondent] of criminal activity," in order to pursue him. *United States v. Cortez*, 449 U.S 411.

California v. Hodari
United States Supreme Court, 499 U.S. 621, 111 S.Ct. 1547 (1991)

Police officers on patrol in an unmarked police car observed four or five youths huddled around a car parked at a curb. All the young men began to run at the approach of the officers' car, so one of the officers chased them on foot. The officer caught up with Hodari and tackled him. Just before he was tackled, Hodari threw to the ground what turned out to be crack cocaine. In holding that the cocaine could be used as evidence against Hodari, the Supreme Court held that:

> assuming that Pertoso's [policeman] pursuit in the present case constituted a "show of authority" enjoining Hodari to halt, since Hodari did not comply with that injunction he was not seized until he was tackled. The cocaine abandoned while he was running was in this case not the fruit of a seizure, and his motion to exclude evidence of it was properly denied.

Denial of Ownership as a Form of Abandonment

Persons who deny ownership of property to a law enforcement officer relinquish their right of privacy in the property and do not later have standing to challenge the use of evidence obtained from the property. The following are a few of the hundreds of denial cases that have come before criminal courts in recent years:

- Airport denial case where the defendants denied ownership in their luggage at airports. Because of their denials, the defendants could not later challenge searches of their luggage by law officers. Illegal drugs and other contraband obtained from the luggage was used as evidence against the defendants.[5]

- Train passenger's denial of a garment bag under his feet.[6]

- Denial of luggage in the trunk of car.[7]

- Denial of a satchel that the defendant hid after a car accident.[8]

- Denial of ownership of an apartment.[9]

Evidence Obtained from Garbage or Trash

Trash receptacles kept in a home or garage have Fourth Amendment constitutional protection while located in such places. Evidence obtained from these places without valid consent or a search warrant would be suppressed and could not be used, even if it were proven that the trash was abandoned.

In *California v. Greenwood*,[10] police asked the regular trash collector to turn trash collected at the curb in front of the Greenwood home over to them without commingling it with trash from other homes. Inspection of the Greenwood trash revealed evidence of drug use, which was used to obtain a search warrant of the Greenwood home. Greenwood was then charged and convicted of felony drug charges. In affirming the drug convictions, the U.S. Supreme Court held that the defendants "could have no reasonable expectation of privacy in . . . the plastic garbage bags left on or at the side of the public street . . ."[11]

A few state courts, however, impose stricter standards. These states include New Jersey, Washington, and Vermont.[12]

Abandoned Motor Vehicles

The phenomena of abandoned and stolen vehicles is a constant problem in every American city and state. Many states have statutes that define when a vehicle is legally abandoned. For example, Section 342.40(i) of the Wisconsin Statutes provides that if a vehicle is left unattended on a public highway or private or public property "under such circumstances as to cause the vehicle to reasonably appear to have been abandoned" for more than 48 hours, "the vehicle is deemed abandoned and constitutes a public nuisance."

In the following case, a court held that a suitcase in a vehicle was abandoned.

United States v. Oswald
U.S. Court of Appeals, Sixth Circuit, 783 F.2d 663 (1986)

The defendant was transporting $300,000 worth of cocaine north from Florida in a stolen car when the car caught on fire on an interstate highway. Oswald ran from the car in fear that the car would blow up. Oswald did not report the fire or the car on the highway because the car was stolen and had cocaine in a suitcase in the trunk. Local authorities put out the fire, which extensively damaged the vehicle. Before having the vehicle towed away, a deputy sheriff took the valuables out of the car. After attempting to determine the identity of the owner of the vehicle and why they had not reported the incident, the sheriff (more than an hour and a half later) began to go through the items he had taken from the car. When the sheriff pried open a metal suitcase, the cocaine in the suitcase cleared up the mystery of why no one had claimed the property. In affirming Oswald's conviction, the trial court and the Court of Appeals held that Oswald had abandoned the suitcase when he made no efforts to preserve his right of privacy in the metal suitcase.

Police Searches of Trash Barrels

In a two-part article entitled "*Katz*[a] in the Trash Barrel," in the *FBI Law Enforcement Bulletin* (February and March 1979), the following conclusions were presented on the seizure of abandoned personal property:

> Criminals who dispose of contraband and other evidence of criminal offenses in their trash cans are unskilled practitioners. They assume the risk that their discards will be seized by, or turned over to, law enforcement officers for use against them. Such items can be used directly as evidence in a criminal prosecution, or indirectly by forming the basis for issuance of a search warrant.

The following conclusions also can be drawn from an analysis of the Federal and State trash search decisions:

1. A search warrant is the best assurance that evidence seized from a trash container will not be challenged successfully on constitutional grounds.

2. One who disposes of personal property in a trash receptacle placed at curbside for collection, or in a commonly used receptacle, or in a refuse pile accessible to the public, generally is held to have abandoned the property.

3. A former possessor retains no reasonable expectation of privacy in abandoned property, and thus has no standing to object to its seizure or inspection.

4. Warrantless entry by police or their agents to a constitutionally protected area, such as the yard or garage, in order to gain access to trash, may taint the search or seizure, regardless of the intent of the possessor to abandon; and

5. Officers contemplating a warrantless trash inspection should be thoroughly familiar with State as well as Federal principles governing the search or seizure of trash, since State courts may impose under State constitutions more restrictive rules than those announced by Federal courts.

[a]See the U.S. Supreme Court case of *Katz v. United States* in section B, "Wiretapping and Electronic Surveillance," in Chapter 15.

Expiration of Rental Agreements for Motels and Lockers as a Form of Abandonment

Many courts have held that the expiration of a motel room agreement or the expiration of the rental time for a storage looker was a form of abandonment. In those cases, courts held that defendants had no standing to challenge evidence obtained by police searches.

In the 1990 case of *United States v. Reyes*,[13] the evidence was obtained twelve days after the expiration of the rental of a bus terminal storage locker. The defendant did not remove the contraband used as evidence because he had been arrested and was in custody.

E EVIDENCE DISCOVERED IN OPEN FIELDS WILL NOT BE SUPPRESSED

Curtilage is that area close to a home where persons assert a right of privacy. The protection of the Fourth Amendment extends to the home and to the curtilage. The U.S. Supreme Court defined *curtilage* as follows in 1984:[14]

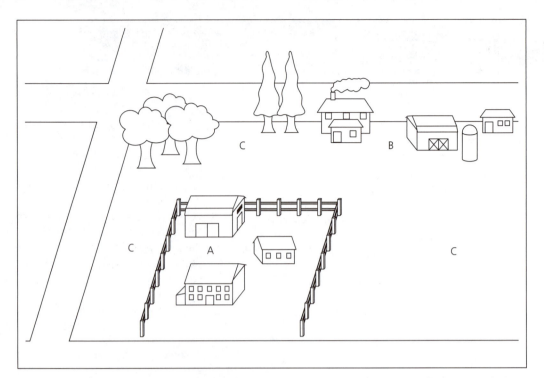

Persons living in a single-family home have a greater expectation of privacy in their curtilage (A and B above) than the privacy rights in the curtilage around a large apartment building. There are no privacy rights by the owner or other persons in open fields (C above).

At common law, the curtilage is the area to which extends the intimate activity associated with the "sanctity of a man's home and the privacies of life," *Boyd v. United States,* 116 U.S. 616, 630, 6 S.Ct. 524, 532, 29 L.Ed. 746 (1886), and therefore has been considered part of the home itself for Fourth Amendment purposes. Thus, courts have extended Fourth Amendment protection to the curtilage; and they have defined the curtilage, as did the common law, by reference to the factors that determine whether an individual reasonably may expect that an area immediately adjacent to the home will remain private.

In 1987 the U.S. Supreme Court held that curtilage questions should be resolved with particular reference to four factors:[15]

- The proximity of the area claimed to be curtilage to the home
- Whether the area is included within an enclosure surrounding the home
- The nature of the uses to which the area is put
- The steps taken by the resident to protect the area from observation by people passing by

The Plain-View or Open-View Doctrine[a]

If a law enforcement officer is where the officer has a right to be and sees evidence or contraband of a crime in plain view, the evidence may be seized and will be admissible at a trial.

The plain-view doctrine was stated as follows in the case of *Texas v. Brown,* 103 S.Ct. 1535 (1983):

> First, the police officer must lawfully make an "initial intrusion" or otherwise properly be in a position from which he can view a particular area.
>
> Second, the officer must discover incriminating evidence "inadvertently," which is to say, he may not "know in advance the location of . . . evidence and intend to seize it," relying on the plain-view doctrine only as a pretext.
>
> Finally, it must be "immediately apparent" to the police that the items they observe may be evidence of a crime, contraband, or otherwise subject to seizure.

Plain View and the Five Human Senses

Most plain-view cases occur when an officer, who is where he or she has a right to be, sees evidence or contraband of a crime. However, plain view is not limited to visual observations. Any of the five human senses could provide infor-mation that makes it "immediately apparent" to the police that the object is evidence of a crime.

- *Plain smell.* In 1948, the U.S. Supreme Court held that odors may be "found to be evidence of the most persuasive character." *Johnson v. United States,* 333 U.S. 10, 13, 68 S.Ct. 367, 368 (1948).

- *Plain hearing.* The "naked ear" or plain hearing rule applies to things that are heard without the use of any electronic or mechanical devices.

- *Plain touch.* If, in making a lawful pat-down, the officer touches what is immediately apparent to be a concealed pistol, plain touch has occurred. See also *United States v. Mulligan,* 488 F.2d 732 (9th Cir.1973).

- *Plain taste.* The sense of taste is rarely used to provide information to a law enforcement officer. No reported decisions can be found on this point.

[a]See the U.S. Supreme Court Case of *Coolidge v. New Hampshire,* 91 S.Ct. 2022 (1971), where a writer for the Court stated that the terms *plain view* and *open view* differ. This distinction, however, has not been followed. *Plain view* is now the term used broadly without any distinction from *open view.*

See *United States v. Agapito,* 620 F.2d 324 (2d Cir. 1980), *United States v. Mankani,* 738 F.2d 538 (2d Cir., 1984, *United States v. Lopez,* 475 F.2d 537 (7th Cir., 1973), *United States v. Fisch,* 474 F.2d 1071 (9th Cir., 1973).

There is a high degree of privacy in the curtilage, or backyard, of a one-family dwelling that is fenced in so as to be protected from observation from people passing by. However, there is a much lesser degree of privacy in the curtilage of a fifty-unit apartment building because all occupants of the apartment can use the common area available to them.[16]

But should Fourth Amendment protection extend beyond the curtilage to open fields? The U.S. Supreme Court noted in 1974 that the Supreme Court refused in the 1924 case of *Hester v. United States,*[17] "to extend the Fourth Amendment to sights seen in the open fields."[18] In the *Hester* case, government agents were trespassing on the defendant's land when they observed the defendant running away from them and throwing contraband to the ground in open fields. In holding that the contraband could be used as evidence to obtain a conviction against the defendant, the U.S. Supreme Court ruled that:

> The special protection accorded by the Fourth Amendment to the people in their "persons, houses, papers and effects," is not extended to the open fields. The distinction between the latter and the house is as old as the common law. 4Bl.Comm. 223, 225, 226.

"Open fields include any unoccupied or undeveloped area outside of the curtilage. An open field need be neither 'open' nor a 'field' as those terms are used in common speech."[19] An **open field** can consist of woods, swamps, meadows, or fields of farm crops.

Ⓔ EVIDENCE DISCOVERED IN GOOD FAITH OR HONEST MISTAKE WILL NOT BE SUPPRESSED

The Good Faith Exception

In the 1984 U.S. Supreme Court case of *United States v. Leon*,[20] police officers executed a search warrant that they believed to be valid but was defective. The evidence obtained under the defective warrant was permitted to be used because the police believed in good faith that the search warrant was valid. In holding that the evidence could be used, the U.S. Supreme Court held that "the exclusionary rule is designed to deter police misconduct rather than punish the errors of judges and magistrates."

The *Leon* **good faith** rule permits the use of evidence where a search warrant contains a technical error that does not violate a fundamental constitutional right of a suspect.[21] However, not all states have adopted this good faith exception that permits the use of evidence because of a mistake by a judge, prosecutor, police dispatcher, or computer.

The Honest Mistake Rule

After an armed robbery, California police had probable cause to arrest Hill for the robbery. They obtained Hill's home address and his description. A man who "exactly fit [Hill's] description" answered the door to Hill's home but denied that he was Hill. However, the police arrested the man, believing that he was Hill. In the search incident to the arrest of the man, the police found and seized evidence that incriminated Hill. The police later became aware that they had arrested the wrong man. They released the man and within a short time arrested Hill.

Because probable cause existed to arrest the man in Hill's home, the U.S. Supreme Court held in the 1971 case of *Hill v. California*,[22] that the "arrest (of the wrong man) and subsequent search were reasonable and valid under the Fourth Amendment" and therefore the evidence could be used in the trial and conviction of Hill.

In the 1987 U.S. Supreme Court case of *Maryland v. Garrison*,[23] a search warrant was issued to search a third-floor apartment. The police reasonably believed that only one apartment was on the third floor of the building and did not become aware of the second apartment, which belonged to Garrison, until after they found heroin, cash, and drug paraphernalia there. In holding that the evidence could be used to convict Garrison of drug violations, the Supreme Court pointed out that the Court has "recognized the need to allow some latitude for **honest mistakes** that are made by officers in the dangerous and difficult process of making arrests and executing search warrants."

Ⓖ OTHER AREAS WHERE THE EXCLUSIONARY RULE DOES NOT APPLY

Source of Evidence or Use of Evidence	Court Rulings
Common carriers (airlines, parcel services, truckers, railroads, and so on)	"Common carriers have a common-law right to inspect packages they accept for shipment, based on their duty to restrain from carrying contraband."[24]
U.S. Customs Service	"The U.S. Government has the undoubted right to inspect all incoming goods at a port of entry . . . [but like the common carriers] it would be impossible for customs officers to inspect every package."[25]
Grand jury proceedings	". . . it is unrealistic to assume that application of the rule of grand jury proceedings would significantly further [the] goal of deterrence of police misconduct. . . . The grand jury's investigative power must be broad if its public responsibility is adequately to be discharged."[26]
Probation or parole revocation hearings	". . . the overwhelming number of reported cases have held that the Fourth Amendment's 'exclusionary rule' was not applicable under the circumstances to probation revocation proceedings or qualitatively comparable proceedings to revoke parole. . . .

(continued on next page)

Source of Evidence or Use of Evidence	Court Rulings
	The only reservation expressed by several courts in denying application of the 'exclusionary rule' to a revocation proceeding might occur in situations where police harassment of probationers is demonstrated."[27] In 1998 the U.S. Supreme Court followed the ruling of a state court in a parole revocation case.[28]
Searches by probation or parole officers	". . . a probation agent who reasonably believes that a probationer is violating the terms of probation may conduct a warrantless search of a probationer's residence. . . . A probation agent has a duty to see that a probationer is complying with the terms of his probation."[29] In 1987 the U.S. Supreme Court affirmed Griffin's conviction for possession of a handgun holding that the "search of Griffin's home satisfied the demands of the Fourth Amendment because it was carried out pursuant to a regulation that itself satisfies the Fourth Amendment reasonableness requirement." The U.S. Supreme Court affirmed another probation search in 2001 in *United States v. Knights.* Knights was on probation and had signed a consent to search agreement to obtain the benefits of probation. Detectives had reasonable suspicion that Knights had started an arson fire. Without a search warrant, the detectives searched Knight's apartment, relying on the probation consent to search. The U.S. Supreme Court affirmed the use of the evidence obtained[30]. . . .
Military discharge proceeding	A military administrative discharge proceeding is a civil proceeding and not a military criminal proceeding. Illegally seized drugs could be used as evidence. The Court held that to force the military to keep a serviceman who uses drugs "is a price which our society cannot afford to pay."[31]

Source of Evidence or Use of Evidence	Court Rulings
Child protective proceedings	"... because a child protective proceeding ... is not punitive in nature ... the State's interest in protecting its children mandates the admissibility of relevant evidence seized during an illegal search."[32]
Civil tax proceedings and civil deportation proceedings	The U.S. Supreme Court refused to extend the exclusionary rule to civil tax proceedings[33] and to civil deportation proceedings.[34]
"Community caretaking functions" by police	During the thousands of traffic accidents that occur monthly, police are performing "community caretaking functions" such as moving a damaged vehicle to allow traffic to move. If evidence or contraband is seen under such circumstances, it may be used as evidence as the plain-view doctrine would apply. The U.S. Supreme Court pointed out that the conduct of law officers under these circumstances are "totally divorced from the detention, investigation or acquisition of evidence relating to the violation of a criminal statute ..." *Cady v. Dombrowski*, 93 S. Ct. 2523 (1971).
Evidence obtained in foreign countries by foreign officials	To deter the estimated $50-billion-a-year illegal drug industry in the United States, evidence seized in foreign countries by foreign officials is being used to prosecute both American and foreign citizens. Evidence obtained by a foreign official is admissible even if the search or seizure violated the suspect's rights under the U.S. Constitution. Two exceptions to this are: (1) The conduct of the foreign official was extremely inhumane or outrageous, or (2) there was substantial participation by an American law officer in the seizure.[35]

Source of Evidence or Use of Evidence	Court Rulings
Important witness testimony against the defendants	In seeking to apprehend a robber, police improperly took Crews into custody on mere suspicion. A photo taken of Crews while he was in custody caused a robbery victim to identify Crews as the offender. The woman was a witness at Crews's trial and again identified him as she had in the photo array and in a lineup. The U.S. Supreme Court affirmed Crews's conviction and the use of the in-court witness.[36] A case with some similarities was affirmed by the Illinois Supreme Court.[37]
Sentencing proceedings after criminal conviction	Holding that evidence seized by the police in violation of the Fourth Amendment is not necessarily unreliable, courts have held that sentencing courts should consider all "reliable" evidence in doing so.[38]

SUMMARY

The exclusionary rule (or the rule of exclusion of evidence) generally applies as follows:

The Exclusionary Rule Does Apply to Law Officers who Improperly or Illegally

- Obtain physical and other evidence (Chapter 14)
- Obtain confessions and statements to be used as evidence (Chapter 12)
- Obtain evidence by use of search warrant, wiretapping, or trained dogs (Chapter 15)
- Obtain identification evidence (Chapter 13)
- Obtain fingerprints and DNA evidence (Chapters 16 & 18)
- Obtain evidence from the crime scene (Chapter 16)
- Obtain scientific evidence (Chapter 18)
- Obtain videotapes, photographs, documents, or writings for use as evidence (Chapter 17)

The Exclusionary Rule Does *Not* Apply to

- Evidence obtained by private persons lawfully or illegally
- Civil cases and proceedings and applies only to criminal cases
- Situations where a defendant does not have standing or no right of privacy of a defendant has been violated
- Abandoned property that is used as evidence against a defendant
- Evidence found in open fields or when evidence is discovered in plain view

- Evidence is obtained where the "good faith" rule or the "honest mistake" rule apply
- Evidence obtained by a law officer who has lawful authority to seize the evidence
- Evidence that is obtained or used in any of the functions or sources listed in section G of this chapter

PROBLEMS

A defense lawyer files motions to suppress in an attempt to prevent the use of evidence against a defendant:

AVAILABLE ANSWERS

a. The evidence would be suppressed and cannot be used against the defendant.

b. The evidence cannot be suppressed as the evidence was lawfully and properly obtained.

c. The evidence was not lawfully obtained but can be used as evidence.

1. Police officers stopping a speeding car see objects thrown out of the window of the car. The officers pick up the objects and find them to be packages of cocaine.

2. Officers investigating an armed robbery seek to determine the owner of a jacket found on a table in a tavern. All persons present deny ownership. Cocaine and the identity of the owner are found in the pockets of the jacket. The owner of the jacket was present in the tavern and denied ownership.

3. A burglar caught in the act of committing a burglary turns evidence of a serious felony over to police that the burglar stole from the home of the defendant.

4. When evidence in a criminal tax fraud case is suppressed, the Internal Revenue agents then use the same evidence in a case of civil fraud in a civil action against the defendant.

5. The defendant does not have standing in his (or her) motion to suppress.

6. In a Fourth Amendment motion to suppress, the defendant cannot show that his (or her) right of privacy had been violated by the police.

7. The murder weapon with the defendant's fingerprints and DNA is found in a public park.

8. Trash collectors find the weapon in question 7 and turn the weapon over to the police.

9. A police officer illegally enters the defendant's motor vehicle and obtains the weapon in question 7.

10. The defendant's probation officer making a routine check finds the weapon in question 7.

INFOTRAC COLLEGE EDITION EXERCISES

1. Go to InfoTrac College Edition and using the search term "Fourth Amendment" find the 2000 article in the *American Criminal Law Review* by David Moran that discusses high-tech surveillance and privacy rights. What are some of the newest forms of surveillance equipment and when does the Fourth Amendment prohibit their use without probable cause?

2. Go to InfoTrac College Edition and using the search term "Fourth Amendment" find the 2001 article in the *Journal of Criminal Law and Criminology* titled "Fourth Amendment Privacy Interests . . . ," by William Hefferman. How should "privacy interests" be defined for Fourth Amendment purposes? The layperson's expectation of privacy versus the world? Or the expectation of privacy from the police? How do these expectations differ?

NOTES

1. Chapter 14 discusses the Fourth Amendment exclusionary rule in more detail.

2. Virtually all states follow the *Burdeau* rule. See N. Lafave, *Search and Seizure: A Treatise on the Fourth Amendment,* 3d ed. (St. Paul: West, 1996), sec. 1.8, note 16.

3. 428 U.S. 433.

4. 864 F.2d 843 (D.C. Cir.).

5. *United States v. Tolbert,* 692 F.2d 1041 (6th Cir., 1982); *United States v. Sanders,* 719 F.2d 882 (6th Cir., 1983); *United States v. Roman,* 849 F.2d 920 (5th Cir., 1988).

6. *United States v. Carrasquillo,* 877 F.2d 73 (D.C. Cir., 1989).

7. *United States v. McBean,* 861 F.2d 1570 (11th Cir., 1988).

8. *Commonwealth v. Anderl,* 477 A.2d 1356 (Pa. Super., 1984).

9. *Hayes v. State,* 158 N.W.2d 545 (Wis., 1968).

10. 486 U.S. 35 (1988).

11. In the 1998 case of *Redmon v. United States,* 138 F.3d 1109, the city of Urbana, Ill., forbade leaving trash at the curb, so Redmon placed his cans for collection at the top of his 28-foot-long driveway. The cans were located outside the attached two-car townhouse garage that Redmon shared with another townhouse. The only approach to the front door of the townhouses required that visitors walk up the driveway to a walkway that ran along the side of the garage. Walkways to and from a front door, although on private property, are generally regarded as open to the public. Because Redmon had no control over visitors to his neighbor's townhouse, the court pointed out the area was open to the public.

Drug enforcement agents had Redmon under surveillance and searched the garbage cans outside his garage, where they found evidence of cocaine that enabled the DEA agents to obtain a search warrant. The search of Redmon's townhouse resulted in additional evidence. On appeal to the 7th Circuit Court in Chicago, the conviction was upheld in an 8 to 5 vote.

12. New Jersey: *State v. Hempele,* 576 A.2d 793 (1990); Washington: *State v. Boland,* 48 CrL 1205 (1990); Vermont: *State v. Morris,* 1996 WL 135179 (1996).

13. 908 F.2d 281 (8th Cir.).

14. *Oliver v. United States,* 466 U.S. 170, 140 S.Ct. 1735 (1984).

15. *United States v. Dunn,* 480 U.S. 294, 107 S.Ct. 1134 (1987), where the four factors were used to determine that the defendant's barn lay outside the curtilage of his ranch house.

16. In the case of *United States v. Acosta,* 1992 WL 109641 (1992), the Third Circuit Court of Appeals held that occupants of a three-story apartment building did not have any legitimate expectation of privacy in the backyard of the apartment building. Therefore, the defendant did not have standing and could not challenge the use of evidence thrown out of his bathroom window and picked up by law officers in the backyard of the apartment building.

17. 265 U.S. 57, 44 S.Ct. 445.

18. *Air Pollution Variance Board of Colorado v. Western Alfalfa Corp.,* 416 U.S. 861, 94 S.Ct. 861 (1974).

19. *Oliver v. United States,* 466 U.S. 170, 180, 104 S.Ct. 1735, 1742 (1984), n.11.

20. 104 S.Ct. 3405.

21. The U.S. Supreme Court followed the *Leon* case in the 1995 case of *Arizona v. Evans,* 115 S.Ct. 1185. Evans was stopped by Arizona police for a traffic violation. The officers checked their in-car computer and received information that there was an outstanding arrest warrant for Evans. The police then arrested Evans and, in the search incident to Evans's arrest, found marijuana. This evidence was used to obtain a conviction for the possession of marijuana.

The use of the evidence was challenged because the warrant had been canceled seventeen days before Evans's arrest. The incorrect information was in the computer due to an error by a court clerk. Following *Leon,* the U.S. Supreme Court held that the evidence of the marijuana could be used because there had been a good faith reliance by the police on the incorrect information.

22. 91 S.Ct. 1106.

23. 107 S.Ct. 1013.

24. *Illinois v. Andreas,* 463 U.S. 765, 769 n.1, 103 S.Ct. 3319, 3323 n.1 (1983).

25. Idem.

26. *United States v. Calandra*, 414 U.S. 338, 94 S.Ct. 613 (1974).

27. Supreme Court of Illinois in *People v. Dowery*, 340 N.E.2d 529 (Ill., 1975).

28. *Pennsylvania Board of Probation and Parole v. Scott*, 118 S.Ct. 2014.

29. *Wisconsin v. Griffin*, 388 N.W.2d 535 107 S.Ct. 3164 (1987).

30. *United States v. Knights*, 534 U.S. 112 (2001), and also see 483 U.S. 868.

31. *Garrett v. Lehman*, 751 F.2d 997 (9th Cir., 1985).

32. *In re Diane P.*, 494 N.Y.S.2d 881, 38 CrL 2168 (App. Div., 1985).

33. *United States v. Janis*, 96 S.Ct. 3021 (1976).

34. *INS v. Lopez-Lopez-Mendoza*, 104 S.Ct. 3479 (1984).

35. *United States v. Verdugo-Urquidez*, 112 S.Ct. 2986 (1992); *United States v. Alvarez-Machain*, 112 S.Ct. 2188 (1992).

36. *United States v. Crews*, 100 S.Ct. 1244 (1980).

37. *People v. Winsett*, 606 N.E.2d 1186 (1993).

38. *United States v. McCrory*, 930 F.2d 63 (D.C. Cir., 1991); *United States v. Lynch*, 934 F.2d 1226, 49 CrL 1361 (11th Cir., 1991).

11

Evidence Is Admissible If Obtained During an Administrative Function Under the "Special Needs" of Government

In 1987, the U.S. Supreme Court held that "the probable cause standard is peculiarly related to criminal investigations" and "may be unhelpful in analyzing the reasonableness of routine administrative functions.[1]

Thousands of administrative searches and functions are conducted every day by local, state, and federal employees. The majority of these employees are not law enforcement officers. They are not conducting criminal investigations but are conducting **administrative functions** that are related to the **special needs of government** and the community.

The U.S. Supreme Court and hundreds of lower courts have held that neither probable cause nor search warrants are required in most of these routine administrative functions. Evidence obtained as a result of any of the following would be admissible if the administrative function was within the guidelines established by law.

Ⓐ SECURITY SCREENING AT AIRPORTS, COURTHOUSES, AND OTHER PUBLIC BUILDINGS AND PLACES

At airports alone in the United States, over 1 billion security screenings of persons and personal belongings occur each year. Since 9/11 security screening has been extended to courthouses, public buildings, sporting events, rock concerts, and some other public functions.

Thousands of illegal weapons and other illegal objects are confiscated as a result of these administrative security screenings. Many of the seized items are then used as evidence in courts throughout the United States. In holding that the objects are admissible evidence, most courts hold that security screenings are administrative searches under special government need for security.

Other courts hold that such evidence is admissible because once an individual presents their person and their property to a security checkpoint for screening, they have consented to the screening and that consent cannot be withdrawn during the screening process.[2]

However, such evidence could be held inadmissible if a defense lawyer can establish that the "security officers looked to considerations other than safety in conducting the screening, such as when they are on the lookout for evidence of drug trafficking, the search loses its protective character."[3]

Ⓑ FIRE, HEALTH, AND HOUSING INSPECTIONS

All large cities have very valid concerns for the health and fire safety within their community. Health and fire concerns are higher in areas of cities where buildings are crowded, old, and decaying. Efforts are always being made to prevent fires, the collapse of buildings, the infestation of rodents or insects, and to preserve the community in a safe and healthful condition.

The U.S. Supreme Court held that fire, health, and housing inspection programs "touch at most upon the periphery of the important interests safeguarded by the Fourteenth Amendment's protection against official intrusion."[4]

Most property owners consent to inspections by health, fire, or housing inspectors. However, if a homeowner or the owner of commercial property refuses to allow an inspection, a search warrant must be obtained and the owner of the property cannot be punished for refusal to consent to a search.

The U.S. Supreme Court set a much lower standard for obtaining a fire, health, or housing inspection search warrant in the case of *Camara v. Municipal Court*,[5] holding:

> . . . The warrant procedure is designed to guarantee that a decision to search private property is justified by a reasonable governmental interest. But reasonableness is still the ultimate standard. If a valid public interest justifies the intrusion contemplated, then there is probable cause to issue a suitably restricted search warrant.

Some states have passed laws or have established procedures where area search warrants may be issued when health and sanitation risks exist. For example, if there were an infestation of rats in an area of a city, an area search warrant could be issued to find the source (or sources) of the problem and eliminate the health risk.

In the case of *See v. City of Seattle*,[6] the U.S. Supreme Court made it clear that a search warrant was not needed in an emergency situation such as seizure of contaminated food, compulsory smallpox vaccinations, health quarantines, or destruction of tubercular cattle.

C SCHOOL SEARCHES ON REASONABLE SUSPICION

The U.S. Supreme Court held that "the (search) warrant requirement . . . is unsuitable to the school environment and requiring a teacher to obtain a warrant before searching a child suspected of infraction of school rules (or the criminal code) would unduly interfere with maintenance of the swift and informal disciplinary procedures needed in the schools."[7]

The general rule in the United States is to permit school officials in school and quasi-school settings to conduct searches of students on reasonable suspicion.

In regulating school property and student activities, schools can make it known to students and parents that school lockers and other storage areas are the property of the school and subject to random searches at any time. Schools in the City of Milwaukee followed this procedure, and when a handgun was found in the locker of a student, a trial court permitted the handgun to be used as evidence. The Supreme Court of Wisconsin held that Milwaukee students have no right of privacy in school lockers in view of the written policy and notice given to students.

D DRUG TESTING WITHOUT PROBABLE CAUSE OR A SEARCH WARRANT

Of Law Officers and Other Persons in Critical Occupations

Private businesses may conduct drug testing of employees without fear of Fourth Amendment rights since the Fourth Amendment does not apply to searches by private persons. However, the Fourth Amendment does apply to drug testing by government.

In 1989, the U.S. Supreme Court decided two cases involving drug testing of government employees. In the case of *National Treasury Employees Union v. Von Raab,*[8] the Supreme Court sustained a U.S. Customs requirement that employees seeking transfers or promotions submit to urinalysis. In *Skinner v. Railway Labor Executive's Association,*[9] a similar requirement was approved for workers involved in certain train accidents or incidents. In these cases the Supreme Court stated

> . . . where a Fourth Amendment intrusion serves special governmental needs, beyond the normal need for law enforcement, it is necessary to balance the individual's privacy expectations against the Government's interests to determine whether it is impractical to require a (search) warrant or some level of individualized suspicion in the particular context. *Von Raab,* 489 U.S. at 665, *Skinner,* 489 U.S. at 617–18.

The U.S. Supreme Court identified three governmental interests that are sufficiently compelling to justify drug testing where there is no information causing suspicion of drug abuse. These interest are

1. Ensuring that certain employees "have unimpeachable integrity and judgment." 489 U.S. at 670
2. Enhancing public safety. 489 U.S. at 628
3. "Protecting truly sensitive information." 489 U.S. at 676

Suspicionless drug testing is now required by many federal, state, or local governmental agencies of employees with secret and top secret security clearance, detectives, police officers, guards, firefighters, fire protection specialists, nurses, employees who handle or inspect hazardous wastes, motor vehicle operators, heavy equipment operators, locomotive operators, brake-switching employees, employees required to carry firearms, and other employees with duties "fraught with such risks of injury to others that even a momentary lapse of attention can have disastrous consequences" (109 S.Ct. at 1419). Random drug testing of persons within these groups has been sustained by courts by virtue of being a "heavily regulated industry." *Policemen's Benevolent Ass'n v. Township of Washington,* 850 F.2d 133 (3d Cir. 1988), review denied 490 U.S. 1004, 109 S.Ct. 1637, 45 Crl. 4002 (1989).[10]

Drug Testing on Reasonable Suspicion

The Supreme Court of Hawaii pointed out that law officers have a diminished expectation of privacy because of their employment and "must always be mentally and physically alert

Invalid State Laws that Required Drug Testing Without Probable Cause

State Statute Held Void as Probable Cause Was Needed in Each Case If the Purpose of the Search Is to Obtain Evidence for Criminal Prosecution	Case
Georgia law requiring candidates for public office to take a drug test and test negative.	*Chandler v. Miller,* 117 S.Ct. 1295, U.S. Supreme Court (1997)
Because of concerns for babies born with crack addiction, a South Carolina law required pregnant women being treated at a state hospital to submit to a urine test to determine if they were using cocaine.	*Ferguson v. Charleston, S.C.,* 532 U.S. 67, U.S. Supreme Court (2001)
Illinois law required drivers who caused accidents where there was personal injury to take chemical or breath testing.	*King v. Ryan,* No. 72392, Illinois Supreme Court (1992)

while driving motor vehicles, and must exercise good judgment in the use of guns." *McCloskey v. Honolulu Police Department,* 799 P.2d 953 (1990). In the following cases, drug testing was held to be constitutionally based upon reasonable suspicion:

- Reasonable suspicion to believe that a police officer was using drugs. *Copeland v. Philadelphia Police Department,* 840 F.2d 1139, (3d Cir. 1988), review denied 490 U.S. 1004, 109 S.Ct. 1636, 45 Crl. 4001 (1989).

- An anonymous telephone call that an airman with Air Force flight operations had recently used marijuana was held to provide "reasonable suspicion" for a drug test. *United States v. Blair,* 32 M.J. 404 (1991), review denied U.S. Supreme Court, 112 S.Ct. 438, 50 Crl. 3077 (1991).

School Boards May Require Random Drug Testing of Student Athletes

In the 1995 case of *Vernonia School District v. Acton,*[11] the U.S. Supreme Court upheld the random, suspicionless urinalysis testing of public school students participating in interscholastic sports. The school district had required this testing in its custodial capacity to combat growing drug use by students and to protect the health and safety of student athletes.

The U.S. Supreme Court held that the procedure was not an unreasonable search, citing "special needs, beyond the normal need for law enforcement (making) the warrant and probable cause requirement (of the Fourth Amendment) impractical . . ." The Supreme Court listed the following for approving the reasonableness of the procedure:

1. Student athletes have a reduced expectation of privacy.

2. The intrusion on the student athletes' privacy by urine collection was "negligible."

3. The government (school authorities) had an important and compelling interest in curbing drug use by student athletes as part of the effort to curb drug use.

School Boards May Require Random Drug Testing of Students Participating in Extracurricular Activities

The U.S. Supreme Court stated in the 1969 case of *Tinker v. Des Moines Independent School District*[12] that ". . . children do not shed their constitutional rights . . . at the schoolhouse gate." That statement remains true today but under the "special needs" of government doctrine, elected school boards may, if they deem necessary, require random drug tests of not only student athletes but also of students participating in any extracurricular activities. The Supreme Court concluded in 2002 that ". . . We find that testing students who participate in extracurricular activities is a reasonably effective means of addressing the school district's legitimate concerns in preventing, deterring and detecting drug use."

Federal courts in the 1998 case of *Todd v. Rush County Schools*[13] held that school boards may require drug testing of any student who wanted to participate in any extracurricular activity. Without comment, the U.S. Supreme Court refused to hear the case and left standing the rule of the lower court. The following similar 2002 case was decided by the U.S. Supreme Court after oral arguments and many written briefs:

Board of Education of Pottawatomie County v. Earls
United States Supreme Court, 122 S. t. 2559 (2002)

Petitioners were students at a public high school run the by the respondent Board of Education. The Board passed a rule that required all students participating in extracurricular activities to submit to a urinalysis test for illegal drugs, and to submit to random testing during that participation. The petitioners objected to the drug testing rule, contending that it violated their Fourth Amendment rights because the tests were given without any level of "individualized suspicion." In rejecting that contention the Supreme Court described the "special needs" exception to the "particularized suspicion" usually required by the Fourth Amendment in normal criminal investigations:

> It is true that we generally determine the reasonableness of a search by balancing the nature of the intrusion on the individual's privacy against the promotion of legitimate governmental interests . . . But we have long held that "the Fourth Amendment imposes no irreducible requirement of [individualized] suspicion." "[I]n certain limited circumstances, the Government's need to discover such latent or hidden conditions, or to prevent their development, is sufficiently compelling to justify the intrusion on privacy entailed by conducting such searches without any measure of individualized suspicion." 122 S.Ct., at 2563-2564.

Ⓔ SEARCHES WITHOUT PROBABLE CAUSE OR SEARCH WARRANTS OF "CLOSELY REGULATED BUSINESSES"

The U.S. Supreme Court held that a "businessman, like the occupant of a residence, has a constitutional right to go about his business free from unreasonable official entries upon his private commercial property." *See v. City of Seattle*, 387 U.S. 541, 543, 87 S.Ct. 1737, 1739 (1967).

Search warrants, therefore, are generally required for the administrative searches of commercial properties. However, search warrants are not required for searches of "closely regulated" industries where courts have held that the owner's privacy interests are adequately protected by detailed state or federal laws that authorize inspections (searches) without warrants. The U.S. Supreme Court held in 1978 that "the closely regulated industry . . . is the exception, and ". . . when an entrepreneur embarks upon such a business, he has voluntarily chosen to subject himself to a full arsenal of governmental regulation."[14]

States and the federal government can address major social problems "both by way of an administrative scheme and through penal sanctions. . . . An administrative statute establishes how a particular business in a 'closely regulated' industry should be operated, setting forth rules to guide an operator's conduct of the business and allowing government officials (sometimes the police) to ensure that these rules are followed. Such a regulatory approach contrasts with that of the (criminal) laws, a major emphasis of which is the punishment of individuals for specific acts of behavior." (The U.S. Supreme Court in the 1987 case of *New York v. Burger*, 482 U.S. 691, 107 S.Ct. 2636.)

In the *Burger* case, the U.S. Supreme Court established the following three requirements needed to authorize inspections without search warrants of **closely regulated businesses:**

1. There must be a "substantial" government interest that informs the business operator of the "regulatory scheme" to which the inspection is to be made. For example, in the *Burger* case, the closely regulated industry was the junkyard business. These businesses are regulated because of the serious problem of stolen cars and stolen vehicle parts. Five police officers entered Burger's junkyard to inspect the junkyard as permitted by New York state law. Burger stated that he did not have a license, or records of vehicles he was required to have. The officers then found stolen cars and stolen vehicle parts. Burger was charged with the possession of stolen property. The New York law was found to be constitutional by the U.S. Supreme Court.

2. The inspection without a search warrant must be "necessary to further the regulatory scheme."

3. The regulatory law must perform the two basic functions of a search warrant: (a) it must advise the business owner that a search is to be made pursuant to the law: and (b) the law must limit the discretion of the inspecting officers.

Examples of industries that have "such a history of government oversight that no reasonable expectation of privacy . . . could exist for proprietors over the stock of such an enterprise" *Marshall v. Barlow's Inc.*, 436 U.S. at 313, 98 S.Ct. at 1821, include liquor

[*Colonnade Catering Corp. v. United States,* 397 U.S. 72, 90 S.Ct. 774 (1970)]; firearms [*United States v. Biswell,* 406 U.S. 311, 92 S.Ct. 1593 (1972)]; coal mines [*Donovan v. Dewey,* 452 U.S. 594, 101 S.Ct. 2534 (1981)]; pharmacies [*State v. Del City,* 947 F.2d 432 (10th Cir. 1991)]; horse racing [*State v. Williams,* 417 A.2d 1046 (N.J.1980)]; taverns [*State v. Rednor,* 497 A.2d 544 (N.J.1985)]; common carriers in trucking industry [*United States v. Dominguez-Prieto,* 923 F.2d 464 (6th Cir. 1991)]; and other businesses and industries regulated by specific state or federal statutes.

Ⓕ WORK-RELATED SEARCHES IN GOVERNMENT OFFICES (THE *ORTEGA* RULE)

Private employers may make **work-related searches** of employees' desks, files, and company-owned computers as they wish. This could be done if an employee is sick and another person is filling in for the absent employee. Or there could be suspicion that theft or fraud is occurring.

Should government supervisors have the same ability? The U.S. Supreme Court held that to require "the Government to procure a warrant for every work-related intrusion would conflict with 'the common-sense realization' that government offices could not function if every decision became a constitutional matter" *O'Connor v. Ortega.*[15]

Public supervisors have wide latitude to search public employee's offices, desks, and files without search warrants or probable cause to believe that the search will uncover evidence of wrongdoing. However, the Court noted that it would require greater justification to search personal items such as "a piece of closed personal luggage, a handbag or a briefcase that happens to be within the employer's business address."

Ⓖ ROADBLOCKS OR VEHICLE CHECKPOINT STOPS

Roadblocks and vehicle stops were used during the October 2002 sniper shootings in the Washington, D.C., area. Law officers aided by the military used the roadblocks in attempts to apprehend the snipers who killed ten people before they were apprehended.

If challenged regarding the roadblocks, the government would point to the very specific goal and purpose of the roadblocks, which were addressed to the "special needs" of the emergency situation.

Highway checkpoints are used in the United States for many reasons. There are weight and inspection checkpoints for trucks [*Delaware v. Prouse,* 440 U.S. 648, 663 no. 26, 99 S.Ct. 1391, 1401 n. 26 (1979)]; checkpoints to detect illegal aliens [*United States v. Martinez-Fuerte,* 428 U.S. 543, 96 S.Ct. 3074 (1976)]; checkpoints to check driver's licenses [*Texas v. Brown,* 460 U.S. 730, 103 S.Ct. 1535 (1983)]; checkpoints to check for drunk drivers [*Michigan State Police v. Sitz,* 496 U.S. 444, 110 S.Ct. 2481 (1990)]; and for other public safety reasons.

The U.S. Supreme Court affirmed the conviction and the use of evidence obtained in the drunk driver case of *Michigan State Police v. Sitz,*[16] holding that a "special government need" existed as "drunk drivers cause an annual death toll of over 25,000 and . . . nearly one million personal injuries and more than five billion dollars in property damage."

In the roadblock to check driver's licenses (*Texas v. Brown*),[17] the officer shined a flashlight into Brown's car and bent down at an angle where the officer saw loose white powder in small plastic vials and a green party balloon with white powder. The U.S. Supreme Court affirmed the use of the heroin as evidence obtained in a plain-view seizure and affirmed Brown's illegal drug conviction.

In the 2000 case of *City of Indianapolis v. Edmonds*,[18] the U.S. Supreme Court held that law officers may not simply set up roadblocks in high-crime neighborhoods as general crime-fighting procedures but must have an "immediate vehicle-bound threat to life and limb."

The Supreme Court held the stops were unconstitutional. The purpose of the checkpoint was not to deal with some special need like a particular hazard related to the checkpoint, such as drunk driving in the *Sitz* case, but rather the police's "general interest in crime control." The Court reasoned that if such checkpoints were permitted, then the police could set up a checkpoint to see if motorists were violating any criminal law.

The Court identified some of the circumstances where special needs would justify suspicionless highway stops. They include:

- Detecting drunk drivers
- Verifying driver's licenses and vehicle registration
- Intercepting illegal aliens on border highways
- Apprehending fleeing criminals
- Thwarting terrorist activity or attack

Ⓗ CORRECTIONAL PROGRAMS, HEARINGS, OR REQUIREMENTS THAT MAY CAUSE A PRISON INMATE TO INCRIMINATE HIMSELF

In 2002, the U.S. Supreme Court wrote of the seriousness of sexual assaults in the United States as follows: ". . . In 1995 an estimated 355,000 rapes and sexual assaults occurred nationwide . . . imprisoned sex offenders (have) increased at a faster rate than for any other category of violent crime . . . victims of sexual assault are most often juveniles . . . (n)early 4 in 10 violent sex offenders said their victims were 12 or younger . . . sex offenders (when released from prison) are much more likely than any other type of offender to be rearrested for a new rape or sexual assault. . . ." *McKune v. Lile*, 153 L Ed 2d at p. 56.

Because of the seriousness of this problem, Sexual Assault Treatment Programs (SATP) are in place in state and federal prisons in which inmates must disclose and accept responsibility for "the crimes for which they have been sentenced" and also "all prior sexual activities" whether lawful or whether "the activities constitute uncharged criminal offenses." The following SATP case came before the U.S. Supreme Court in 2002:

Case	Punishment If Inmate Refused to Disclose Uncharged Crimes	Ruling of the U.S. Supreme Court
McKune v. Lile 153 L Ed 2d 47 (2002)	Lile was convicted of the rape and sexual assault on a high school student. As an inmate in a Kansas prison, he challenged the Kansas SATP. Punishment for failure to comply in Kansas would be reduction and curtailment of visitation rights, earnings, work opportunity, access to television, sending money to family and purchases in the canteen. Lile would also be transferred to a potentially more dangerous maximum-security unit.	"Acceptance of responsibility is the beginning of rehabilitation . . . "The Kansas SATP represents a sensible approach to reducing the serious danger that repeat offenders pose to many innocent persons, most often children." (The fact that Kansas does not offer legal immunity from prosecution for disclosures does not render the Kansas SATP invalid.)

Other Requirements or Hearings

Minnesota v. Murphy 104 S.Ct. 1136 (1984)	As a condition of probation defendant agreed to be truthful with his probation officer in all matters. Because defendant feared being returned for 16 months if he remained silent, defendant confessed to a rape and murder. Murphy was tried and convicted for these crimes.	Murphy obtained probation from prison by agreeing in writing to be truthful with his probation officer. Convictions for rape and murder were affirmed.
Ohio Adult Parole Authority v. Woodard, 118 S.Ct. 1244 (1998)	A death row inmate at his voluntary clemency interview chose to incriminate himself rather than be silent and cause "the clemency board (to) construe that silence against him."	The defendant faced "a choice quite similar to the sorts of choices that a criminal defendant must make in the course of criminal proceedings, none of which has ever been held to violate the Fifth Amendment." The Court held it was not an unconstitutional compulsion.
Baxter v. Palmigiano, 96 S.Ct. 1551 (1976)	A state prisoner objected to the fact that his silence at a prison disciplinary hearing would be held against him. The prisoner faced 30 days in punitive segregation. The Supreme Court held the disciplinary board could draw an inference of guilt from the prisoner's silence.	Prison disciplinary hearings "involve the correctional process and important state interests" and are unlike a criminal trial where a jury is forbidden from drawing an inference of guilt from a defendant's failure to testify.

❶ OTHER "SPECIAL GOVERNMENT NEEDS" WHERE NEITHER PROBABLE CAUSE NOR SEARCH WARRANTS ARE NEEDED

The need to supervise persons on probation and parole closely. *Griffin v. Wisconsin,* U.S. Supreme Court 483 U.S. 868, 107 S.Ct. 3164 (1987)

In the *Griffin* case, the U.S. Supreme Court upheld the search by a probation officer under a Wisconsin statute that authorized such searches on the basis of reasonable suspicion. The Supreme Court held that the "special needs of the probation system requires the need to supervise persons on probation and parole closely.

Not only do many states have such statutes, but it is also a common practice to include consent to search sections in parole and probation agreements, which persons being placed on parole or probation must sign to receive such status.

Illegal aliens. *United States v. Martinez-Fuerte,* U.S. Supreme Court 428 U.S. 543, 96 S.Ct. 3078 (1976)

In permitting checkpoints for illegal aliens, the U.S. Supreme Court held that "requiring particularized suspicion before routine stops on major highways near the Mexican border would be impractical because the flow of traffic tends to be too heavy to allow the particularized study of a given car that would enable it to be identified as a possible carrier of illegal aliens." 428 U.S. at 557, 96 S.Ct. at 3082, and 489 U.S. at 668, 109 S.Ct. at 1392.

Safety in jails and prisons. *Bell v. Wolfish,* U.S. Supreme Court 441 U.S. 520. 99 S.Ct. 1861 (1979)

As persons in jails and prisons have a reduced right to privacy, they are subject to random searches for weapons and contraband without any showing of suspicion. In the case of *Bell v. Wolfish,* the U.S. Supreme Court held that visual body cavity searches may be made of inmates to find weapons and drugs and to maintain safety in jails and prisons.

Obtaining Evidence In Foreign Countries

Sometimes evidence of serious crimes about to be committed (or being committed) in the United States becomes available in foreign countries (including Mexico or Canada). The general rules for the admissibility of such evidence in American courts was presented in the *FBI Law Enforcement Bulletin* of July 2002 entitled, "Investigating International Terrorism Overseas: Constitutional Considerations." The general rules stated by article are:

- When law officers in the foreign country acting alone and independently obtain the evidence, the FBI article states: "Generally, American legal standards do not apply to the seizure of evidence . . . where a foreign country is conducting the investigation independently and seizes evidence that is later introduced into an American court."[a]

- "If American investigators are acting alone in seeking to obtain evidence in a foreign country, they should always comply with the laws of that country and should conduct their investigation as if they were operating in the United States."

- "When American investigators are working jointly with foreign officials, they should remember that searches or interrogations . . . will invoke (American) constitutional protections on the part of the subject (of the search or interrogation)."

Another way of obtaining evidence from foreign countries is through the use of Mutual Legal Assistance Treaties (MLAT), which the United States signed with thirty-four countries including Canada and Mexico. If an MLAT does not exist, authority may be requested from a federal court to request the assistance of officials in a foreign country to obtain evidence. This is called a "letter rogatory." Subpoenas could also be issued on persons or corporations in the United States who have constructive possession of evidence located in foreign countries.[b]

[a]American courts would refuse to use evidence obtained by foreign government officials if the conduct of the foreign officials in obtaining the evidence shocked the conscience of the U.S. court. See the case of *United States v. Callaway*, 446 F. 2d 753 (3rd Cir., 1971), where Canadian police who were not acting in connection or cooperation with American law enforcement officials obtained criminal evidence that was used to convict Callaway in a New Jersey court. As the actions of the Canadian police were not so outrageous as to shock the conscience of the trial court, the evidence was admitted, and Callaway's conviction was affirmed.

[b]The U.S. Supreme Court ruled in the 1999 case of *Flippo v. West Virginia*, 120 S.Ct. 7, that American courts do not have the authority to issue search warrants authorizing searches in foreign countries.

SUMMARY

Local, state, and federal governments provide many services that are not related to criminal investigations. Many of these are routine administrative functions. The U.S. Supreme Court and other courts have held that the Fourth Amendment requirement of "reasonableness" has to be viewed differently "when analyzing the reasonableness of routine administrative functions" (489 U.S. 656, 668).

Evidence that is obtained in any of the administrative functions presented in this chapter is admissible evidence if the guidelines established by law or the courts have been complied with.

The "special needs" of government are needs of safety, health, education, and concern for the well-being of the society as a whole.

PROBLEMS

1. In the *Vernonia* and *Earls* cases discussed in this chapter, the Supreme Court upheld suspicionless drug testing of public high school students engaged in extra-curricular activities. Would the "special needs" identified by the Court in those cases justify a similar drug-testing policy for public school employees? For a custodian at an elementary school? See *Aubrey v. School Board of Lafayette Parish,* 148 F.3d 559 (5th Cir., 1998).

2. The Michigan Welfare Department concluded that the principal obstacle to getting people off the welfare roles and into the workforce was substance abuse. It therefore instituted a program authorizing department employees to require suspicionless drug tests of persons enrolled in welfare programs. (The testing program was permitted but not required under Federal Welfare Statutes.) The results of such tests were not given to police, but a recipient who failed to participate in substance abuse treatment programs was disqualified from receiving welfare benefits. Is the Michigan testing program constitutional? See *Marchwinski v. Howard,* 113 F.Supp.2d. 1134 (E.D. Mich., 2000).

3. An airline ticket agent became concerned about the contents of a passenger's checked luggage when the passenger refused to consent to a search of carry-on luggage and then brought the carry-on luggage to the counter to be checked.

The ticket agent summoned a police officer, and in his presence began searching the luggage. In the process of that search the police officer reached around the agent and took a wrapped bag out of the luggage. The bag contained illegal drugs, and the passenger was charged with illegal possession of cocaine. At his trial he moved to suppress the evidence because the search of his luggage occurred without a search warrant in violation of the Fourth Amendment. Should the evidence be suppressed? Does it matter that the agent, if left on her own, would have found the cocaine? See *United States v. Hernandez-Cano,* 808 F.2d 779 (11th Cir., 1987).

4. While driving on an interstate highway, defendant saw a sign stating "drug checkpoint ahead." To avoid the "checkpoint" defendant exited the interstate. While doing so he saw police cars at the end of the exit. His passenger threw a bag containing drugs out of the car, but officers hiding along the exit saw her do so and found the bag, which contained illegal drugs. The "checkpoint" was a ruse. At his trial defendant moved to suppress the evidence of illegal drugs, contending the search was illegal under *City of Indianapolis v. Edmonds,* 531 U.S. 32 (2000). Should the evidence be suppressed? What is the best argument for the prosecution? See *United States v. Flynn,* 309 F.3d 736 (10th Cir., 2002).

INFOTRAC COLLEGE EDITION EXERCISES

1. Go to InfoTrac College Edition and using the search term "roadside sobriety tests" find the 2003 article in the *FBI Law Enforcement Bulletin* titled "Battling DUI: A Comparative Analysis of Checkpoints and Saturation Patrols," by Jeffery Greene. This article reviews arrests for DUI from both sobriety checkpoints and saturation patrols in areas where extensive driving under the influence of alcohol is found. The correlation between such checkpoints and saturation patrols and traffic fatalities is also shown.

2. Go to InfoTrac College Edition and using search term "airport security" and the subdivision "analysis" find the 2002 article in *Insight on the News* titled "Losing the War for Civil Libertarians . . . ," by Kelly Patricia O'Meara. Civil libertarians on both the political right (including this periodical) and the left (such as the American Civil Liberties Union) have condemned the USA Patriot Act passed after the events of September 11. This article lists some of these groups' grievances with the act. How do you regard their concerns? Real? Imagined?

NOTES

1. *National Treasury Employee Union v. Von Raab,* 489 U.S. 656, 668, and *Colorado v. Bertine,* 479 U.S. 367, 371.

2. *People v. Heimel,* 812 P.2d 1177 (1991). For similar rulings, see *State v. Plante,* 594 A.2d 165 (N.H. 1991) and *United States v. Vigil,* 989 F.2d 337 (9th Cir. 1993).

3. *Klarfeld v. United States* (9th Cir., 1992) 962 F. 2d 866.

4. *Frank v. Maryland,* 359 U.S. 360.

5. *Camara v. Municipal Court,* 387 U.S. 523 (1967).

6. 387 U.S. 541 (1967).

7. *New Jersey v. T.L.O.,* 469 U.S. 340 at 340 (1985).

8. 489 U.S. 656.

9. 489 U.S. 602.

10. Not all courts go along with the reasoning in the U.S. Supreme Court *Von Raub* decision. In the 1991 case of *Guiney v. Police Commissioner of Boston,* 582 N.E.2d 523, the Massachusetts Supreme Judicial Court held that "unannounced, warrantless, suspicionless, random" urinalysis testing of Boson police officers violated the Masschusetts constitution even if permitted under the U.S. Constitution.

11. 115 S.Ct. 2386 (1995).

12. 393 U.S. 503 (1969).

13. No. 97–2021 (1998).

14. *Marshall v. Barlow's Inc.,* 436 U.S. 307 (1978).

15. 480 U.S. 709 (1987).

16. 496 U.S. 444 (1990).

17. 460 U.S. 730 (1983).

18. 531 U.S. 32 (2000).

12

Obtaining Statements and Confessions for Use as Evidence

A confession is like no other evidence. Indeed, the defendant's own confession is probably the most probative and damaging evidence that can be admitted against him . . . [T]he admissions of a defendant come from the actor himself, the most knowledgeable and unimpeachable source of information about his past conduct.[1]

These words by U.S. Supreme Court Justice White underscore both the evidentiary value and risk associated with **confessions** and **incriminating statements.**[2] If true, confessions are the best evidence of guilt. On the other hand, if untrue and given by the defendant because of coercion or pressure, confessions carry a high risk of misleading the jury.

For those and other reasons, the law governing the use of confessions and incriminating statements in criminal trials has a long and complex history. In many respects, it is still developing. In this chapter we explore some of those developments.

Ⓐ CAN A CONFESSION ALONE SUSTAIN A CRIMINAL CONVICTION?

The Corpus Delicti Rule

Frank Connelly approached a police officer on a Denver street and confessed to a murder.[3] If the police could find no other evidence of the murder, could Connelly be charged and convicted of a murder solely on the basis of his confession? The answer is no, because a confession alone will not sustain a conviction.

In using a confession as evidence, corroborating evidence must also be provided to prove **corpus delicti** (that the crime was committed). This requirement originated in England and, as the Supreme Court of California pointed out in 1991, was used "to protect the defendant against the possibility of fabricated testimony which might wrongfully establish the crime and the perpetrator."[4]

In the 1991 case of *People v. Jennings,* the defendant bragged to persons on how he would pick up prostitutes, pay them for sex, and then later kill them and take their money before burying the bodies. The state of California produced evidence corroborating the confessions to three murders and other felonies such as kidnapping and robberies of the women. In affirming the convictions and death penalty in the *Jennings* case, the Supreme Court of California quoted another court in sustaining the corpus delicti rule holding:

> As one court explained, "Today's judicial retention of the rule reflects the continued fear that confessions may be the result of either improper police activity or the mental instability of the accused, and the recognition that juries are likely to accept confessions uncritically." [*Jones v. Superior Court,* (1979) 96 Cal.App.3d 390, 397, 157 Cal.Rptr. 809.]
>
> Viewed with this in mind, the low threshold that must be met before a defendant's own statements can be admitted against him makes sense; so long as there is some indication that the charged crime actually happened, we are satisfied that the accused is not admitting to a crime that never occurred.

Other examples illustrate that confessions must be corroborated by proof of corpus delicti:

- In 1988 Marty James appeared on the ABC *Nightline* show and admitted that he had helped a friend with AIDS commit suicide. After questioning by reporters a day later, James stated that he assisted at least eight men with AIDS commit suicide. Relatives of the men accused James of murder, but prosecutors stated that investigations did not turn up evidence to corroborate James's confessions. Because the corpus delicti rule could not be satisfied, criminal charges could not be filed against James. (Marty James was suffering from AIDS himself and died of an overdose of sleeping pills in 1992.)[5]

- The defendant's conviction for first-degree sexual assault was reversed in *State v. Torwirt*.[6] The defendant stated in recorded phone conversations with a friend and with a police officer that she touched and placed her lips on the genital area of a 3-year-old child she was babysitting. Because no physical evidence of the touching could be shown and no other corroboration existed, the Nebraska Court of Appeals held in 2000 that the confession alone could not support conviction.

- Proof of corpus delicti was presented to sustain confessions in the following cases: armed robbery,[7] embezzlement,[8] drug use by military personnel,[9] and manslaughter.[10]

B THE REQUIREMENT THAT CONFESSIONS AND INCRIMINATING STATEMENTS BE VOLUNTARY

In fifteenth-century England, confessions to crimes were often obtained by courts and law officers by torture and violence. These abuses caused the English courts to create the concept that "no man is bound to accuse himself" (*nemo tenetur prodere*). This maxim meant that persons ought not to be put on trial for a crime and compelled to answer incriminating questions until after they had been properly accused by a grand jury.

To protect against the historic abuses that occurred in England, Europe, and colonial United States, the Fifth Amendment of the U.S. Constitution adopted in 1791 requires that no person "... shall be compelled in a criminal case to be a witness against himself, nor be deprived of life, liberty, or property, without due process of law...."

It has never been held that interrogations by police are *per se* unconstitutional. However the **voluntariness test** used today requires that confessions and admissions by a suspect must be voluntarily and freely given. If the police or a prosecutor obtain a confession or an incriminating admission by means that overbears the will of the accused, that statement or confession cannot be used as evidence, on the grounds that it is a denial of the Fifth and Fourteenth Amendment requirements of due process of law.

Using Violence to Obtain Confessions

Until 1936, each state established its own voluntariness test and determined for itself what "due process of law" meant within that state. In the following important U.S. Supreme Court case, the U.S. Supreme Court reversed murder convictions in the State of Mississippi and, in a strongly worded decision, held that the confessions used as evidence were involuntarily obtained.

Brown v. Mississippi[11]
United States Supreme Court, 297 U.S. 278, 56 S.Ct. 461 (1936)

When a murder occurred in Mississippi in 1934, the defendants, three black men, were taken into custody by law enforcement officers. By means of whippings, beatings, and the actual hanging of one of the defendants by a rope to the limb of a tree, confessions to the murder were obtained from the defendants. With practically no other evidence and with the rope mark "plainly visible" on the neck of the defendant who was hanged, the criminal trial charging the defendants of murder began. The defendants were convicted despite the fact that a state witness (a deputy sheriff) admitted that brutality and violence were used to obtain the confessions. In reversing the convictions, the U.S. Supreme Court held that:

> The question in this case is whether convictions, which rest solely upon confessions shown to have been extorted by officers of the state by brutality and violence, are consistent with the due process of law required by the Fourteenth Amendment of the Constitution of the United States.
>
> . . . The rack and torture chamber may not be substituted for the witness stand.
>
> . . . In the instant case, the trial court was fully advised by the undisputed evidence of the way in which the confessions had been procured. The trial court knew that there was no other evidence upon which conviction and sentence could be based. Yet it proceeded to permit conviction and to pronounce sentence. The conviction and sentence were void for want of the essential elements of due process, and the proceeding thus vitiated could be challenged in any appropriate manner.

The Totality-of-the-Circumstances Test Used to Determine Whether a Confession or Statement Is Voluntary

Confessions and statements can be involuntarily obtained from a suspect not only by torture and violence but by many other means. For example, if a confession was obtained by withholding food, heat, clothing, or other essentials of life from a prisoner, courts would refuse to allow the confession to be used as evidence because it was involuntarily induced and would be a violation of due process.

Defendants in criminal cases can be convicted only on reliable, relevant evidence. To be admissible as evidence, confessions and statements must be made voluntarily and freely. If the police obtain a confession or admission by means that overbear the will of the accused, the statement or confession will not be admitted for use as evidence on grounds that a denial of due process of law occurred.

In determining whether a confession or a statement may be used as evidence, courts use the **totality-of-the-circumstances test.** In looking at the "whole picture" (totality of the circumstances), all of the following factors are considered:

Why Did Five Teenagers Confess to a Rape That Evidence Now Shows They Did Not Commit?

In 1989 a woman jogger was beaten, raped, and left for dead in New York's Central Park. A series of assaults and robberies had occurred in the park that evening. News media throughout the United States reported the shocking events that occurred.

New York police picked up five 14- and 15-year-old youths from Harlem who admitted to kicking and fondling the jogger and beating her with a pipe. None admitted to personally committing the rape itself, but they did incriminate one another.

Based primarily on five videotaped and written confessions, the five teenagers were convicted and sentenced in two jury trials for the beating and rape of the woman.

In January 2002, a serial rapist and murderer confessed that he alone had raped the woman jogger in Central Park. His confession was backed by a DNA match. This led to a reexamination of the evidence obtained to convict the five teenagers in 1989.

The new evidence was submitted to a court along with a report that stated that a reconstruction of the events that occurred suggest that the five youths could not have raped the jogger be-cause they were elsewhere in the park—assaulting, robbing, and harassing joggers, bikers, and other persons. One of the youths had used the term *wilding* to describe their conduct.

In December 2002, the convictions were vacated for the five young men who had already completed their prison terms and were back in civilian life. Questions were asked about how this could have happened.

At first, the police were faulted. But investigators and videotapes showed that the police had used lawful procedures in questioning the youths. Different investigative panels came up with different theories as to what had occurred in New York's Central Park that night.

Two different trial judges and two juries found the confessions to be voluntary and reliable. All of the teenagers had been vigorously represented by competent defense lawyers, who had challenged the confessions and other evidence at pretrial hearings and during the criminal trials. There have been no reports of civil lawsuits, and in view of the findings of the different panels, it does not appear that any civil lawsuits will be filed.

- *Suspect vulnerabilities:* Age (very young or very old), education, mental impairment, or physical condition that could make the suspect vulnerable. Was the suspect an alcoholic, a drug addict, or chain smoker in need of a cigarette, a drink, or a fix?

- *Interrogating factors:* Did the questioning overbear the will of the accused? (Length of questioning; number of officers; time of day or night; denial of food, water, heat, sleep, or other basic necessities?)

- *Place of questioning:* Was questioning done in an isolated area of a police station, or did it occur in the suspect's home or office or in a public place?

- *Use of the following:* Were any (1) threats, (2) promises, (3) deception, lies, or trickery used?

Hundreds of state and federal court cases address the question of when lies, threats, promises, deceits, or trickery could cause a confession to be held to be involuntary. Some of the *FBI Law Enforcement Bulletin* articles reviewing this area of the law are: "Magic Words to Obtain Confessions" and "Conducting Successful Interrogations" (October 1998); "Ensuring Officer Integrity and Accountability" (August 1998); and "Lies, Promises, or Threats: The Voluntariness of Confessions" (July 1993).

ⓒ THE *MIRANDA* REQUIREMENTS

For many years, the voluntariness test was the only test used to determine the admissibility of confessions and statements as evidence. In 1966, the U.S. Supreme Court added a new requirement to be used in addition to the voluntariness requirement.

In the 1966 case of *Miranda v. Arizona*,[12] the U.S. Supreme Court made the admissibility of confessions and statements turn not only on a finding of volunariness, but also on proof by a prosecutor that procedural safeguards were complied with. In the case of *Miranda v. Arizona*, the U.S. Supreme Court ruled that:

> The prosecution may not use statements, whether exculpatory or inculpatory, stemming from custodial interrogation of the defendant unless it demonstrates the use of procedural safeguards effective to secure the privilege against self-incrimination.

The well-known ***Miranda* requirements** were established by the U.S. Supreme Court as part of the procedural safeguards. The *Miranda* requirements are that: (1) the suspect must be told of his right to remain silent; (2) that anything he says may be used against him in a court of law; (3) that he is entitled to the presence of an attorney; and (4) if he cannot afford an attorney one will be appointed to represent him.

The *Miranda* requirements do not have to be complied with unless the following two conditions exist:

- The suspect must be in custody (custody is defined as "the functional equivalent of formal arrest").
- A government official (police, sheriff, and so on) seeks to interrogate the suspect as to his (or her) suspected criminal conduct ("questioning initiated by a law enforcement officer after a person has been taken into custody or otherwise deprived of his freedom of action in any significant way").

When a prosecutor seeks to use statements as evidence, which are the product of custodial interrogation, the prosecutor must demonstrate the following procedural safeguards in order to have the statements used as evidence:

- Sufficient and adequate warnings were given to the suspect.
- The suspect understood the warnings.
- The suspect waived his (or her) rights to remain silent and to have an attorney present during the questioning.

When *Miranda* Warnings Are Not Required

1. *Miranda* warnings are not required if the person is not in custody, or if a suspect is in custody and there is no intention or effort by a law officer to interrogate the suspect as to the crime for which the suspect has been arrested.

Some police and sheriff departments require that *Miranda* warnings be given after every arrest. This, then, would be a requirement of that department or within that state, but the U.S. Supreme Court does not require *Miranda* warning under these circumstances.

2. *Miranda* is not required when a person volunteers information. The U.S. Supreme Court held that "There is no requirement that police stop a person who enters a police station and states that he wishes to confess to a crime, or a person who calls the police to offer a confession or any other statement he desires to make. Volunteered statements of any kind are not barred by the Fifth Amendment and their admissibility is not affected by our holding today."[13] As an example, a deputy sheriff asked a prisoner awaiting trial, "How's it going, Ashford?" Ashford answered with a statement that incriminated him. The court held that the deputy could testify about Ashford's incriminating statement.[14]

   Other examples of volunteered statements include the cases in which the defendant surprised everyone by admitting while he was on the witness stand that he killed the victim;[15] the defendant walked into a police station and told the police that he had shot his wife;[16] and the defendant voluntarily stated he had a gun under the front seat of his automobile.[17]

   The Maryland Court of Appeals pointed out that there is no privilege against inadvertent self-incrimination, or even stupid self-incrimination, but only against self-incrimination.[18] In that case, the defendant blurted out he had a lot of illegal drugs in his car.

3. "*General on-the-scene questioning* as to facts surrounding a crime or other general questioning of citizens in the fact-finding process is not affected by our holding. It is an act of responsible citizenship for individuals to give whatever information they may have to aid in law enforcement. In such situations the compelling atmosphere inherent in the process of in-custody interrogation is not necessarily present."[19] Consider the following examples:

   - When a deputy sheriff working in a jail saw one of two men held in a drunk tank lying on the floor in a pool of blood, he asked the other man sleeping on a wall bench, "What happened?" The man answered, "I killed the son of a bitch last night; he would not shut up." The Supreme Court of Utah held that the defendant's response was properly admitted in evidence.[20]

   - Minutes after a shooting occurred on a street, a police officer arrived at the scene. A young boy at the scene told the officer that the assailant had run away between two houses. The officer proceeded in that direction and saw a man step out of a doorway. The officer (who had his revolver out) asked the man if he had been involved in the shooting. The man answered, "Yeh, I shot him." After the man was arrested, the murder weapon was found in his pocket. The statement of the defendant and the weapon were held to be properly admitted in evidence by the Wisconsin Supreme Court.[21]

   - In investigating crimes, peace officers are required to ask questions and talk to persons who are *material witnesses* to crimes. In some instances, the investigation could reveal that a material witness is the person who committed the crime. In the 1991 case of *Wallace v. State*,[22] it was held that an officer called to a store to investigate a forged check was not obligated to give *Miranda* warnings to Wallace, who was viewed as a material witness when questioned.

4. *Miranda* is not required for investigative detentions (stop and inquiry) based upon reasonable suspicion to believe that the person is committing, has committed, or is about to commit a crime. In 1984, the U.S. Supreme Court stated this rule again as follows:[23]

Under the Fourth Amendment, we have held, a policeman who lacks probable cause but whose "observations lead him reasonably to suspect" that a particular person has committed, is committing, or is about to commit a crime, may detain that person briefly in order to "investigate the circumstances that provoke suspicion." *United States v. Brignoni-Ponce,* 422 U.S. 873, 881, 45 L.Ed.2d 607, 95 S.Ct. 2574 (1975). "[T]he stop and inquiry must be 'reasonably related in scope to the justification for their initiation.'" Ibid. [quoting *Terry v. Ohio,* supra, at 29, 20 L.Ed.2d 889, 88 S.Ct. 1868). Typically, this means that the officer may ask the detainee a moderate number of questions to determine his identity and to try to obtain information confirming or dispelling the officer's suspicions. But the detainee is not obliged to respond. And, unless the detainee's answers provide the officer with probable cause to arrest him, he must then be released. The comparatively nonthreatening character of detentions of this sort explains the absence of any suggestion in our opinions that *Terry* stops are subject to the dictates of *Miranda.*

5. *Miranda* is not required in "ordinary traffic stops." The U.S. Supreme Court ruled in the 1984 case of *Berkemer v. McCarty*[24] that both the investigative stop and a traffic stop are similar in that both have "noncoercive aspect(s)," with traffic stops usually being temporary, brief, and public. The Court ruled that "persons temporarily detained pursuant to (traffic) stops are not 'in custody' for the purposes of *Miranda.*" The reasons for this ruling were explained as follows by the U.S. Supreme Court:

Two features of an ordinary traffic stop mitigate the danger that a person questioned will be induced "to speak where he would not otherwise do so freely," *Miranda v. Arizona,* . . . First, detention of a motorist pursuant to a traffic stop is presumptively temporary and brief. The vast majority of roadside detentions last only a few minutes. A motorist's expectations, when he sees a policeman's light flashing behind him, are that he will be obliged to spend a short period of time answering questions and waiting while the officer checks his license and registration, that he may then be given a citation, but that in the end he most likely will be allowed to continue on his way. In this respect, questioning incident to an ordinary traffic stop is quite different from stationhouse interrogation, which frequently is prolonged, and in which the detainee often is aware that questioning will continue until he provides his interrogators the answers they seek.

Second, circumstances associated with the typical traffic stop are not such that the motorist feels completely at the mercy of the police. To be sure, the aura of authority surrounding an armed, uniformed officer and the knowledge that the officer has some discretion in deciding whether to issue a citation, in combination, exert some pressure on the detainee to respond to questions. But other aspects of the situation substantially offset these forces. Perhaps most importantly, the typical traffic stop is public, at least to some degree. Passersby, on foot or in other cars, witness the interaction of officer and motorist. This exposure to public view both reduces the ability of an unscrupulous policeman to use illegitimate means to elicit self-incriminating statements and diminishes the motorist's fear that, if he does not cooperate, he will be subjected to abuse. The fact that the detained motorist typically is confronted by only one or at most two policemen further mutes his sense of vulnerability. In short, the atmosphere surrounding an ordinary traffic stop is substantially less "police dominated" than that surrounding the kinds of interrogation at issue in *Miranda* itself, and in the subsequent cases in which we have applied *Miranda*.

However, if a motorist (or a passenger in a vehicle) is arrested or taken into custody, *Miranda* becomes applicable. In the *Berkemer v. McCarty* case, the defendant should have been given the *Miranda* warnings after his arrest for drunken driving and before police interrogation after his arrest.

6. Routine booking questions are exempt from *Miranda's* coverage. In the 1990 case of *Pennsylvania v. Muniz*,[25] the U.S. Supreme Court held that questions and answers as to "name, address, height, weight, eye color, date of birth, and current age—did not constitute custodial interrogation . . . (and) fall within a *routine booking question exception,* which exempts from *Miranda's* coverage questions to secure the 'biographical data necessary to complete booking or pretrial service' 873 F.2d 180, 181 n.2." The U.S. Supreme Court pointed out with approval that the trial court in the *Muniz* case held that these questions were "requested for record-keeping purposes only" and therefore "appear reasonably related to the police's administrative concerns."

Booking questions about employment are also routinely asked and were sustained in the 1991 case of *People v. Abdelmassih*.[26] In the 1991 case of *State v. Mallozzi*,[27] the defendant made incriminating statements during the booking process after an FBI agent informed him of the charges against him. Because no questions other than routine booking questions were asked, the defendant's statements were admissible in evidence against him.

7. The *Miranda* warnings are not imposed upon private persons who ask questions. For example, a family member asks "Why did you do it, Joe?" Or an employer or other private person asks questions that could produce incriminating answer. Since *Miranda* is not required of private persons, any incriminating statement could be admitted as evidence in both civil and criminal cases. The following cases further illustrate:

   - A shoplifter made incriminating statements in response to questions from a store clerk. The Georgia Court of Appeals held *Miranda* is applicable only to law enforcement officers; the store clerk was not required to give the *Miranda* warnings before questioning.[28]

   - A journalist gathering material for a book visited John Joubert in a Nebraska prison where Joubert was sentenced to death. Joubert made statements incriminating him in the death of an 11-year-old boy in Maine. The Supreme Court of Maine held the admissions were admissible because the journalist

Can the U.S. Congress Overturn *Miranda*?

Two years after the *Miranda* decision, opponents to the *Miranda* rule attached a provision to a bill that overturned *Miranda* when it became law. The 1968 enactment provided that if a confession or incriminating statement was voluntary, the confession or statement should be admitted as evidence in federal criminal cases whether *Miranda* had been complied with or not.

U.S. presidents for more than thirty years instructed the Justice Department to ignore 18 U.S.C. Section 3501 until 1999 when a federal appeals court in Richmond, Virginia, ruled in the case of *Dickerson v. United States* that the U.S. Congress was free to overturn *Miranda* and had done so in Section 3501.

In the *Dickerson* case, Dickerson's incrimination statements as to his involvement in a bank robbery were suppressed because *Miranda* warning had not been given to Dickerson. The federal court of appeals in Virginia ruled that as the statements were voluntary, they were admissible under Section 3501. The U.S. Supreme Court reversed, holding the statements were not admissible and held in the case of *Dickerson v. United States,* 530 U.S. 428 (2000), that the *Miranda* doctrine could not be overruled by the U.S. Congress, holding:

> . . . *Miranda* has become embedded in routine police practices [in the United States] to the point where the warnings have become part of our national culture . . .

. . . we conclude that *Miranda* announced a constitutional rule that Congress may not supersede legislatively.

Does the Police Procedure in the Following Case Do An "End Run" Around *Miranda*?

In the 1985 case of *Oregon v. Elstad,* 470 U.S. 298, police inadvertently failed to give the *Miranda* warnings. After the defendant confessed (the "cat was out of the bag"), the police then complied with the *Miranda* rule, and the defendant confessed again. The U.S. Supreme Court held that as both confessions were voluntarily made, the second confession was admissible as evidence and affirmed the defendant's conviction.

In the 2003 case of *Missouri v. Seibert,* 123 S. Ct. 2041, now before the U.S. Supreme Court, the police deliberately failed to give the *Miranda* warnings to a woman suspected of arson. After Ms. Seibert confessed to the arson, the police turned on a tape recorder and complied with the *Miranda* rule, reminding the defendant of her incriminating statements.

Because the police admitted to routinely using this two-step interrogation technique in an effort to obtain confessions and incriminating statements, the Missouri Supreme Court reversed Ms. Seibert's conviction, calling the procedure an "end run" around *Miranda*. The case is now before the U.S. Supreme Court, and as of this writing, a ruling has not been handed down.

was not acting as an agent of the police. No *Miranda* warnings were given or required.[29]

- Most courts hold that private security officers do not come under the *Miranda* requirements. The state of New York courts held:

To hold that the conduct of [a] private store detective was governed by *Miranda* would be an extravagant expansion of the intended scope of that decision, and would constitute an unnecessary and unauthorized interference with the right of a merchant to protect his property by lawful means. *Id.* at 287, 480 N.W.2d at 1068, 491 N.Y.S.2d at 285. The duty of giving "*Miranda* warnings" is limited to employees of governmental agencies whose function is to enforce the law, or to those acting for such law enforcement agencies by direction of the agencies; . . .

In also holding that *Miranda* does not apply to private security persons, the Virginia Court of Appeals reviewed state court cases with similar rulings in the 1991 case of *Mier v. Commonwealth.*[30]

8. The *Miranda* requirements have been held *not* to be applicable in the following cases:

- To offenders (sexual and other offenses) who are required by conditions of their probation or parole to participate in treatment programs and be truthful "in all matters" or risk revocation of their parole or probation: In the 1984 case of *Minnesota v. Murphy,*[31] Murphy was in such a program and confessed to an unsolved rape and murder. The U.S. Supreme Court held his admissions could be used to sustain his conviction.

- Undercover officers conducting investigations while not disclosing their true identity do not have to give *Miranda* warnings and do not have to identify themselves. See the 1990 case of *Illinois v. Perkins,*[32] where an undercover officer went into a prison cell, and the 1966 case of *Hoffa v. United States,*[33] where an undercover agent was obtaining information against former Teamster Union President James Hoffa.

- When a probation or parole officer is doing a presentence interview on behalf of the trial court, it has been repeatedly held that *Miranda* is not applicable.[34]

The Public Safety Exception and the Rescue Doctrine as Exceptions to *Miranda* Requirements

The *Miranda* requirements must be complied with if answers to police questions are to be admitted into evidence in criminal cases. The following two exceptions permit police questioning before *Miranda* warning are given:

THE PUBLIC SAFETY EXCEPTION The *public safety exception* was established by the U.S. Supreme Court in the 1984 case of *New York v. Quarles,*[35] In that case, an armed rapist was fleeing police in New York City. The man fled to an A&P supermarket, carrying a gun. He hid the gun somewhere in the store before being captured by police officers. After the man was handcuffed, he was asked where the gun was, without being given the *Miranda* warnings. The suspect (Quarles) nodded in the direction of some empty cartons and answered, "the gun is over there." In addition to rape, Quarles was convicted of criminal possession of a weapon. The weapon and the statement by Quarles were used as evidence against him. In affirming the convictions and creating the public safety exception to *Miranda,* the U.S. Supreme Court held:

> . . . The exception will not be difficult for police officers to apply because in each case it will be circumscribed by the exigency which justifies it. We think police officers can and will distinguish almost instinctively between questions necessary to secure their own safety or the safety of the public and questions designed solely to elicit testimonial evidence from a suspect.

Ernesto Miranda leaving court. Miranda was the defendant in a rape case from which the Miranda *warnings developed. In 1963 Miranda was charged with rape and armed robbery. (He was not charged and convicted of kidnapping, which he should have been because he transported the victim some distance.) He confessed to the crimes during a police interrogation in which he was not informed that he had a right to have an attorney present or that anything he said could be used against him in court. Although subsequently convicted, he successfully appealed to the U.S. Supreme Court, which overturned his conviction and established the* Miranda *warning to guard a citizen's right to protection against self-incrimination.*

Bettmann/Corbis

The facts of this case clearly demonstrate that distinction and an officer's ability to recognize it. Officer Kraft asked only the question necessary to locate the missing gun before advising respondent of his rights. It was only after securing the loaded revolver and giving the warnings that he continued with investigatory questions about the ownership and place of purchase of the gun. The exception which we recognize today, far from complicating the thought processes and the on-the-scene judgments of police officers, will simply free them to follow their legitimate instincts when confronting situations presenting a danger to the public safety.

OTHER CASES CONCERNING PUBLIC SAFETY The public safety exception to *Miranda* has been used many times since it was created in 1984. Following are a few of the many cases where it was held that police questions before giving suspects *Miranda* warnings were prompted by a concern for public safety:

- A man suspected of stealing vials of freeze-dried bacteria that could cause bubonic plague was questioned about the location of the vials.[36]
- Prior to executing search warrants for illegal drugs, defendants were asked if they had weapons.[37]
- Police arriving on an emergency call for help asked White what had happened. White stated he cut his girlfriend's throat.[38]
- Police questions about the location of the defendant's gun;[39] questions about the location of a gun in a motel room that concerned only the safety of the police;[40]

When Does a Person Have a Right to an Attorney?

If a person has a right to an attorney and is indigent (does not have the resources to hire a private attorney), the state or federal government must provide a lawyer at taxpayers' expense. The state or federal government cannot proceed with custodial questioning or commence a criminal trial until the person's Fifth or Sixth Amendment right to an attorney is complied with. A right to an attorney exists:

- During custodial interrogation (if the person is not in custody, or if there is no police interro-

gation, there is no right to an attorney). This is a Fifth and Sixth Amendment right. (*Miranda v. Arizona,* 384 U.S. 436, 1966).

- Once criminal charges are initiated against the person, a defendant has the right to an attorney at all critical stages of that prosecution under the Sixth Amendment. (*Kirby v. Illinois,* 406 U.S. 682, 1972).

Evidence Obtained by Threats of Loss of a Job or License

When complaints are filed against a law enforcement officer, lawyer, teacher, doctor, or another person with a license, it is common practice to request that a written response to the complaint be submitted. Failure to submit a written response could result in disciplinary action. Must police officers, lawyers, teachers, doctors, and others face disciplinary action or the loss of their license if they do not incriminate themselves?

This question was before the U.S. Supreme Court in the 1967 case of *Spevack v. Klein,* 87 S.Ct. 625, where a lawyer lost his license to practice law. The Supreme Court held:

Lawyers are not excepted from the words "No person . . . shall be compelled in any criminal

case to be a witness against himself"; and we can imply no exception. Like the school teacher in *Slochower v. Board of Higher Education of City of New York,* 350 U.S. 551, . . . and the policemen in *Garrity v. State of New Jersey,* 87 S.Ct. 616, . . . lawyers also enjoy first-class citizenship.

Law enforcement agencies, employers, and licensing agencies can obtain reports concerning job-related incidents by stating on the request for information that answers provided would not be used as evidence in criminal prosecutions [see the case of *Broderick v. Police Commissioner of Boston,* 330 N.E.2d 199 (Mass., 1975)].

concern for people in nearby motel rooms justified asking for the location of a gun in a motel room.[41]

THE CALIFORNIA RESCUE DOCTRINE The *California rescue doctrine* was adopted in the 1965 case of *People v. Modesto.*[42] California officers asked questions of an arrested suspect because of their concern for the safety of a missing or kidnapped victim. Statements of the defendant were admitted even though he had not been given the *Miranda* warnings.

Can the Failure to Give *Miranda* Warnings Be the Basis for a Civil Lawsuit?

The 2003 Case of *Chavez v. Martinez*, 123 S. Ct. 1994

Two police officers stopped Martinez while he was riding his bicycle at night. During a subsequent search a struggle ensued. One officer shouted, "He's got my gun," and the other officer shot Martinez several times. Martinez was brought to a hospital, and while receiving emergency treatment, a police supervisor, Chavez, questioned him about the altercation, including questions that related to criminal actions Martinez may have taken. Martinez was not given his *Miranda* warning.

No criminal charges were brought against Martinez, and his statements made to Chavez were never used in any prosecution against him. Martinez brought a civil action against Chavez under federal civil rights laws, alleging that Chavez violated his Fifth Amendment rights by questioning him without a *Miranda* warning. The 9th Circuit held that Martinez's Fifth Amendment rights had been violated.

The United States Supreme Court reversed, holding that no Fifth Amendment rights had been violated because the statements were never used in a criminal case brought against Martinez. Noting that the Fifth Amendment provides that "No person . . . shall be compelled in any criminal case . . ." to be a witness against himself, the Court concluded that in the absence of such a criminal case the Fifth Amendment did not apply. Thus, neither the *Miranda* rule nor the Fifth Amendment were violated by the police interrogation. The Court also noted that if the police use torture or other abuse in questioning of a suspect, but never attempt to use the resulting statements in a criminal case, the Fourteenth Amendment would provide a remedy for the torture or other abuse inflicted on the suspect.

When Does a Conversation with a Defendant Become "Interrogation"?

Whether conversations with a defendant in custody constitute "interrogation" requiring a *Miranda* warning can sometimes be difficult to determine. For example, in *Drury v. State,* 793 A.2d 567 (Md. Ct. App., 2002), police took a defendant to the police station for questioning concerning a burglary. The door of a store was pried open with a tire iron, which was found near the crime scene. Before being advised of his *Miranda* rights, police showed the defendant the tire iron and some other articles found near the crime scene and told the defendant the items were to be sent out for fingerprints. The defendant then made incriminating statements, which were used against him at his trial. On appeal, the court held that showing the defendant the evidence found near the crime scene was the functional equivalent of interrogation, since the police should have known that it would evoke an incriminating response from the defendant.

Other courts have reached the opposite result. In *United States v. Allen,* 247 F.3d 741 (8th Cir., 2001), the court held that it was not interrogation to inform the defendant in custody that three of four witnesses identified the defendant as present at the scene of a crime; the court said that information was merely describing the state of the investigation.

Other states have adopted this exception. The 1978 California case of *People v. Riddle*,[43] was appealed to the U.S. Supreme Court where review was denied.[44] *People v. Riddle* holds that *Miranda* warnings are excused when the following conditions exist:

(1) an urgent need and no other course of action promises relief; (2) the possibility of saving human life by rescuing a person in danger; and (3) rescue as the primary purpose and motive of the interrogator.

In the 1992 case of *State v. Provost*,[45] the defendant, who smelled of gasoline, walked into a police station and asked to be locked up because he had burned his wife. Officers were concerned about the safety of the woman and asked where she was. Because the defendant was not coherent, he was placed in handcuffs after he agreed to take them to his wife. His statements and evidence of the murder were held admissible by the Minnesota Supreme Court, which adopted the rescue doctrine, noting that it was similar to but not the same as the public safety exception to the *Miranda* requirements.

Ⓓ THE *MASSIAH* Limitation

Until a person is formally charged with a crime, the only tests used to determine whether a confession can be used are the voluntariness test and the *Miranda* requirements. After a suspect is formally charged with a crime, it is "entirely proper [for law officers] to continue an investigation of the . . . criminal activities of the defendant and his alleged confederates."[46]

However, law enforcement officers must remember that "once adversary proceedings have commenced against an individual, he has a right to legal representation when the government interrogates him"[47] (***Massiah*** limitation). Failure to observe a defendant's Sixth Amendment right to an attorney by questioning without that attorney violates that amendment, as the following two cases held.

Massiah v. United States
United States Supreme Court, 377 U.S. 201, 84 S.Ct. 1199 (1964)

The defendant (a merchant seaman) and a man named Colson were charged with importing, concealing, and facilitating the sale of cocaine. The defendants were indicted for these offenses and released on bail. A few days later, and without Massiah's knowledge, Colson agreed to cooperate with the federal agents and permitted a radio transmitter to be installed under the front seat of his automobile. Then, according to a prearranged plan, Colson carried on a lengthy conversation with Massiah while federal agents listened in another car a short distance away. At Massiah's trial, one of the federal agents testified as to the incriminating statements he overhead by means of the radio transmitter. Although this investigative technique and procedure is a permissible means of obtaining evidence before suspects are indicted or charged, the U.S. Supreme Court held that Massiah's Sixth Amendment

---

rights were violated because he had already been indicted and was awaiting trial. In reversing Massiah's conviction, the Court held that:

> . . . the [defendant] was denied the basic protection of [the Sixth Amendment] when there was used against him at his trial evidence of his own incriminating words, which federal agents had deliberately elicited from him after he had been indicted and in the absence of his counsel.

Brewer v. Williams[48]
United States Supreme Court, 430 U.S. 387, 97 S.Ct. 1232 (1977)

Williams was arrested and charged in Davenport, Iowa, for the abduction of ten-year-old girl. Since the crime was committed in Des Moines, Iowa, Williams had to be transported 160 miles back to Des Moines.

The police officers driving Williams to Des Moines were told by the lawyer appointed to represent Williams that they were not to question Williams without his presence. Williams had stated to the officers that "when I get to Des Moines . . . I will tell you the whole story." The officers, however, believed that the little girl was dead, and one of the officers persuaded Williams to tell the officers where he had buried the girl's body.

The trial court allowed all the evidence obtained during the automobile trip, holding that Williams had waived his Sixth Amendment right to an attorney. The U.S. Supreme Court held that it was error to use the evidence of how the girl's body was recovered. In ordering a new trial, the Supreme Court held:

> . . . the clear rule of Massiah is that once adversary proceedings have commenced against an individual, he has a right to legal representation when the government interrogates him. It thus requires no wooden or technical application of the Massiah doctrine to conclude that Williams was entitled to the assistance of counsel guaranteed to him by the Sixth and Fourteenth Amendments.

Texas v. Cobb
United States Supreme Court 121 S. Ct. 1335 (2001)

While Cobb was under arrest for an unrelated offense, he confessed to a home burglary. But Cobb denied knowledge of the disappearance of a woman and a child from the home. He was indicted for the burglary, and a lawyer was appointed to represent him. Cobb later confessed to his father that he killed the woman and child. His father contacted the police and the police questioned Cobb without the presence of his attorney but after obtaining a waiver to Cobb's *Miranda* rights. Cobb confessed to the double murder and was convicted of capital murder and was sentenced to death.

On appeal, Cobb contended his Sixth Amendment rights were violated because his lawyer was not present during the police interrogation that led to his confession to the double murders.

The U.S. Supreme Court held that the Sixth Amendment right to counsel is "offense specific" (limited here to the burglary Cobb was charged with) and was not "factually related" (to the two murders related to the burglary). The Court ruled ". . . burglary and capital murder are not the same offense. . . . The Sixth Amendment right to counsel did not bar police from interrogating (Cobb) regarding the murders, and (Cobb's) confession was therefore admissible."

Ⓔ THE *BRUTON* Rule

Major crimes are often committed by more than one person. For example, three men commit an armed robbery. One of the men, X, is apprehended and makes statements incriminating himself and the other two men (Y and Z). On the basis of this information, arrest warrants and/or search warrants are obtained, and Y and Z are taken into custody.

If the victim and witnesses can identify all three men, the state now has a good case to go to trial. But if witnesses can only identify X and the state cannot otherwise incriminate Y and Z, a *Bruton* problem is going to occur when X's lawyer becomes aware of the situation.

X's confession and incriminating statements can be used as evidence against X but cannot be used against Y unless X takes the witness stand and incriminates Y. Y has a Sixth Amendment right to be confronted with the witness against him (or her).

But X does not have to take the witness stand and cannot be forced to incriminate himself and his friend. His confession can only be used against him unless X takes the witness stand. This is where the bargaining begins. To get around this **Bruton rule,** the prosecutor ordinarily has the following options available:

1. Make concessions to X (lowering or dropping criminal charges or sentence concessions) to get him to become a state witness and incriminate himself and Y and Z.

2. If X will not cooperate or if it is decided that concessions should not be made, drop the criminal charges against Y and Z and proceed to trial against X (failure to cooperate could result in a greater sentence).

In situations where there is sufficient evidence to go to trial against Y and Z, the following options would also be available:

1. Try the defendants in two trials, which would permit using X's confession in the trial against him, or

2. Redact (reduce or edit) X's statements to eliminate any references to Y and Z and use the statements in a joint trial.[49]

The 1968 *Bruton* case, which established this rule of law, follows:

Bruton v. United States
United States Supreme Court, 391 U.S. 123, 88 S.Ct. 1620 (1968)

The defendant (Bruton) and a codefendant (Evans) were tried together and convicted of armed postal robbery. Evans had confessed and admitted that he had an accomplice whom he would not name. The confession was used as evidence against Evans and the trial judge "instructed the jury that although Evans' confession was competent evidence against Evans it was inadmissible hearsay against petitioner (Bruton) and therefore had to be disregarded in determining petitioner's (Bruton's) guilt or innocence." In reversing Bruton's conviction, the Supreme Court held that:

> Here the introduction of Evans' confession posed a substantial threat to petitioner's right to confront the witnesses against him, and this is a hazard we cannot ignore. Despite the concededly clear instructions to the jury to disregard Evans' inadmissible hearsay evidence inculpating petitioner, in the context of a joint trial we cannot accept limiting instructions as an adequate substitute for petitioner's constitutional right of cross-examination. The effect is the same as if there had been no instruction at all. . . .
> Reversed.

F QUESTIONING PEOPLE IN JAIL OR PRISON

Prisons and jails in the United States have almost 2 million inmates. The presence of a career or violent criminal in a jail or prison presents an opportunity to investigate and attempt to obtain evidence as to unsolved crimes or additional evidence as to crimes for which the person is incarcerated. There now is a substantial body of federal and state case law detailing the application of the four major tests as to evidence obtained from prisoners.

An article entitled "Constitutional Rights to Counsel During Interrogation" in the September 2002 *FBI Law Enforcement Bulletin* points out the similarity between questioning by an undercover law enforcement officer and questioning by a cellmate informant or an undercover law officer posing as a prisoner. *Miranda* warnings are not required in either situation because, as the article points out, ". . . (as) the subjects of the questioning do not know that the government is interrogating them, they cannot feel the coerciveness *Miranda* was designed to protect against. Consequently, the practice of using cellmate informants does not contravene the *Miranda* rule." The following U.S. Supreme Court decisions illustrate this rule of law:

An informant was placed in Wilson's jail cell and told only to listen and not to ask any questions. The informant complied with these directions.	*Kuhlmann v. Wilson,* 477 U.S. 436, 106 S. Ct. 2616 (1986)	". . . . the defendant must demonstrate that the police took some action, beyond merely listening, that was designed deliberately to elicit incriminating remarks."

Henry's cell mate deliberately elicited information about the bank robbery that Henry was charged with and awaiting trial.	*United States v. Henry,* 447 U.S. 264, 100 S.Ct. 2183 (1980)	Conviction reversed because the testimony of the cell mate information violated Henry's Sixth Amendment right to counsel. (a *Massiah* violation)
Perkins was in prison for assault. An undercover agent was placed in his cell to gain information about an unsolved murder. Perkins bragged about committing the murder when asked if he had ever "done" anyone. It was held *Miranda* warnings were not required.	*Illinois v. Perkins,* 496 U.S. 292, 110 S. Ct. 2394 (1990)	The court held that "The use of undercover agents is a recognized law enforcement technique, often employed in the prison context to detect violence against correctional officials or inmates, as well as for the purposes served here. The interests protected by *Miranda* are not implicated in these cases, and the warnings are not required to safeguard the constitutional rights of inmates who make voluntary statements . . ."
A paid information promised to protect the defendant from other inmates in the prison if he confessed to a murder. The defendant admitted he killed his 11-year-old-stepdaughter.	*Arizona v. Fulminante,* 499 U.S. 279, 111 S.Ct. 1246 (1991)	It was held that the confession was coerced because there was a threat of physical violence unless the defendant confessed. However, the use of the confession might have been harmless error.
Moulton was in jail for burglary and theft. Incriminating statements of these crimes were obtained by recording his conversations with an undercover cellmate.	*Maine v. Moulton,* 106 S.Ct. 477 (1985)	The state could intercept conversations of other uncharged offenses but not the crime the defendant is in jail for because of Sixth Amendment violation of right to an attorney.

Other U.S. Supreme Court Prison Questioning Cases

After the murder of a prison employee, a strip search of inmates in the area began. Blood was seen on the defendant's clothes; he was questioned and admitted that he committed the murder. No *Miranda* warnings were given.	*Bradley v. Ohio,* 541 N.E. 2d 78 (Ohio, 1989), review denied 497 U.S. 1011, 110 S.Ct. 3258 (1990)	Was held by the Ohio courts to be "on-the-scene questioning," and this ruling was let stand by the U.S. Supreme Court.
After a prison inmate falsely obtained income tax refunds, IRS agents came into the prison and questioned the defendant who made incriminating statements.	*Mathis v. United States,* 391 U.S. 1, 88 S.Ct. 1503 (1968)	Statements of the defendant could not be used because no *Miranda* warnings and waiver of rights occurred.

The Four Major Tests Controlling the Use of Confessions[a]

1. The *voluntariness test,* which is used at all times during the criminal proceeding, requires that confessions be freely and voluntarily given. Violations occur when the government obtains a confession by means that overbear the will of the accused. The resulting confession would be excluded as evidence on the grounds that there was denial of due process law.

2. The *Miranda test* is required when (a) a suspect is in custody and (b) a law officer seeks to obtain incriminating information through questioning. *Miranda* must be complied with if answers are to be used as evidence. *Miranda* requires that:
   - Warnings (cautions) be given.
   - Suspect states or acknowledges that he or she understands warnings.
   - Suspect waives rights and answers some or all questions.

3. After a suspect is charged with a crime, his Sixth Amendment right to an attorney must be observed. A *Massiah violation* could occur if a defendant who has already been charged with a crime is questioned in regard to that crime in violation of the defendant's Sixth Amendment **right to an attorney.** (See the U.S. Supreme Court cases of *Massiah v. United States* and *Brewer v. Williams* in this chapter.)

4. A confession by one suspect cannot be used against another suspect unless the second suspect has an opportunity to cross-examine the source of the accusation against him (or her). A *Bruton violation* could occur unless:
   - The first suspect agrees to take the witness stand and testify.
   - The suspects are tried in separate trials.
   - The suspects are tried in one trial with reference to the second suspect taken out of the confession.
   - If all else fails, charges against the second suspect are dropped.

[a]The federal government and most (if not all) states have statutes or court decisions requiring that arrested persons be taken before a court promptly or within a reasonable time. Failure to do this could jeopardize the use of any statements or confessions as evidence if the statements or confessions were obtained during the unreasonable delay. The federal rule in this area is sometimes called the *McNabb–Mallory rule* [*McNabb v. United States,* 63 S.Ct. 608 (1943) and *Mallory v. United States,* 77 S.Ct. 1356 (1957)]. 18 U.S.C. sec. 3501(c) (1968) severely limited *McNabb–Mallory;* however, in *Gerstein v. Puagh,* 420 U.S. 103 (1975), the Court found a requirement in the Fourth Amendment that one arrested be brought before a judicial officer within a reasonable time for a probable cause hearing.

Ⓖ POLYGRAPH TEST RESULTS AS EVIDENCE

Persons charged or suspected of a crime cannot be ordered to take a polygraph test (lie detector) because such compulsion would violate their Fifth Amendment privilege against self-incrimination.[50] Nor does a defendant charged with a crime have a right to take a polygraph test to prove his or her innocence.[51]

Miranda

The U.S. Supreme Court has "never insisted that *Miranda* warnings be given in the exact form described . . ." [*Duckworth v. Eagan,* 492 U.S. 195, 109 S.Ct. 2875 (1989), and *California v. Prysock,* 453 U.S. 355, 101 S.Ct. 2806 (1981)].

A defendant who states he or she is willing to make an oral statement but is unwilling to make a written statement without his attorney has waived the rights stated in the *Miranda* warnings [*Connecticut v. Barrett,* 479 U.S. 523, 107 S.Ct. 828 (1987)].

Undercover law enforcement officers do not have to give *Miranda* warnings and do not have to disclose their true identity. (Undercover officer was placed in Perkin's prison cell block.) [*Illinois v. Perkins,* 110 S.Ct. 2394 (1990).] (Undercover officer pretended to be a friend of James Hoffa.) [*Hoffa v. United States,* 385 U.S. 293, 87 S.Ct. 408 (1966).]

Police do not have to tell a suspect undergoing interrogation that a lawyer hired by someone else has agreed to represent the suspect and has offered to be present. (The suspect was about to confess to the brutal slaying of a young woman.) [*Moran v. Burbine,* 475 U.S. 412, 106 S.Ct. 1135 (1986).]

Police do not trick a suspect when they fail to inform him as to all the crimes he may be questioned about. (Instead of just questioning about stolen firearms, ATF agents also questioned Spring about a murder to which he confessed.) [*Colorado v. Spring,* 479 U.S. 564, 107 S.Ct. 851 (1987)].

Custody for *Miranda's* purposes is based upon facts and circumstances known to the suspect and not on the uncommunicated suspicions of the police [*Stansbury v. California,* 114 S.Ct. 1526 (1994)].

"Interrogation" by police is not limited to express questioning. The term also includes "any words or actions on the part of the police . . . that the police should know are reasonably likely to elicit an incriminating response from the suspect" [*Rhode Island v. Innis,* 446 U.S. 291 (1980)].

"A person may assert his constitutional rights at any time. He may answer questions if he wishes, but he may stop at any time" [*Miranda v. Arizona,* 384 U.S. 436, 86 S.Ct. 1602, 16 L.Ed.2d 694 (1966)].

After a suspect lets the "cat out of the bag" and admits his guilt, *Miranda* warnings may be given (if they were not already given) and a second admission of guilt taken. "The relevant inquiry is whether, in fact, the second statement was also voluntarily made" [*Oregon v. Elstad,* 470 U.S. 298, 105 S.Ct. 1285 (1985)].

Juveniles have the same rights as adults and should be given *Miranda* warnings prior to interrogation while in custody [*Fare v. Michael C.,* 442 U.S. 707, 99 S.Ct. 2560 (1979)].

Involuntary Confessions

A federal court reviewing the use of a confession in a state court is not bound by a state court finding and has a "duty to make an independent evaluation of the record"[*Mincey v. Arizona,* 437 U.S. 385, 98 S.Ct. 2408 (1978); *Miller v. Fenton,* 474 U.S. 104, 106 S.Ct. 445 (1985)].

However, it is reported that more than 1 million polygraph tests are given each year in the United States. Many of these tests are given by private companies, and some are administered within the criminal justice system. Prosecutors or a law enforcement agency might ask persons to voluntarily take a lie detector test, to affirm statements they have made or to demonstrate their innocence.

In 1998 the U.S. Supreme Court noted that "(m)ost states maintain per se rules excluding polygraph evidence" and pointed out that "New Mexico is unique in making polygraph evidence generally admissible without prior stipulation of the parties and without significant restriction."[52] The reasons generally given by states for forbidding polygraph evidence entirely, or for placing severe restrictions on the use of polygraph evidence in criminal or civil trials, are:

- A belief that polygraph results are not sufficiently reliable and trustworthy.
- The tendency of juries to rely too heavily on the report of polygraph examiners who appear as "expert" witnesses in criminal or civil cases and testify whether persons taking lie detector tests were truthful or not truthful.
- The inability of trial courts to judge the competency of polygraph examiners.

The Controversy over Polygraph Testing[53]

Polygraph testing is very controversial. Persons who oppose the use of lie detector tests refer to the tests as degrading and humiliating. The late U.S. Senator Sam Ervin called the tests "twentieth-century witchcraft." On the other hand, defense lawyer F. Lee Bailey testified before the U.S. Congress in 1986 that polygraphy tests are "useful investigative tools" and that when "properly run in good hands, it is a good test."

After it was discovered in 2001 that a high-ranking FBI agent (Robert Hanssen) had been selling secret information to Russia for more than fifteen years, the FBI was criticized for not giving more lie detector tests to key FBI agents.

However, in 2002 a panel of leading scientists confirmed a U.S. congressional study done in 1983, with both studies reporting that lie detector tests do a poor job of identifying spies or other national security risks and are likely in security screening to produce false accusations about innocent people. The 1983 congressional report stated that spies "may well be the most motivated and perhaps the best trained to avoid detection" by developing skills necessary to deceive polygraph machines and operators.

The 2002 panel of scientists acknowledged that their report would cause much debate and would probably reduce some of the tens of thousands of security lie detector tests that were being given yearly. The panel acknowledged that there is a place for polygraphs in the investigation of specific crimes.

Polygraph Testing in the American Criminal Justice System

Polygraph testing is occasionally used by law enforcement agencies from the FBI to local police and sheriff departments, primarily for investigative and advisory purposes. Some defense lawyers also use lie detector tests in efforts to establish defense positions or arguments for their clients. Most states forbid the use of lie detector evidence in civil and criminal trials, but some states allow such evidence upon prior stipulation of both parties. The following cases and material show some of the other uses of polygraph testing:

- While working undercover for the U.S. Air Force, Scheffer was required to periodically take drug tests and polygraph tests. When a drug test revealed the presence of an illegal drug in the airman's urine, a polygraph test was given, and it supported Scheffer's statement that he did not knowingly take the illegal drug. At his trial for wrongfully using methamphetamine, the trial court excluded the evidence of the polygraph test because the military have a pro se ban on the use of polygraph evidence. The U.S.

Supreme Court affirmed the ban on evidence of polygraph testing imposed on military courts, holding that "(s)tate and federal governments . . . have a legitimate interest in ensuring that reliable evidence is presented to the trier of fact in criminal trials."[54]

- In the 1995 case of *Wood v. Bartholomew,*[55] the state of Washington's ban on the use of polygraph evidence even for impeachment purposes was sustained by the U.S. Supreme Court. In that case, a prosecutor failed to disclose that a witness had failed a polygraph test. The Supreme Court held this failure did not deprive the defendant of "material" evidence under the *Brady* rule.

- In the 1991 case of *People v. Suly,*[56] the Supreme Court of California approved the use of a required lie detector test in a plea-bargain agreement. The defendant in this case was convicted of six murders and sentenced to death. His alleged accomplice who testified against him was required by the plea agreement to pass a lie detector test showing that she had not herself committed any of the murders.

- Governors and the president of the United States have the power to pardon and commute criminal sentences (including the death sentence). In 1992 the governor of Virginia ordered a polygraph test for Roger Keith Coleman who faced execution in Virginia's electric chair. Coleman failed a lie detector test and was executed. His case received wide public attention.

- Several states have established polygraph testing as a condition of probation. In agreeing to the conditions of probation, defendants would agree to periodic polygraph examinations. If the defendant failed the test, the sentencing judge would reassess the case and could revoke probation, and place the defendant in jail. Such programs are being used in several states for sexual offenders and child abusers.

- A few courts have held that the results of lie detector tests could be used for establishing probable cause for search warrants. Courts that have approved of such use of polygraph tests are the Fifth Federal Court of Appeals,[57] the Court of Appeals of State of Washington,[58] and an Oregon court.[59] However, the Court of Appeals of Maryland held that the results of polygraph examinations could not be used to establish probable cause to arrest or charge a suspect with a crime.[60]

- In some instances, people make incriminating admissions or confessions either before, during, or after a polygraph test is given. The polygraph operator or examiner may testify as to these statements if (1) the statements were voluntarily made, and (2) the *Miranda* warnings were given and a waiver obtained in situations where the polygraph operator is a law enforcement officer. The *Miranda* warnings should also be given by private polygraph examiners if the suspect is in police custody.

Ⓗ VOICE SPECTROGRAPHY EVIDENCE

There have been many attempts to use voiceprints (spectrographic voice identification) as evidence over the years. Most courts using the old *Frye* test have held that spectrographic voice identification was inadmissible. The stricter and higher standards for the admission of scientific evidence established by the U.S. Supreme Court in the 1993 *Daubert* case (see Chapter 18 on scientific evidence) make it more difficult to use voiceprints as evidence unless dramatic improvements are made in voiceprints.

In seeking to use voiceprints as evidence, a lawyer is attempting to prove the identification of a speaker on a tape or wiretap recording. The technique could be used to evaluate the voice (or voices) heard on taped conversations and compare the results to other taped conversations of an identified person.

Some courts have admitted voice spectrography evidence; see, for example, *United States v. Smith*, 869 F.2d 348 (7th Cir., 1989), *United States v. Love*, 767 F.2d 1052 (4th Cir., 1985), cert. denied 474 U.S. 1081 (1986). Those decisions were reached before the *Daubert* decision and may not accurately represent the current approach to voice spectrography. In a 2000 decision, the 8th Circuit Court of Appeals excluded voice spectrography evidence offered by a defendant to prove his voice was not the voice heard on a federal wiretap. The court found that the expert testimony did not meet the *Daubert* standards for reliability. *United States v. Bahena*, 223 F.3d 797 (8th Cir., 2000).

SUMMARY

To be admissible as evidence, confessions and incriminating statements must be relevant, not in violation of the hearsay rule, and obtained in a manner that does not violate the exclusionary rule.

In addition, a violation of any of the following could cause the confession or incriminating statement to be held inadmissible as evidence:

1. The voluntariness test, which requires that the confession or statement be freely and voluntarily given. If the government used means to overbear the will of the accused, a violation of this test has occurred.

2. If the suspect is in custody and the government seeks to obtain incriminating statements, the following procedural safeguards must be shown in court: (a) that *Miranda* warnings were given; (b) that the suspect understood the warnings; and (c) that the suspect waived his (or her) rights and answered some or all of the questions.

3. Once a suspect has been charged or indicted for a crime, the suspect's Sixth Amendment right to an attorney commences. Questioning a defendant about the crime with which she (or he) have been charged without the presence of the defense attorney is a Sixth Amendment *Massiah* violation. If your state follows the *Cobb* rule, defendants can be questioned about other crimes but not the crime charged. (See *Texas v. Cobb* in this chapter.)

4. A *Bruton* violation occurs if a confession by one suspect is used against another suspect unless the second suspect has an opportunity to cross-examine the source of the accusation against him (or her).

PROBLEMS

AVAILABLE ANSWERS

a. *Cannot* be used as evidence because was not a voluntary statement.

b. *Cannot* be used as evidence because violated *Miranda* requirements.

c. *Cannot* be used as evidence because violated *Massiah* requirement.

d. *Cannot* be used as evidence because violated *Bruton* rule.

e. Is admissible as evidence as no violation occurred.

CONFESSIONS AND INCRIMINATING STATEMENTS WERE OBTAINED UNDER THE FOLLOWING CONDITIONS:

1. The defendant was given no food or water until he waived *Miranda* and confessed.

2. The defendant walked into a police station and confessed before *Miranda* could be given to him.

3. During a traffic stop, the driver stated he drank six beers in response to the officer's request that he step out of the vehicle.

4. A person stopped for shoplifting admitted the theft before police arrived at the store.

5. In answer to a parole officer's question, the parolee confessed to a crime.

6. A stockbroker confessed to his boss that he was guilty of theft.

7. After being charged with abduction, Williams voluntarily confessed to the crime without being questioned.

8. After being charged with abduction, Williams confessed after repeated questions by police after waving his *Miranda* requirements.

9. The police questioned a person they believed to be a material witness to a felony without giving *Miranda* warnings.

10. During a valid investigative detention, the person stopped makes incriminating statements before *Miranda* warnings are given.

11. The defendant, who was charged with a robbery and murder, was placed in a jail cell with a police informant. The informant overheard the defendant make incriminating statements that he passed on to the police. Can the informant appear as a witness and testify about the statements he heard if he took no action other than merely listening to what the defendant had to say? Should the evidence of the defendant's statements be admissible if there was a prior arrangement of the police to put the informant in a position where he could overhear the defendant's statements? If the informant "deliberately elicited" the statements from the defendant by questions and conversation, should the

evidence be admissible? Explain. [*Kuhlmann v. Wilson*, 106 S.Ct. 2616 (U.S. Sup. Ct., 1986)].

12. Federal IRS agents from the Intelligence Division met with the defendant at a private home where the defendant occasionally stayed. The agents identified themselves and their function of investigating his federal income tax liability. The agents read a statement to the defendant from a printed card, but they did not give the defendant the *Miranda* warnings and receive a waiver of his rights. For about three hours, the agents conversed with the defendant in what they described as a "friendly" and "relaxed" manner. In separate cars, the parties then went to the defendant's place of business where the defendant supplied his books to the agents after being informed that he was not required to furnish any books or records. The defendant was not arrested at the time but was later charged with criminal tax fraud. Were the statements and other evidence that the tax agents obtained at the voluntary meeting at the private home and then at defendant's place of business properly obtained and properly used as evidence in defendant's criminal trial? [*Beckwith v. United States*, 425 U.S. 341, 96 S.Ct. 1612 (1976)].

13. An officer of the state police investigated a theft at a residence near Pendleton, Oregon. He asked the lady of the house that had been burglarized if she suspected anyone. She replied that the defendant was the only one she could think of. The defendant was a parolee and a "close associate" of her son. The officer tried to contact the defendant on three or four occasions, with no success. Finally, about twenty-five days after the burglary, the officer left his card at the defendant's apartment, with a note asking him to call because "I'd like to discuss something with you." The next afternoon the defendant did call. The officer asked where it would be convenient to meet. The defendant had no preference, so the officer asked if the defendant could meet him at the state patrol office in about an hour and a half, about 5:00 P.M. The patrol office was about two blocks from defendant's apartment. The building housed several state agencies.

The officer met the defendant in the hallway, shook hands, and took him into an office. The defendant was told he was not under arrest. The door was closed. The two sat across a desk. The police radio in another room could be heard. The officer told the defendant that he wanted to talk to him about a burglary and that his truthfulness would possibly be considered by the district attorney or judge. The officer further advised that the police believed that the defendant was involved in the burglary and [falsely stated that] the defendant's fingerprints were found at the scene. The defendant sat for a few minutes and then said he had taken the property. This occurred within five minutes after defendant had come to the office. The officer then advised defendant of his *Miranda* requirements and took a taped confession.

At the end of the taped conversation, the officer told the defendant that he was not arresting him at this time; he was released to go about his job and return to his family. The officer said he was referring the case to the district attorney, to determine whether criminal charges would be brought. It was 5:30 P.M. when the defendant left the office.

The defendant was then charged days later with burglary. Can all the incriminating statements the defendant made be used in evidence against him? Were any improper promises made to the defendant? Did the officer's false statement that the defendant's fingerprints were found at the scene of the burglary prevent the use of any of the evidence? Were the defendant's confessions made voluntarily? Was *Miranda* properly complied with? [*Oregon v. Mathiason*, 429 U.S. 492, 97 S.Ct. 711 (1977)].

14. Police were investigating a shooting death outside a cafe in Dallas, Texas. Defendant Orozco had left the scene of the shooting and had returned to his boardinghouse to sleep. At about 4 A.M. four police officers arrived at the petitioner's boardinghouse, were admitted by an unidentified woman, and were told that the petitioner was asleep in the bedroom. All four officers entered the bedroom and began to question the petitioner. From the moment he gave his name, according to the testimony of one of the officers, petitioner was not free to go where he pleased but was "under arrest." The officers asked him if he had been to the El Farleto restaurant that night; when he answered yes, he was asked if he owned a pistol. Petitioner admitted owning one. After being asked a second time where the pistol was located, he admitted that it was in the washing machine in a backroom of the boardinghouse. Ballistics tests indicated that the gun found in the washing machine was the gun that fired the fatal shot.

Should the statements of the defendant be admitted as evidence? Should the gun be admitted as evidence? Explain your answer. [*Orozco v. Texas*, 394 U.S. 324, 89 S.Ct. 1095 (1969)].

INFOTRAC COLLEGE EDITION EXERCISES

1. Go to InfoTrac College Edition and using the search term "exclusionary rule" find the 2002 *Duke Law Journal* article titled "Miranda's Final Frontier." Does *Miranda* apply to interrogations of non-Americans that take place in foreign countries, the results of which are then used in criminal trials in this country?

2. Go to InfoTrac College Edition and using the search term "exclusionary rule" find the 2002 *Yale Law Journal* article titled "Are Police Free to Disregard *Miranda*?" After the decision in *Dickerson*, which held that *Miranda* imposed a constitutional requirement, some questions remain. Among them is the question of whether or not police who disregard *Miranda* can be sued under civil rights laws. Is *Miranda* a rule that governs police conduct or simply a rule of admissibility of evidence? This article attempts to answer that question.

NOTES

1. U.S. Supreme Court case of *Arizona v. Fulminante,* 499 U.S. 279 (1991).
2. A confession is generally viewed the same as a guilty plea in open court. An incriminating statement differs from a confession in that a confession directly acknowledges guilt whereas an incriminating statement "is any statement or conduct from which guilt of the crime can be inferred" [*People v. Stanton,* 158 N.E.2d 47 (Ill., 1959)]. Sometimes even silence can constitute an incriminating statement. In *Key-el v. State,* 709 A.2d 1305 (Md., 1999), the prosecution introduced evidence that the defendant had remained silent when his wife, in the presence of a police officer, accused him of battering. The evidence was held properly admissible under the *tacit admission* rule, and the defendant's conviction was affirmed.
3. This occurred in the U.S. Supreme Court case of *Colorado v. Connelly,* 479 U.S. 157, 107 S.Ct. 515 (1986). In the *Connelly* case, the defense lawyer argued that Connelly was suffering from a psychosis that prevented Connelly from understanding his rights and motivated his confession. Because the confession had been corroborated, it was held to be admissible evidence and Connelly's conviction was affirmed.
4. *People v. Jennings,* 807 P.2d 1009.
5. See the *New York Times* obituary of Marty James, 16 January 1992.
6. 9 Neb. App. 52 (2000).
7. *People v. Cotton et al.,* 478 N.W.2d 681 (Mich. App., 1991).
8. *United States v. Chimal,* 976 F.2d 608 (10th Cir., 1992).
9. *United States v. Maio,* 34 MJ 215 (U.S. CMA, 1992).
10. *Thornburgh v. State,* 815 P.2d 186 (Okla. Crim. App., 1991).
11. In the 1953 case of *Stein v. New York,* 346 U.S. 156, 73 S.Ct. 1077, the U.S. Supreme Court pointed out why confessions obtained by physical violence are considered involuntary and unreliable:

> Physical violence or threat of it by the custodian of a prisoner during detention serves no lawful purpose, invalidates confessions that otherwise would be convincing, and is universally condemned by the law. When present, there is no need to weigh or measure its effects on the will of the individual victim. The tendency of the innocent, as well as the guilty, to risk remote results of a false confession rather than suffer immediate pain is so strong that judges long ago found it necessary to guard against miscarriages of justice by treating any confession made concurrently with torture or threat of brutality as too untrustworthy to be received as evidence of guilt. *Stein,* 346 U.S. at 182, 73 S.Ct. at 1091 [emphasis added].

12. 384 U.S. 436 (1966).
13. *Miranda v. Arizona,* 384 U.S. 436, 86 S.Ct 1602 (1966).
14. *People v. Ashford,* 71 Cal. Rptr. 619 (Cal. App., 1968).
15. *People v. Gonzales,* 554 N.E.2d 1269 (N.Y. 1990).
16. *State v. Jackson,* 600 So.2d 739 (La. App., 1992).
17. *Commonwealth v. Daniels,* 590 A.2d 778 (Pa. Super., 1991).
18. *Ciriago v. State,* 471 A.2d 320 (1984).
19. *Miranda v. Arizona,* 384 U.S. 477, 86 S.Ct. 1629 (1966).
20. *State v. Bennett,* 517 P.2d 1029 (Utah, 1973).
21. *Britton v. State,* 170 N.W.2d 785 (Wis., 1969).
22. 813 S.W.2d 748 (Tex. App.).
23. 468 U.S. 420, 104 S.Ct. 3138 (1984).
24. 468 U.S. 420, 104 S.Ct. 3138 (1984).
25. 496 U.S. 582, 110 S.Ct. 2638.
26. 577 N.E. 2d 861 (Ill. App.).
27. 588 A.2d 389 (N.J. Super.).
28. *Glean v. State,* 397 S.E.2d 459 (Ga. App., 1990).
29. *State of Maine v. Joubert,* 603 A.2d 861 (1992).
30. 407 S.E.2d 342.
31. 465 U.S. 420, 104 S.Ct. 1136.
32. 496 U.S. 292, 110 S.Ct. 2394.
33. 385 U.S. 293, 87 S.Ct. 408.
34. *United States v. Rosengard,* 949 F.2d 905 (7th Cir., 1991); *United States v. Cortes,* 922 F.2d 123 (2d Cir., 1990).
35. 467 U.S. 649, 104 S.Ct. 2626.
36. *United States v. Harris,* 961 F.Supp. 1127 (S.D. Ohio, 1997).
37. *People v. Simpson,* 76 Cal. Rptr. 2d 851 (Calif. App. 4th, 1998); *State v. Harris,* 384 S.E.2d 50 (N.C. App., 1989).
38. *State v. White,* 619 A.2d 92 (Maine, 1993).

39. *Commonwealth v. Bowers,* 583 A.2d 1165 (Pa. Super., 1990).

40. *State v. Trangucci,* 796 P.2d 606 (N.M App., 1990).

41. *State v. McKessor,* 785 P.2d 1332 (Kans., 1990).

42. 42 Cal.Rptr. 417, 398 P.2d 753.

43. 148 Cal. Rptr. 170 (App.).

44. 440 U.S. 937, 99 S.Ct. 1283 (1979).

45. 490 N.W. 2d 93 (Minn.).

46. *Massiah v. United States,* 377 U.S. 201, 84 S.Ct. 1199 (1964).

47. *Brewer v. Williams,* 430 U.S. 387, 97 S.Ct. 1232 (1977).

48. This case was before the U.S. Supreme Court again in 1984 under the title of *Nix v. Williams,* 467 U.S. 431, 104 S.Ct. 2501 (1984), discussed in Chapter 9, p. 125.

49. The U.S. Supreme Court has decided two redacting cases. In *Richardson v. Marsh,* 481 U.S. 200 (1987), the Court upheld a conviction in a joint murder trial of two defendants. One defendant, Williams, made a confession implicating the codefendant, Marsh. This confession was introduced at Marsh and Williams's joint trial but was redacted to omit any reference to Marsh and also any reference to Marsh's existence. The Supreme Court held this redaction took the case outside the *Bruton* rule. In *Gray v. Maryland,* 523 U.S. 185, 118 S.Ct. 1151 (1998), Bell and Gray were jointly tried for murder. Bell confessed and this confession was introduced in the joint trial. It was redacted to delete any reference to Gray, but where Gray's name appeared in the confession the police officer reading the confession in court said "deleted." For example, the confession read "Question: Who was in the group that beat Stacey?" Answer: "Me, deleted, deleted, and a few other guys." The Supreme Court said keeping the "deleted" spaces in the confession invited the jury to tie the confession to Gray and held the *Bruton* rule applicable.

50. See the 1992 case of *Melvin v. State,* 606 A. 2d 69, 50 CrL 1575 (Del.), where the state of Delaware produced evidence during the trial showing that the defendant was in possession of cocaine. After the evidence was presented, the trial judge stated that he was "going to give this (juvenile) an opportunity to prove me wrong" by taking a polygraph test as to whether the cocaine belonged to the defendant. When the defendant refused to take the test, the judge found him guilty, stating "I gave him an opportunity to clear himself."

The Supreme Court of Delaware reversed the conviction and ordered a new trial for the violation of the Fifth Amendment privilege against self-incrimination.

51. In the 1977 case of *Sandlin v. Oregon Women's Correctional Center,* 28 Or. App. 519, 559 P.2d 1308, the defendant argued that she had a right to a polygraph test. However, a test was not given to her. In affirming the defendant's conviction, the court held that due process did not require the state to grant the defendant's request for a polygraph test.

52. *United States v. Scheffer,* 118 S.Ct. 1265 (1998).

53. After holding public hearings on the use of polygraph testing, the U.S. Congress enacted the Employee Polygraph Protection Act, which generally forbids employers engaged in interstate commerce from using lie detector tests for either employment screening (i.e., as part of a job application procedure) or during employment with certain exceptions. One of the exceptions permits polygraph testing when an investigation into a money loss or other theft is being conducted.

54. *United States v. Scheffer,* 118 S.Ct. 1261 (1998).

55. 116 S.Ct. 7.

56. 812 P.2d 163.

57. *Bennett v. City of Grand Prairie,* 883 F.2d 400 (1989).

58. *State v. Cherry,* 810 P.2d 940 (1991).

59. *State v. Coffey,* 788 P.2d 424 (1990).

60. *Kairys v. Douglas Stereo, Inc.,* 577 A.2d 386 (1990).

13

The Law Governing Identification Evidence

Ⓐ EVIDENCE NEEDED TO CONVICT OF A CRIME

To convict a person of a crime, the government must prove:

1. That the crime charged did occur (proof of corpus delicti)
2. That the defendant committed or was a party to the crime charged

Identification of the defendant as the person who committed or was a party to the crime must be made in all criminal cases. This can be done by direct or circumstantial evidence, or a combination of both direct and circumstantial evidence. Identification evidence could consist of one or more of the following:

- Identification by the victim of the crime.
- Identification by an eyewitness to the crime. (In a July 2002 release, *NCJ* reported that bystanders are present in 70% of simple and aggravated assaults, 52% of robberies, and 29% of rapes/sexual assaults. See *NCJ* 189100.)
- Confessions, admissions, or incriminating statements by the defendant or his associates showing that the defendant committed the crime or was a party to the crime.
- DNA fingerprinting, regular fingerprints, tire tracks, and the like, which place the defendant at the scene of the crime.
- Other physical evidence left at the scene of the crime or obtained later by the police that implicates the defendant as the perpetrator of the crime (for example, the gun that killed the victim is found in the defendant's possession the day after the crime was committed).
- Photos or videos from a surveillance camera or hand-held video taken as the defendant committed the crime.
- Voice identification or, if admissible, voiceprints (spectrographic) evidence that identifies the defendant as the perpetrator of the crime or as a party to the crime.

It is the trier of the facts (the jury or the judge) who determines whether the identification evidence is sufficient to carry the burden of proof beyond reasonable doubt.

Examples of cases where unusual identification evidence was presented include *People v. Sutterland,*[1] where a shoeprint found on the victim's back and tire tracks were held to be sufficient evidence to sustain kidnapping, sexual assault, and murder of a 10-year-old girl; *Culbreath v. State,*[2] where the victim's caller ID was used as evidence to sustain a stalking prosecution; *People v. Campbell,*[3] where clear and unique shoeprints plus flight from an officer three days after the crime were held to be sufficient; *Spence v. State,*[4] where bite mark evidence on the body of the victim was used to link the defendant to the crime; *State v. Faircloth,*[5] where hair evidence (most often used in rape and murder cases) was used in identifying the offender (The court pointed out that while hair—unlike DNA—cannot positively identify an offender, it can be relevant evidence for identification purposes.); and *State v. Jells,*[6] where footprints (as distinguished from shoeprints) were used as evidence for a murder conviction and the use of the death penalty.

Using Biometrics for Identification and Authentication

Fingerprints are the best-known type of biometrics. Other means of identification and authentication through biometrics include:

- Iris-based systems, which in the future may equal or exceed fingerprints in accuracy.

- Hand-geometry systems, which have better access and control and can be vital in prisons and jails where high levels of accuracy and security are required.

- Voice recognition, which is the least accurate but is the best available to verify identity over a telephone.

- Facial-recognition systems, which present opportunities to identify people unobtrusively and without their cooperation in video surveillance and other means.

The article "Biometrics: Solving Cases of Mistaken Identity and More" in the June 2000 issue of the *FBI Law Enforcement Bulletin* reviews the present use of biometrics for identification and authentication. The article points out that:

> Biometric technology creates new opportunities for law enforcement and crime prevention by accurately identifying people when they cash checks, collect welfare benefits, use automated teller machines (ATMs), cross borders into the United States, sign on to computer networks, or enter secure buildings.

After an arrest is made, a suspect is fingerprinted to verify the identity that the suspect has given and to determine if the suspect's fingerprints have been found at other crime scenes. Some states are already using other forms of biometrics for identification and authentication of suspects in addition to fingerprinting.

B THE PROBLEM OF MISTAKEN EYEWITNESS IDENTIFICATION

In the 1960s, the International Association of Chiefs of Police recognized that eyewitness "identification and description is regarded as a most unreliable form of evidence and causes more miscarriages of justice than any other method of proof."[7]

Mistaken eyewitness identification could cause the accusation or conviction of an innocent person; and it could cause a guilty person to avoid identification and conviction. As the extent of this problem is unknown, it is hoped that it occurs in only a very small percentage of the hundreds of thousands of criminal cases handled by criminal courts each year in the United States. Mistaken identification can happen if:

- Stress and excitement caused by the shock of witnessing or being the victim of a crime could cause the mistaken eyewitness identification.

- A look-alike situation occurred between an innocent person and the person who actually committed a crime.

- A suspect's story and claim of innocence are not checked carefully.

- Other leads are not checked carefully. Such leads could be fingerprints, blood, sperm, alibi stories, and so on.

Mistaken identification is also more likely to occur in cases where no corroborative evidence is presented to support eyewitness identification by a victim or a witness. Good defense lawyers should attack eyewitness identification, pointing out shortcomings and the possibility of error. The following eyewitness identification cases illustrate:

EXAMPLE: *Case where eyewitness identification was not corroborated.* A Wisconsin man served nine years for the attempted murder and rape of a 15-year-old girl who had identified him as her attacker. Neither the police, the prosecutor, nor the defense lawyer had the semen found on the victim's clothing tested. When it was tested, it showed that the attacker had type B blood. The man in prison had type A blood and sued his defense lawyer upon release from prison, recovering a settlement of $500,000. (This case occurred before DNA evidence became available.)

EXAMPLE: *Case where eyewitness identification was corroborated.* A woman who was raped in a wooded rural area identified the defendant as her attacker. To corroborate the rape victim's testimony, the police took soil samples and vegetation from under the defendant's car and found that they matched soil and vegetation from the crime area.[8]

Criminal convictions of the wrong person have been lessened by increased DNA testing, building up of DNA databanks, better-equipped state and national crime labs, and computerized fingerprint searches.

❸ USING SHOWUPS TO OBTAIN IDENTIFICATION EVIDENCE

A **showup** differs from a lineup in that in a showup law enforcement officers permit witnesses or the victim of a crime to view a suspect in police custody singly instead of as part of a group. In commenting on showups in 1967, the U.S. Supreme Court stated that "(t)he practice of showing suspects singly to persons for the purposes of identification and not as part of a lineup, has been widely condemned."[9]

Showups are therefore suggestive and should not be used by law enforcement officers unless they are necessary under the circumstances. However, suggestiveness alone would not justify a ruling by a court that there has been a violation of the defendant's due process rights. To rule that the defendant's due process rights have been violated, there must have been impermissible suggestiveness to such a degree as to make the identification unreliable as a matter of law and resulting in a possible miscarriage of justice.

The U.S. Supreme Court has repeatedly held that the question of whether there has been a violation of the defendant's due process rights must be determined "on the totality of the circumstances."[10] In using the totality of the circumstances test, the Supreme Court and other courts have held that showups do not violate the due process rights of defendants when the following occur:

- The showup was held a short time after the crime was committed in a scene-of-the-crime, on-the-spot, or short detour confrontation and viewing. Courts have approved of such showups because the memory of the witness is very fresh and officers can make an immediate determination as to whether they have taken the right person into custody. For example, a woman's purse is snatched. Witnesses to the incident chase the purse-snatcher and after several blocks catch the person. A police officer immediately brings the man and the recovered purse back to ask the victim if the purse was hers and if the man in custody is the man who snatched the purse.[11]

- Though showups are generally held a short time after the crime and are generally held at or near the crime scene, they have also been approved under the following circumstances by the U.S. Supreme Court:

1. The showup was necessary because the victim or witness was in critical condition and could die at any time. In the case of *Stovall v. Denno*,[12] one of the victims of a criminal attack was dead, and his wife was in critical condition because of eleven stab wounds. Two days after the crime, Stovall was taken in handcuffs to the victim's hospital room where she identified him as the perpetrator of the crime. In affirming Stovall's convictions and the use of this procedure, the U.S. Supreme Court quoted a lower court, holding that:

   Here was the only person in the world who could possibly exonerate Stovall. Her words and only her words, "He is not the man," could have resulted in freedom for Stovall.

2. The suspect is in possession of property recently stolen from a victim. In the case of *Kirby v. Illinois*,[13] the defendant was arrested in downtown Chicago with traveler's checks and a Social Security card taken from a man who had been robbed the day before. The holdup victim was driven to the police station where he identified Kirby as one of the holdup men. In affirming Kirby's conviction and in holding there is no right to an attorney during showups, the U.S. Supreme Court held that:

   In this case we are asked to import into a routine police investigation an absolute constitutional guarantee historically and rationally applicable only after the onset of formal prosecutional proceedings. We decline to do so.

3. The showup did not create a very substantial likelihood of irreparable misidentification—for example, if the victim or witness knew the offender or had seen the offender on previous occasions or if the victim or witness to the crime gives the police such a specific description of the suspect so as to clearly distinguish the offender from other persons, as occurred in the U.S. Supreme Court case of *Neil v. Biggers*[14] (this cases follows in section D).

The Importance of Obtaining Prior Descriptions of Offenders

It is important that investigating officers have the witnesses give them as detailed a description of the offender as is possible soon after the crime is reported. The officer should assist the victim and the witness in searching their memories (without being in any way suggestive) for details of physical appearances and clothing, no matter how insignificant such details may seem. Such prior descriptions are important in that:

- They will authorize stops in the neighborhood and elsewhere for investigative detentions of persons reasonably matching these descriptions.

- The descriptions may be compared to descriptions given by victims and witnesses of other crimes and further aid in the apprehension of the offender.

- Detailed descriptions matching the defendants can significantly increase the reliability of identifications made later by victims and witnesses.

- Testimony by the investigating officers in court concerning prior descriptions provides important evidence for juries and judges in the determination of the issue of guilt or innocence.

Ⓓ DETERMINING THE RELIABILITY OF IDENTIFICATION EVIDENCE

The U.S. Supreme Court ruled that "It is the reliability of identification evidence that primarily determines its admissibility [as evidence in a trial]."[15]

The guidelines for determining the reliability of identification evidence were established by the U.S. Supreme Court in the case of *Neil v. Biggers,* which follows. The Supreme Court pointed out that, when eyewitness identification evidence is presented, defense lawyers can "both cross-examine the identification witness and argue in summation as to factors causing doubts as to the accuracy of the identification. . . ."[16]

Neil v. Biggers
United States Supreme Court, 409 U.S. 188, 93 S.Ct. 375 (1972)

A nurse was assaulted in her home and then taken outside where she was raped in a criminal incident that lasted between 15 and 30 minutes on a bright moonlit night. The victim gave the police a very specific description of her assailant. In the months that followed, she viewed many lineups and photo arrays but made no identification.

Seven months after the rape, the defendant was taken into police custody for another offense. When the police noticed the similarity of the defendant to the description given by the rape victim, the police attempted to make up a lineup but could find no one fitting the defendant's "unusual physical description."

When the rape victim arrived at the police station, a showup was used. After hearing the defendant repeat "Shut up or I'll kill you," the victim identified the defendant as her assailant. The defendant appealed his rape conviction, arguing that the identification evidence obtained in the station house showup was so suggestive that it violated due process. The Supreme Court held that the identification evidence was properly admitted, ruling that: "Weighing all the factors, we find no substantial likelihood of misidentification. The evidence was properly allowed to go to the jury."

"The Primary Evil to Be Avoided . . . a Very Substantial Likelihood of Irreparable Misidentification"

U.S. Supreme Court in *Neil v. Biggers*, 409 U.S. 188, 93 S.Ct. 375 (1972) and *Simmons v. United States*, 390 U.S. 377, 384, 88 S.Ct. 967, 971 (1968)

Identification evidence could be denied admission for use as evidence in a trial if the evidence was not reliable, or if the evidence was obtained in a manner that was so impermissibly suggestive as to cause a "very substantial likelihood of irreparable misidentification."

"It Is the Reliability of Identification Evidence that Primarily Determines Its Admissibility [for Use as Evidence in a Criminal Trial]"

U.S. Supreme Court in *Manson v. Brathwaite*, 432 U.S. 98, 113–14, 97 S.Ct. 2243 (1977)

Reliability is determined by the tests stated in the U.S. Supreme Court case of *Neil v. Biggers*, 409 U.S. 188, 93 S.Ct. 375 (1972). Defense lawyers "can both cross-examine the identification witnesses and argue in summation as to factors causing doubts as to the accuracy of the identification—including reference to both any suggestibility in the identification procedure and any countervailing testimony such as alibi" [*Watkins v. Sowders*, 449 U.S. 341, 101 S.Ct. 654, 28 CrL 3037 (1981)].

Guidelines Used to Determine the Reliability and Accuracy of Eyewitness Identification

To minimize the possibility that an innocent person will be identified as a criminal and sent to prison, the following factors are used to determine whether the evidence is sufficiently accurate and reliable to present to a jury for their deliberation:[17]

- What was the witness's opportunity to observe the criminal at the time of the crime? Factors are length of time of the encounter; distance between the witness and the suspect; lighting conditions; whether the witness's view was unobstructed; the witness's state of mind at the time.

- Was the witness a casual observer, or did the witness show a high degree of attention? A witness who observed a person hurry down a hall or a street might be a very casual observer and may not be able to accurately describe or identify that person a short time later. On the other hand, the victim of a rape or a robbery would ordinarily have a very high degree of attention, which could result in a more accurate and more reliable identification of the perpetrator of the crime.

- How accurate was the witness's prior description of the criminal? How accurate was the description recorded by the investigating officers? Did it record unusual features such as scars, moles, birthmarks, tattoos, and distinctive clothing, which could establish an independent basis of identification and make the identification highly reliable? How well did the testimony of the witness in court stand up under cross-examination? Was the witness able to explain why she identified the defendant as the person who committed the crime? Any discrepancies between the prior identification and the actual appearance of the defendant would ordinarily be brought out in cross-examination.

- What was the level of certainty demonstrated by the witness at the confrontation? Did the witness immediately identify the suspect? Was there hesitancy? Was there a misidentification?

- What time element elapsed between the commission of the crime and identification of the suspect as the perpetrator of the crime? Did the identification occur 10 minutes after the crime or 10 hours, 10 days, or 10 months? This factor, when combined with the other factors, would determine the basis of reliability upon which the decision by the trial judge as to whether to submit the identification evidence to a jury would be determined.

Ⓔ USING LINEUPS TO OBTAIN IDENTIFICATION EVIDENCE

Judges' Rules for Lineups

Lineups should be used whenever practical and must be used in situations where showups would not be authorized. Lineups not only minimize suggestiveness but also increase the reliability of the identification evidence.

Lineups are used to test recognition in a manner that avoids suggestiveness. The National Council of Judges provides the following rules for the lineup procedure:[18]

- Reasonable notice of the proposed lineup shall be given to the suspect and his counsel, and both shall be informed that the suspect may have his attorney present at the lineup. If the suspect is not represented by counsel, he shall be advised of his right to have counsel assigned without charge. He may waive in writing the presence of his attorney.[19]

- The lineup should consist of at least six persons, approximately alike in age, size, color, and dress; and none of them, other than possibly the suspect, shall be known to the witness.

- Persons in the lineup may be requested to speak certain words, identical for each person, for purposes of voice identification.

- Neither directly nor indirectly shall any police officer indicate or allow anyone but the witness to indicate in any way any person in the lineup as the suspect or defendant. Any instructions shall be given to all as a group, not individually.

- The lineup shall be viewed by only one witness at a time, others being excluded from the room and not permitted to discuss the lineup or descriptions of the suspect.

The following U.S. Supreme Court cases of the 1960s reflect why judges' rules on lineups were drafted.

United States v. Wade
United States Supreme Court, 388 U.S. 218, 87 S.Ct. 1926 (1967)

Wade was arrested for robbery of a bank in Texas. A lineup was conducted in the courtroom of a local courthouse without first informing Wade's attorney. The Supreme Court ordered a new hearing before excluding the identification at the trial of Wade by the bank witnesses because of the failure to notify the lawyer. At the hearing, the government was given an opportunity to establish by clear and convincing evidence that the in-court identifications were based upon observations of the suspect other than the lineup identification.

Gilbert v. California
United States Supreme Court, 388 U.S. 263, 87 S.Ct. 1951 (1967)

Gilbert was arrested for the robbery of a savings and loan association and the murder of a police officer during the robbery. Gilbert was also charged with other robberies. A lineup was held without notifying Gilbert's lawyer. The lineup was held on a stage with "upwards of 100 persons in the audience," each an eyewitness to one of the robberies charged to Gilbert. Bright lights prevented the persons in the lineup from seeing the audience. Persons in the audience would call out the number of the man they could identify in the lineup. It is not known whether the audience talked to one another during the lineup, but they did talk to one another after the lineup. In holding that the lineup was illegal, the Court stated that:

> The admission of the in-court identifications without first determining that they were not tainted by the illegal lineup but were of independent origin was constitutional error. United States v. Wade, supra. We there held that a post-indictment pretrial lineup at which the accused is exhibited to identifying witnesses is a critical stage of the criminal prosecution; that police conduct of such a lineup without notice to and in the absence of his counsel denies the accused his Sixth Amendment right to counsel and calls in question the admissibility at trial of the in-court identifications of the accused by witnesses who attended the lineup.

F USING PHOTOGRAPHS TO OBTAIN IDENTIFICATION EVIDENCE

Photographs are often used for identification purposes in criminal investigations. The Metropolitan Police Department of the District of Columbia (Washington, D.C.) issued the following instructions in regard to the use of photographs:

1. The use of photographs for identification purposes prior to an arrest is permissible provided the suspect's photograph is grouped with at least eight[20] other photographs (mug shots) of the same general description.[21]

2. Adequate records of the photographs shown to each witness must be kept so that the exact group of photographs from which an identification was made can be presented in court at a later date to counteract any claim of undue suggestion and enhance the reliability of the in-court identification. This information shall be recorded in the statement of facts of the case.

3. Each witness shall view the photographs independently, out of the immediate presence of the other witnesses.

Failure to preserve the photographs used to make an identification creates serious problems. The court cannot then determine whether law officers complied with due process and whether identification was made without excessive suggestiveness. In the 1980 case of *Branch v. Estelle,* the Federal Court of Appeals for the 5th Circuit held that "in situations where the police fail to preserve the **photographic array,** there shall exist a presumption that the array is impermissibly suggestive."[22]

Using a Single Photograph for Identification

In the 1989 case of *People v. Kelly,* the Illinois Court of Appeals pointed out that as "a rule, the use of a single-photograph display is unduly suggestive and gives rise to a substantial likelihood of irreparable misidentification if the totality of the circumstances surrounding the identification renders it unreliable."[23]

Single-photograph showings are suggestive; however, a prosecutor and the police could show by testimony or other evidence that the identification was sufficiently reliable. Reliability is determined by the factors established in the U.S. Supreme Court cases of *Neil v. Biggers* (discussed in this chapter).

Problem 1 at the end of this chapter presents the U.S. Supreme Court case of *Manson v. Brathwaite.* In the *Manson* case, a single photograph was used between police officers after one of the officers had made a heroin buy but did not know the identity of the heroin seller. Using the guidelines to determine the reliability of identification evidence (*Neil v. Biggers* factors), the Supreme Court answered the questions as to whether the identification evidence was sufficiently reliable to use and whether the use of only one photograph under the circumstances caused a substantial likelihood of irreparable misidentification. Compare the facts in Problem 1 to the *Neil v. Biggers* factors and state what you think the logical ruling of this case should be. Can the evidence be used, and should the criminal conviction stand?

Ⓖ OBTAINING IDENTIFICATION EVIDENCE BY OTHER MEANS

Other means of obtaining identification evidence include:

- *Sketches* **Sketches** can be done by an artist or with an identi-kit with the assistance of one witness or the input of a number of witnesses. "Wanted" posters could be made from a sketch, or the sketch could be published in newspapers or shown on television. The identi-kit, invented by a police officer, has hundreds of facial components (noses, eyes, chins, hairlines, hair, and so on) that can be built into the likeness of a person.[24]

- *Surveillance cameras and camcorders* Many businesses (such as banks and convenience stores) use surveillance cameras, and private persons with camcorders can be seen in many places. It is not unusual to have crime-scene photographs available as evidence. In the case of *United States v. Gray*,[25] bank surveillance photographs and descriptions of the offender from bank employees led to Gray's arrest two weeks after he robbed a bank. In affirming his conviction, the court pointed out that "the reliability of these identification procedures is obvious."

- *Unusual features* Such features as tattoos, scars, gold teeth or other dental feature, hair, weight, or size can increase the reliability of an identification. Such unusual features can be exhibited in a courtroom as identification evidence.

- *Clothing* Clothing is often included in descriptions given by victims or witnesses. Sometimes in rape cases an offender's clothing becomes torn, dirty, or stained in his struggle with the victim. Hats or other items of clothing are sometimes left behind or dropped in a hasty exit. Knowledgeable suspects will sometimes change clothing with other persons in an effort to avoid identification through a hat or jacket.

    The Supreme Court of California held that a defendant's refusal to don a jacket and cap during a showup at a police station can be used as evidence in the trial of the defendant,[26] as can a defendant's refusal to participate in a lineup.[27] Such evidence is not protected by the Fifth Amendment privilege against self-incrimination and can be compelled, with refusal by the defendants used as evidence against them.

    The robbery victim's identification of the defendant's hat and jacket were used as evidence to convict the defendant in the case of *Johnson v. Ross*.[28] The suspect's voice and clothes were used as aids in identification in the case of *State v. Holloman*.[29] The gun carried by one of the defendants was used in identification in the case of *Turner v. State*.[30] In the case of *Holder v. State*,[31] the defendant was required to stand in court and put on a jacket, mask, and cap worn by the robber and to say words spoken by the robber. To minimize such evidence, the defense lawyer also put on the cap and the bandana, but the jury's finding of guilt was sustained by the appellate court.

- *Voice identification* Voice identification has been admissible as evidence for years in the United States. In some cases, the victim has had previous contact with the defendant and recognizes the voice because of the previous contacts. In other cases, the offender is unknown to the victim, but the victim or other persons recall features of the offender's voice. A recording of the offender's voice may be available from a message-recording machine, voice mail, or other means.

    In crimes such as rape and robbery, most victims not only see the offenders but also hear their voices. However, in cases of telephone threats, telephone harassment, and stalking, voice identification alone can be used as evidence if the victim can identify the voice.[32] Victims can ordinarily testify that the voice "sounds like" the voice of the offender. The Supreme Court of Minnesota stated the rule of law for the admissibility of voice identification evidence:

    > It is the rule in this state that the foundation for admission of testimony as to the identity of the voice of a telephone caller is sufficient when it appears that the witness to whom the telephone call is made testifies that he is reasonably certain as to the voice of such caller and can identify it.[33]

A young woman believed to be responsible for six Boston area bank robberies is shown in this bank video surveillance camera image. The woman drew a gun and escaped with thousands of dollars.

AP/Wide World Photos

- *Spectrograms, or voiceprints* If voice recordings become available in such crimes as kidnapping, murder plots, bomb threats, or false alarms, a **spectrogram or voiceprint** could be made in an effort to identify the offender. If a match is made with the voiceprint of a suspect, some state courts will permit the spectrograms to be used as evidence in criminal trials. The highest court in Maryland described the operation of a spectrograph in the case of *Reed v. State*[34]:

> The process involves the use of a machine known as a spectrograph. This machine analyzes the acoustic energy of the human voice into three components—time, frequency, and intensity—and graphically displays these components by generating, through an electric stylus, a series of closely spaced light and dark lines, varying in position, on a sheet of electrically sensitive paper. The resulting graphic representation is what is called a spectrogram or "voiceprint." It reveals certain patterns or "formals" which correspond to the sounds which are analyzed.

Ⓗ COURTROOM IDENTIFICATION OF A DEFENDANT

In criminal trials the state must carry the burden of identifying the defendant beyond a reasonable doubt as the person who committed the crime or as an aider and abettor

Should Changes Be Made in the Way Photos Are Viewed?

Viewing photos to identify wanted suspects is used extensively in the United States. The different types of photo viewing can be illustrated by the following example. Suppose you and eight other persons were customers or employees in a bank when a man held up the bank. You had a good view of the man for 2 or 3 minutes. When the police arrived, you provided as detailed a description of the man as you could. The police might then request:

- That you come down to the police station to view mug shots books of more than a hundred persons, most of whom have been in trouble with the police. In most instances, you will be left by yourself to go through the photos moving back and forth, if you wish, comparing, contrasting, and restudying them at will. You could infer at this stage the police have no major suspect in mind.

- That you meet with an officer so you can view a photo array of eight or more pictures. You infer that in the group of photos is one of a man suspected by the detective of committing the robbery. You view the photos, which are spread out on a table allowing you to compare, contrast, and study them.

  Suppose photo #6 is the man the police suspect, and when you pick #2 as the man, the detective says, "Be sure to look carefully at all the photos." Then after 10 more minutes, you choose #6 and the detective then says, "Tell me why you choose #6." Has this procedure been impermissibly suggestive?

A study in 1999 of twenty-eight criminal cases where criminal convictions were overturned by DNA evidence showed that the strongest evidence in most of the cases was eyewitness identification. The U.S. Justice Department then published a 1999 guide entitled "Convicted by Juries, Exonerated by Science," which recommended changes in how witnesses view suspects. Two of the changes that have been made by some law enforcement agencies in the United States are:

1. Witnesses are not permitted to browse when viewing photos but instead are shown photos one at a time to narrow the risk that a mistake in identification is made. Whether a witness would be permitted a second look could depend upon procedure in that state. If a second look at photos is permitted, the witness would have to view all the photos singly in a new sequence.

2. An officer who did not know which photo was that of the person the police suspect would conduct the photo showing. This might be very difficult to do in a small police or sheriff department.

or a conspirator to the crime. This task can be accomplished through any of the means discussed in this chapter.

During criminal trials, defendants may be required to try on such items as jackets, hats, and glasses, to show whether such items fit the defendant. Defendants could also be required to speak for identification or to display tattoos, scars, or a gold tooth.

Eyewitnesses or earwitnesses are asked by the prosecutor to describe the person who committed the crime or who was seen fleeing from the crime scene. The witness is then asked whether that person is in the courtroom. When the witness answers yes, the witness is then asked to point out the person.

Because the defendant is ordinarily seated next to his or her attorney at the defense table,[35] the witness will then point the person out to the court and the jury. To

Tests that Determine the Admissibility of Eyewitness Identification Evidence

- Were the defendant's Fifth Amendment due process rights violated by identification procedures that were so unnecessarily suggestive as to cause "a very substantial likelihood of irreparable misidentification"? [*Simmons v. United States,* 390 U.S. 377, 384, 88 S.Ct. 967, 974 (1968).]

- Was the defendant's Sixth Amendment right to an attorney observed and complied with during identification proceedings after the defendant was charged or indicted?

The One-on-One Showup

1. Showups are suggestive but not necessarily in violation of the Fifth Amendment due process requirement.

2. The propriety of a showup is determined by the "totality of the circumstances surrounding" the identification (U.S. Supreme Court in *Stovall v. Denno*).

3. The suggestiveness inherent in the one-to-one showup can be outweighed by the following policy considerations:
   - The reliability due to the nearness in time of the identification to the crime committed and the need for immediate release of a person who is innocent.
   - The reliability of a witness, as demonstrated in *Neil v. Biggers,* in which the U.S. Supreme Court stated, "Her record for reliability was thus a good one, as she had previously resisted whatever suggestiveness inheres in a showup."
   - An emergency condition exists, such as in *Stovall v. Denno,* in which two days after a murder, the only witness was in critical condition in a hospital. The U.S. Supreme Court held in *Stovall v. Denno* that an "immediate hospital confrontation was imperative."

Photographic Identification

- The propriety of pretrial photographic identification is determined by the "totality of the circumstances surrounding" the identification and will be set aside "only if the photographic identification was so impermissibly suggestive as to give rise to a very substantial likelihood of irreparable misidentification" [*Simmons v. United States,* 390 U.S. 377, 88 S.Ct. 967 (1968)].

- The suspect's photograph should be grouped with a sufficient number of other photographs of the same general description and shown to witnesses separately. The exact group of photographs should be preserved so it may be presented to the court at a later date to counteract any claim of undue suggestiveness and to enhance the reliability of the in-court identification.

- A suspect has no right to have an attorney present during a photographic identification proceeding [*United States v. Ash,* 413 U.S. 300, 93 S.Ct. 2568 (1973)], unless your state courts have held otherwise.

- A single-photograph identification procedure is suggestive but may not be impermissibly suggestive. The burden would be on the state to show that the identification was sufficiently reliable to be used as evidence in view of the "totality of the circumstances surrounding" the identification procedure used.

clearly establish that the witness has identified the defendant as the person who committed the crime, the witness is then ordinarily requested to further identify the defendant by one or more of the following methods:

- By asking the witness to describe what the defendant is wearing in court and to specifically describe where that person is sitting

- By asking the defendant to stand and asking the witness whether this is the person who committed the crime or was seen fleeing from the crime scene
- By requesting the witness to step down from the stand and to point to or to touch the person who committed the crime or who was seen fleeing from the crime scene

The prosecutor will then request that the court record show that the witness has identified the defendant as the person who was seen committing the crime or was seen fleeing from the crime scene.

Because many jurisdictions permit testimony by eyewitnesses regarding prior out-of-court identification, witnesses may then be asked whether they had previously identified the defendant as the person who assaulted them or committed the crime being charged. Such testimony can be technically considered hearsay, but it is important and meaningful because it gives the jury and judge a full picture of the identification process that was used. Such testimony also buttresses the ritualized **courtroom identification** against possible attack in cross-examination and shows to the jury and the judge the extent of the investigation and deliberation before the decision was made to bring the defendant to trial.

SUMMARY

In the 1960s, the English and American public became aware of serious problems in eyewitness identification evidence when twenty-two honest English citizens testified and falsely convicted a man for a crime he did not commit. The man served seven years in a penitentiary before other evidence showed he was innocent.

In the United States, thirty witnesses testified that the defendant in a forgery case had committed dozens of forgeries. The man was not convicted because he produced evidence showing that he was in jail at the time the forgeries were committed.

Reliable identification evidence is required to carry the burden of proving guilt beyond reasonable doubt to a jury or a judge when the right to a jury has been waived.

The law governing identification evidence such as showups, lineups, and photo arrays is presented in this chapter.

PROBLEMS

All problems are U.S. Supreme Court cases.

1. Connecticut State Trooper Glover was working as an undercover officer in narcotics. He and an informer went to an apartment building in Hartford, where Glover knocked on the door of one of the apartments. A man (the defendant in this case) opened the door and in a 5- to 7-minute period sold $20 worth of heroin to Glover. Glover had never seen the defendant before and did not know the defendant's proper name. Upon leaving the building, Trooper Glover described the man to Officer D'Onofrio, who had been backing him up outside the building. From the description, Officer D'Onofrio suspected that the seller was the defendant. D'Onofrio obtained a single photograph of the defendant and left the picture at Trooper Glover's office. Two days later, Glover viewed the single picture and identified the defendant as the man who sold him the heroin. Based upon this information, the defendant was arrested. Without defense objection, the picture was used as evidence, and Trooper Glover made a positive in-court identification of the defendant.

What improper procedure was used by the officers that caused defense lawyers to appeal this case to the U.S. Supreme Court? Should the evidence of the in-court identification be allowed, and should the defendant's conviction for selling heroin be affirmed? Why? [*Manson v. Brathwaite*, 432 U.S. 98, 97 S.Ct. 2243 (1977).]

2. After the three men robbed a Western Union office, one of the men surrendered to the police and implicated Foster, who had gone into the office with him, and another man. Foster was placed in a three-man lineup for viewing by the only witness (the manager of the office). Foster was about 6 feet tall, whereas the other two men in the lineup were about 5 feet 6 inches tall. Foster wore a leather jacket, which the night manager said he saw the robber wear under coveralls. After viewing the lineup, the night manager of the Western Union office could not positively identify Foster as one of the robbers. The manager was not sure but he thought Foster was one of the robbers. The manager then asked to speak with Foster, who was taken into an office and sat at a table across from the manager. No one else was in the room except prosecuting officials. The manager still could not positively identify Foster. About ten days after the first lineup, the night manager viewed a second lineup. Of the five men in the lineup, Foster was the only person who had been in the first lineup. This time, the manager was "convinced" that Foster was one of the robbers.

Should the identification evidence be permitted in Foster's trial? Should the U.S. Supreme Court affirm Foster's conviction for armed robbery? Why? [*Foster v. California*, 394 U.S. 440, 89 S.Ct. 1127 (1969).]

3. A young man robbed a woman in a woman's restroom at the Washington National Monument. During the robbery, the woman had a good opportunity to see the young man. The woman immediately reported the robbery and described the young man who robbed her. Three days later, a young man (Crews) was improperly and illegally detained. Photographs were taken of the young man and a photographic display (array) was shown to the woman. She immediately identified Crews as the man who robbed her. In a lineup, the woman again identified Crews as the man who robbed her. At Crews's trial for armed robbery, the woman appeared as a witness and identified the defendant as the robber. Crews was convicted and appealed, arguing that the in-court identification was the "fruit of the poisonous tree" and should not be used as evidence.

Should the woman's in-court identification be allowed to be used as evidence, and should the U.S. Supreme Court affirm Crews's conviction? Why? [*United States v. Crews*, 445 U.S. 463, 100 S.Ct. 1244 (1980).]

INFOTRAC COLLEGE EDITION EXERCISES

1. Go to InfoTrac College Edition and using the search term "Hearsay evidence" and the subdivision "psychological aspects" find the 1993 article in the *Journal of Social Psychology* titled "Effects of Lineup Modality on Witness Credibility." This study explores the credibility of "earwitness" versus "eyewitness" testimony.

2. Go to InfoTrac College Edition and using the search term "voiceprints" find the 1999 article in the *American Criminal Law Review* titled "Anything You Say Can and Will Be Used Against You: Spectrographic Evidence in Criminal Cases," by Lisa Rafferty. This article reviews the admissibility of spectrographic evidence in criminal trials and the effect of the *Daubert* decision, discussed in Chapter 18 of the text, on the admissibility question.

NOTES

1. 610 N.E.2d l (Ill. App., 1993).

2. 667 So.2d 156 (Ala. Crim. App., 1995).

3. 586 N.E.2d 1261 (App., 1992).

4. 47 CrL 1252 (Tex. Crim. App., 1990).

5. 394 S.E.2d 198 (N.C. App., 1990).

6. 559 N.E.2d 464 (Ohio, 1990).

7. IACP Training Key #67, entitled "Witness Perception."

8. *State v. Skelton,* 795 P.2d 349 (Kan., 1990).

9. *Stovall v. Denno,* 388 U.S. 293, 87 S.Ct. 1967 (1967).

10. *Stovall v. Denno;* and *Neil v. Biggers,* 409 U.S. 188, 93 S.Ct. 375 (1972).

11. A few of the many one-on-one showups approved by courts include *State v. Valentine,* 570 So.2d 533 (La. App., 1990), within a half hour after the robbery; *State v. Garcia,* 453 N.W.2d 469 (Neb., 1990), "shortly after the crime"; *State v. Moore,* 469 N.W.2d 269 (Iowa App., 1991), within 2 hours after the store robbery; *Letica v. State,* 569 N.E.2d 952 (Ind., 1991), within 30 minutes after the crime; *People v. Duuvon,* 571 N.E.2d 654 (N.Y. Ct. App., 1991), 3 to 4 minutes after the crime; *State v. Severance,* 828 P.2d 1066 (Utah App., 1992), $1\frac{1}{2}$ hours after the robbery; *People v. Roberts,* 591 N.E.2d 1182 (N.Y., 1992), experienced undercover officer confirmed that defendant was the man who sold him cocaine by viewing the man through one-way mirror less than 5 hours after the crime (called "drive-by identification" to confirm right person was arrested); *Rogers v. State,* 415 S.E.2d 49 (Ga. App., 1992), "shortly" after the rape and "as soon as possible after the crime"; *People v. Follins,* 554 N.E.2d 345 (Ill. App., 1990), within 5 minutes of the robbery; *United States v. Clark,* 989 F.2d 1490 (7th Cir., 1993), within $1\frac{1}{2}$ hours of the bank robbery; *Commonwealth v. Brown,* 611 A.2d 1318 (Pa. Super., 1992) less than 2 hours after the assault, the victim identified the defendant at the hospital where the victim was being treated.

12. 87 S.Ct. 1967.

13. 406 U.S. 682, 92 S.Ct. 1877 (1972).

14. 409 U.S. 188, 93 S.Ct. 375 (1972).

15. *Manson v. Brathwaite,* 432 U.S. 98, 97 S.Ct. 2243 (1977).

16. *Watkins v. Sowders,* 449 U.S. 341, 101 S.Ct. 654 (1981).

17. These guidelines and factors for determining the accuracy and reliability of eyewitness identification were established by the U.S. Supreme Court in the case of *Neil v. Biggers.* Model Jury Instruction 52.20 is very similar to these guidelines and factors. This Model Jury Instruction can be found in *State v. Willis,* 731 P.2d 287 (Kans., 1987).

18. "Procedures for Obtaining Pretrial Eyewitness Identification" Series 304, No. 7.

19. In the 1992 case of *State v. Hoyte,* 413 S.E.2d 806, the Supreme Court of South Carolina reversed the defendant's crack cocaine conviction, because a showup without the defendant's attorney was held $5\frac{1}{2}$ months after the last drug sale and after the defendant's arrest. The court held that "there was no lineup; it was a one-man showup without notice to appointed counsel. While showups have been upheld by [this] Court, these situations usually involve either extenuating circumstances or are very close in time to the crime."

20. Courts have held that in view of the totality of circumstances that less than eight photographs are sufficient. The Supreme Court of Nebraska held that five photographs constituted "a fair and adequate array when attempting to identify a single perpetrator" [*State v. Gibbs,* 470 N.W.2d 558 (Neb., 1991)]. In the case of *United States v. Sanchez,* 24 F.3d 1259 (10th Cir., 1994), it was held that six photos were not impermissibly suggestive when there was only a minor difference between the photos. In the *Sanchez* case, the defendant's photo was the only photo depicting a person with his eyes closed. Major difference could consist of using photos depicting persons of different appearances (weight, lack of hair, age, sex, color, dress, etc.) than the defendant.

21. Mug shots are maintained by law enforcement agencies not only for citizen identification purposes but also to acquaint law enforcement officers with known suspects and persons who have criminal records. Mug shots should not be used as evidence, however, because they could easily cause jury members to believe that the defendant had a prior criminal record or prior trouble with the law; this could deny the defen-

dant the right to a fair trial. Evidence of other offenses and prior trouble with the law is inadmissible as part of the government's case against a defendant. [See *Michelson v. United States,* 335 U.S. 469, 69 S.Ct. 213 (1948).]

22. 631 F.2d 1229 (5th Cir.).

23. Cases in which courts held that misidentification in single-photograph showings was a remote possibility due to "the totality of the circumstances" include *People v. Kelly,* 540 N.E.2d 1125 (1989), in which the victims were 5- and 7-year-old children; *United States v. Dring,* 930 F.2d 687 (9th Cir., 1991); *State v. Barnett,* 588 N.E.2d 887 (Ohio App., 1990), the showing of only one photo was held to be "unnecessarily suggestive" but not "impermissibly suggestive"; *State v. James,* 592 So.2d 867 (La. App., 1991), held that an independent basis for identification existed in view of the *Manson* factors.

In the 1992 case of *State v. Martin,* 595 So.2d 592, the Supreme Court of Louisiana held that a single-photograph showing was made under circumstances resulting in substantial likelihood of irreparable misidentification and that there was no independent basis for the undercover police officer's in-court identification of the defendant. Other cases in which criminal convictions were reversed for a new trial include *Commonwealth v. Jarecki,* 1992 WL 104524 (Pa. Super., 1992), where a police officer permitted four witnesses to a store robbery to view a photographic display at the same time and talk among themselves in attempting to select the picture of the robber. In the 1991 case of *Hull v. State,* 581 So.2d 1202, the Alabama Appellate Court reversed the conviction of Hull for a new trial because, in a photo spread of five pictures, only the defendant's picture was a black-and-white photo while the other four photos were colored. The court held that the in-court identification by a witness was not independently reliable.

24. In the 1992 case of *Sanders v. English et al.,* 950 F.2d 1152 (5th Cir.), Sanders was arrested as the result of a composite sketch of the "bicycle bandit" who repeatedly robbed at gunpoint. After holding Sanders for 50 days, a grand jury refused to indict him after concluding that probable cause did not exist. In a civil lawsuit against the police officers involved, Sanders lost on the false arrest claims but was able to sue for the 50 days illegal detention and malicious prosecution.

25. 958 F.2d 9 (1st Cir., 1992).

26. *People v. Smith,* 91 Cal. Rptr. 786 (1970).

27. *People v. Johnson,* 842 P.2d 1 (Calif., 1992).

28. 955 F.2d 178 (2d Cir., 1992).

29. 837 P.2d 826 (Kan. App., 1992).

30. 803 P.2d 1152 (Okl. Crim. App., 1990).

31. 837 S.W.2d 802 (Tex. App., 1992).

32. It is a common practice to have persons in a lineup say words and sentences or to try on hats or clothing. Voice-only lineups could be held by having six or more persons repeat sentences or to tape-record the voices stating the sentence or phrase for replay when necessary. Defense lawyers requested this procedure in the case *Evans v. Superior Court,* 522 P.2d 681 (Calif., 1974). California trial judges have the authority to order voice-only lineups just as they have the authority to order physical lineups. [See *Garcia v. San Joaquin Superior Court,* 50 CrL 1312 (Calif. App., 1991).]

On-the-street and station-house voice identifications in rape cases were held not to be impermissibly suggestive in the cases of *State v. Jones,* 587 N.E.2d 886 (Ohio App., 1990), and *Jefferson v. State,* 425 S.E.2d 915 (Ga. App., 1992).

Voice exemplars, or recorded voice samples, were approved for use as evidence by the U.S. Supreme Court [*United States v. Wade,* 87 S.Ct. 1926 (1967), and *United States v. Dionisto,* 93 S.Ct. 764 (1973)]. Compelling a defendant or suspect to speak for the purposes of identification does not violate a suspect's Fifth Amendment privilege against self-incrimination.

33. *City of St. Paul v. Caulfield,* 94 N.W.2d 263 (Minn., 1959).

34. 391 A.2d 364 (1978).

35. In a few instances, defense lawyers have had persons who look similar to the defendant sit next to them at the defense table with the defendant sitting elsewhere in the courtroom during the trial. If the court is not informed of this situation, contempt charges could result against the defense attorney and the look-alike. In the 1973 case of *Duke v. State,* 298 N.E. 2d 453 (Ind.), the decoy sitting next to the defense lawyer was convicted and temporarily jailed in place of the defendant.

Other cases where defense lawyers were found in direct criminal contempt of court for not informing the trial court that the person sitting next to them was not the defendant include *United States v. Thoreen*, 653 F.2d 1332 (9th Cir., 1981); *People v. Simac*, 603 N.E.2d 97, 52 CrL 1260 (Ill. App., 1992); and *Miskovsky v. State ex rel. Jones*, 586 P.2d 1104 (Okla. Crim. App., 1978).

14

Obtaining Physical and Other Evidence

Physical evidence—or **real evidence,** as it is sometimes called—is often important and critical evidence in many criminal cases. Examples of physical evidence include weapons (guns, knives, and so on), illegal drugs, fingerprints, clothing, documents, footprints, hair, blood, grass marks or other stains on clothing, metal and wood fragments and objects that were stolen, such as merchandise, money, and purses.

Physical evidence could be obtained in a public place where a crime had been committed; it could be obtained from the person of a suspect or the suspect's motor vehicle; or it could be obtained in a home or other place. It could be obtained with lawful consent; it might be observed in plain view; or it might be obtained in a lawful search by a law enforcement officer.

This chapter presents the basic law that must be observed if evidence from constitutionally protected places is to be used in criminal trials.

Ⓐ OBTAINING PHYSICAL EVIDENCE FROM THE PERSON OF A SUSPECT

Obtaining Evidence and Information by Means of Voluntary Conversations

Encounters between citizens and law enforcement officers are of the following three types: (1) the voluntary encounter or voluntary conversation; (2) the investigative stop, or *Terry* **stop,** where the officer has reasonable suspicion to believe the suspect has committed, is committing, or is about to commit a crime; and (3) an arrest that is justified by probable cause to believe that the person has committed a crime.

All persons have a fundamental right in a democracy to move freely about without unnecessary interference by government. The U.S. Supreme Court pointed out that:

> No right is held more sacred, or is more carefully guarded, by the common law, than the right of every individual to the possession and control of their own person, free from all restraint or interference of others, unless by clear and unquestionable authority of law.[1]

Law enforcement officers may attempt to engage a person in a voluntary conversation in a public place such as on a sidewalk or in an airport or train station.[2] The U.S. Supreme Court pointed out that:

> the person approached . . . need not answer any questions . . . indeed, he may decline to listen to the questions at all and may go on his way. . . . He may not be detained even momentarily without reasonable objective grounds for doing so; and his refusal to listen, or answer does not, without more furnish these grounds. . . .[3]

Most persons will engage in voluntary conversations, however, with law enforcement officers. If at some point they wish to discontinue the conversation, they may do so. The test used by American courts to determine whether such situations are voluntary or not is the **free-to-leave test,** which was defined by the U.S. Supreme Court as follows:[4]

Facts in the Case of

***United States v. Drayton* 122 S. Ct. 2105 (2002)** Passengers on a Greyhound bus disembarked at a scheduled stop in Tallahassee, Florida, while the bus was refueled and cleaned. Shortly after the passengers reboarded the bus, three plainclothes police officers boarded as part of a drug and weapons interdiction program. One officer knelt on the driver's seat facing the passengers, a second stood at the back of the bus, while the third walked down the aisle speaking with individual passengers, asking about their travel plans and trying to match them with luggage in the overhead bins. To avoid blocking the aisle, the officer stood next to, or behind, each passenger with whom he spoke. No general announcement was made regarding why the officers were on the bus, and the passengers were never told that they could refuse to consent to any search of their luggage.

An officer approached Drayton and his traveling companion, introduced himself, and told them he was looking for drugs and weapons. The officer asked if the pair had any luggage. They responded that they shared a single bag located in the overhead bin. They gave the officer permission to search the bag, but no contraband was found. The officer then asked permission to frisk Drayton's traveling companion.

He consented to the frisk, and drug packages were found strapped to his inner thighs. He was arrested and escorted off the bus. Drayton was then asked to consent to a pat-down search. Drayton also consented, and similar packages were found in his possession. Drayton and his companion were charged with conspiracy to distribute cocaine and possession with intent to distribute cocaine.

Questions Before the Courts

Should the evidence be suppressed (a) because the passengers were not free to leave the bus, and (b) were the officers obligated to inform the passengers that they could refuse to give consent to search because the passengers did not feel free to refuse to give consent?

Rulings of the Lower Courts

- *Trial Court* The defense motion to suppress the evidence (drug packages) was denied.

- *Court of Appeals* The evidence was suppressed because the officers were obligated to inform the passengers of their right to refuse to give consent to search.

After considering the facts and the law in this case, you will find the U.S. Supreme Court ruling in note 40 of this chapter.

. . . a person has been "seized" within the meaning of the Fourth Amendment only if in view of all the circumstances surrounding the incident, a reasonable person would have believed that he was not free to leave.[5]

Authority Needed to Make an Investigative Detention (*Terry* Stop)

That quantum (amount) of evidence known as **reasonable suspicion** is needed to authorize an investigative detention, or *Terry* stop. Reasonable suspicion is less than probable cause that would authorize an arrest. To make a temporary stop, the officer must be able to "point to specific and articulable facts which, taken together with rational inferences from those facts, reasonably warrant that intrusion."[6]

Reasonable suspicion is therefore more than a "hunch," "gut reaction," or mere suspicion. Reasonable suspicion is that amount of evidence and facts that will cause a reasonable person to believe that the suspect has committed, or is committing, or is about to commit a crime. The totality-of-the-circumstances test is used to determine whether reasonable suspicion exists. That is, looking at the whole picture and all of the circumstances that existed.

Searches that Can Be Justified During an Investigative Detention

Consent searches and protective searches (where the law officer has a valid safety concern) are the only searches that could be justified during an investigative detention.

Consent to search would have to be voluntarily and clearly given. Consent searches would be limited to the area or object consented to the searched. The consent to search could be of luggage, a parcel, a purse, a vehicle, or other object or place.

A **protective search** can be made if an officer who has made a valid investigative stop has reasonable suspicion to believe that the suspect "may be armed and presently dangerous." The U.S. Supreme Court also pointed out that ". . . it would be unreasonable to require that police officers take unnecessary risks in the performance of their duties. American criminals have a long tradition of armed violence, and every year in this country many law enforcement officers are killed in the line of duty and thousands more are wounded."[7]

The protective frisk is strictly limited to the necessity of discovering threatening weapons. If the pat-down causes the officer to reasonably believe that an object detected in the frisk could be a weapon, the object may be removed and may be used as evidence if the object is a weapon or other illegal contraband.

In the 1993 U.S. Supreme Court case of *Minnesota v. Dickerson*,[8] a police officer making a lawful pat-down felt an object that he knew was not a weapon but suspected it was a lump of rock cocaine. The Supreme Court held that once it was immediately apparent that the object was not a weapon, no further search was permissible. If the nature of the unknown object is not immediately apparent and there is not probable cause to believe it is evidence of a crime, it cannot be seized and used as evidence.

In March of 2000 the United States Supreme Court again considered the *Terry* rules in connection with anonymous tips. In *Florida v. J.L.,* 120 S.Ct. 1375 (2000), an anonymous caller told Miami-Dade police that a black male standing at a bus stop was carrying a concealed weapon. The caller identified the man as wearing a plaid shirt but gave no other basis for the caller's belief that the man was carrying a weapon. Police found J.L. at the bus stop and identified him by his plaid shirt. The police had no other basis for suspecting J.L. was carrying a concealed weapon. They searched J.L. and found a concealed weapon.

The Supreme Court held the tip alone did not justify the *Terry* stop. **Anonymous tips** require **"indicia of reliability,"** that is, corroborating information from the person giving the tip showing that person to have "predictive information" about the suspect's behavior that allowed the police to judge the reliability of the anonymous tip. In *White v. Alabama,* for example, the tip included detailed information about the suspect's behavior, which the Court there said indicated the tipster had inside information about the suspect.[9] The *J.L.* court noted that *White* was a close case, on the borderline of permissible *Terry* stops. Since even less corroborating information was provided by the anonymous tip in *J.L.*, the Court held it crossed over the border into impermissible *Terry* stops.

The *J.L.* court also held that there is no "firearm exception" to the *Terry* stop requirements of indicia of reliability, as contended by the State of Florida. Such an exception, the Court reasoned, would permit any person to "set in motion an intrusive, embarrassing police search of the targeted person simply by placing an anonymous call reporting the target's unlawful carriage of a gun," *J.L.*, 120 S.Ct. at 1379–1380. The Court stated, however, that it was reserving ruling on such stops where the risks are particularly great, as for example where a caller informs the police that a person is carrying a bomb.

Obtaining Physical Evidence During and After an Arrest

The Fourth Amendment of the U.S. Constitution requires that **probable cause** exists for either a law enforcement officer or a private citizen[10] to make an **arrest.** The U.S. Supreme Court pointed out that the "requirement of probable cause has roots that are deep in our history" and that "common rumor or report, suspicion, or even 'strong reason to suspect' was not adequate to support a warrant for arrest. . . ."[11]

The famous English lawyer and writer, Sir William Blackstone, defined the legal term *arrest* in his 1760 *Commentaries* as "the apprehending or restraining of one's person, in order to be forthcoming to answer an alleged or suspected crime."

Most traffic stops and all *Terry* stops are not arrests. However, evidence could become available during such stops to support a finding of probable cause to authorize an arrest. Alternatives to an arrest could be used, such as issuing a citation or ordering the person to appear at a police station or a prosecutor's office. In minor incidents, the person could receive a warning or scolding.

Evidence Obtained in Searches Following an Arrest

A search for weapons and evidence of the crime may be made in the **search incident to an arrest.** The U.S. Supreme Court held that this search could be made "of the arrestee's person and the area 'within his immediate control'—construing that phrase to mean the area from within which he might gain possession of a weapon or destructible evidence."[12]

When the arrested person is in a motor vehicle, the U.S. Supreme Court held that the police "may, as a contemporaneous incident of that arrest, search the passenger compartment of that automobile" and the police "may also examine the contents of any containers found within the passenger compartment."[13]

A container could be a box, paper bag, suitcase, briefcase, or anything used to hold objects. The container searched in the *Belton* case was the zipped-up pocket of a black leather jacket belonging to Belton and lying on the backseat. The Supreme Court held that the cocaine found in Belton's leather jacket could be used as evidence to convict Belton of the possession of cocaine.

Terry Stops and the U.S. Supreme Court

Reasonable Suspicion Authorized *Terry* Stops

Case	Reasonable Suspicion that Justified the Stop and Frisk	Incriminating Evidence Admitted for Use at Trial
Terry v. Ohio, 88 S.Ct. 1868 (1968)	A veteran Cleveland detective observed two men who made a dozen trips past a store, looking in and then talking to each other. The officer suspected the men were "casing" the store for a stick-up. The officer approached the men, identified himself, and because he feared for his safety frisked them and seized two pistols.	In affirming the concealed-weapons convictions, the Court held "that where a police officer observes un-usual conduct which leads him rea-sonably to conclude in light of his experience that criminal activity may be afoot and that the persons with whom he is dealing may be armed and presently dangerous . . ." the officer may take protective measures.
Adams v. Williams, 92 S.Ct. 1921 (1972)	A known informant told police that Williams was sitting in a car late at night in a public place and had narcotics and a gun on his person. The tip was corroborated when Williams was seen sitting in the parked car.	After seizing the gun, the police ar-rested Williams and, in the search incident to the arrest, found the drugs. The Court held: "The purpose of this limited search is not to discover evidence of a crime, but to allow the officer to pursue his investigation without fear of violence." Conviction of two crimes were sustained.
Alabama v. White, 110 S.Ct. 2412 (1990)	An anonymous telephone caller told police that White would be driving a brown Plymouth station wagon with a broken right taillight, from her house to a named motel, carrying cocaine. After the tip was corroborated, when White arrived at the motel, a police *Terry* stop was made.	The Court held that there was suffi-cient indication of reliability to jus-tify the stop based upon reasonable suspicion after police corroborated the tip. White gave the police con-sent to search her attaché case and gave the police the combination to the lock.
United States v. Sokolow, 109 S.Ct. 1581 (1989)	The defendant bought airline tickets to travel from Honolulu to Miami (20 hours). He stayed in Miami for 48 hours and then returned to Honolulu. He paid $2,100 in cash for his airfare from a big roll of $20 bills and appeared nervous. A drug-detection dog led to the finding of cocaine in Sokolow's luggage.	The Court held that reasonable sus-picion existed to make the stop, holding that: "Any one of these factors is not by itself proof of ille-gal conduct and is quite consistent with innocent travel. But we think that taken together, they amount to reasonable suspicion."

Cases Where Evidence Could Not Be Used

Case	Facts that Did Not Authorize a *Terry* Stop	Ruling
Brown v. Texas, 99 S.Ct. 2637 (1979)	The defendant was stopped in an alley in an area that had a high incident of drug trafficking. There was no testimony that it was unusual for people to be in the alley.	"The fact that [the defendant] was in a neighborhood frequented by drug users standing alone, is not a basis for concluding that [the defendant] himself was engaged in criminal conduct . . . [the defendant's] activity was no different from activity of other pedestrians in that neighborhood."
Florida v. Royer, 103 S.Ct. 1319 (1983)	Officers at the Miami airport observed Royer and concluded that he fit the "drug courier profile," but their information did not amount to reasonable suspicion. The officers approached Royer and asked for and examined his plane ticket and driver's license. Without returning the ticket or driver's license, they informed Royer he was suspected of transporting drugs and asked him to come with them to a small police room.	The Court held that the police conduct was such a show of police authority that a reasonable person would not have felt free to leave. Royer's consent to search his luggage was held to be "invalid because [it was] tainted by the unlawful confinement."
Dunaway v. New York, 99 S.Ct. 2248 (1979)	The defendant was picked up on the uncorroborated tip from an informant and taken to a police station for questioning about the murder of a pizza parlor owner. After being given *Miranda* warnings and waiving his rights, the defendant incriminated himself.	The Court ruled that the confession could not be used as evidence because it would allow the police "to violate the Fourth Amendment with impunity, safe in the knowledge that they could wash their hands in the 'procedural safeguards' of the Fifth Amendment."
Davis v. Mississippi, 89 S.Ct. 1394 (1969)	Police rounded up more than twenty young black men for questioning about the rape of a white woman and to seek a match for fingerprints and palm prints found at the scene of the crime. Days later, the defendant was picked up a second time and this time was held overnight and transported to another city where the defendant's fingerprints were found to match those found at the crime scene.	In reversing the defendant's convictions and holding that the police roundup procedures violated the Fourth Amendment, the Court held: "Nothing is more clear than that the Fourth Amendment was meant to prevent wholesale intrusions upon the personal security of our citizenry, whether those intrusions be termed 'arrests' or 'investigative detentions.'"

NOTE: Six additional U.S. Supreme Court cases in this area are found as problems at the end of this chapter.

Facts in the Case of

United States v. Arvizu

534 U.S. 266 (2002) Arvizu was observed by a border patrol agent traveling in a remote area of Arizona on an unpaved road frequently used by smugglers. He was traveling in a minivan with a woman and three children. The position of the children in the back seat suggested to the agent that their legs were resting on some cargo on the floor. When Arvizu observed the agent, he immediately slowed the vehicle and avoided eye contact. When the agent began following his vehicle, the children in the back seat began waving in an "abnormal pattern" as if they were following instructions.

A registration check indicated that Arvizu's vehicle was registered to an address in an area that was notorious for alien and drug smuggling. The border patrol agent decided to stop the vehicle after noting that the route taken by Arvizu was designed to avoid area checkpoints and that he was traveling at a time when border patrol agents were changing shifts. Following the stop, Arvizu consented to a search of his vehicle that resulted in the seizure of more than 128 pounds of marijuana.

Arvizu was charged with possession with intent to distribute a controlled substance. He moved to suppress the marijuana on the grounds that there was no reasonable suspicion to stop his vehicle as required by the Fourth Amendment.

Question Before the Courts

Should the evidence (the 128 pounds of marijuana) be suppressed because "reasonable suspicion" to make the vehicle stop did not exist.

Rulings of the Lower Courts

- *Trial Court* Concluded that the observations and inferences drawn from the observations did amount to reasonable suspicion.

- *Court of Appeals* Considered each factor (observation) separately and concluded a majority of the facts were susceptible to innocent explanations. Held the vehicle stop was illegal as reasonable suspicion did not exist.

After considering the facts and the law in this case, you will find the U.S. Supreme Court ruling in note 41 of this chapter.

If during or after an arrest in a home or building there is reason to believe that another person (or persons) may be in a nearby room and may present a security risk, a **protective sweep or safety check** would be justified. This precaution was described as follows in the case of *United States v. Sheikh:*[14]

> Arresting officers have a right to conduct a quick and cursory check of the arrestee's lodging immediately subsequent to arrest—even if the arrest is near the door but outside the lodging—where they have reasonable grounds to believe that there are other persons present inside who might present a security risk.

Evidence Obtained During Inventory Searches

The U.S. Supreme Court listed the following reasons for inventorying property that is being held by the police:

The Three Types of Police–Citizen Contacts

Voluntary Conversation and/or Observation/Surveillance

Voluntary conversations may be used for investigative purposes if the person will talk with the officer. Observation and surveillance may be made of persons in public places without a showing of probable cause or reasonable suspicion. [See *Weber v. Cedarburg,* 370 N.W.2d 791 (1985), in which the Supreme Court of Wisconsin affirmed a ruling that the defendant had no civil cause of action for surveillance without reason to suspect wrongdoing. Police followed Weber to bars, sporting events, and so forth and made notes of his activities.]

Investigative Stop, or *Terry* Stop

Police must have reasonable suspicion to make a *Terry* stop (investigative detention). A detention is made and a *Terry* stop has occurred when a "reasonable person would have believed that he was not free to leave" (*United States v. Mendenhall*).

The free-to-leave test determines when a police encounter is no longer a voluntary conversation. The detention, or *Terry* stop, "must be temporary and last no longer than is necessary" (*Florida v. Royer*). In the 1985 case of *United States v. Sharpe,* the Supreme Court held that a 20-minute stop was not unreasonable "when the police have acted diligently and a suspect's actions contributed to the added delay about which he complains" (470 U.S. at 688, 105 S.Ct. at 1576).

Custody or Arrest

Probable cause, also known as reasonable grounds to believe, must exist to hold a person in custody or make an arrest. Incident to a lawful, custodial arrest, a search may be made of the person and the area under the person's immediate control. Under the delayed search exception of *United States v. Edwards,* searches of the arrestee's person may be made at later times. But if police take control of property or a container, they may only search it at the time of arrest.

1. The protection of the owner's property while it remained in police custody
2. The protection of the police against claims or disputes over lost or stolen property
3. The protection of the police from potential danger[15]

Inventory searches are therefore not searches for incriminating evidence. They are a common and sensible police procedure to determine what the law enforcement agency is responsible for. They are "not an independent legal concept but rather an incidental administrative step following arrest and preceding incarceration."[16]

In the U.S. Supreme Court case of *Illinois v. Lafayette,*[17] the defendant was arrested for fighting with a theater manager. At the police station, the defendant was told to empty his pockets and purse-type shoulder bag he was carrying, as part of the established police inventory procedure being used. Ten amphetamine pills were found inside a cigarette package. In holding that the pills could be used as evidence, the Supreme Court held that:

> . . . it is not "unreasonable" for police, as part of the routine procedure incident to incarcerating an arrested person, to search any container or article in his possession, in accordance with established inventory procedure.

The Fourth Amendment

The Fourth Amendment of the U.S. Constitution consists of one long sentence with two clauses:

The Rights Clause

The right of the people to be secure in their persons, houses, papers, and effects against unreasonable searches and seizures shall not be violated, and

The Warrant Clause

no Warrants shall issue, but upon probable cause, supported by Oath or affirmation, and particularly describing the place to be searched, and the persons or things to be seized.

Regarding the Rights Clause, the U.S. Supreme court held:

- "The Fourth Amendment is not a guarantee against all searches and seizures, but only against *unreasonable* searches and seizures."[a]

- "The ultimate standard set forth in the Fourth Amendment is reasonableness."[b]

- The touchstone of the court's analysis under the Fourth Amendment "is always 'the reasonableness in all the circumstances of the particular governmental invasion of a citizen's personal security.'"[c]

- A basic principle of Fourth Amendment law is "that searches and seizures inside a home without a warrant are presumptively unreasonable."[d]

[a]*United States v. Hensley,* 469 U.S. 221, 105 S.Ct. 675 (1985).
[b]*Camera v. Municipal Court,* 387 U.S. 523, 87 S.Ct. 1727 (1967).
[c]*Terry v. Ohio,* 392 U.S. 1, 19, 88 S.Ct. 1868, 1878.
[d]*Payton v. New York,* 445 U.S. at 586, 100 S.Ct. at 1380.

B OBTAINING EVIDENCE BY POLICE ENTRY INTO PRIVATE PREMISES

The Fourth Amendment of the U.S. Constitution protects the "right of the people to be secure in their persons, houses, papers and effects."[18] The U.S. Supreme Court has held that an illegal or improper police "physical entry of the home is the chief evil against which the wording of the Fourth Amendment is directed."[19]

The right of privacy in the home has deep roots in Anglo-Saxon law. The U.S. Supreme Court quoted the following statement attributed to William Pitt in 1763:

> The poorest man may in his cottage bid defiance to all the forces of the Crown. It may be frail—its roof may shake—the wind may blow through it—the storm may enter—the rain may enter—but the King of England cannot enter—all his force dares not cross the threshold of the ruined tenement![20]

As early as 1461, an English court held that it was unlawful for a sheriff to break down the door of a man's house to arrest him in a civil suit for debt or trespass.

Sir William Blackstone wrote in 1822 in *4 Blackstone's Commentaries* that "the law of England has [such] . . . regard to the immunity of a man's house, that it styles it his castle, and will never suffer it to be violated with impunity . . ." (p. 222).

The home of a person could be worth millions, or it could be a very poor and simple building. It could be an apartment in a large building, or it could be a motel or hotel room. A person could be living alone or could be living with other persons. A tent pitched lawfully on public or private land was held to be a home in the cases of *United States v. Gooch,*[21] and *LaDuke v. Nelson.*[22] In whatever form, a person's home is protected by the privacy clause of the Fourth Amendment of the U.S. Constitution.[23]

Authority Needed by Police Officers to Enter Private Premises

Probable cause alone will not authorize a law enforcement officer to enter private premises. In the following cases, the U.S. Supreme Court held that the evidence obtained by police officers who entered private premises with only probable cause could not be used in criminal trials:

Vale v. Louisiana
United States Supreme Court, 90 S.Ct. 1969 (1970)

After arresting Vale on the front steps of his house, police had probable cause to believe illegal narcotics were in the house. The narcotics that police seized in the house could not be used as evidence and were suppressed.

Payton v. New York and Riddick v. New York
United States Supreme Court, 100 S.Ct. 1371 (1980)

The Supreme Court combined these cases where police entered private premises to arrest the two defendants without either arrest warrants or search warrants. Police had probable cause to arrest Payton for murder and Riddick for two armed robberies. The Court held that evidence obtained in both cases could not be used in the two criminal trials.

Search warrants and arrest warrants will authorize police entry into private premises. However, the following must be complied with by law enforcement officers who have valid warrants to enter private premises:

ARREST WARRANTS As an **arrest warrant** "carries with it the limited authority to enter a dwelling in which the suspect lives when there is reason to believe the suspect is within,"[24] police may enter under the following limitations:

1. Entry with an arrest warrant is limited to a suspect's *own residence,* and

2. "Where there is reason to believe the suspect is within."[25]

If these conditions do not exist, law officers should obtain a **search warrant** in addition to the arrest warrant; or they could wait until the suspect appears in a public place to make an arrest.

SEARCH WARRANTS AND ARREST WARRANTS Prior to entry into private premises with either a search warrant or an arrest warrant, law enforcement officers are obligated to knock, identify themselves, state their purpose, and await a refusal or silence before entering. There are two reasons for imposing these requirements and forbidding unannounced police entries into private premises:

- *Possibility of mistake* "[C]ases of mistaken identity are surely not novel in the investigation of crime. The possibility is very real that the police may be misinformed as to the name or address of a suspect, or as to other material information. . . . Innocent citizens should not suffer the shock, fright or embarrassment attendant upon an unannounced police intrusion."[26]

- *Protection of the officers* "[It] is also a safeguard for the police themselves who might be mistaken for prowlers and be shot down by a fearful householder."[27]

Although knock-and-announce entries are the most usual type of police entry, a no-knock entry would be justified if one or more of the following conditions can be shown:

- Such notice would be likely to endanger the life or the safety of the officer or another person.

- Such notice would be likely to result in the evidence subject to seizure being easily and quickly destroyed or disposed of.[28]

- Such notice would be likely to enable the escape of a party to be arrested.

- Such notice would be a useless gesture.

In order to justify a no-knock entry when no prior notice was given, the officer would have to point to evidence that would give the officer the authority to enter without announcement.

Police may detain and prevent owners and occupants from entering private premises while the police are in the process of obtaining a search warrant for the premises. In the 2001 case of *Illinois v. McArthur,* 531 U.S. 326, the U.S. Supreme Court held that the police lawfully denied the defendant access to the premises during the 2 hours that it took to obtain a search warrant, unless an officer accompanied the defendant into the building.

Exceptions to the Warrant Requirement to Enter Private Premises

The Fourth Amendment of the U.S. Constitution forbids "unreasonable searches and **seizures**" and requires a search warrant unless the government can show that a court-recognized exception to the warrant requirement of the Fourth Amendment exists.

Consent that is voluntarily given by a person who either has sole control of the property or has such mutual use of the premises to have joint access and control of the premises will authorize law enforcement officers to enter the premises.[29]

The *emergency search doctrine* (also known as the **exigent circumstances**) is also a court-recognized exception to the warrant requirement of the Fourth Amendment and will authorize entry by not only law enforcement officers but also firefighters and emergency medical personnel. In 1963, former Chief Justice Warren Burger, while a Court of Appeals judge, wrote the following of the emergency search doctrine:

A warrant is not required to break down a door to enter a burning home to rescue occupants or extinguish a fire, to prevent a shooting or to bring emergency aid to an injured person. The need to protect or preserve life or avoid serious injury is justification for what would be otherwise illegal absent an exigency or emergency. Fires or dead bodies are reported to police by cranks where no fires or bodies are to be found. Acting in response to reports of "dead bodies," the police may find the "bodies" to be common drunks, diabetics in shock, or distressed cardiac patients. But the business of policemen and firemen is *to act,* not to speculate or meditate on whether the report is correct. People could well die in emergencies if police tried to act with the calm deliberation associated with the judicial process. Even the apparently dead often are saved by swift police response. A myriad of circumstances could fall within the terms "exigent circumstances" . . . e.g., smoke coming out a window or under a door, the sound of gunfire in a house, threats from the inside to shoot through the door at police, reasonable grounds to believe an injured or seriously ill person is being held within.[30]

Situations that would fall under the exigency, or emergency, search doctrine may be classified as follows:

- When an officer has reason to believe that a life may be in jeopardy
- When an officer is in hot pursuit of a person who has committed a crime, or there is danger of escape by criminals
- Now-or-never situations in which evidence or contraband such as drugs will be destroyed or moved to another place before a search warrant can be obtained

If an entry into premises by a law enforcement officer is lawful and proper, the officer then has the right to be where he or she is. What the officer then sees in plain view (and unexpectedly) comes under the plain-view doctrine and can be seized if there is reason to believe it is evidence of a crime.

C OBTAINING EVIDENCE IN TRAFFIC STOPS AND VEHICLE SEARCHES

Studies show that motor vehicles are involved in some manner in over 75 percent of the crimes committed every year in the United States. Vehicles are used as instrumentalities of most crimes; crimes are committed in vehicles; and motor vehicles are the object of criminal efforts, because more than 1 million motor vehicles are stolen every year in the United States. Motor vehicles that are illegally driven cause thousands of deaths and hundreds of thousands of injuries every year in the United States.

May a Police Officer Stop a Motor Vehicle for No Reason?

A vehicle stop may be made by a law enforcement officer for many valid reasons: The driver may be speeding or may have violated other sections of the traffic code; there may be an equipment violation, such as a headlight out; there may be probable cause

Most Traffic Stops Are Temporary, Brief, and Public

In pointing out that most traffic stops are temporary, brief, and public, the U.S. Supreme Court stated in footnote 26 of *Berkemer v. McCarty,* 104 S.Ct. 3138, 3149 (1984), that "no state requires that a detained motorist be arrested unless he is accused of a specified serious crime, refuses to promise to appear in court, or demands to be taken before a magistrate."

However, a motorist who fails to furnish satisfactory self-identification or an out-of-state motorist who is unable to post bail or to pay a traffic fine or a citation is likely to be detained until the matter is cleared.

or reasonable suspicion to arrest or question the driver or a passenger in the vehicle. But can a vehicle be stopped with no reason? That question was before the U.S. Supreme Court in the 1979 case of *Delaware v. Prouse*.[31] In that case, the officer making the vehicle stop testified, "I saw the car in the area and wasn't answering any complaints, so I decided to pull them off." In holding that such stops are unreasonable under the Fourth Amendment, the Court ruled that:

> except in those situations in which there is at least articulable and reasonable suspicion that a motorist is unlicensed or that an automobile is not registered, or that either the vehicle or an occupant is otherwise subject to seizure for violation of law, stopping an automobile and detaining the driver in order to check his driver's license and the registration of the automobile are unreasonable under the Fourth Amendment.

A traffic stop significantly interferes with the freedom of movement, not only of the vehicle driver but also of the passengers, but, again, most traffic stops are temporary, brief, and public police stops. In the 1984 case of *Berkemer v. McCarty*,[32] the U.S. Supreme Court pointed out the consequences to a motorist of failing to obey a law enforcement officer's signal to stop:

> It must be acknowledged at the outset that a traffic stop significantly curtails the "freedom of action" of the driver and the passengers, if any, of the detained vehicle. Under the law of most States, it is a crime either to ignore a policeman's signal to stop one's car or, once having stopped, to drive away without permission. . . .
> . . . Certainly few motorists would feel free either to disobey a directive to pull over or to leave the scene of a traffic stop without being told they might do so. Partly for these reasons, we have long acknowledged that "stopping an automobile and detaining its occupants constitute a 'seizure' within the meaning of [the Fourth] Amendmen[t], even though the purpose of the stop is limited and the resulting detention quite brief." *Delaware v. Prouse,* 440 U.S. 648, 653.

Obtaining Evidence During Routine Traffic Stops

On routine traffic stops, evidence of violations often becomes available as law enforcement officers enact the following routine:

1. Officers may and do request a driver's license and other required documents.[33] Because operating a motor vehicle on public highways is a privilege rather than a right, it is constitutional to require a lawfully stopped driver to produce a driver's license upon request, the vehicle registration, and other documents required by statute. The acquisition of the information contained in these documents gives an officer important facts to assist him in determining whether he is confronting innocent or criminal conduct. Inconsistencies between documents or between what is found in the documents and what the officer is told by the driver may provide clues to criminal behavior that might otherwise be overlooked. Refusal to produce required documents will almost universally constitute criminal behavior under State statutes. Thus, demand for and examination of required documentation by a police officer is a sound early step in investigating a stopped vehicle and its driver.

2. Officers may question the occupants of the vehicle. A police officer gathering information may also briefly question a stopped car's driver and other occupants of the car where the car and occupants have been lawfully stopped.[34] The U.S. Supreme Court has made clear that such questioning may take place without any prior *Miranda*-type warnings, so long as the persons questioned have not been placed under arrest or subjected to arrest-type treatment.[35] This is true even where an officer may have determined that she has lawful grounds for arrest and has decided to effect such an arrest. Despite the fact that no warnings are required, persons being questioned do enjoy a constitutional right not to respond, and although a failure to respond may be taken into consideration as an officer weighs facts in assessing whether probable cause to arrest or search exists, a person's failure to respond probably cannot constitute in itself a criminal offense, since the person is merely exercising a right guaranteed by the Constitution.

3. Officers sometimes request consent to search. An officer who has lawfully stopped a car may request that the person in lawful control of the car (generally the driver) waive his or her Fourth Amendment rights and give consent to a search of the car.[36] If such a consent is obtained, the officer should be prepared to prove at a later time that the consent was voluntarily given, that the person giving the consent was in lawful control of the items searched, and that the search performed was within the scope of the consent that was given.

4. Officers may make plain-view observations of parts of the vehicle exposed to public view.[37] The Fourth Amendment does not require officers who approach a lawfully stopped car to wear blinders. The exterior of a car on a public highway is exposed to the public view, and it is unreasonable for a person to expect that a car's exterior appearance is therefore private. Consequently, an officer's visual inspection of the exterior of a stopped car does not constitute a search for Fourth Amendment purposes. Portions of the interior that are likewise exposed to the public view due to the placement of windows are also not private, and an officer's

visual examination of these areas from outside the car is also not a Fourth Amendment search. As a result, officers approaching a lawfully stopped vehicle frequently are exposed to a wealth of information that they may lawfully use for investigative purposes.

Obtaining Evidence in Searches of Vehicles, Drivers, and Passengers

The following two U.S. Supreme Court Cases illustrate the protective measures law enforcement officers may take in traffic stops and while investigating an accident. The U.S. Supreme Court sustained the use of the evidence and affirmed the criminal convictions:

Pennsylvania v. Mimms
United States Supreme Court, 98 S.Ct. 330 (1977)

Mimms's vehicle was stopped because of an expired license plate. Mimms was asked to step out of the car, and as he did a bulge was noticed under his sport coat. The officer reached under the coat and removed a revolver from Mimms's waistband. The Supreme Court sustained the use of the evidence, holding that "In these circumstances, any man of 'reasonable caution' would have conducted the 'pat-down.'"

Michigan v. Long
United States Supreme Court, 103 S.Ct. 3469 (1983)

Long lost control of a speeding car late at night on a country road and crashed in a ditch. Long was the only occupant of the car and appeared to be under the influence of something when officers saw him standing at the rear of the car. When he was asked to show his driver's license, Long began to return to the open door of the car. Before allowing Long in the car, the officers checked the interior of the car for weapons. A large hunting knife was found on the floor of the driver's side of the car. Marijuana was then found in the car, and Long was arrested. The Supreme Court held that officers may make a limited search of the interior of vehicles to locate and control weapons when officers reasonably suspect the presence of weapons.

The next case illustrates the legality of searches incident to the lawful arrest of a driver or passenger of a vehicle.

New York v. Belton
United States Supreme Court, 101 S.Ct. 2860 (1981)

After a car was stopped for speeding, officers smelled marijuana. The four occupants of the car were directed to get out of the vehicle, and a search incident to the arrest was made. Cocaine was found in the jacket pocket of Belton's coat, which was on the backseat. Belton was a passenger in the vehicle. The case is important because the Supreme Court answered the question of whether the interior of a vehicle can be searched when the arrested person is outside the vehicle. Yes. May containers within the vehicle be searched? Yes, all containers.

Permissible Searches Under the Automobile Exception

Over the years since motor vehicles have been used as means of transportation, the courts have consistently noted the constitutional difference between motor vehicles and fixed structures such as homes and other types of buildings. In the 1976 case of *South Dakota v. Opperman*,[38] the U.S. Supreme Court stated that:

> This Court has traditionally drawn a distinction between automobiles and homes or offices in relation to the Fourth Amendment. Although automobiles are "effects" and thus within the reach of the Fourth Amendment, . . . warrantless examinations of automobiles have been upheld in circumstances in which a search of a home or office would not.

The **automobile exception** (or the *Carroll rule*, or the *probable cause rule*) is a simple rule. It authorizes a law enforcement officer who has probable cause to believe a vehicle contains evidence of a crime to search the vehicle and to seize the evidence. Probable cause alone will not get a law enforcement officer into a home to make an arrest or a search for evidence. However, probable cause alone will authorize entry into a vehicle to seize evidence. The rule, which originated during Prohibition in the 1925 case of *Carroll v. United States,* is stated by the following cases.[39]

Carroll v. United States
United States Supreme Court, 45 S.Ct. 280 (1925)

Officers had probable cause to believe that Carroll's roadster had gin and whiskey in it, in violation of the National Prohibition Act. The evidence found in the car was held to be lawfully obtained and could be used to sustain Carroll's conviction.

Chambers v. Maroney
United States Supreme Court, 90 S.Ct. 1975 (1970)

Four armed robbers were arrested late at night. After the suspects were in a jail cell, officers went out to the robbers' vehicle, which had been moved to the police station, and obtained incriminating evidence that the police had probable cause to believe was in the vehicle. The Supreme Court sustained the use of the evidence, holding that a "careful search [at the place of the arrest] was impractical and perhaps not safe for the officers."

Obtaining Evidence from Motor Vehicles (Includes Aircraft, Watercraft, Snowmobiles, Trucks, Buses, and Others)

Authority	Requirements
Plain-view observations and smells of vehicles exposed to public view	• The officer is where she or he has a right to be; if vehicle was stopped by the police, the stop must be lawful. • The contraband is in plain view and it is "immediately apparent" that the item may be evidence of a crime. • The officer may seize the contraband if the officer has a lawful right of access to the object.
Consent to search	Officer must show that the consent was voluntarily given, that the person giving consent could give consent, and that the search was within the scope of the consent that was given.
Reasonable suspicion would justify • An investigative stop. • A frisk or search for weapons if there was justifiable concern for safety.	To make a *Terry* stop, the officer "must have a particularized and objective basis for suspecting the particular person stopped of criminal activity."
• A search of the passenger compartment of a vehicle for weapons.	The officer has reasonable suspicion that "the suspect is dangerous and the suspect may gain immediate control of weapons" [*Michigan v. Long,* 463 U.S. 1032, 103 S. Ct. 3469 (1983)].
If a lawful custodial arrest is made of the occupant of a motor vehicle	The officer may, at the time of the arrest and the place of the arrest • Search the "passenger compartment of that automobile." • Search opened or closed containers in the vehicle. (Some states have statutes or court rulings that limit this authority.)

United States v. Ross
United States Supreme Court, 102 S.Ct. 2157 (1982)

Police had probable cause to believe that Ross was selling heroin out of the trunk of his car in Washington, D.C. After stopping the defendant, they found a pistol in the glove compartment. The police arrested Ross and took his keys to open the car trunk. They opened a brown paper bag in the trunk and found glassine bags containing white powder. They then took Ross and his car to a police station where it was determined that the white powder was heroin. A further search of the trunk produced additional evidence. In sustaining the convictions and the use of the evidence, the Supreme Court held that: "If probable cause justifies the search of a lawfully stopped vehicle, it justifies the search of every part of the vehicle and its contents that may conceal the object of the search."

Authority	Requirements
The automobile exception (or the *Carroll* rule, or probable cause rule)	Probable cause to believe that a vehicle contains evidence of a crime. A search of "a lawfully stopped vehicle" can then be made. The search can be "of every part of the vehicle and its contents that may conceal the object of the search" [U.S. Supreme Court in *United States v. Ross* (see case in this chapter)].
Authority to inventory property in lawful custody of a law enforcement agency[a]	An inventory is a search but it is *not* a search for evidence to incriminate a suspect. The purpose of an inventory is to • Protect the owner's property. • Protect police against claims or disputes over property. • Protect police from potential danger.
Community caretaking function	A **community caretaking function** is a task or job that has to be done or that should be done in the best interests of the community. The officer is not looking for evidence of a crime but, while he is performing the community caretaking function, comes upon evidence of a crime. For example, an accident blocks traffic lanes on a busy street. To open the street to traffic, an officer gets into one of the cars and moves it to the curb. While in the vehicle, the officer sees contraband. [See the U.S. Supreme Court case of Cady v. Dombrowski, 93 S.Ct. 2523 (1973)].

[a]U.S. Supreme Court cases having to do with the inventory of vehicles are *Cooper v. California,* 386 U.S. 58, 87 S.Ct. 788 (1967), and *Harris v. United States,* 390 U.S. 234, 88 S.Ct. 992 (1968). The *Harris* case is described as follows in *Cady v. Dombrowski* (93 S.Ct. 2523): "In *Harris,* petitioner was arrested for robbery. As petitioner's car had been identified leaving the site of the robbery, it was impounded as evidence. A regulation of the District of Columbia Police Department required that an impounded vehicle be searched, that all valuables be removed, and that a tag detailing certain information be placed on the vehicle. In compliance with this regulation, and without a warrant, an officer searched the car and, while opening one of the doors, spotted an automobile registration card, belonging to the victim, lying face up on the metal door stripping. This item was introduced into evidence at petitioner's trial for robbery. In rejecting the contention that the evidence was inadmissible, the Court stated: 'Once the door had lawfully been opened, the registration card . . . was plainly visible. It has long been settled that objects falling in the plain view of an officer who has a right to be in the position to have that view are subject to seizure and may be introduced in evidence.'" 390 U.S., at 236, 88 S.Ct., at 993.

Wyoming v. Houghton
United States Supreme Court, 526 U.S. 295, 302 (1999)

Police had probable cause to believe an automobile contained illegal drugs, after seeing a hypodermic syringe in the driver's pocket and being told by the driver he used the syringe to take drugs. The police searched the automobile and found a black container in the back seat that when opened was found to contain illegal drugs. The container belonged to Houghton, a passenger in the car. At her trial on the charge of possession of a controlled substance, Houghton argued the search of her property violated the Fourth Amendment. The Supreme Court held it did not:

When there is probably cause to search for contraband in a car, it is reasonable for police officers—like customs officials in the Founding era—to examine packages and containers without a showing of individualized probable cause for each one. A passenger's personal belongings, just like the driver's belongings or containers attached to the car like a glove compartment, are "in" the car, and the officer has probable cause to search for contraband *in* the car.

SUMMARY

The U.S. Supreme Court has repeatedly pointed out that the Fourth Amendment forbids only "unreasonable" searches and seizures. This chapter presents cases and material on lawful searches and seizures that have been held to be "reasonable" under the Fourth Amendment. The following are "reasonable" if done within the guidelines set by the U.S. Supreme Court:

investigative detentions

protective searches

consent searches

arrests

searches incident to a lawful arrest

inventory searches

entry into a private premise

- with consent
- under authority of a search warrant
- under authority of an arrest warrant
- life endanger exigency
- "hot-pursuit" exigency
- now-or-never exigency

lawful vehicle stop

search of a vehicle

- with consent
- plain view
- protective searches
- searches incident to an arrest
- searches under the automobile exception
- inventory searches

community caretaking functions

Profiles identify the characteristics and likely conduct of people involved in a given type of criminal activity. There are many types of profiles such as shoplifting profiles, terrorist profiles, drug courier profiles, airline hijacker profiles, and so on. The Maryland Court of Appeals stated that:

> The use of profiles is simply a means by which the law enforcement team communicates its collective expertise and empirical experience to the officer in the field and by which the officer, in turn, explains the special significance of his observations to the court.[a]

A profile is not evidence but is an investigative tool. In the 1989 case of *United States v. Sokolow,*[b] a DEA agent testified in court to facts that amounted to reasonable suspicion to authorize a detention of Sokolow by the agent. The agent then testified that Sokolow's behavior "had all the classic aspects of a drug courier."

In affirming Sokolow's conviction, the U.S. Supreme Court held that the fact that Sokolow's behavior was consistent with the DEA drug profile did not alter the conclusion that reasonable suspicion existed to make an investigative stop of Sokolow. The Court held that "the fact that these factors may be set forth in a 'profile' does not somehow detract from their evidentiary significance as seen by a trained agent."

Improper Racial Profiling Is Illegal

Guidelines similar to those used by many states were issued by President Bush in 2003 forbidding racial profiling by the seventy federal law enforcement agencies. These guidelines forbid the use of race or ethnicity by law officers in their routine investigations. The following examples were used:[c]

Example of Forbidden Racial Profiling in Routine Investigations

- Law officers cannot focus on a specific neighborhood only because of its racial makeup.

- A man going into a courthouse passes through a metal detector, which shows nothing suspicious. The man cannot be ordered to undergo a more extensive search "solely because he appears to be of a particular ethnicity."

- An uncorroborated tip states that a man of a certain race will buy an illegal weapon at a bus terminal. Officers cannot use that information to single out men of that race in the terminal because "the information is neither sufficiently reliable nor sufficiently specific."

Proper Use of Racial Information

- An "all points bulletin" or an "Amber alert" describes a fleeing felon by race, hair color, age, weight, and color of car. Officers may use all of the above to decide which drivers to pull over.

- Information that terrorists of a particular ethnicity plan to hijack a plane in California in the next week. Officers may subject men of that ethnicity who are boarding planes in California to "heightened security."

- Computer software on patterns of drug arrest show that the majority of drug arrests occur in neighborhoods occupied primarily by people of a single race. Law enforcement operations in these areas may be increased "so long as they are not motivated by racial animus."

[a]*Derricot v. State,* 578 A. 2d 791 (1990).
[b]490 U.S. 1, 109 S. Ct. 1581 (1989).
[c]Examples and quotations are from the June 2003 "U.S. Justice Department Guidance Regarding the Use of Race by Federal Law Enforcement Agencies."

PROBLEMS

All the following problems are from U.S. Supreme Court cases.

1. A police officer patrolling in downtown New York City saw the defendant "continually from the hours of 4:00 P.M. to 12:00 midnight." The officer saw the defendant talking to six or eight people, who the officer knew from experience were narcotic addicts. The officer did not overhear any of the conversations, nor did he see anything pass between the defendant and the people. Later in the evening, the officer saw the defendant enter a restaurant and speak to three more known addicts inside the restaurant. Once again, nothing was overheard, and nothing was seen to pass between them. The defendant ordered pie and coffee in the restaurant, and as he was eating, the officer approached him "and told him to come outside." Outside, the officer said to the defendant, "You know what I am after." The defendant "mumbled something and reached into his pocket." The officer also thrust his hand into the same pocket of the defendant and came out with several glassine envelopes, which contained heroin.

Was the heroin lawfully obtained in an authorized search? Explain. Can the heroin be used as evidence in charging the defendant with possession of heroin? Explain. Should the U.S. Supreme Court affirm the defendant's conviction? [*Sibron v. New York,* 392 U.S. 40, 88 S.Ct. 1899 (1968).]

2. An off-duty police officer was drying himself after a shower in his apartment when he heard a noise at his door. However, the telephone then rang, and he answered the telephone. When he looked out of the peephole in his front door into the hall, he saw two men tiptoeing toward the stairway. The officer called the police, put on some clothes, and armed himself with his service revolver. Looking out of the peephole again, he saw the men continuing to tiptoe. The officer had lived in the apartment building for twelve years but did not recognize either of the men as ten-

ants. Believing that the men were attempting to burglarize an apartment, the officer opened the door, stepped out into the hall, and slammed the door loudly behind him. The men immediately ran down the stairs from the sixth floor. The officer caught defendant Peters between the fourth and fifth floors. With Peters in tow, the officer tried to catch the other man but could not. Peters said he was in the building to visit a girlfriend, but because she was a married woman he would not give her name. The officer patted down Peters for weapons and discovered a hard object in his pocket. The officer testified that the object did not feel like a gun, but because the object might have been a knife, he removed it from Peters's pocket. It was an opaque plastic envelope containing burglar's tools.

Was the stop and search lawful and proper? Explain. Did the U.S. Supreme Court permit the use of the evidence in Peters's trial for possessing burglary tools? Why? [*Peters v. New York,* 392 U.S. 40, 88 S.Ct. 1899 (1968).]

3. Detectives first noticed the defendant at a ticket counter in the Miami airport. Their attention was drawn to the defendant because he and his two companions behaved in an unusual manner as they left the counter. The other two men talked to each other but not to the defendant. When one of the men saw the detectives who were following the three men, he turned and talked to the other man. When the second man saw the detectives as the men were getting off an escalator, he turned to the defendant and said, "Let's get out of here." He repeated in a lower voice, "Get out of here." The defendant then saw the detectives. A detective testified that the defendant attempted to move away, but his "legs were pumping up and down very fast and not covering much ground, but his legs were as if the person were running in place." Finding that he was not leaving the presence of the detectives, defendant turned to a detective and uttered a vulgar expression.

A detective then showed his badge to the defendant and asked if they might talk. The defendant agreed and the detective suggested they move a short distance to where the other two men and the other detective stood. Both detectives had been identified to all of the men, and as they stood in the public area of the airport, the defendant was asked for identification and if he had an airline ticket. When a ticket was produced by one of the other men, the officers asked for consent to search the defendant's luggage. Defendant handed the officer a key to the luggage, and three bags of cocaine were found in a suit bag.

Was the procedure used by the officers proper and lawful? Explain. Can the evidence obtained be used in the trial of the three men? Should they be charged with possession with intent to deliver? [*Florida v. Rodriguez*, 469 U.S. 1, 105 S.Ct. 308 (1984).]

4. Police officers were investigating the robbery of a grocery store and other robberies in the Montgomery, Alabama, area. A man held in jail on an unrelated charge told a police officer that "he had heard that Omar Taylor was involved in the [grocery store] robbery." The man did not tell the police where he heard the information, did not provide any details of the crime, and had never provided information to the police before.

Police officers arrested Omar Taylor, and upon arrival at the police station, gave him the *Miranda* warnings. Taylor was fingerprinted, questioned, and placed in a lineup. When victims of the robbery were unable to identify Taylor, he was told that his fingerprints matched those found on objects at the crime scene. After Taylor had a short visit with his girlfriend and a male companion, he signed a waiver of rights form and executed a written confession. The form and confession were admitted into evidence.

Were the procedures used by the police lawful and proper? Why? Was the form and confession properly used as evidence? Why? Should the Supreme Court affirm the use of the evidence and Taylor's conviction? [*Taylor v. Alabama*, 457 U.S. 687, 102 S. Ct. 2664 (1982).]

5. Portland, Oregon, police officers were investigating the strangulation murder of the defendant's wife in her home. The defendant was not living with his wife and voluntarily came into the police station with an attorney for questioning. The defendant was not arrested but probable cause to arrest him existed on the following facts:

- The fact that there were no signs of a struggle, break-in, or robbery at the scene of the crime "tended to indicate a killer known to the victim rather than a burglar or other stranger."
- "The decedent's son, the only other person in the house that night, did not have fingernails which could have made the lacerations observed on the victim's throat."
- "The defendant and his deceased wife had a stormy marriage and did not get along well."
- The defendant admitted being at the home of his wife on the night of the murder but claimed that he drove back to central Oregon without entering the house or seeing his wife.
- The defendant "volunteered a great deal of information without being asked, yet expressed no concern or curiosity about his wife."

While the defendant and his attorney were in the police station, officers noticed dark spots on the defendant's finger and under his fingernails. The police asked Murphy if they could take a sample of scraping from under his fingernails. Murphy refused and put his hands in his pockets, and was attempting to clean his nails with objects in his pockets.

Was there any way that the police could get samples of scrapings from under Murphy's nails before he destroyed what might be important evidence of the murder? Explain. [*Cupp v. Murphy*, 412 U.S. 291, 93 S.Ct. 2000 (1973).]

6. After overhearing from a public telephone what appeared to be arrangements for a drug transaction, a Florida police officer followed the defendant's car. When Jimeno committed a traffic violation, the officer stopped his car. The officer told Jimeno that he believed that Jimeno was carrying narcotics in his car and asked for consent to search the car. After Jimeno said that he had nothing to hide and gave consent, the officer opened a door on the passenger side and saw a folded brown paper bag on the floor of the car. The officer picked up the bag, opened it, and found cocaine inside. The Supreme Court of Florida held that the consent to search a vehicle does not extend to a closed container found inside the vehicle. Did the consent to search authorize opening the brown paper bag? Explain. Should the evidence be permitted for use against the defendant? Why or why not? [*Florida v. Jimeno,* 111 S.Ct. 1801 (1991).]

INFOTRAC COLLEGE EDITION EXERCISES

1. Go to InfoTrac College Edition and using the search term "*Terry* stop" find the 2002 *New York Defender Digest* article titled "May Police, in *Terry*-Type Stop, Reach into a Suspect's Pocket, Prior to a Pat-Down and Absent Probable Cause?" What must be shown for a *Terry* stop? In a *Terry* stop, what may the officer do to frisk or search the person stopped? What must the officer's reasons be for that activity?

2. Go to InfoTrac College Edition and using the search term "warrants (law)" and the subdivision "cases" find the 2003 article in the *FBI Law Enforcement Bulletin* titled "Consent Once Removed," by Edward Hendrix. When can consent to enter a private dwelling given to an undercover police officer or informant be used by other police officers to enter the dwelling for a search or arrest? How should the undercover officer convey that consent to the other officers?

NOTES

1. *Terry v. Ohio,* 88 S.Ct. 1868 (1968).
2. Witnesses to crimes or accidents have a civic obligation as good citizens to provide what information they have to law officers who are investigating the incident. If a material witness will not provide his identification, he may be detained and could if necessary be taken to a police station and charged. See the section on "Obeying Lawful Police Orders" in Chapter 11 of *Criminal Law: Principles and Cases,* 7th ed., by Thomas Gardner and Terry Anderson (Belmont, Calif.: Wadsworth, 1999).
3. *Florida v. Royer,* 103 S.Ct. 1319 (1983).
4. Courts will consider the following in determining whether a citizen–police encounter was voluntary or an illegal police seizure:

- Was there physical contact (touching, holding) by the officer or private security person?
- How many police officers were present (one or ten)? Backup officers should stay in the background unless safety is a problem.
- Were weapons unnecessarily displayed or pointed?

- Did the officers or their vehicle block a clear path for the suspect to leave the area? Was the person free to leave?
- Was the suspect told to go to another location instead of asking the person to voluntarily move to another place?
- Was the language and tone of voice intimidating? Was a police badge flashed repeatedly?
- If identification or plane or bus tickets were examined by the police officer, were they returned promptly? Because a citizen will need his driver's license or bus ticket, he is not free to leave until the item is returned.

See the *FBI Law Enforcement Bulletin* article, "Voluntary Encounter or Fourth Amendment Seizure?" (January 1992) for a further discussion and case citations of these factors.
5. *United States v. Mendenhall,* 100 S.Ct. 1870 (1980).
6. *Terry v. Ohio,* 88 S.Ct. 1868 (1968).
7. Idem.
8. 113 S.Ct. 2130. A situation similar to *Minnesota v. Dickerson* was before the U.S.

Supreme Court in April of 2000. In *Bond v. United States,* 120 S.Ct. 1462 (2000), the defendant was a passenger in a public bus. He placed carry-on luggage in a public luggage rack. When the bus properly stopped at a border checkpoint, a Border Patrol officer entered the bus and verified immigration status. After doing so the officer "squeezed" soft carry-on luggage in the public bins. He detected a hard, bricklike object in Bond's luggage, which on inspection turned out to be illegal drugs. Bond was convicted over his Fourth Amendment objection to the search of his luggage.

The Supreme Court reversed, finding that Bond had sought to preserve privacy in his luggage by placing it in the bin above him, and he did not expect the kind of exploratory touching done by the border officer. As a result, Bond's reasonable expectation of privacy was violated without probable cause, and the Fourth Amendment required exclusion of the drugs.

The rule in *Bond* may have little effect in airline security cases. Passengers who have soft carry-on luggage on airline flights must expect careful scrutiny of such bags and thus have no reasonable expectation of privacy.

9. Courts to this point have split on the permissibility of stops under these circumstances. Some upheld such stops. See e.g. *United States v. DeBerry,* 76 F.3d 884 (7th Cir., 1996) and *United States v. Clipper,* 973 F.2d 944 (C.A.D.C. 1992). After *J.L.* it seems likely that state and federal courts will look more closely at the reliability factors in anonymous tips.

10. Citizen's arrest goes back to England and early America when law officers were scarce or did not exist in some areas. Under such circumstances, private citizens then had to assume the burden of maintaining public order. The common-law doctrine of private person arrest usually limits the authority to misdemeanor breaches of the peace committed in presence of the private person and to felonies committed in the presence of the private persons. The law of your state should be determined before assuming this authority exists.

In some states, the general authority of a private citizen to make a citizen's arrest, or *private person arrest,* is set forth in a statute. In most states, the authority to make a citizen's arrest is

part of the common law of that state (that is, it is found in the court decisions of that state).

State statutes giving private persons the authority to make arrests could include some or all of the following:

- Shoplifting statutes, which give merchants and their adult employees authority to make either an arrest or a detention of a person where there is solid, probable cause to believe the person has shoplifted.
- Railroad and bus employees.
- Private citizens who are asked or ordered to aid and assist a law officer could be given the "same power as that of a law enforcement officer"—Wisconsin statute 968.07(2).
- Surety or extradition statutes could give private citizens authority to make an arrest under circumstances set forth in such statutes.

Law officers who are off-duty or out of their jurisdiction (city or state) could have the authority to make a citizen's arrest in another city or state.

11. *Henry v. United States,* 361 U.S. 98 (1959).
12. *Chimel v. California,* 89 S.Ct. 2034 (1969).
13. *New York v. Belton,* 101 S.Ct. 2860 (1981).
14. 654 F.2d 1057 (5th Cir., 1981), review denied U.S. Supreme Court, 102 S.Ct. 1617 (1982).
15. *Illinois v. Lafayette,* 462 U.S. 640, 103 S.Ct. 2605 (1983).
16. Idem.
17. Idem.
18. See Appendix A, where the "Applicable Sections of the U.S. Constitution" are presented.
19. *Payton v. New York,* 445 U.S. 573, 585, 100 S.Ct. 1371–79 (1980).
20. In the 1958 case of *Miller v. United States,* 357 U.S. 301, 78 S.Ct. 1190 (1958), the U.S. Supreme Court quoted from the *Oxford Dictionary of Quotations* (2d ed., 1953), attributing the statement to William Pitt in 1763. The Supreme Court traces the history of the Fourth Amendment in the case of *Stanford v. Texas,* 379 U.S. 476, 85 S.Ct. 506 (1965).
21. 6 F.3d 673 (9th Cir., 1993).
22. 762 F.2d 1318 (9th Cir., 1985).
23. In the 1991 case of *State v. Mooney,* 588 A.2d 145 (Conn.), law officers searched under a highway bridge in a place they knew that the defendant regarded as his home. They found

additional evidence of the crime for which the defendant had been arrested. The majority of the Supreme Court of Connecticut (three judges dissenting) held that the defendant had a reasonable right and expectation of privacy in the duffel bag and cardboard box from which the officers obtained the evidence. The evidence was suppressed and could not be used against the defendant.

Mobile homes are homes to some people. However, the U.S. Supreme Court has held that mobile motor homes are motor vehicles if they can be quickly driven away. In the 1985 case of *California v. Carney,* 471 U.S. 386, 105 S.Ct. 2066, the U.S. Supreme Court held that mobile motor homes have a reduced expectation of privacy and are classified under the law as motor vehicles where the automobile exception can apply.

24. *Payton v. New York,* 445 U.S. 573, 100 S.Ct. 1371 (1980).

25. *Steagald v. United States,* 451 U.S. 204, 101 S.Ct. 1642 (1981).

26. U.S. Supreme Court in *Ker v. California,* 83 S.Ct. 1623 (1963).

27. U.S. Supreme Court in *Miller v. United States,* 78 S.Ct. 1190 (1958).

28. See *Ker v. California,* 83 S.Ct. 1623 (1963).

29. When illegal drug complaints are received from neighbors and landlords, one of the options available is to knock and talk to the occupant of the suspect home or apartment. The *FBI Law Enforcement Bulletin* article, "Knock and Talk" (November 1991) discusses this option. Consent to search could be requested, to check on the validity of the complaint. Because small drug houses have drugs in inventory only at certain times of the day or week, this tactic may or may not work.

30. *Wayne v. United States,* 318 F.2d 205 (D.C. Cir., 1963), cert. denied 375 U.S. 860 (1963).

31. 440 U.S. 653.

32. 4 S.Ct. 3138.

33. The facts and ruling of the U.S. Supreme Court in 1986 case of *New York v. Class,* 475 U.S. 106, 106 S.Ct. 960, follow: After New York police officers stopped the defendant for exceeding the speed limit and driving with a cracked windshield (both are offenses in New York), one of the officers looked for the VIN on the defendant's car. Because some papers were obscuring the area of the dashboard where the VIN should be located, the officer reached in to move the papers. As he did so, he saw the handle of a gun protruding about one inch from under the driver's seat. The officer seized the gun, and the defendant was arrested. In holding that law enforcement officers making a lawful stop of a vehicle have a right and duty to inspect the VIN, the Court affirmed the defendant's conviction of criminal possession of a gun, ruling that:

We hold that this search was sufficiently unintrusive to be constitutionally permissible in light of the lack of a reasonable expectation of privacy in the VIN and the fact that the officers observed respondent commit two traffic violations. Any other conclusion would expose police officers to potentially grave risks without significantly reducing the intrusiveness of the ultimate conduct— viewing the VIN—which, as we have said, the officers were entitled to do as part of an undoubtedly justified traffic stop.

We note that our holding today does not authorize police officers to enter a vehicle to obtain a dashboard-mounted VIN when the VIN is visible from outside the automobile. If the VIN is in the plain view of someone outside the vehicle, there is no justification for governmental intrusion into the passenger compartment to see it.

34. See *Berkemer v. McCarty,* 468 U.S. 420, 104 S.Ct. 9, (1984).

35. In the 1988 case of *Pennsylvania v. Bruder,* 488 U.S. 9, 109 S.Ct. 205, a police officer stopped Bruder who was driving erratically and ran a red light. Because the officer smelled alcohol and observed Bruder's stumbling movements, he administered field sobriety tests, which included reciting the alphabet and questions regarding alcohol. When Bruder failed the sobriety tests, he was placed under arrest and given *Miranda* warnings. However, because of Bruder's intoxicated condition, waiver or understanding of the warnings could not be shown and Bruder's answers were suppressed for lack of *Miranda* warnings. The U.S. Supreme Court held that Bruder's answers to roadside questions were admissible. The Court compared this case to *Berkemer v. McCarty* holding that:

In *Berkemer v McCarty,* which involved facts strikingly similar to those in this case, the Court concluded that the "noncoercive aspect of ordinary traffic stops prompts us to hold that persons temporarily detained pursuant to such stops are not 'in custody' for the purposes of *Miranda."* 468 U.S. at 440.

The Court reasoned that although the stop was unquestionably a seizure within the meaning of the Fourth Amendment, such traffic stops typically are brief, unlike a prolonged station house interrogation. Second, the Court emphasized that traffic stops commonly occur in the "public view," in an atmosphere far "less 'police dominated' than that surrounding the kinds of interrogation at issue in Miranda itself." The detained motorist's "freedom of action [was not] curtailed to 'a degree associated with formal arrest.'" . . .

Accordingly, he was not entitled to a recitation of his constitutional rights prior to arrest, and his roadside responses to questioning were admissible.

36. *Schneckloth v. Bustamonte,* 412 U.S. 218, 93 S.Ct. 2041 (1973).

37. In the 1990 case of *Horton v. California,* 496 U.S. 128, 110 S.Ct. 2301, the U.S. Supreme Court held that the following requirements are necessary for a plain view or open view seizure of evidence by law officers:

- Officers must be in a place where they have a right to be.
- The object or evidence must be in plain or open view and "immediately apparent" to be illegal or evidence of a crime.
- Not only must the officer be lawfully located to see the object, but the officer must also have a lawful right of access to the object. (For example, an officer who is where he or she has a right to be and sees con-traband in a home but has no authority to enter the home does not have a lawful right of access to the immediately apparent evidence.)

38. 96 S.Ct. 3092 (1976).

39. The U.S. Supreme Court has repeatedly held that only probable cause is needed to search an automobile in police custody without a search warrant. A showing of exigent circumstance is not needed as was held in the 1989 case of *Boyd*

v. Alabama, 542 So.2d 1276 (Ala.), review denied U.S. Supreme Court, 493 U.S. 883, 110 S.Ct. 219, 46 CrL 3033 (1989).

40. The U.S. Supreme Court affirmed the criminal convictions of Drayton et al. and held that the evidence showed the bus passengers were free to leave. The Court held:

> Law enforcement officers do not violate the Fourth Amendment's prohibition of unreasonable seizures merely by approaching individuals on the street or in other public places and putting questions to them if they are willing to listen. . . . Even when law enforcement officers have no basis for suspecting a particular individual, they may pose questions, ask for identification, and request consent to search luggage—provided they do not induce cooperation by coercive means. See Florida v. Bostick, 5501 U.S., at 434–435, 111 S.Ct. 2382 (Citations omitted). If a reasonable person would feel free to terminate the encounter then he or she has not been seized.
>
> . . . (This) Court has rejected in specific terms the suggestion that police officers must always inform citizens of their right to refuse when seeking permission to conduct a warrantless consent search. . . . "While knowledge of the right to refuse consent is one factor to be taken into account, the government need not establish such knowledge as the sine qua non of an effective consent." Nor do this Court's decisions suggest that even though there are no per se rules, a presumption of invalidity attaches if a citizen consented without explicit notification that he or she was free to refuse to cooperate. Instead, the Court has repeated that the totality of the circumstances must control, without giving extra weight to the absence of this type of warning. . . . Although Officer Lang did not inform respondents of their right to refuse the search, he did request permission to search, and the totality of the circumstances indicates that their consent was voluntary, so the searches were reasonable.
>
> In a society based on law, the concept of agreement and consent should be given a weight and dignity of its own. Police officers act in full accord with the law when they ask citizens for consent. It reinforces the rule of

law for the citizen to advise the police of his or her wishes and for the police to act in reliance on that understanding. When this exchange takes place, it dispels inferences of coercion.

In *Bond v. United States,* 529 U.S. 334 (2000), the Supreme Court found a violation of the Fourth Amendment when a police officer boarded a bus at a border patrol checkpoint, and after determining that all passengers were lawfully in the United States, walked along the bus squeezing the overhead luggage. The officer found a hard object in the defendant's canvas bag that turned out to be methamphetamine. He was charged with illegal possession and at his trial moved to suppress the evidence found in his bag. The trial court and the Court of Appeals found that no "search" within the meaning of the Fourth Amendment occurred, because the defendant should have expected that others would touch his bag in a public baggage compartment.

The Supreme Court disagreed, holding that a search occurred and because no probable cause existed for that search, it violated the Fourth Amendment. The Court stated that although a passenger on public transportation expects that his bag will be handled by employees and other passengers for one reason or another, he does not expect that it will be felt in an "explorative" manner. Since the officer handled the bag in a manner different from the defendant's reasonable expectations, it was an unlawful search, and the evidence obtained from the search must be suppressed.

41. The U.S. Supreme Court held that reasonable suspicion did exist to authorize the vehicle stop in the *Arvizu* case. the *F.B.I. Law Enforcement Bulletin* wrote as follows on the U.S. Supreme Court *Arvizu* decision:

In *United States v. Arvizu,* the U.S. Supreme Court rejected an attempt by the Court of Appeals for the Ninth Circuit to "describe and delimit" factors that can be used to determine "reasonable suspicion." The Supreme Court reaffirmed its earlier decisions requiring a determination of "reasonable suspicion" be based on a totality of circumstances. . . .

. . . the Supreme Court repudiated the approach taken by the court of appeals and reaffirmed earlier case law requiring courts to use a "totality of circumstances" approach when determining the existence of "reasonable suspicion." Even though when viewed alone some factors may lend themselves to an innocent explanation, they still may be considered along with other more probative factors when reaching a determination of "reasonable suspicion." Applying the "totality of circumstances" approach to the facts presented in Arvizu, the Court concluded that the stop was lawful.

15

Obtaining Evidence by Use of Search Warrants, Wiretapping, or Dogs Trained to Indicate an Alert

Ⓐ SEARCH WARRANTS

When evidence is obtained without a **search warrant,** the burden is upon the government to show that the evidence was obtained under one of the "established and well-delineated exceptions" to the search warrant requirement. The U.S. Supreme Court pointed out that the exceptions to the search warrant requirement are "jealously and carefully drawn."[1]

The Fourth Amendment to the U.S. Constitution states that ". . . no Warrant shall issue, but upon probable cause supported by Oath, or affirmation, and particularly describing the place to be searched and the persons or things to be seized" (see Appendix A).

A search warrant must be issued by a neutral and detached judge or magistrate who determines that probable cause exists to issue the search or arrest warrant.[2] The search warrant must particularly describe the place to be searched and the persons or things to be seized. The oath or affirmation supporting the search warrant is in most instances made by a law enforcement officer. Search warrants are always executed by law enforcement officers.

Luggage or a package may be detained to obtain a search warrant where probable cause exists to believe that the package or luggage contains evidence of a crime. In the U.S. Supreme Court case of *United States v. Van Leeuwen,*[3] a package was held up in the U.S. mail for 29 hours, and in the case of *State v. Morrison,*[4] the delay was 3 hours. Both delays were held to be reasonable and necessary under the existing circumstances.

Types of Search Warrants

NIGHTTIME SEARCH WARRANTS Most states and the federal government have statutes requiring that search warrants be served and executed during daylight hours. However, such laws permit a magistrate or judge to authorize a nighttime search. Federal Rule of Criminal Procedure 41(c) permits the authorization of a nighttime search when "there be cause for carrying on the unusual nighttime . . . search . . . upon a showing (that) convinces the magistrate that it is reasonable."

NO-KNOCK OR UNANNOUNCED ENTRIES Law enforcement officers must knock, identify themselves, state their purpose, and await a refusal or silence before entering private premises.

An unannounced or no-knock entry can be made if it is specifically authorized by the search warrant or if the officers can show that such notice by knocking would be likely to (1) endanger the safety of the officers or another person, (2) result in the evidence subject to seizure being easily and quickly destroyed or disposed of, (3) enable the party to be arrested or searched to escape, or (4) be a useless gesture.

ANTICIPATORY SEARCH WARRANTS Occasionally, law enforcement officers will have information that evidence—usually illegal drugs—will be at a particular place at a future time. For example, police have specific, reliable information that a large ship-

When in Doubt, Get a Search Warrant

The most basic constitutional rule in this area is that "searches conducted outside the judicial process, without prior approval by judge or magistrate, are per se unreasonable under the Fourth Amendment—subject only to a few specifically established and well-delineated exceptions." The exceptions are "jealously and carefully drawn," and there must be "a showing by those who seek exemption . . . that the exigencies of the situation made that course imperative. . . . [T]he burden is on those seeking the exemption to show the need for it."[a]

When a search warrant is obtained, the judge's determination that probable cause exists is given great deference, and the burden shifts to those challenging a search or arrest warrant to prove that it is invalid.

[a]U.S. Supreme Court in *Coolidge v. New Hampshire,* 403 U.S. 443, 91 S.Ct. 2022 (1971).

ment of drugs will come into a city to a specific address in the next few days. But the officers do not have reliable information about where the drugs are now, what day and time the drugs will arrive, and how they are being transported.

Because most stocks of illegal drugs are dispersed rapidly due to the danger of a police raid or a snatching by a rival gang, an anticipatory search warrant would solve the problem presented to law enforcement officers in such situations. An anticipatory search warrant could be directed toward the search of a person or it can be used for a "controlled delivery."[5]

SNEAK-AND-PEEK ENTRY WARRANTS Sneak-and-peek warrants permit law officers to make an entry into premises for various reasons. In the 1993 case of *United States v. Pangburn,* the entry was made to photograph the contents of a suspected clandestine methamphetamine lab.[6]

The entry could be made into private premises to plant listening devices as was done in the Waco, Texas, Branch Davidian case and also the Arlington, Virginia, home of Alrich Ames, a high-ranking officer of the CIA who was arrested in 1994 for spying against the United States for the Russians.

In the 1979 U.S. Supreme Court case of *Dalia v. United States,*[7] a search warrant was issued to implant a listening device in a business office. Three weeks later, another entry was made to remove the device. The U.S. Supreme Court affirmed the defendant's conviction holding that

> Nothing in the language of the Constitution or in this Court's decisions . . . suggest that . . . search warrants . . . must include a specification of the precise manner in which they are to be executed. . . . It is generally left to the discretion of the executing officers to determine the details of how best to proceed with the performance of a search authorized by warrant—subject of course to the general Fourth Amendment protection "against unreasonable searches and seizures."

SEARCHES OF COMPUTERS AND OTHER DOCUMENTARY SOURCES Computers and other places where records are stored can be important sources of evidence. If consent cannot be obtained but probable cause exists, a search warrant could be obtained to make such searches.

Search warrants are subject to attack if they are overbroad in their language or fail to specify, with particularity, the items to be seized. In the case of *United States v. Hall,*[8] the search warrant authorized the seizure of image files that contained child pornography. The defendant had taken his computer to a repair shop, and in the course of making repairs, the child pornography was observed. The FBI was called, and the defendant was charged with possession of child pornography. The court found no Fourth Amendment violation.

The Privacy Protection Act of 1980[9] gives special protection to documentary material prepared or gathered for dissemination to the public (newspapers, magazines, and so forth), and a subpoena rather than a search warrant would have to be used unless one of the exceptions in the Privacy Protection Act would permit the use of a search warrant.

Ⓑ WIRETAPPING AND ELECTRONIC SURVEILLANCE

Prior to 1968 the United States did not have any laws governing **wiretapping** and **electronic surveillance.** However, the 1967 case of *Katz v. United States,*[10] caused the U.S. Congress to act. In the *Katz* case, FBI agents attached an electronic listening and recording device to the outside of a public telephone booth that Katz was using to lay off Los Angeles gambling bets in Miami, Florida. The U.S. Supreme Court held that the FBI had violated Katz's Fourth Amendment privacy rights and that the evidence obtained should not have been used to obtain Katz's criminal gambling conviction.

In 1968 Congress enacted the Federal Wiretapping and Electronic Surveillance Act.[11] Most states followed by enacting similar state laws making the following changes in the law of electronic surveillance:

- The laws authorize court orders permitting wiretapping and/or electronic surveillance by law enforcement officers in much the same manner as search warrants are issued.[12]
- The act makes wiretapping and electronic surveillance done in violation of the act a felony. The distribution, possession, and advertising of mechanical and electronic devices used for wiretapping and electronic surveillance is also made a felony (see section 2513 of the act).

Thermal-Imaging Devices

Advances in technology now make it possible to obtain information about activities occurring in houses, cars, and other places. The question of whether police may use such technological advances in investigations of crimes without traditional search warrants has been before the Supreme Court many times. In some cases technology opens what was once private spaces to public, and hence official, observation. For example, in *California v. Ciraolo*, 476 U.S. 207 (1986), the Court held that the uncovered portions of a house and its curtilage have become open to general observation by air travel and are thus no longer private for purposes of the Fourth Amendment.

To what extent may police use technological advances that enable an observer to sense what is inside a private place, like a house? An Internet Web site maintained by the National Law Enforcement and Corrections Technology Center, *www.nlectc.org/technproj/*, describes several radar and ultrasound devices that enable an observer to detect individuals through interior walls. The Supreme Court considered one of these kinds of devices, thermal-imaging, in the following case:

Kyllo v. United States
United States Supreme Court, 533 U.S. 27 (2001)

Federal agents suspected Kyllo was growing marijuana in his home. Using a thermal-imaging device, which detects infrared radiation and converts to a colored image based upon intensity of the radiation, the police believed that Kyllo was using high-intensity lamps to grow marijuana. Based on this and other evidence, the police obtained a search warrant and searched Kyllo's home, discovering over 100 marijuana plants. At his trial for the illegal manufacture of marijuana, Kyllo moved to suppress the evidence seized from his home. The trial court and court of appeals upheld the validity of the search warrant, holding it did not expose any intimate details of Kyllo's life, but only "hot spots" on the roof and exterior walls.

The Supreme Court reversed, holding that use of the thermal-imaging device constituted a search of Kyllo's house and could not be used without a search warrant:

... We think that obtaining by sense-enhancing technology any information regarding the interior of the home that could not otherwise have been obtained without physical "intrusion into a constitutionally protected area" ... constitutes a search—at least where (as here) the technology in question is not in general public use.

Techniques of Lawful Electronic Surveillance

Telecommunication corporations are not only required by federal law to cooperate in conducting lawfully authorized electronic surveillances, but they are also required to modify their equipment, facilities, and services to ensure that lawful electronic surveillance actually can be performed. The three primary techniques of electronic surveillance available to law enforcement agencies are pen registers, trap and trace devices, and interception of the content of the message:

- Pen registers and trap and trace devices are the most frequently used surveillance techniques used. They identify calling numbers or dialed numbers (outgoing or incoming). They can trap or lock lines when threatening or harassing calls are made, if necessary.

- The third form of lawful electronic surveillance includes identification of outgoing and incoming calls and also the content of messages. The federal government and forty-five states permit this technique, but only in investigations to obtain evidence of felony offenses such as kidnapping, extortion, murder, illegal drug trafficking, organized crime, terrorism, and national security matters. Court authorization will only be granted when it is shown that the needed evidence cannot be obtained by other means or would be too dangerous.

Tactics Used by Suspects to Avoid Electronic Surveillance

To avoid having conversations regarding criminal activities intercepted and used as evidence against them, suspects who are aware of government electronic surveillance could try the following tactics:

- "Walk and talk" meetings to avoid bugged rooms, vehicles, and other types of electronic surveillance. One suspect would meet and talk in the middle of a busy city street with trucks, buses, and cars coming dangerously close on either side. This made the use of a parabolic directional mike more difficult, and the surrounding noise level interfered with reception to a wire planted on a person cooperating with the government.

- Use of a series of public or private telephones. To counter this tactic, the U.S. Congress enacted in 1986 a federal statute authorizing "roving wiretaps" 18 U.S.C.A. 2518 (11), which permits authorized law officers to anticipate and follow a suspect using a series of public or private telephones.

Situations Where Court Orders Are Not Required

OVERHEARD CONVERSATIONS ("PLAIN HEARING") Law enforcement officers may use artificial means of aiding their vision such as bifocals, binoculars, or telescopes, but they may not use mechanical or electronic listening devices that intrude and violate the privacy of another person without a court order.

People who are talking about criminal activity sometimes become careless and do not exercise a right of privacy. We have all been in restaurants, hotel rooms, taverns, on aircraft, or other places where we have overheard the conversations of other people. If law enforcement officers are where they have a right to be,[13] they may testify in court about statements overheard or heard inadvertently. The following cases illustrate:

- Law enforcement officers were invited into an apartment where they could hear the defendant talking in a loud voice in the next apartment about illegal drug transactions. The conversations were heard without use of anything but the human ear. Based upon this information, the officers obtained a wiretap warrant and then a search warrant. In affirming the defendant's convictions in the 1988 case of *State v. Benton*,[14] the Court held:

  . . . It has widely been recognized, in cases involving apartments and hotel or motel rooms, that . . . overhearing of statements does not constitute a search under the Fourth Amendment. This view has been consistently upheld regardless of whether the eavesdropper was positioned in a common hallway of an apartment building, motel or hotel, or in an adjoining motel or hotel room. These cases do not hinge upon the single fact that the defendant is within the confines of his dwelling, but rather rely for their determination upon the conjunction of various facts, including especially the lack of sensory enhancement, the fact that the eavesdropping government agent was lawfully in position to overhear the statements, and that the presence of a person in that place could reasonably be anticipated.

- Law enforcement officers rented the motel room next to the defendants and listened to their conversations as the defendants were having a party and talking in loud voices.[15]

- A federal narcotics agent stood in the hall of an apartment and listened to the loud voices of the defendants within the apartment. Because the apartment door was hanging imperfectly, the officer could also see the defendants through a small crack in the door. The court held that such evidence was admissible because the "conversations [were] knowingly exposed to the public."[16]

- Testimony of what an officer heard coming from a motel room as the officer stood in the motel parking lot was held to be admissible as evidence.[17]

- The defendant's yelling during a telephone conversation was overheard by a law enforcement officer.[18]

UNDERCOVER OFFICERS MAY TESTIFY ABOUT WHAT WAS SAID IN THEIR PRESENCE All witnesses, including undercover officers, may testify about what was said in their presence unless a privilege exists (husband–wife, and so on). The following two U.S. Supreme Court cases illustrate two cases of this type.

Lewis v. United States
United States Supreme Court, 385 U.S. 206, 87 S.Ct. 424 (1966)

An undercover federal narcotics officer was invited into the defendant's home, where the defendant sold narcotics to the officer. In affirming the defendant's conviction and in holding that testimony about what the defendant said and did was properly used as evidence, the U.S. Supreme Court ruled that:

> A government agent, in the same manner as a private person, may accept an invitation to do business and may enter upon the premises for the very purposes contemplated by the occupant. Of course, this does not mean that, whenever entry is obtained by invitation and the locus is characterized as a place of business, an agent is authorized to conduct a general search for incriminating materials.

Hoffa v. United States
United States Supreme Court, 385 U.S. 293, 87 S.Ct. 408 (1966)

The former union official, James Hoffa, made incriminating statements in the presence of a paid government informer. Testimony about what Hoffa said was permitted as evidence in Hoffa's trial on criminal charges. The U.S. Supreme Court affirmed the defendant's conviction, holding that no violation occurred of Hoffa's

Sixth Amendment right to confer privately with his attorneys out of the presence of government agents and informers.

USE OF POCKET TAPE RECORDERS AND THE CRIME OF BRIBERY The availability of inexpensive pocket tape recorders contribute to the ease with which conversations are secretly recorded. The *Wall Street Journal* reports that secret recordings of conversations are on the increase in the United States.[19]

Federal law allows such secret taping as long as one of the parties to a conversation knows about it. However, in more than a dozen states, the law requires that all the parties to a conversation must know of the recording in order to use it as evidence in a civil or criminal trial if no prior court order has been obtained.

Bribery has always presented a problem for law enforcement investigators, whether the case involves a government official seeking to bribe a private citizen or vice versa. The offender will likely deny the wrongdoing; and unless other corroborating evidence is available, the word of the victim standing alone could be insufficient evidence to sustain a conviction. The following U.S. Supreme Court case illustrates the usual solution to the problem:

United States v. Caceres
United States Supreme Court, 440 U.S. 741, 99 S.Ct. 1465 (1979)

The defendant was having federal tax problems and offered to bribe a federal tax agent to fix his tax audits. Unknown to the defendant, three of his face-to-face conversations with the IRS agent were recorded by means of a radio transmitter concealed on the agent's person. However, IRS regulation required that prior authorization be obtained before taping, and the tax agent did not obtain the required permission. The U.S. Supreme Court held that the evidence was admissible despite the federal tax agency requirement. The Court referred to and quoted a similar case (*Lopez v. United States*) and stated that:

> Nor does the Constitution protect the privacy of individuals in respondent's position. In Lopez v. United States, 373 U.S. 427, 439, 83 S.Ct. 1381, 1388, 10 L.Ed.2d 462, we held that the Fourth Amendment provided no protection to an individual against the recording of his statements by the IRS agent to whom he was speaking. In doing so, we repudiated any suggestion that the defendant had a "constitutional right to rely on possible flaws in the agent's memory, or to challenge the agent's credibility without being beset by corroborating evidence that is not susceptible of impeachment," concluding instead that "the risk that petitioner took in offering a bribe to [the IRS agent] fairly included the risk that the offer would be accurately reproduced in court, whether by faultless memory or mechanical recording."

DO SUSPECTS HAVE A RIGHT OF PRIVACY IN CONVERSATIONS HELD IN POLICE VEHICLES, JAILS, OR OTHER POLICE BUILDINGS? Suspects and other people do not have a right of privacy in police vehicles, jails, or police or sheriff stations. The Sep-

Was There An Expectation of Privacy in the Following Secret Tapings?

The following secret tapings came to the public's attention during the 2002 election campaigns and received considerable attention by the news media. In both cases, it was determined that there was neither a legal expectation of privacy nor a violation of someone's right of privacy. The situations are:

- In Wisconsin, an assistant district attorney secretly taped his boss's conversation as his boss bragged of an explicit sexual encounter that the district attorney had in the office with a woman (not his wife) during office hours. The assistant district attorney then ran against his former boss for the office of district attorney of that county. The tape was released to the media during the election campaign. Both the district attorney and the assistant district attorney were defeated in the election, and a third person was elected to the office.

- In the race for the job of U.S. senator in Iowa, a strategy session was scheduled and 750 people were invited. The meeting was held in a Des Moines hotel, with the principal speaker being a U.S. congressman. People from the opposition party attended the meeting without protest and secretly taped what was said at the meeting. Both federal and state prosecutors stated that as no federal or state laws were violated, no criminal or civil charges were filed. However, the two men involved in the taping lost their jobs.

There was no expectation of privacy in either situation, as parties to the Wisconsin conversation and people at the Iowa meeting stated publicly what had been said. The lead Iowa prosecutor stated, "There were 750 people invited; there's 22 present; you're in a political campaign, and you're a public figure making comments. . . ."

---

tember 1993 issue of the *FBI Law Enforcement Bulletin* has an excellent article, entitled "Surreptitious Recording of Suspects' Conversations." This article points out that the "effective investigative technique" of surreptitiously recording conversations of suspects in such places will be admissible as evidence if the following points are followed:

> . . . (1) Because the technique does not amount to "interrogation" for purposes of *Miranda,* it is not necessary to advise suspects of their constitutional rights and obtain a waiver prior to using this technique. . . . (2) To avoid a Sixth Amendment problem, this technique should not be used following the filing of formal charges or the initial appearance in court, unless the conversation does not involve a government actor, the conversation involves a government actor who has assumed the role of a "listening post," or the conversation pertains to a crime other than the one with which the suspect has been charged. (3) . . . suspects should not be given any specific assurances that their conversations are private.

In the following cases, either the recordings of conversations were held to be admissible or a witness could testify about what was said:

- Two robbery suspects were arrested, placed in the back seat of a squad car, and left unattended. Before leaving, one of the officers activated a tape recorder on the front seat of the car. Unaware that their conversation was being recorded, the suspects engaged in an extremely incriminating conversation that was used in their criminal trial.[20]

- Perkins was in jail for aggravated assault. Because he was suspected of a murder unrelated to the assault, an undercover officer was placed in the cell with him. During the planning of a prison break, the undercover officer asked Perkins whether he had ever "done" anyone. Perkins then described in detail the murder-for-hire killing he had committed. The testimony of the officer was held admissible by the U.S. Supreme Court.[21]

- An informer was placed in a jail cell with instructions to just listen and not to question his cell mate. The cell mate, who was formally charged with a crime, made incriminating statements. The U.S. Supreme Court affirmed the defendant's conviction, holding that "the defendant must demonstrate that the police and their informant took some action, beyond merely listening."[22]

- A juvenile who was arrested for murder asked to speak with his mother after being given the *Miranda* warnings. The defendant and his mother talked alone in an interrogation room with the door closed. The juvenile admitted his part in the murder, not knowing the conversation was being recorded. In holding the recording could be used as evidence, the Court held that "no representations or inquiries were made as to privacy or confidentiality" and that "walls have ears."[23]

- During an investigative stop on reasonable suspicion, the police were given consent to search the suspect's car. The two suspects were asked to sit in the back of a police car while the car was searched by the officers. Not knowing that a tape recorder was turned on, the two suspects made incriminating statements in their conversation while being left alone in the police car. The court held that the statements could be used as evidence against them.[24]

WHEN ONE PARTY TO A TELEPHONE CONVERSATION CONSENTS TO THE POLICE LISTENING AND/OR RECORDING THE CONVERSATION The Federal Wiretapping Act of 1968 provides that a person who is a party to a wire, oral, or electronic communication may intercept such conversation "unless [the interception] is . . . for the purpose of committing any crime or tortious act."[25]

Therefore, one of the parties to a telephone call may consent to a law enforcement officer listening to or recording the call without disclosing this fact to the other party. Most states follow this rule, although a few states require a court order for this procedure.

The following cases illustrate the use of this investigative technique:

- In a drug investigation, law enforcement officers recorded telephone conversations with the consent of one of the parties to the conversations. The use of the evidence and the conviction was affirmed.[26]

- A cooperative witness consented to the tape recording of telephone conversations with a murder suspect. The tape recording along with the testimony of an Illinois Assistant State's Attorney who had listened to the defendant's confession in the telephone conversations were held to properly admitted as evidence.[27]

- In a tax fraud investigation, evidence of the tax fraud was obtained by the tape recording of telephone conversation with the consent of one of the parties to the conversations.[28]

- An interpreter listened from an extension telephone while an informant talked in Spanish with a suspected drug dealer. The Supreme Court of Nevada held the resulting evidence to be admissible.[29]

OBTAINING EVIDENCE BY USE OF THE CONFRONTATIONAL TELEPHONE CALL If the victim of a crime or a witness is cooperative, law enforcement officers could ask the person to telephone a suspect in a *confrontational call*. Such telephone calls would have to be made before criminal charging. The following cases illustrate situations in which this technique was used successfully:

- A minor victim of sexual abuse telephoned her stepfather who made incriminating admissions while unaware that the conversation was being recorded and a law officer was listening. The stepfather's admission corroborated the victim's accusations and led to criminal charging and conviction.[30]

- In a child molestation case, the child's mother telephoned the defendant who admitted that he had fondled the child. The defendant was charged with child molestation, and the tape recording of the telephone call was used as evidence to obtain a conviction.[31]

- A woman who participated in the armed robberies of convenience stores agreed to telephone Walton who made incriminating statements not knowing that the conversation was being recorded and that a police officer was listening.[32]

- Minnesota officers investigating a murder went into Wisconsin to talk to a woman who was being used as an alibi. After the woman admitted she was being paid $1,000 for her story, she agreed to telephone the two defendants who made incriminating statements in conversations that were recorded. The defendants were then charged with murder and convicted in Minnesota. Because Wisconsin is one of the few states where evidence obtained in this manner is not admissible unless a prior court order is obtained, the question before the Minnesota courts was whether Wisconsin law or Minnesota law should be used. The Minnesota Supreme Court affirmed the murder convictions, holding that Minnesota law would be used in a Minnesota murder trial.[33]

However, defendants who have been charged with a crime have the right to an attorney, and use of a confrontational call after a defendant has been charged with a crime would in most instances violate the *Massiah* rule (see Chapter 12). The following case illustrates an exception.

Jenkins v. Leonardo
U.S. Court of Appeals, Second Circuit, 991 F.2d 1033 (1993)

After the defendant was charged with rape and was represented by an attorney, he began calling the victim to harass her. The victim contacted the police, and they provided her with recording equipment and encouraged her to have the defendant talk about the facts of the crime.

During the next telephone call, the recorder was activated, and the defendant made incriminating statements, unaware that his statements were being recorded. The victim testified about the statements, and the recording was used as evidence in the trial, which resulted in the defendant's conviction. The U.S. Court of Appeals held that the defendant waived his right to an attorney in making such telephone calls to harass the rape victim.

USING BODY WIRES OR RADIO TRANSMITTERS Undercover officers, informants, or other people are sometimes fitted with "body wires" or radio transmitters for any or all of the following reasons:

1. To alert backup officers should the undercover officer or the police agent be in danger or need assistance.

2. To keep nearby officers informed about what is being said and the events that are occurring (with informants, this is a method of controlling the informant and preventing double dealing).

3. Besides recording of the incident, the listening officers could also testify in court as to what they heard.

Federal law permits the use of radio transmitters as demonstrated by the two following U.S. Supreme Court cases. Most states follow the federal rule, but in some states a prior court order would have to be obtained to permit the use of such evidence in a criminal trial.

On Lee v. United States
United States Supreme Court, 343 U.S. 747, 72 S.Ct. 967 (1952)

Federal narcotics agents wired an undercover agent with a small microphone and radio transmitter. The agent then purchased a pound of opium from the defendant after conducting conversations with the defendant in his laundry and on the streets in New York City. The undercover agent did not testify at the defendant's trial, but one of the federal narcotics agents who overheard the conversations by means of the radio transmitter was permitted to testify about what he heard and saw. In affirming the defendant's conviction and the use of this evidence, the Supreme Court held that: "No good reason of public policy occurs to us why the Government should be deprived of the benefit of On Lee's admissions because he made them to a confidante of shady character."

United States v. White
United States Supreme Court, 401 U.S. 745, 91 S.Ct. 1122 (1971)

A government informant made a drug buy while federal drug agents listened to the conversations between the informant and the defendant by means of a concealed radio transmitter worn by the informant. At the time of the defendant's trial, the informer could not be located to testify, and the narcotics agents were permitted to testify about what they heard. The Supreme Court affirmed the defendant's conviction and the use of the officer's testimony as evidence, holding that:

> Concededly a police agent who conceals his police connections may write down for official use his conversations with a defendant and testify concerning them, without a warrant authorizing his encounters with the defendant and without otherwise violating the latter's Fourth Amendment rights. . . . For constitutional purposes, no different result is required if the agent in-

stead of immediately reporting and transcribing his conversations with defendant, either (1) simultaneously records them with electronic equipment which he is carrying on his person, . . . (2) or carries radio equipment which simultaneously transmits the conversations either to recording equipment located elsewhere or to other agents monitoring the transmitting frequency. On *Lee v. United States*. . . . If the conduct and revelations of an agent operating without electronic equipment do not invade the defendant's constitutionally justifiable expectations of privacy, neither does a simultaneous recording of the same conversations made by the agent or by others from transmissions received from the agent to whom the defendant is talking and whose trustworthiness the defendant necessarily risks.

MAY ONE FAMILY MEMBER WIRETAP AND RECORD TELEPHONE CALLS OF ANOTHER FAMILY MEMBER? Electronic surveillance and wiretapping is governed by Title III of the 1968 Omnibus Crime Control and Safe Streets Act.[34] The act makes it unlawful for any person to intercept or attempt to intercept any wire, oral, or electronic communication "except as otherwise specifically permitted" by the act. Willful disclosure of the contents of communications by a person who knows or has reason to know that the information was obtained through an unlawful interception is also forbidden.[35] No exception in federal law permits electronic surveillance or wiretapping by one family member on another. The following cases illustrate:

- In the 1992 case of *Heggy v. Heggy*,[36] a woman sued her former husband and won a money award against him for recording her telephone conversations.

- After a mother used a microcassette device attached to an extension telephone and recorded conversations between her son and a drug dealer, she turned the recordings over to the police. The recordings were used to obtain a search warrant. In holding the search warrant invalid, the North Carolina court cited *Rickenbaker v. Rickenbaker.*[37]

- A California man recorded telephone conversations between his wife and her lover. The man was then murdered, and his wife and her lover were convicted of the murder with the telephone recordings being used as evidence. The California Supreme Court reversed the convictions following the majority rule, holding that because the recordings were unlawful they could not be used as evidence.[38]

In discussing listening in on an extension telephone and wiretapping, the Supreme Court of California said:

The differences between casually overhearing part of a conversation on an extension phone and intentionally wiretapping all incoming and outgoing calls are substantial; the former requires the physical presence of the eavesdropper, which inherently limits the extent and frequency of the invasion; the latter, by contrast, requires no supervision, is of potentially unlimited duration, and is wholly indiscriminate. . . . Whatever Congress might have intended concerning the occasional use of an extension phone by a parent, we find no evidence of a legislative intent to create a wholesale exception for systematic interspousal wiretapping.

Informants come from all walks of life. They may be private citizen who contact the police, or they may use 911 with information regarding a crime. Informants are also persons who could be involved in crime and are providing information for money or to avoid a long prison term.

Some informants are known to law officers and have provided reliable information in the past. Other callers remain anonymous. A caller who is reporting drug or other criminal activity by a neighbor may fear retaliation if their identity is disclosed. Some anonymous calls are maliciously made to harm another person or to harass the police. However, police must respond to 911 calls because as the court in the case of *United States v. Holloway*[a] stated, "If law enforcement could not rely on information conveyed by anonymous 911 callers, their ability to respond effectively to emergency situations would be severely curtailed."

Much of the information from informants is of no or little value to a law enforcement agency. Some information, however, could start an investigation that results in curtailing serious criminal activity. Other information could establish reasonable suspicion to make an investigative stop of a person or vehicle. Information from an informant could also establish probable cause to make an arrest or to obtain a search warrant.

U.S. Supreme Court Cases Where the Informant Was Known

Case and Crime	Type of Tip	Additional Information and Action by Law Officers
Draper v. United States, 79 S. Ct. 329 (1959), drug peddler	Known paid informer who had provided accurate and reliable information in the past	Detailed information corroborated by federal agents, justified arrest
McCray v. Illinois, 87 S. Ct. 1056 (1967), drug trafficking	Specific information from known, reliable informant	"Officers did rely in good faith upon credible information by a reliable informant," justified arrest
Adams v. Williams, 92 S. Ct. 1921 (1972), concealed weapon and possession of drugs	". . . Given in person by known informant who had provided information in the past"	". . . Carried sufficient indicia of reliability to justify a forcible stop." Protective search revealed illegal weapon. Search incident to arrest resulted in finding illegal drugs.

Anonymous Tips Where the Identity of the Informer Is Unknown

In two of the following U.S. Supreme Court cases, the Supreme Court stated that:

. . . Unlike a tip from a known informant whose reputation can be assessed and who can be held responsible if her allegations turn out to be fabricated, an anonymous tip alone seldom demonstrates the informant's basis of knowledge or veracity." 110 S. Ct. 2412 and 146 L Ed 260

U.S. Supreme Court Case and Crime	Type of Anonymous Tip	Was Sufficient Indicia of Reliability Shown?
Illinois v. Gates, 103 S. Ct. 2317 (1983), trafficking in drugs	An Illinois police department received a handwritten letter telling how Mr. and Mrs. Gates (address given) were buying and selling drugs out of their home. The letter stated detailed facts and information regarding the Gates.	Yes, extensive police investigation corroborated major portions of the letter, causing an Illinois judge to issue a search warrant for the Gates's home and car where drugs were found. Convictions affirmed.

U.S. Supreme Court Case and Crime	Type of Anonymous Tip	Was Sufficient Indicia of Reliability Shown?
Alabama v. White, 110 S. Ct. 2412 (1990), possession of cocaine and marijuana	"Police received an anonymous tip asserting that a woman was carrying cocaine and predicting that she would leave an apartment building at a specific time, get into a car matching a particular description, and drive to a named motel." 146 L Ed 2d at 260	Yes, the Court held "(k)nowledge about a person's future movements indicates some familiarity with the person's affairs, but having such knowledge does not necessarily imply that the informant knows, in particular, whether that person is carrying contraband. We accordingly classified White as a 'close case."
Florida v. J.L., 120 S. Ct. 1375 (2000), illegal possession of a firearm (minor)	". . . An anonymous caller reported to the (police) that a young black male was standing at a particular bus stop and wearing a plaid shirt was carrying a gun." Six minutes later, officers arrived at the bus stop and saw J.L. but did not see a firearm. "J.L. made no threatening or otherwise unusual movements." A frisk revealed a concealed weapon.	No, the Court held that "all the police had to go on in this case was the bare report of an unknown, unaccountable informant who neither explained how he knew about the gun nor supplied any basis for believing he had inside information about J.L."

When a Tip Warns of Possible Great Danger

Because public safety requires police to respond quickly to tips of great public danger, the following statements were made by the U.S. Supreme Court in the case of *Florida v. J.L.*:

Justice Ginsburg for the Majority of the Court

We do not say, for example, that a report of a person carrying a bomb need bear the indicia of reliability we demand for a report of a person carrying a firearm before the police can constitutionally conduct a frisk. Nor do we hold that public safety officers in quarters where the reasonable expectation of privacy is diminished, such as airports and schools, cannot conduct protective searches on the basis of information insufficient to justify searches elsewhere.

Justice Kennedy and the Chief Justice

. . . There are many indicia of reliability respecting anonymous tips that we have yet to explore in our cases. . . . One such feature, as the Court recognizes, is that the tip predicts future conduct of the alleged criminal. There may be others. . . .

Justice Kennedy then uses the example of three similar calls by a voice that sounds the same each time and states that this situation "ought not to be treated automatically like the tip in the case now before us." Justice Kennedy also points out that as the police have instant caller identification, police cars can be sent to the location used by the informant. As it is a crime to make false reports to the police, the identity of the informant might then be "a factor which lends reliability . . ."

[a]*United States v. Holloway,* 290 F. 3d at 1339, review denied, 2003 WL 138487 (2003).

In sum, we follow a majority of the courts in declining to read into Title III an exception for interspousal or domestic wiretapping. Neither the text, the history nor the purposes of Title III permit the conclusion that defendants' conversations were lawfully intercepted.

ⓒ OBTAINING EVIDENCE BY USE OF DOGS TRAINED TO INDICATE AN ALERT

Dogs have a sense of smell that is reported to be several thousand times greater than the average human. For years, dogs have been used to pursue fugitives, locate escaped convicts, find missing persons, detect drugs and explosives, and in recent years to identify suspects in a lineup.

The article "Detection Dog Lineup" in the January 1996 *FBI Law Enforcement Bulletin* tells of a Colorado bloodhound named Yogi who tracked the scent of a kidnapped 5-year-old girl for 7 hours over a 14-mile trail. After the girl's body was found, Yogi then led officers to the suspect in a nearby apartment complex. Yogi has been used in four kidnapping cases, 45 homicide cases, and 350 other criminal cases.

The article reports that Yogi has been used in more than twenty-five dog detection lineups and describes the methods for using detection dogs to identify suspects in detection dog lineups. The article cites three appellate court cases where detection dog lineup evidence was used to obtain criminal convictions.[39]

Drug and Bomb Detection Dogs

Drug and bomb detection dogs have become a common and very effective tool used by law enforcement agencies throughout the United States. In a 1983 ruling, the U.S. Supreme Court held that luggage exposed to a trained drug detection dog in a public place "did not constitute a search within the meaning of the Fourth Amendment."[40]

An *FBI Law Enforcement Bulletin* article[41] observes that drug-detection dogs "have proven highly effective and reliable in detecting illegal narcotics" and that the U.S. Supreme Court and "most lower courts have granted particular deference to the olfactory abilities of police drug detection dogs." In reviewing the court rulings of the 1990s, the FBI article concludes that:

- "The use of drug detection dogs has met with few real challenges in the courts."
- "A dog's positive alert alone generally constitutes probable cause to search a vehicle. . . ."
- "As long as the [motor] vehicle is not detained beyond the time necessary to accomplish the purposes of the traffic stop . . . the exterior of the vehicle is available for a sniff."

In using dog-detection evidence in criminal courts, keeping and maintaining updated records on the dog and its handler is essential because the challenge to this evidence generally is the dog's reliability. When presenting drug cases where dogs have alerted the presence of the illegal drugs, dog-detection handlers should be prepared to establish the reliability of the dog by testimony regarding:

AP/Wide World Photos

Dogs trained to smell drugs or explosives are used to patrol airline and train terminals. Persons using such public places subject their luggage to dog sniff tests. The use of dog-detection evidence in court is dependent on up-to-date records verifying the dog's reliability.

- The training that the dog received to detect the odors for particular drugs
- The dog's success rate in detecting these drugs
- The method used to train the dog to indicate an alert
- Whether the dog alerted in the proper manner
- Proof of the dog's certification
- Proof that the dog has continued to meet certification requirements and has continued to receive necessary training on a regular basis[42]

SUMMARY

Search warrants have always been an important tool to obtain evidence during the investigation of a criminal case. When a search warrant is issued, the determination by the judge or magistrate issuing the warrant is given great deference, and the burden of proving that probable cause did not exist shifts to persons challenging the warrant.

Today, telecommunication systems have become the cornerstones of everyday life. Dependence upon computers, data services, and mobile communications has become increasingly important for business and personal use. To cope with the many changes, law enforcement must, upon occasion, obtain authority to use electronic surveillance to obtain evidence when dealing with terrorism, organized crime, or sophisticated illegal drug trafficking.

Detection dogs are another important tool needed by law enforcement upon occasion to obtain evidence or to find a missing person, locate illegal drugs, or a bomb.

PROBLEMS

1. Lopez was having federal tax problems and attempted to bribe an IRS agent. After the IRS agent reported the matter to his superior, he was instructed to keep an appointment with Lopez. However, at the second meeting the IRS agent had a tape recorder in his pocket and recorded the conversation in which Lopez again attempted to bribe the agent to fix his tax problems with the federal government. Lopez was then charged with attempted bribery and at his trial took the witness stand in his own behalf. After Lopez denied under oath that he attempted to bribe the tax agent, the tape recorder was introduced into evidence to show that Lopez had not told the truth under oath.

Should the U.S. Supreme Court hold that the evidence of the tape recorder was properly used in the federal trial of Lopez? Explain. Should the U.S. Supreme Court affirm Lopez's conviction for bribery? Why? [*Lopez v. United States,* 373 U.S. 427, 83 S.Ct. 1381 (1963)].

2. A police officer made a proper stop of a vehicle, having reasonable suspicion to believe the driver was driving while intoxicated. The officer, who was in full uniform, talked with the defendant (driver). The defendant did not know that the officer was tape-recording the conversation and made statements incriminating himself.

Would the tape recording be admissible as evidence in your state in a trial for drunken driving? Explain. [*City and Borough of Juneau v. Quinto,* 684

P.2d 127 (Alaska, 1984)]. Would a videotaping of the defendant after he was arrested for drunken driving be admissible as evidence? Explain. [*Palmer v. State,* 604 P.2d 1106 (Alaska, 1979)].

3. Florida police investigating the murder of a psychologist who was shot five times in his office thought at first they had a hard case to solve. There were no witnesses, nor did anyone hear the shots. But to their surprise, the police found that the psychologist had tape-recorded the business meeting between himself and the defendant. The sounds of the two men quarrelling, a gun being cocked, five shots, groans by the victim, gushing of blood, and the victim falling to the floor could be heard on the tape.

If this murder had occurred in your state, could the recording be used as evidence in a criminal trial? Explain. [*State v. Inciarrano,* 473 So.2d 1272 (Fla., 1985)].

4. The latest development in investigating driving while intoxicated is the Passive Alcohol Sensor (PAS). This flashlight with a built-in breathalyzer enables an officer to analyze a driver's breath without the driver's participation or consent. Does use of this device, which could be called a "sense-enhancing" device because it enables an officer to sense something not otherwise possible without the device, constitute a search under *United States v. Kyllo*? Why or why not?

INFOTRAC COLLEGE EDITION EXERCISES

1. Go to InfoTrac College Edition and using the search term "wiretapping" and the "periodical" view find the 2003 article in *Business Week Online,* titled "These Are Not Your Father's Wiretaps," by Jane Black. This article explores the FBI's "carnivore" program for intercepting emails and its new program to do the same for Voice Over Internet Protocol (VOIP) transmissions. What are some of the privacy problems presented by law enforcement programs such as these? How should they be resolved?

2. Go to InfoTrac College Edition and using the search term "electronic surveillance" and the "periodical" view find the 2002 *Security Manage-* *ment* article titled "Facing Facts: Crooks Can't Bet on Anonymity," by Douglas L. Florence Sr. This article discusses new facial recognition technology that can be used in public places to identify known offenders or others wanted by the police. Are there any constitutional problems with the use of this technology? Where is the best place for its use by police?

NOTES

1. The U.S. Supreme Court has repeatedly held that searches "without prior approval by a judge . . . are per se unreasonable under the Fourth Amendment—subject only to a few specifically established and well-delineated exceptions" [*Collidge v. New Hampshire,* 91 S. Ct. 2022 (1971)]. Therefore, evidence obtained as a result of an unreasonable search would be suppressed and could not be used.

2. The U.S. Supreme Court held in the case of *United States v. Leon,* 104 S.Ct. 3405 (1984), that "the courts must also insist that the magistrate purport to perform his neutral and detached function and not serve merely as a rubber stamp for the police."

3. 90 S.Ct. 1029 (1970).

4. 500 N.W.2d 547 (Nebr., 1993).

5. The U.S. Supreme Court defined "controlled delivery" in the 1983 case of *Illinois v. Andreas,* 463 U.S. 765, 103 S.Ct. 3319, and affirmed the manner in which the law enforcement officers acted:

> Controlled deliveries of contraband apparently serve a useful function in law enforcement. They most ordinarily occur when a carrier, usually an airline, unexpectedly discovers what seems to be contraband while inspecting luggage to learn the identity of its owner, or when the contraband falls out of a broken or damaged piece of luggage, or when the carrier exercises its inspection privilege because some suspicious circumstance has caused concern that it may unwittingly be transporting contraband. Frequently, after such a discovery, law enforcement agents restore the contraband to its container, then close or reseal the container, and authorize the carrier to deliver the container to its owner. When the owner appears to take delivery he is arrested and the container with the contraband is seized and then searched a second time for the contraband known to be there.

6. Federal Rule of Criminal Procedure 41 requires that a covert entry under a sneak-and-peek warrant be followed within seven days by notice to the person whose property has been entered. However, for cases where this was not done, see *United States v. Pangburn,* 983 F.2d 449, 52 CrL 1417 (2d Cir., 1993); and *United States v. Freitas,* 800 F.2d 1451 (9th Cir., 1986).

7. 441 U.S. 238, 99 S.Ct. 1682.

8. 142 F.3d 988 (7th Cir., 1998).

9. 42 U.S.C. 2000(a)(a).

10. 88 S.Ct. 507.

11. Title 18, Chapter 119 of the Omnibus Crime Control and Safe Streets Act of 1968 (18 U.S.C., Sec. 2510).

12. In footnote 1 of the case of *Dalia v. United States,* 441 U.S. 238, 99 S.Ct. 1682 (1979), the U.S. Supreme Court stated the difference between wiretapping and bugging as follows:

> All types of electronic surveillance have the same purpose and effect: the secret interception of communications. As the Court set forth in *Berger v. New York,* 388 U.S. 41, (1967), however, this surveillance is performed in two quite different ways. Some surveillance is performed by "wiretapping," which is confined to the interception of communication by telephone and telegraph and generally may be performed from outside the premises to be monitored. . . . At issue in the present case is the form of surveillance commonly known as "bugging," which includes the interception

of all oral communication in a given location. Unlike wiretapping, this interception typically is accomplished by installation of a small microphone in the room to be bugged and transmission to some nearby receiver.

The issue before the U.S. Supreme Court in the 1979 case of *Dalia v. United States* was whether a separate court order was necessary to authorize the FBI entering an office building to place a listening device and then, several weeks later, entering again at night to remove the device. The majority held that court orders were not necessary.

13. The word *eavesdropping* is an old English word meaning "to sneak under the eaves of a home and listen to conversations within the home." This conduct was forbidden under old English law and is forbidden under present law. See the case of *State of Texas v. Gonzales,* 388 F.2d 145 (5th Cir., 1968), where law officers sneaked into the defendant's yard at night and listened to conversations in the house. Because the defendant's Fourth Amendment right of privacy was violated, the evidence obtained was suppressed.

14. 10 Conn App. 7, 521 A.2d 204 (1987), review denied 486 U.S. 1056, 108 S.Ct. 2823.

15. *United States v. Fisch,* 474 F.2d 1071 (9th Cir., 1973), review denied 412 U.S. 921, 93 S.Ct. 2742 (1973); *United States v. Jackson,* 588 F.2d 1046 (5th Cir., 1979).

16. *United States v. Llanes,* 398 F.2d 880 (2d Cir., 1968).

17. *Ponce v. Craven,* 409 F.2d 621 (9th Cir., 1969).

18. *Pappas v. Municipality of Anchorage,* 698 P.2d 1236 (Alaska App., 1985).

19. See the article "Secret Taping of Supervisors Is on the Rise, Lawyers Say," 3 November 1992, p. B1. The article points out that labor lawyers report an increase in secret taping of supervisors by employees seeking to protect their jobs in a tight labor market.

20. *Stanley v. Wainwright,* 604 F.2d 379 (5th Cir., 1979), review denied 100 S.Ct. 3019 (1980).

21. *Illinois v. Perkins,* 496 U.S. 292, 110 S.Ct. 2394 (1990).

22. *Kuhlmann v. Wilson,* 477 U.S. 436, 106 S.Ct. 2616 (1986).

23. *Ahmad A. v. Superior Court,* 263 Cal. Rptr. 747 (1989), review denied 498 U.S. 834, 111 S.Ct. 102 (1990).

24. *State v. Fedorchenko,* 630 So.2d 213 (Fla. App., 1993).

25. 18 U.S.C.A., sec. 2511(2)(d).

26. *State v. Kedoranian,* 828 P.2d 45 (Wash. App., 1992).

27. *People v. Griffin,* 592 N.E. 2d. 930 (Ill. App., 1992). Illinois law requires a prior court order for one-party consent to the monitoring of a private conversation through the use of an eavesdropping device.

While investigating an arson, Illinois police officers listened to a telephone conversation between Shinkle (one of the wrongdoers) and a man who admitted to committing the arson and who allowed the police to listen to the conversation. The police officer picked up an extension phone and placed his hand over the mouthpiece. Shinkle made incriminating statements that were used to convict him. The Illinois Supreme Court held that the extension phone did not become an eavesdropping device because the officer cupped his hand over the mouthpiece in the 1989 case of *People v. Shinkle,* 539 N.E.2d 1238, 45 CrL 2211.

28. *United States v. Dale,* 991 F.2d 819 (D.C. Cir., 1993).

29. *State v. Reyes,* 808 P.2d 544 (Nev., 1991).

30. *State v. Allgood,* 831 P.2d 1290 (Ariz. App., 1992).

31. *Lawrence v. State,* 393 S.E.2d 475 (Ga. App., 1990).

32. *State v. Walton,* 809 P.2d 81 (Ore., 1991).

33. *State v. Lucas,* 372 N.W.2d 731 (Minn., 1985).

34. 18 U.S.C.A., sec. 2510–21.

35. 18 U.S.C.A., sec. 2511(1)(c).

36. 944 F.2d 1537 (10th Cir.), review denied 112 S.Ct. 1574 (1992).

37. *State v. Shaw,* 404 S.E. 2d 887, 49 Crl 1340 (N.C. App., 1991);*Rickenbaker v. Rickenbaker,* 226 S.E. 2d 347 (N.C., 1976).

38. *People v. Otto,* 831 P.2d 1178 (Calif., 1992), review denied U.S. 113 S.Ct. 414 (1992).

39. See *Ramos v. State,* 4966 So. 2d 121 (Fla., 1986); *United States v. McNiece,* 558 F. Supp. 612 (E.D.N.Y., 1983); and *State v. Roscoe,* 700 P. 2d 1312 (Ariz., 1984), cert. denied 417 U.S. 1094.

40. In the case of *United States v. Place,* 462 U.S. 696, the U.S. Supreme Court pointed out that a dog's sniff is nonintrusive and reveals only the presence of illegal drugs. Place was not required

to open his luggage and expose his personal belongings to public view. The Supreme Court, however, reversed Place's conviction not because of the dog sniff but because the 90-minute wait for the arrival of the dog at the airport was held to be too long to be reasonable; the officers did not act with due diligence.

A 90-minute detention based upon reasonable suspicion has been held to be reasonable in cases where officers acted with due diligence to get a dog to the scene. In the case of *United States v. $64,765.00*, 786 F.Supp. 906 (Ore., 1991), the officers' efforts and diligence in getting a dog to the scene caused the court to rule that the delay was reasonable under the circumstances.

41. "Drug Detection Dogs: Legal Considerations" (January 2000).

42. Ibid., 32.

IV

Crime–Scene, Documentary, and Scientific Evidence

16

The Crime Scene, the Chain of Custody Requirement, and the Use of Fingerprints and Trace Evidence

Ⓐ OBTAINING EVIDENCE FROM A CRIME SCENE

Crimes occur in both public and private places. If a crime occurs on a street or sidewalk or in premises, such as a tavern or store, open to the public, law officers would not have to show authority such as consent, a search warrant, or an exigency to justify their entry.

When a crime occurs in a private premise such as a home, apartment, office, or factory, law enforcement officers most often enter with the consent of victims, family members, or someone having control of the premise. Other situations conferring authority to enter includes:

- Exigency, where a person's life or safety is endangered; where there is concern for an elderly person or other person; where a shooting, fire, or explosion, has occurred (see Chapter 14 for cases and the law about exigent entry into private premises).

- Search warrants, which are usually necessary to enter premises where there is probable cause to believe that nonemergency crimes have or are occurring (such as drug houses, or places where nonviolent crimes are believed to be occurring).

Law enforcement officers may stay in a **crime scene** for a reasonable period of time to perform whatever tasks they are obligated to do. The question of how long officers may stay in a premise was presented in the following 1978 case where the U.S. Supreme Court held that there was no "murder scene exception" to the Fourth Amendment of the U.S. Constitution:

Mincey v. Arizona
United States Supreme Court, 437 US. 385, 98 S.Ct. 2408 (1978)

In a drug raid of the defendant's apartment in Tucson, Arizona, Officer Headricks was shot and later died. Police officers seized the apartment and held it for four days. The U.S. Supreme Court described the police search as follows:

> . . . Their search lasted four days, during which period the entire apartment was searched, photographed, and diagrammed. The officers opened drawers, closets, and cupboards, and inspected their contents; they emptied clothing pockets; they dug bullet fragments out of the walls and floors; they pulled up sections of the carpet and removed them for examination. Every item in the apartment was closely examined and inventoried, and 200 to 300 objects were seized. In short, Mincey's apartment was subjected to an exhaustive and intrusive search. No warrant was ever obtained.

In reversing the defendant's convictions and ordering a new trial, the Court held:

> In sum, we hold that the "murder scene exception" created by the Arizona Supreme Court is inconsistent with the Fourth and Fourteenth Amendments—that the warrantless search of Mincey's apartment was not constitutionally permissible simply because a homicide had recently occurred there.

What Can Police Search for in Premises Where a Serious Crime Has Recently Occurred?

In the *Mincey* case, the U.S. Supreme Court also decided what police may search for in premises where a serious crime has recently occurred. The Court held in *Mincey* that law enforcement officers may make "warrantless entries and searches when they reasonably believe that a person within is in need of immediate aid" (**emergency situations**). The Court stated:

1. Law officers "may make a prompt warrantless search of the area to see if there are other victims or if a killer is still on the premises . . ."

2. The police "may seize any evidence that is in plain view during the course of their legitimate emergency activities . . ."[1]

In holding that the police search in the *Mincey* case went too far and exceeded the limits of "emergency activities," the Court held:[2]

> But a warrantless search must be "strictly circumscribed by the exigencies which justify its initiation," *Terry v. Ohio,* 392 U.S., at 25–26, 88 S.Ct., at 1882, and it simply cannot be contended that this search was justified by any emergency threatening life or limb. All the persons in Mincey's apartment had been located before the investigating homicide officers arrived there and began their search. And a four-day search that included opening dresser drawers and ripping up carpets can hardly be rationalized in terms of the legitimate concerns that justify an emergency search.

Obtaining Evidence After a "Hot-Pursuit" Entry into Private Premises

The following two U.S. Supreme Court cases state the law about the admissibility of evidence obtained by police in lawful "hot-pursuit" entries into homes.[3]

Warden, Md. Penitentiary v. Hayden
United States Supreme Court, 387 U.S. 294, 87 S.Ct. 1642 (1967)

Immediately after the defendant robbed a Baltimore cab company, his flight was observed by two cab drivers who reported that he entered a nearby home. Within minutes, police arrived at the home. Having been given a description of the defendant, they requested entrance and when Mrs. Hayden offered no objections, the police began a search of the home for the defendant. Before the police found Hayden in the home, they found a pistol in a toilet flush tank that was running, and ammunition for the pistol was found under the mattress of Hayden's bed. A shotgun was found, and ammunition for it was found in a bureau drawer. Clothing similar to the type worn by the fleeing felon was found in a washing machine. All the seized items were used as evidence. In affirming the use of the evidence and the conviction of the defendant, the Court held that:

They [the police] acted reasonably when they entered the house and began to search for a man of the description they had been given and for weapons which he had used in the robbery or might be used against them. The Fourth Amendment does not require police officers to delay in the course of an investigation if to do so would gravely endanger their lives or the lives of others. Speed here was essential, and only a thorough search of the house for persons and weapons could have insured that Hayden was the only man present and that the police had control of all weapons which could be used against them or to effect an escape. . . .

. . . The permissible scope of search must, therefore, at the least, be as broad as may reasonably be necessary to prevent the dangers that the suspect at large in the house may resist or escape.

United States v. Santana
United States Supreme Court, 427 U.S. 38, 96 S.Ct. 2406 (1976)

In a "buy-and-bust" operation, a police informant bought heroine from Santana and paid for it in marked money. Police officers then had probable cause to arrest Santana. The officers identified themselves to the defendant as she stood in the doorway of her home. The defendant retreated into the house, and the officers followed and caught her in the vestibule of the home. In holding that the arrest and the evidence obtained in the search incident to the arrest were lawful, the Supreme Court reversed the lower-court's ruling and held that:

The only remaining question is whether her act of retreating into her house could thwart an otherwise proper arrest. We hold that it could not. In *Warden v. Hayden,* 387 U.S. 294, 87 S.Ct. 1642 (1967), we recognized the right of police, who had probable cause to believe that an armed robber had entered a house a few minutes before, to make a warrantless entry to arrest the robber and to search for weapons. This case, involving a true "hot pursuit," is clearly governed by Warden; the need to act quickly here is even greater than in that case while the intrusion is much less. The District Court was correct in concluding that "hot pursuit" means some sort of a chase, but it need not be an extended hue and cry "in and about [the] public streets." The fact that the pursuit here ended almost as soon as it began did not render it any the less a "hot pursuit" sufficient to justify the warrantless entry into Santana's house. Once Santana saw the police, there was likewise a realistic expectation that any delay would result in destruction of evidence. . . . Once she had been arrested the search, incident to that arrest, which produced the drugs and money was clearly justified.

We thus conclude that a suspect may not defeat an arrest which has been set in motion in a public place, and is therefore proper under *Watson v. United States,* 96 S.Ct. 820 (1976), by the expedient of escaping to a private place.

Obtaining Evidence in Now-or-Never Exigency Situations

An exigency exists if law officers have no time to obtain a search warrant and have probable cause to believe that evidence will be destroyed or moved to an unknown place. The burden is on the law officers to show that a now-or-never situation exists; that is, the police must show that they needed to act immediately or would lose the opportunity to seize the evidence because it would be destroyed or moved to an unknown place.

In the 1966 case of *Schmerber v. California*,[4] the defendant was involved in a car accident where both he and others were injured. Police had probable cause to believe that Schmerber was driving while intoxicated. Since the human body quickly destroys evidence of intoxication and the police did not have time to obtain a search warrant for intoxication evidence within Schmerber's body, a now-or-never situation existed.

Because of the compelling public interest in highway safety, the U.S. Supreme Court held in both the *Schmerber* case and in the 1983 case of *South Dakota v. Neville*,[5] that, because there was no time to obtain a search warrant, immediate action was required by law officers to obtain and preserve evidence of intoxication by obtaining blood or breath for testing and use as evidence. All states have now passed an implied consent law: Drivers who use the highways imply their consent to such tests if probable cause exists to believe that the driver is operating a motor vehicle while intoxicated. Failure to consent to testing under such circumstances is a crime.

In the following case, the U.S. Supreme Court held that a now-or-never entry into an apartment was lawful to seize illegal drugs as evidence.

Ker v. California
United States Supreme Court, 374 U.S. 23, 83 S.Ct. 1623 (1963)

Law enforcement officers observed Ker make a large illegal drug buy from a drug dealer. They followed Ker's car but lost it in traffic when Ker made a sudden turn. Believing that Ker knew that he was being followed, the officers then obtained the address of Ker's apartment from his automobile license number. When Ker's car was found parked at his apartment, the officers obtained a key to his apartment from the apartment manager. Believing that evidence would be destroyed if they made an entry by knocking, the officers made a "no-knock" entry into Ker's apartment by use of the key. In holding that the officer's testimony sustained an exception to the California "knock" requirement, the Supreme Court affirmed the defendant's conviction and the use of the narcotics seized as evidence in Ker's trial, holding that:

> Here . . . the criteria under California law clearly include an exception to the notice requirement where exigent circumstances are present. . . .
>
> . . . Here justification for the officers' failure to give notice is uniquely present. In addition to the officers' belief that Ker was in possession of narcotics, which could be quickly and easily destroyed, Ker's furtive conduct in eluding them shortly before the arrest was ground for the belief that he might well have been expecting the police. We therefore hold that in the particular circumstances of this case the officers' method of entry, sanctioned by the law of California, was not unreasonable under the standards of the Fourth Amendment as applied to the States through the Fourteenth Amendment.

Obtaining Evidence in Emergency Aid Situations[6]

Thousands of emergency aid cases have come before U.S. courts. Evidence found when police are responding to an emergency may be used in criminal trials. Examples where courts sustained the action of the police are the following:

- To aid physicians who are treating a person suffering from a drug overdose, police may search for the substance the person took and seize it to assist in the person's treatment. In the case of *State v. Follett,*[7] police arrested a driver who was under the influence of some substance. Police could search for and seize the substance the person took (cocaine) to aid the treating physician and to use as evidence. This also has been done in attempted suicides.

- The Supreme Court of Delaware held that when police receive a report indicating that emergency aid might be needed, "it was the duty of the police to act forthwith upon the report of the emergency—not to speculate upon the accuracy of the report or upon legal technicalities regarding search warrants. . . ."[8]

- An injured driver left the scene of a vehicle accident and was traced by a police officer to his home. When the officer observed the man through a window lying on a bed unconscious and bleeding, an emergency entry into the home was authorized. Evidence of drunk driving was then lawfully obtained.[9]

- Police had reasonable suspicion to stop cars leaving an area where shots were heard. In the 1993 case of *United States v. Reedy,*[10] a citizen told the police of the gunshots; in the 1992 case of *Williamson v. United States,*[11] a police officer heard the shots fired. Evidence obtained in the car stops could be used.

Defendants Must Have Standing to Challenge the Use of Evidence Obtained from Crime Scenes

To have *standing* and challenge the manner in which police obtained evidence from a crime scene, a defendant must show that he or she had a legitimate expectation of privacy in the crime scene.

A burglar who illegally entered a home has no legitimate expectation or right of privacy in the home and therefore no standing to challenge evidence against him that police obtained from the home. The following cases illustrate:

- Michael Perry was convicted of five murders and sentenced to death. Among the murder victims were his mother and father who had their own home where defendant could not enter without the consent of his parents and in which he had no belongings. In the 1986 case of *State v. Perry,*[12] the Supreme Court of Louisiana held that: "There was no living person who had a privacy interest in the house at 810 Seventh Street. (Defendant had killed all of the occupants of the house.) Therefore the entries of the house were not in violation of anyone's privacy interest."

- The defendant's girlfriend was murdered in a house that the defendant had built for her, to which he possessed a key and in which he occasionally stayed overnight. But the defendant lived elsewhere, and the victim paid for the building supplies used to build the home. The defendant was charged with the murder and challenged the evidence the police had obtained from the victim's home, which was going to be used against him. The Tennessee courts held that the defendant did not have standing to challenge the use of the evidence because he was only a casual visitor who had no right to exclude others from the premises and had insufficient interest to object to the search that turned up the evidence.[13]

Protecting and Searching a Crime Scene[14]

Testimony of a trained law enforcement officer of the observations and findings of a crime scene is vitally important in many criminal cases. Improper protection of a crime scene could result in the contamination, loss, or unnecessary movement of physical evidence. Therefore, the first officer to arrive at the scene of the crime automatically incurs the serious and critical responsibility of securing the crime scene from unauthorized intrusions. Even though the officer who arrives first will also search it for physical evidence, the necessity to immediately take precautions to protect it remains unchanged.

To prove that evidence is genuine and authentic and to show that the object is what it is claimed to be, a witness would have to be able to:

- Testify about where and how the object was obtained.
- Identify the object by a serial number if a serial number is on the object. For example, a serial number would probably be on a handgun, and it would be identified in this manner.
- Identify the object based upon personal knowledge and observations. This could be done by an officer scratching his or her initials and the date on the object to make it readily identifiable.[15] A *chain of custody* (see next section) is not needed if the object is positively identified at trial and the evidence is not susceptible to tampering, contamination, substitution, or mistake.[16]
- "If the evidence is not readily identifiable or is susceptible to alteration by tampering, substitution, or contamination, the party must establish a chain of custody; in this event, the chain of custody must be of sufficient completeness to render it improbable that the evidence has been tampered with or substituted."[17]

Crime Scenes Are No Place for a Crowd

A Michigan forensic scientist asked many of his fellow technicians to name the biggest problem on the job. The same answer came from technicians around the country: "crime scenes contaminated by curious officers, detectives, and supervisors."[18] The technician wrote the following description of the problems caused by "pointless tourism":

Lost Evidence, Lost Opportunities

Widespread trampling of crime scenes can prove very damaging to investigations. Often, it results in several of the more sensitive forensic techniques—such as trace analysis, bloodspatter interpretation, and DNA comparison—not being used to their fullest potential. Crime scene technicians know the futility of collecting hair or fiber samples after a roomful of officers have shed all over the scene. Footwear and tire track evidence is rarely recognized as valuable in

Case	Strongest Evidence Available to Government	Arguments by Defense Lawyers
Unknown snipers terrorized the Washington, D.C., area for twenty-three days in October 2002. The snipers are linked to twenty shootings, which caused thirteen deaths in five states and the District of Columbia.	Thousands of law officers searched for evidence to identify the snipers. An angry telephone call was the linchpin to fingerprints identifying the snipers, who were arrested in their car as they slept. The 18-year-old suspect made extensive incriminating statements, which were held to be admissible at his preliminary hearing.	In trials that will be held in 2003 or 2004, defense lawyers will have to attack the incriminating statements, ballistic and fingerprint evidence, and the sniper car, which was modified into a mobile killing machine.
Arthur Anderson, Inc. (89-year-old accounting firm with 27,000 employees), convicted in 2002 of the crime of obstruction of justice	Mass destruction of thousands of documents and thousands of email messages. Prosecutors argued that Anderson destroyed potential criminal evidence against the Enron Corporation and Anderson because they expected a police investigation.	This was a routine disposal of documents and messages and was not the intentional destruction of potential evidence.
In 1976, a 15-year-old girl was murdered in a wealthy Connecticut community. At the time, there was not sufficient evidence to charge a neighbor boy. But twenty-six years later, the State charged and convicted the boy (now a man) of the crime.	The defendant's words to others and how his story changed caused the jury to perceive this evidence as the defendant's "consciousness of guilt." The jury believed the testimony of a witness that the defendant, Michael Skakl, had stated, "I'm going to get away with murder. I'm a Kennedy."	There was no direct evidence of the murder that had occurred twenty-six years prior to the trial of 41-year-old Michael Skakl.

departments where officers routinely wander unimpeded through crime scenes. On occasion, this can seriously hamper investigations.

Not long ago, a sheriff's department was forced to conduct a mass fingerprinting of its detective unit after a particularly sensational homicide crime scene became overrun with curious personnel. Considerable time and effort went into eliminating officers' fingerprints from the pool of legitimate prints. In another case involving a different agency, a set of crime scene photographs showed supervisory personnel standing on a blood-soaked carpet.

Unsolved Murder Cases Where Insufficient Evidence Exists to Charge or Convict

Anthrax attacks in Washington, D.C., New York City, Boca Raton, Florida, and Reno, Nevada, killed five people and caused others to become ill.

Who murdered JonBenet Ramsey, age 6, in her home in Boulder, Colorado, on December 26, 1996? Hundreds of persons disappear every year in the United States and are not heard of again. The 1975 disappearance of former union boss Jimmy Hoffa continues to make the news. Was Hoffa murdered? What did happen to him? News media again covered the story in 2002 when DNA testing showed that hair from Mr. Hoffa was in a Mafia-owned car driven that day by a prime suspect.

Deadly, potent, pure strains of anthrax were sent through the U.S. mail. The source of the anthrax is believed to be domestic, but there is insufficient evidence to identify the terrorist. A large reward has been offered for information.

Much has been written and published on this murder with some writers stating the murder investigation was bungled, causing the loss of evidence. Despite the efforts of Colorado governors, grand juries, police, and prosecutors, no one has been charged or indicted for the crime.

Hoffa, the father of the current Teamster's president, disappeared from the parking lot of a fashionable restaurant in a Detroit suburb where Hoffa was to meet Mafia bosses from New Jersey and Detroit. All of these persons deny involvement in Hoffa's disappearance, as does the prime suspect, Charles O'Brien. Hoffa's family states that only a close friend such as O'Brien could persuade Hoffa to get into the car O'Brien was driving that day. New DNA technology now shows Hoffa hair in the car O'Brien was driving. Michigan prosecutors stated this was insufficient evidence to charge, even though the vehicle belonged to a high Detroit Mafia leader.

B THE CHAIN OF CUSTODY REQUIREMENT

To use physical evidence in a criminal or civil trial, the party offering the evidence has the burden of proving that the evidence is genuine and authentic. This requires testimony establishing an adequate foundation about where and how the object was obtained and that the object offered in evidence is the object that it claims to be.

If the evidence (such as fingerprints or illegal drugs) could be subject to alteration by tampering, substitution, or contamination, a **chain of custody** must be shown. This requires that all persons who had possession of the evidence must appear as witnesses

Was the Following "Crime Scene" Search Lawful?

The U.S. Supreme Court case of *Thompson v. Louisiana,* 105 S. Ct. 409 (1984):

A despondent woman decided to end her life. She shot her husband of many years; wrote a suicide note; then took an overdose of sleeping pills. While waiting to die, she changed her mind and called her daughter for help.

The daughter quickly notified the sheriff's office and rushed to her parents' home. When sheriff's deputies arrived at the home, the daughter admitted them to the scene of the homicide and the attempted suicide. The unconscious woman was taken to a hospital and after searching the house for other victims or suspects, the officers secured the house.

Thirty-five minutes later, homicide investigators arrived and went into the house to begin a "general exploratory search for evidence of a crime." Every room in the house was examined during a two-hour search. Three important items of evidence were seized: a pistol found in a chest of drawers, a torn note found in a bathroom wastepaper basket, and a suicide note tucked inside a Christmas card on top of a chest of drawers.

The detectives had neither consent nor a search warrant for their search. Was their search within the scope of the emergency that had existed in this home? Can the three pieces of evidence be used against the woman who survived and was charged with the second-degree murder of her husband?[a]

[a]The U.S. Supreme Court's ruling is found in note 19 at the end of this chapter.

---

to testify that the fingerprints or illegal drugs had not been tampered with, substituted, or contaminated while the witness had custody and control of the evidence. In handling evidence requiring a chain of custody, it is therefore best that as few people as possible have custody of the evidence.

Besides illegal drugs and fingerprints (regular and DNA), the following court cases have held that chains of custody must be presented for the use of the following as evidence: videotapes,[20] a crack pipe,[21] a suitcase full of marijuana,[22] forensic evidence,[23] shell casing,[24] blood samples,[25] note found next to murder victim,[26] human hair and fibers from carpet,[27] semen and blood,[28] forged check,[29] specimens from human body,[30] and body of murder victim.[31]

Failing to Show a Sufficient Chain of Custody

To use evidence that could be subject to tampering, substitution, or contamination, the state must, by the use of witnesses, establish a chain of custody to "show a reasonable probability that the [evidence] was not tampered with."[32] The following cases illustrate situations in which the state did *not* prove a sufficient chain of custody for critical evidence in criminal cases:[33]

- A rape victim identified her panties and blouse in the criminal trial. The semen and blood stains on the panties and the wool fiber on the blouse seriously incriminated the defendant, but there was no showing about where the clothing was during the time after the crime and before the trial. The Supreme Court of Virginia reversed the defendant's conviction of rape and remanded for a new trial in the case of *Robinson v. Commonwealth.*[34]

- The court reversed and remanded for a new trial because the state did not show where the cocaine used as evidence was or how it was kept for a period of twenty days.[35]

- A gap in the chain of custody between seizure of drugs and the vouching for them at the police station caused reversal for a new trial in the 1993 case of *People v. Rivera.*[36]

- Failure of the drug-testing laboratory to complete the chain of custody form for a urine sample caused reversal for a new trial.[37]

Situations Not Requiring a Chain of Custody

A chain of custody is not required if the object to be used as evidence is not subject to alteration by tampering, substitution, or contamination. The following cases illustrate:

- A chain of custody is not required in most shoplifting and theft cases. The Supreme Court of Nebraska held that a chain of custody was not required in the shoplifting case of *State v. Sexton.*[38]

- A pistol was held to be admissible without showing a chain of custody (no fingerprint or ballistic testimony used) in the 1991 case of *Outland v. State.*[39]

- Twenty-two silver dollars stolen from a pawn shop were admitted for use in evidence although the victim could not specifically identify them as the silver dollars stolen. In affirming the defendant's conviction, the court in the 1991 case of *State v. Simmons*[40] stated

  . . . The court does not need a positive and indisputable description of the object in order to admit it into evidence. *Gresham v. State,* 456 P.2d 119 (Okla. 1969). Lack of positive identification goes to weight, not admissibility. See also *State v. Amaya-Ruiz,* 166 Ariz. 152, 800 P.2d 1260 (1990), *cert. denied* 111 S.Ct. 2044, 114 L.Ed.2d 129 (1991); *State v. Skelton,* 129 Ariz. 181, 629 P.2d 1017 (App. 1981); *State v. Baker,* 219 Kan. 854, 549 P.2d 911 (1976); *Young v. State,* 701 P.2d 415 (Okla. 1985); *State v. Mitchell,* 56 Wash. App. 610, 784 P.2d 568 (1990). Further, because of the physical nature of coins and currency, to sufficiently identify the money to make it admissible as relevant evidence, it is not necessary that the witness identify each bill or coin separately, rather, the witness may testify that the money appears to be the same money alleged to have been stolen after considering its amount, denomination, packaging, and general appearance.

C FINGERPRINTS AS EVIDENCE

Historians believe that the Chinese used thumbprints to sign important documents before the birth of Christ. But it was not until the 1870s that a British civil servant in India used fingerprints to record persons on pensions and of prisoners in jail. Police in Argentina were reportedly the first law officers to use fingerprinting in 1891.

A criminal today who carelessly leaves fingerprints at the scene of a crime leaves what are called **latent fingerprints.** Latent fingerprints taken from a crime scene can

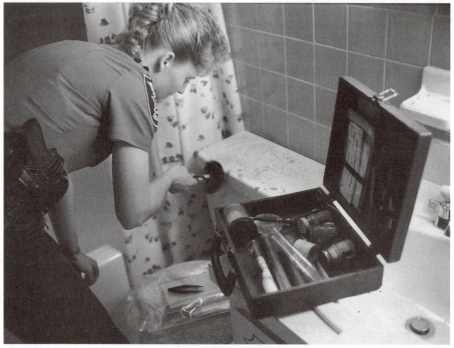

An officer dusts for fingerprints at a crime scene. Fingerprints are a highly reliable form of physical evidence because each person's fingerprints are unique and unchanging.

be compared with fingerprints on file in local, state, or FBI files. The FBI has millions of fingerprints on file and receives more than 20,000 fingerprints a day from law enforcement agencies throughout the country.

> "Fingerprints are perhaps the most common form of physical evidence, and certainly one of the most valuable. They relate directly to the ultimate objective of every criminal investigation . . . the identification of the offender. . . . Since a print of one finger has never been known to exactly duplicate another fingerprint, even of the same person or identical twin, it is possible to identify an individual with just one impression . . . a person's fingerprints have never been known to change. The unchanging pattern thus provides a permanent record of the individual throughout life."[41]

The U.S. Supreme Court stated in the case of *Davis v. Mississippi* that "fingerprinting is an inherently more reliable and effective crime-solving tool than eyewitness identification or confessions and is not subject to such abuses as the improper lineup and the 'third-degree.'"[42]

Obtaining Fingerprints

Persons in lawful police custody are routinely fingerprinted and photographed. Persons who have served in the military have their fingerprints on file, as do many government employees and people who receive licenses for such occupations as bartending, driving a taxicab, working in private security, or obtaining a government security clearance.

People can also consent to having their fingerprints taken, as occurred in the Gainesville, Florida, area in 1990 when five college students were slain in a two-month period. Law officers focused on persons on foot, mopeds, bicycles, and motorcycles. If any question arose concerning why the person was in the area, a voluntary stop was made, and the individual was asked to consent to fingerprinting. In 1994 the killer was apprehended and confessed to the killings.

A number of states have statutes authorizing juvenile judges to order a juvenile who is not arrested or in custody to submit to fingerprinting when probable cause does not exist. The Supreme Court of Colorado[43] and the Supreme Court of Ohio[44] found such statutes constitutional.

The U.S. Supreme Court held in the cases of *Davis v. Mississippi*[45] and *Hayes v. Florida*,[46] that courts may order fingerprinting "under narrowly defined circumstances . . . found to comply with the Fourth Amendment even though there is no probable cause in the traditional sense." Rapes had occurred in both the *Davis* and *Hayes* cases, where the police had fingerprints of the offenders but could not match them up with and identify the defendants, who were not in custody.

Proving that Fingerprints Were Impressed at the Time of the Crime

Fingerprints are circumstantial evidence from which inferences must be drawn. It is "impossible . . . to determine the age of [a] latent print" because the print could have been on an object for a long time before the crime was committed.

As a general rule, the prosecution must first introduce fingerprint evidence by use of an expert witness and show a chain of custody to prove the evidence is authentic, genuine, and has not been tampered with. The government must then show that the fingerprints "could only have been impressed at the time when the crime was committed. The U.S. Department of Justice work entitled *Crime Scene Search and Physical Evidence Handbook*" (note 14) states that: "It is impossible . . . to determine the age of a latent print . . . to determine the age or sex of the person leaving the print . . . to identify the race of the suspect, nor the occupation (unless they are a bricklayer) . . ."[47]

To prove that fingerprints were impressed at the time of the crime, the following evidence could be used:

- Testimony of the victim or a witness that the defendant touched or handled the object on which the fingerprints were found (rape, assault, theft, robbery cases where victim or witness was present at the time of the crime and is available as a witness)
- Testimony that the surface had been washed or cleaned just prior to the crime
- Fingerprints found in a home or an area to which the defendant did not have access (burglary, theft, and sometimes homicide cases)

However, a murder conviction was reversed in the 1991 California case of *Mikes v. Borg*.[48] The court held that the mere fact the defendant's fingerprints were found on the murder weapon was not sufficient to prove that the defendant was the murderer. The court stated, "[T]he prosecution introduced no evidence placing the defendant at the scene of the crime—either on the day of the murder or on any other occasion."[49]

Automated Fingerprint Identification Systems

For years, fingerprints found at a crime scene had to be compared manually with cards on file—one card at a time. The search was a slow, time-consuming process, limiting fingerprint searches in most cities to only the most serious crimes. Victims of burglaries were often shocked to find that burglary was not considered serious enough to qualify in most instances.

In 1985 the new automated fingerprint system (AFIS) for the Los Angeles Police Department was activated. The AFIS permits latent fingerprints to be electronically compared by a computer with a large database.

The first assignment given to the Los Angeles AFIS was fingerprints found at the scene of one of the killings by the "Night Stalker," who had terrorized Los Angeles for months. Within three minutes, the AFIS identified a suspect.

Los Angeles, like other large American cities, arrests 40,000 or more people each month. Comparing fingerprints from these people to fingerprints found at the scenes of crimes and fingerprints of suspects on wanted lists would be an impossible task without AFIS. The largest database in the United States is at the FBI, with 41 million fingerprint files and 24 million crime history records.

Today, all states and all large cities have their own databases (or have access to a database) that can electronically identify fingerprints lifted at a crime scene—often within hours. Fingerprints found in old cases are processed by an AFIS. With fingerprint and other circumstantial evidence, states have been taking cases into criminal courts that for months and years have been unsolved crimes.

Fingerprints and the *Daubert* Test

Prior to 1993, there rarely were attacks by defense lawyers on fingerprint evidence, unless there was a break or weakness in the chain of custody foundation necessary to qualify the fingerprints as admissible evidence.

When an expert witness matched fingerprints found at a crime scene with those of the suspect, this evidence was viewed as a fact, as it is widely accepted that no two people have the same fingerprints.

In the 1993 case of *Daubert v. Merrill Dow Pharmaceuticals Co.*,[50] the U.S. Supreme Court said there are no certainties in science, only probabilistic results. Forensic fingerprint identification evidence then came under attack. It became known that the same finger will not produce the same print twice in a row and that the impression of a small area of a fingerprint may match any number of different fingers.

Since 1993, higher standards for fingerprint technicians and experts have been established. New proficiency testing and new qualitative and quantitative analyses have been established. Fingerprint science has had to "reconstruct itself."

In the *Daubert* case, the U.S. Supreme Court tells American judges that they are bound by the Rules of Evidence, specifically Rule 702 (see Appendix B of this text).

The *Daubert* case emphasizes rigorous testing and organized skepticism. Persons working as fingerprint technicians and experts have been working hard to meet these new standards.

ⓓ TRACE EVIDENCE: THE SMALLEST THINGS CAN MAKE THE BIGGEST DIFFERENCE

When two objects come into contact, there will frequently be a transfer of small amounts of the material from one to the other. This is nearly always the case when fabrics come in contact with a rough surface. Therefore, when a suspect comes in contact with the victim and objects at the crime scene, he frequently leaves behind traces of himself and takes with him traces of the things he has touched. Materials transferred in this way are normally referred to as trace evidence. The term **trace evidence** is usually very loosely defined; however, it most often is applied to minute or microscopic bits of materials that are not immediately apparent to even a trained investigator. Thus, trace evidence is usually in the hard-to-find category. Because trace materials resulting from exchanges are less likely to excite the attention of the criminal, or even to be apparent to him, there is far less probability that they will be deliberately eliminated by him than is the case with larger items of evidence or latent prints.

The following hypothetical situation illustrates the potential for the exchange of physical evidence during a series of fairly typical criminal actions.

The criminal crosses the back porch of a residence and steps on a brown paper bag lying on the floor. To gain entry, he breaks a small glass pane in the back door and reaches into unlock the door. After gaining entry, he is surprised by the homeowner and struggle follows. During the struggle the victim's nose begins to bleed. The suspect flees the scene.

In a situation of this type, the following exchanges of materials are entirely possible:

- The suspect's shoe print to the brown paper bag on the back porch
- Fibers from the suspect's clothing to the edge of the broken pane of glass in the back door (or blood on the glass from a cut on the suspect's arm)
- Fingerprints to the glass on the back door, and possibly to other surfaces along the suspect's route of entry
- Fibers from the suspect's clothing to the victim's clothing during the struggle, and vice versa

The following (transferred) evidence may be found on or in possession of the suspect.

- Glass fragments or small paint chips on the outer garments of the suspect from the back door window pane and frame
- Blood or hair from the victim to the suspect's clothing
- Bruises or lacerations suffered by the suspect in the struggle with the victim
- Fibers from the rug or furniture at the crime scene on the shoes or garments of the suspect

It is apparent from this example that the possibilities for exchanges of trace materials are great. Even if the shoe prints and fingerprints are excluded from the array of physical evidence potential, there are still abundant opportunities to link the suspect with the crime scene, if proper collections are made at the scene and from the person of the suspect.

The Example of the Missing 5-Year-Old in Virginia

The following example of the use of trace evidence is used in the May 2002 publication of the *Office of Justice* (NCJ #191717). A 5-year-old girl disappeared from a Christmas party in Virginia in 1989. Witness tips authorized a maintenance man to be taken into police custody. The man worked in the building where the child lived. When found, he was washing his jacket and shoes and a sheath from a knife.

The man never denied the abduction of the child but challenged the police to prove it. After learning what clothes the girl wore at the time of the abduction, the police found that only a limited number of the suits the girl wore had been made and were sold through J.C. Penny's. Fliers were sent out, and a man who had bought one of the outfits for his granddaughter donated his outfit to the investigation.

Several blue acrylic fibers were recovered from the suspect's car that were consistent with the make of the outfit the girl had been wearing when she disappeared. In addition, fibers that matched a black dyed rabbit-hair coat the girl's mother had been wearing the night of the abduction were also found in the suspect's car. It could be inferred that the rabbit-hair fiber transferred from the mother to the little girl and was then transferred to the suspect's vehicle.

The little girl's body was never recovered. The man was convicted based upon the trace evidence, which corroborated his incriminating statements and the observations of witnesses placing him at the time and place of the abduction.

Ⓔ OTHER TYPES OF EVIDENCE

Palm Prints and Lip Prints as Evidence

Palm prints are considered part of fingerprinting and, in some cases, are found at crime scenes or on victims of crimes. Cases where palm prints were important evidence in obtaining criminal convictions are the murder case of *State v. Inman*,[51] the armed robbery of a post office in the case of *United States v. Moore*,[52] and the rape and robbery case of *Yelder v. State*.[53]

An article, entitled "Focus on Forensics: Lip Prints," was published in the November 1992 issue of the *FBI Law Enforcement Bulletin*. The article reported on studies of lip prints done by the Japanese. The author of the article stated that findings indicate that "every individual has unique lip prints—no two were identical in any case." No court cases were cited by the author, Dr. Mary Lee Schnuth.

Footprints and Shoe Prints as Evidence

There are very few footprint cases because the majority of criminals wear shoes! One of the more notable cases is the 1984 murder case of *State v. Bullard*,[54] where the

Supreme Court of North Carolina discussed the art of footprint identification in affirming the defendant's conviction.

In many cases, however, shoe prints provide important identification evidence. Shoe prints are obtained from surfaces with snow, mud, dust, dirt, paint, or other substances that cause an imprint to be made. Identification testimony would have to establish enough matching characteristics—such as size, length, width, type, wear patterns, and individual characteristics, such as nicks, cuts and scratches—to establish a match between the print or prints left at the crime scene and the defendant's shoes.

In the 1992 home burglary case of *People v. Campbell*,[55] the Supreme Court of Illinois held that "shoeprint evidence, standing alone, is sufficient to convict." The court pointed out that shoe-print evidence, like fingerprint evidence, is circumstantial evidence. To support the shoe-print evidence was further evidence that the defendant had the opportunity to commit the burglary, as well as evidence of flight.

In the 1990 murder case of *State v. Jells*,[56] the Supreme Court of Ohio affirmed the defendant's conviction and permitted a lay witness (a police officer) to testify as to the similarities between the prints and the defendant's shoes. The Supreme Court of Nebraska affirmed the attempted sexual assault conviction in the 1989 case of *State v. Rhodes*,[57] where shoe-print evidence was used. Burglary convictions that were affirmed on shoe-print evidence include *State v. Tincher*,[58] *State v. Ingold*,[59] and *State v. Johnson*.[60]

Bite Marks as Evidence

To use bite-mark evidence, a chain of custody must be shown of the evidence, and an expert witness must be used, such as a dentist with training and experience as a forensic odontologist.

Bite marks could result from fighting; they could be sexual, attacking, or sadistic. In the 1990 case of *Commonwealth v. Henry*,[61] the Supreme Court of Pennsylvania stated that:

> . . . The essence of the distinction is that fighting bite marks are less well defined because they are done carelessly and quickly, whereas attacking or sadistic bite marks are made slowly and produce a clearer pattern. According to Dr. Asen, the sadistic bite mark is one of the most well-defined. Sexual bite marks are also well defined, but usually have a red center, produced by sucking tissue into the mouth. The dentist testified that the bite marks produced in this case were extremely well-defined, and were attacking or sadistic in nature. The legal significance of this testimony is that it might have been considered by the jury as part of their determination that the homicide was committed by means of torture.

In 1986 a Wisconsin Court of Appeals found that no state "has rejected the admission of [bite marks]."[62] Bite-mark evidence is probably used primarily in criminal homicide cases in which police need to establish the identity of the defendant. Examples of such murder cases are *State v. Richards*[63] and *People v. Marsh*.[64]

Tire Tracks as Evidence

In the 1974 U.S. Supreme Court case of *Cardwell v. Lewis*,[65] the defendant parked his car in a commercial parking lot and then went into a police building for questioning regarding a murder. After the police arrested the defendant for the murder, they took his car keys and without a court order or warrant had his car towed to a police lot where tire prints and paint scrapings were taken. This evidence was used to obtain the murder conviction of the defendant.

The U.S. Supreme Court affirmed the conviction and held that no right of privacy was violated, saying:

> In the present case, nothing from the interior of the car and no personal effects, which the Fourth Amendment traditionally has been deemed to protect, were searched or seized and introduced in evidence. With the "search" limited to the examination of the tire on the wheel and the taking of paint scrapings from the exterior of the vehicle left in the public lot, we fail to comprehend what expectation of privacy was infringed.
>
> Under circumstances such as these, where probable cause exists, a warrantless examination of the exterior of a car is not unreasonable under the Fourth and Fourteenth Amendments. (417 U.S. at 592, 94 S.Ct. at 2470).

In the 1991 case of *State v. Tillman*,[66] the manager of a Goodyear tire store was held to have sufficient training and experience in tire thread patterns to testify as an expert witness on tire tracks. The witness testified as to the similarities between tire tracks found at the scene of a murder and tires on the defendant's car. The defendant's conviction for murder was affirmed.

SUMMARY

To use physical or real evidence in a criminal trial, the government must show:

- That the evidence was obtained under the authority of a search warrant, or that the evidence was obtained under one of the "established and well-delineated exceptions" to the search warrant requirement
- That the evidence is genuine and authentic, and the object is what the government claims it is
- That all persons who had custody or access to evidence that could be altered, tampered with, or substituted have testified that the evidence is genuine and authentic (proof of a chain of custody)

Higher standards requiring rigorous testing and organized skepticism have been established for scientific evidence such as fingerprinting and trace evidence under the *Daubert* case by the U.S. Supreme Court.

PROBLEMS

1. Claudine Longet (Mrs. Andy Williams) was arrested after she shot and killed her lover, professional skier "Spider" Sabich. The officer in charge of the investigation was informed that Longet had been seen in a bar earlier in the day. After Longet was in custody, the officer noticed a faint smell of liquor coming from her person. He then ordered that Longet be taken to a hospital for blood and urine tests. Other officers and a hospital technician stated that she did not appear to be under the influence of alcohol or drugs. Ms. Longet objected to the tests, but the body fluids were obtained over her objections.

Should the trial court and the Supreme Court of Colorado permit the results of the urine and blood tests to be used as evidence? Give reasons for your answer. [*People v. Williams,* 192 Colo. 249, 557 P.2d 399 (1976).]

2. After the assassination of President Kennedy in 1963, Dallas police officers found a rifle that they believed was the murder weapon in the School Book Depository Building. The rifle was not moved until after photographs were taken of the rifle and the surrounding area. After a live shell was ejected from the rifle, a police officer scratched his name and date on the rifle (his initials and date on the shell). The serial number on the rifle was C-2566.

If fingerprints and palm prints had been found on the rifle, which the government wanted to use as evidence, and should the case go to trial, what foundation must the government present to prove that both the rifle, the fingerprints, and the palm prints were genuine and authentic evidence? If no fingerprints, palm prints, or ballistic evidence were obtained from the rifle, what foundation would be needed to use the rifle as evidence?

3. The seminude "beaten, lifeless" body of a woman was found in her apartment. A latent palmprint impression was found on the floor next to the body. Suspicion focused on the defendant because (1) he had known the victim and had previously rented an apartment in the building; (2) the "crime, including its sexual overtones, was strikingly similar to a crime for which" the defendant had been previously indicted; and (3) the defendant had fresh scratches on his hands, neck, and face, and abrasions on his elbows "of the type . . . which a woman under sexual attack might inflict." The police wanted palm prints from the defendant. What procedures could they use to obtain palm

prints from the defendant after it was determined that there were none on file at either the state or federal governments? To obtain palm prints, police officers followed the defendant's automobile. When he was observed speeding, he was then arrested and prints were obtained at that time. The defendant's lawyer argued that the state should not be permitted to use the palm prints as evidence because they were obtained from a "sham" arrest.

Did the Supreme Judicial Court of Maine permit the use of this evidence? [*State v. Inman,* 301 A.2d 348 (Main Sup. Jud. Ct., 1973).]

4. One shoe print of a gym shoe (sneaker) was found in a gas station that had been vandalized. The police officer investigating the criminal damage to property and the burglary observed the shoe print. The officer then observed the defendant hitchhiking several miles away and observed that the defendant was wearing a popular brand of running shoes. There was no evidence that the defendant was fleeing or acting in a suspicious manner. The officer then arrested the defendant and later developed other evidence used in charging and convicting the defendant of the offense.

Was the arrest lawful? Should the conviction be affirmed? [*State v. Reynolds,* 453 A.2d 1319 (N.H., 1982).]

5. A law enforcement officer investigating a burglary asked the victim if she suspected anyone. The victim replied that the defendant was the only one she could think of. The officer then contacted the defendant, who was on parole for another offense, and arranged for a meeting. At the meeting, the officer falsely told the defendant that his fingerprints were found at the scene of the burglary. The defendant, after a few minutes of silence, admitted that he had committed the burglary.

Should the officer's false statement about the fingerprints cause the court to rule that the confession of the defendant could not be used as evidence? Explain. [*Oregon v. Mathiason,* 429 U.S. 492, 97 S.Ct. 711 (1977).]

INFOTRAC COLLEGE EDITION EXERCISES

1. Go to InfoTrac College Edition and using the search term "crime scene" find the 1999 article in the *FBI Law Enforcement Bulletin* titled "The Benefits of Scent Evidence," by Robert Hunt. Are human scents sufficiently different to enable investigators to use a suspect's scent to locate the suspect and link him to a crime scene? This article shows how scent may be used to identify and find a suspect.

2. Go to InfoTrac College Edition and using the search term "crime laboratories" and the "periodical" view find the 1998 article in the *American Journal of Law and Medicine* titled "Juries and Crime Labs: Correcting Weak Links in the DNA Chain," by Ryan McDonald. This article discusses extensively the problems with chain of custody and controlled testing of DNA samples to be used in criminal cases. It also contains recommendations about changes to the way DNA evidence is admitted and used in trials. Should courts adopt the recommendations? Why or why not?

3. Go to InfoTrac College Edition and using the search term "fingerprints" and the subdivision "identification" find the 2000 article in the *FBI Law Enforcement Bulletin* titled "Biometrics," by Stephen Coleman. Biometrics involves the use of physical characteristics to distinguish one person from another. This article reviews the use of fingerprints, eyes, faces, hands, voices, and other physical characteristics for identification purposes.

NOTES

1. To seize evidence in plain view, it must be "immediately apparent" to the law officer that the object is evidence of a crime. In the U.S. Supreme Court case of *Arizona v. Hicks,* 107 S.Ct. 1149 (1987), police officers were in an apartment building because a man was wounded when a bullet came through the ceiling of his apartment. The police immediately went into Hicks's apartment, where the bullet came from, to search "for the shooter, for other victims, and weapons."

While lawfully in Hicks's apartment, police saw expensive stereo equipment that they suspected was stolen property. To determine whether the stereo equipment was stolen, an officer picked up stereo parts, to read and record the serial numbers, which he called in to the stolen property division. The U.S. Supreme Court held that as it was not "immediately apparent" that the equipment was stolen; thus, the seizure was unlawful and the evidence could not be used against Hicks on the criminal charge of possession stolen property.

2. An example of a state case where the police exceeded the limits of an emergency search is *People v. Williams,* 557 P.2d 399 (Colo., 1976). After Claudine Longet (Mrs. Andy Williams) shot her lover, professional skier "Spider" Sabich, police were in the couple's home after the body was removed. The gun used in the shooting had been seized, and photographs of the crime scene had been taken. The police then went into dresser drawers where they found Longet's diary, which they seized. The Colorado Supreme Court held that the diary could not be used as evidence in the homicide case because it was seized without consent or a search warrant.

Can the police cordon off and maintain control of major crime scenes so that they may reenter without consent or a search warrant? This issue was before a number of California courts. In the 1991 case of *People v. Boragno,* 49 CrL 1394, police officers continued to enter a murder scene for thirteen hours after the apartment was cordonned off, and the police retained exclusive control of the apartment. The police continued to take photographs and search for blood and hair samples. The California Court of Appeals held that searches after the first sweep of the apartment were invalid. But the valid and good evidence against the defendant was so overwhelming that "it is not reasonably probable a result more favorable to [the defendant] would have occurred."

320 Part IV Crime-Scene, Documentary, and Scientific Evidence

In the case of *People v. Neulist*, 43 A.D.2d 150, 350 N.Y.S.2d 178 (1973), medical examiners first set the cause of the death of a woman in her home as natural. The police, however, posted a guard at the room where the body was found. However, a physician then discovered that a murder had occurred. The police returned to the crime scene within an hour, and the highest court in New York held that evidence obtained could be used against the defendant.

3. Most (if not all) states will authorize "hot-pursuit" entries into private premises for misdemeanor crimes, such as drunk driving, that threaten public safety. However, "hot pursuit" would not be justified of a person who had committed a civil offense. The U.S. Supreme Court reversed the conviction in *Welsh v. Wisconsin*, 104 S.Ct. 2091 (1984) holding that, at the time of Welsh's arrest for first-offense drunk driving, the offense was a civil offense punishable in civil court. No imprisonment was possible for the noncriminal, civil forfeiture offense. At the time, Wisconsin was the only state that made first-offense drunk driving a civil offense.

4. 86 S.Ct. 1826.

5. 103 S.Ct. 916.

6. The U.S. Supreme Court held in two cases that when law enforcement officers make a lawful entry into private premises because of an emergency they may not make a second entry after the emergency no longer exists, without a search warrant or consent.

In the case of *Michigan v. Tyler*, 98 S.Ct. 1942 (1978), the Supreme Court held that an entry 27 days after a fire to obtain evidence of arson was not a lawful entry. The Court held: ". . . we hold that an entry to fight a fire requires no warrant, and that once in the building, officials may remain there for a reasonable time to investigate the cause of the blaze. Thereafter, additional entries to investigate the cause of the fire must be made pursuant to the warrant procedures governing administrative searches. . . ."

7. 840 P.2d 1298 (Ore. App.).

8. *Patrick v. State*, 227 A.2d 486 (Del., 1967).

9. *City of Troy v. Oblinger*, 475 N.W.2d 54, 50 CrL 1006 (Mich., 1991).

10. 990 F.2d 167 (4th Cir.).

11. 607 A.2d 471 (D.C. App.).

12. 502 So.2d 453 (La.), cert. denied 108 S.Ct. 205 (1987).

13. *State v. Vann*, 1990 WL 51763, 49 CrL 3042 (Tenn. Crim. App., 1990), cert. denied 111 S.Ct. 2015 (1991).

14. Much of the following material in this section is taken from U.S. Department of Justice Law Enforcement Assistance Administration book entitled *Crime Scene Search and Physical Evidence Handbook* (Washington, D.C.: Government Printing Office, 1973).

15. Police training manuals and directives recommend that objects likely to be used as evidence be identified by having the collecting officer scratch his initials or name and date on the object if practical. The officer can then readily identify the object as the evidence recovered at the crime scene or other place. Firearms, spent cartridges, bullets, clothing, currency, and many other objects have been identified and authenticated as genuine in this manner. Weapons used in the commission of a felony are ordinarily identified not only by the serial number but also by initials and date scratched on the object by a law enforcement officer.

If the weapon is also to be used as the basis for evidence, such as fingerprints or ballistic reports, a chain of custody must then be established and used to show that the evidence has not been altered or tampered with.

16. See *State v. Gustin*, 826 S.W.2d 409 (Mo. App., 1991); *People v. Winters*, 422 N.E.2d 972 (Ill. App., 1981); and *United States v. Clonts*, 966 F.2d 1366 (10th Cir., 1992).

17. *People v. Kabalia*, 587 N.E.2d 1210 (Ill. App., 1992).

18. "Sound Off: Protecting the Crime Scene," by D. H. Garrison, Jr., in the September 1994 issue of the *FBI Law Enforcement Bulletin*. While this problem was noted in 1994, there is reason to believe that it continues today (hopefully, to a lesser degree).

19. There was no exigency (emergency) when the detectives arrived at the defendant's home, as the unconscious woman had been taken to the hospital, and the house had been secured. A search warrant should have been obtained as the daughter did not have such control of the premises so that she could have given consent to search the home of her parents.

The case was remanded, and the State of Louisiana could try the defendant again but without the use of the three important (and probably critical) pieces of evidence obtained during the improper search.

20. *Schultz v. State*, 811 P.2d 1322 (Okla. Crim. App., 1991).

21. *Hunter v. State*, 805 S.W.2d 918 (Tex. App., 1991).

22. *United States v. Clonts*, 966 F.2d 1366 (10th Cir., 1992).

23. *United.States v. Gilliam*, 975 F.2d 1050 (4th Cir., 1992).

24. *Van Pelt v. State*, 816 S.W.2d 607 (Ark., 1991); *State v. Clay*, 817 S.W.2d 565 (Mo. App., 1991).

25. *Moorman v. State*, 574 So.2d 953 (Ala. Crim. App., 1990).

26. *English v. State*, 575 N.E.2d 14 (Ind., 1991).

27. *Kennedy v. State*, 578 N.E.2d 633 (Ind., 1991); *Davasher v. State*, 823 S.W.2d 863 (Ark., 1992).

28. *State v. Jackson*, 821 P.2d 1374 (Ariz. App., 1991).

29. *Turner v. State*, 610 S.2d 1198 (Ala. Crim. App., 1992).

30. *Snowden v. State*, 574 So.2d 960 (Ala. Crim. App., 1990).

31. *Holder v. State*, 584 So.2d 872 (Ala. Crim. App., 1991).

32. *Bell v. State*, 339 So.2d 96 (Ala. Crim. App., 1976).

33. One of the authors sat on a jury in 1999 where the defendant was charged criminally for dealing rock cocaine. Because two adjournments had already been granted in the case, the trial judge announced in open court that it had been agreed by both parties and the court that no further adjournments would be granted.

After the rock cocaine had been legally seized by the police under the authority of a search warrant, it was delivered to a young lab technician at the state crime lab. After the lab technician testified to receiving the evidence, she testified that two different tests were performed on the substance, and both tests showed that the substance was rock cocaine. After testifying that the rock cocaine was stored in a secured locker, the lab technician was then asked if the storage area was locked at all times and who had a key to the locker. The lab technician answered that the storage area was locked at all times and that she and her two supervisors all had keys to the storage locker. Because the two supervisors who had access to the storage locker were not in court to testify and show a sufficient chain of custody, the charges against the defendant were dismissed, and the state could not file new criminal charges because of the doctrine of double jeopardy.

When a defendant appeals the criminal conviction and wins a reversal of the conviction, as in the four cases cited and used in this section, the state may retry the case. The prosecutors in those cases had another chance to prove the chain of custody for the critical evidence. Today, prosecutors in busy criminal courts had better do a good job at the first trial, or they are going to lose cases because of failure to prove a chain of custody for evidence that can be falsified or tampered with.

34. 183 S.E.2d 179 (Va., 1971).

35. *Laws v. State*, 562 So.2d 305 (Ala. Crim. App., 1990).

36. 184 A.D.2d 153 (N.Y.A.D.).

37. *Byerly v. Ashley*, 825 S.W.2d 286 (Ky. App., 1991).

38. 482 N.W.2d 567 (Nebr., 1992).

39. 810 S.W.2d 474 (Tex. App.).

40. 818 P.2d 787 (Idaho App.).

41. *Crime Scene Search and Physical Evidence Handbook*, 47.

42. 394 U.S. 721 (1969).

43. *People v. Madson*, 638 p.2d 18 (Colo., 1981).

44. *In re Order Requiring Fingerprinting of a Juvenile*, 537 N.E.2d 1286, 45 CrL 2164 (1989).

45. 89 S.Ct. 1394 (1969).

46. 105 S.Ct. 1643 (1985).

47. See the 1992 case of *State v. Hamilton*, 827 P.2d 232, where the Supreme Court of Utah reviewed many cases from throughout the United States concerning the general approaches to the weight that may be afforded fingerprint evidence.

48. 947 F.2d 353 (9th Cir.), review denied 112 S.Ct. 3055 (1992).

49. Cases where the state was able to obtain convictions by proving that fingerprints of the defendant were made at the time of the crime (or created a strong inference to that effect) include: murder and theft case of *Commonwealth v. Servich*, 602 A.2d 1338 (Pa. Super., 1992); where a glass touched by the defendant was washed on the morning of the murder, *Commonwealth v. Hall*, 590 N.E.2d 1177 (Mass. App., 1992); where the robber touched a lavatory doorknob while forcing a witness into a room, *State v. Jackson*,

582 So.2d 915 (La. App., 1991)—a case of theft from a supermarket where the general public did not have access to the area and the defendant was not an employee of store and had never been seen in store before; a home burglary case of *Tyler v. State,* 402 S.E.2d 780 (Ga. App., 1991), where the defendant testified that he had never been in the home and did not know where it was located, but his fingerprints were found in the home; the burglary of an auto sales and repair business case of *Commonwealth v. Baptista,* 585 N.E.2d 335 (Mass. App., 1992), where fingerprints found inside a closed, locked Pepsi vending machine justified the inference that the defendant had cut the lock and entered the machine; a home burglary case of *Jones v. State,* 825 S.W.2d 529 (Tex. App., 1992), where fingerprints on a kitchen window screen and mud marks showed that the screen was laid in the mud; the home burglary case *State v. Evans,* 392 S.E.2d 441 (N.C. App., 1990), where the defendant's fingerprints found on a broken piece of glass from the window broken to gain entry; a car theft case of *In the Interest of N.R.,* 402 S.E.2d 120 (Ga. App., 1991), where juvenile fingerprints were found on the inside of the driver's window of a recently stolen car; the burglary case of *Brown v. State,* 837 S.W.2d 457 (Ark., 1992), where fingerprints were found inside the broken glass door of a home; the murder case of *Hanson v. Commonwealth,* 416 S.E.2d 14 (Va. App., 1992), where police went into the murder victim's trash and found the defendant's fingerprints on envelopes, which were used to show his presence at the crime scene; the murder case of *Cavazos v. State,* 779 P.2d 987 (Okla. Crim. App., 1989), where the defendant's fingerprints were found on the victim's unclothed back; a rape and robbery case of *People v. Himmelein,* 442 N.W.2d 667 (Mich. App., 1989), where the defendant's fingerprints were found on a yardstick used to strike a rape victim.

50. 509 U.S. 579 (1993). See *United States v. Plaza,* 188 F. Supp. 2d 549 (2002), for a discussion on fingerprinting.
51. 350 A.2d 528 (Maine, 1976).
52. 936 F.2d 1508 (7th Cir., 1991).
53. 575 So.2d 131 (Ala. Crim. App., 1990).
54. 322 S.E.2d 370 (N.C.).
55. 586 N.E.2d 1261 (Ill.).
56. 559 N.E.2d 464 (Ohio).
57. 445 N.W.2d 622 (Nebr.).
58. 797 S.W.2d 794 (Mo. App., 1990).
59. 450 N.W.2d 344 (Minn. App., 1990).
60. 464 N.W.2d 167 (Nebr., 1991).
61. 569 A.2d 929.
62. *State v. Stinson,* 397 N.W.2d 137.
63. 804 P.2d 109 (Ariz. App., 1990).
64. 441 N.W.2d 33 Mich. App., 1989).
65. 417 U.S. 583, 94 S.Ct. 2464.
66. 405 S.E.2d 607 (S.C. App.).

17

Videotapes, Photographs, Documents, and Writings as Evidence

Ⓐ PHOTOS AND VIDEOTAPES AS EVIDENCE

Videocameras are everywhere. Hundreds of thousands of people have them. Banks, stores, private businesses, schools and apartments have installed them as part of security systems. Some squad cars and buses have them. They are commonly used in drunk-driving cases, as well as traffic and investigative stops by the police. Videocameras have filmed murders, armed robberies, shoplifting, and other crimes (see Federal Rule 1001 in Appendix B).

Since the "Zapruder" film of the assassination of President Kennedy in 1964, and then the Los Angeles beating cases of Rodney King and Reginald Denny, videotapes have brought street events to the American public and evidence into criminal trials. Fixed surveillance cameras and handheld videocameras regularly provide information to law officers for the identification and arrest of offenders.

If the filming is in a public place where a defendant does not have a right of privacy and if a witness verifies that the tape is a reliable reproduction of the events that occurred, the tape is ordinarily admissible as evidence. The following examples illustrate the thousands of cases where photos and videotapes are used as evidence each year:

- When Winona Ryder walked out of the Hollywood Saks Fifth Avenue store with $5,560 worth of stolen merchandise, she was unaware that closed-circuit cameras had recorded the felony shoplifting. Photo evidence and the testimony of two security officers caused the jury to convict her in November 2002. Her lawyer argued that the evidence used against Ryder was fabricated and planted.

- In the 1990 case of *Pennsylvania v. Muniz*,[1] the U.S. Supreme Court held that videotaped evidence of the defendant's answers to routine booking questions at a police station were admissible as evidence. The tape showing his slurred speech, his poor performance of various sobriety tests, and his unsolicited incriminating statements were used in evidence, which resulted in his conviction and were held not to violate his *Miranda* rights, except for the incrimination caused by asking the defendant for the year of his sixth birthday.

- The Florida Supreme Court pointed out that either the person taping a street arrest can be ordered to appear as a witness or the tape ordered produced in the 1991 case of *CBS, Inc. v. Jackson*.[2] Television news reporters do not enjoy a First Amendment privilege when they are eyewitness observers to an event that is relevant in a criminal trial.

- A murder victim's videotaped dying declaration was held admissible in the 1992 murder case of *Grayson v. State*.[3] The physician withheld all pain medication prior to the videotaping, and the victim responded to most questions by nodding his head and sometimes motioning with his hands.

- An undercover officer's videotape of a drug buy and the videotape of a controlled drug buy were used as evidence in the cases of *Hall v. State*[4] and *Edwards v. State*.[5]

- A videotape of the defendant cultivating marijuana in a field was used as evidence in the 1992 case of *Pfaff v. State*.[6]

- A defendant, while being booked on an assault charge, became disruptive and was also charged with disorderly conduct. The videotape of the scene was admitted as evidence in the 1991 case of *State v. Warmsbecker*.[7]

- Videotapes of the defendant refusing to submit to blood alcohol testing and refusing to perform field sobriety tests while in police custody were admissible as evidence to obtain a criminal conviction in the 1991 case of *Commonwealth v. McConnell.*[8]

- A videotape of the defendant's arrest and a search of the immediate premises was admissible in the 1991 case of *People v. Schaaefer.*[9]

- A videotape simulation of a highway accident by the Minnesota Highway Patrol was held admissible in the 1990 case of *State v. Rasinski.*[10] In reconstructing the accident, the state stayed within the objective evidence (measurements, placement of the skid marks, and the final resting place of the vehicles at the accident). But video reenactment of a fight at a jail was held inadmissible because the version was biased in favor of what the state believed had occurred (*State v. Hopperstad*).[11]

- When the defendant approached a man with regard to committing an armed robbery, the man went to the police. A videotape then captured the defendant soliciting a police informant for armed robbery. The authenticated videotape was used in evidence, resulting in the defendant's conviction (*Powell v. State*).[12]

- Store security videotapes and apartment lobby videotapes were held admissible for use as evidence in the cases of *MacFarland v. State*[13] and *Smith v. United States.*[14]

- Videotapes of drug dealers, prostitutes, and car thieves taken by people living in the neighborhood are sometimes turned over to local police.

When Is a Warrant Needed to Install and Conduct Videotape Surveillance?

Search warrants must be obtained to conduct **videotape surveillance** when a suspect has a right of privacy in the place where the videotape surveillance is to be conducted (for instance, suspect's home, apartment, or office). The following cases illustrate:

- Law enforcement officers obtained a warrant to install a hidden microphone and videocamera in a hotel room that the officers had rented. The defendant came to the room and offered to buy 185 pounds of marijuana for $121,000. The defendant was arrested when he returned with the money and bought the marijuana. Because the defendant did not have a right of privacy in the hotel room rented by the law officers, the Supreme Court of Massachusetts held that the defendant did not have standing in court to challenge the use of the surveillance tapes as evidence against him (*Commonwealth v. Price*).[15]

- As a general rule, a search warrant is not necessary to search a public employee's workplace (desk, files, and so on) to investigate work-related misconduct under the U.S. Supreme Court case of *O'Connor v. Ortega.*[16]

    In the 1991 case of *United States v. Taketa,*[17] federal agents suspected Taketa (a law officer) of improper wiretapping. The federal agents entered Taketa's office at night to investigate possible work-related misconduct. This was lawful without a warrant under *O'Connor v. Ortega,* but the federal agents also placed a hidden videocamera in the office without a warrant. Their failure to obtain a warrant for the video surveillance spoiled the evidence obtained by the camera.

- A hidden video surveillance camera was installed in the employee break room of a Hawaii post office where it operated for a year. The camera picked up evidence of illegal gambling against the defendant. The Supreme Court of Hawaii held that the postal employees had a reasonable expectation of privacy in the break room, which was neither a public place nor open to public view or hearing. Because the offense was not work related to postal work, it was held not to fall under *O'Connor v. Ortega* (*State v. Bonnell*).[18]

- In 1992 Secret Service agents permitted a CBS camera crew to go with them in the search of a New York home under the authority of a search warrant. The agents had the authority to search for illegal credit cards; however, they had no authority under a search warrant to permit private citizens to accompany them. Only a woman and her 4-year-old son were present in the home, and no evidence of any crime was found.

  A civil lawsuit against CBS and the federal government was settled by damage payments to the family. The trial judge, in the case of *Ayeni v. CBS et al.,*[19] stated that "CBS had no greater right than that of a thief to be in the home. . . . [T]he television crew took from the home, for the purpose of broadcasting them to the world at large, pictures of intimate secrets of the household, including sequences of a cowering mother and child resisting the videotaping."

Where Videotaping Can Be Done Without a Warrant

Videotaping can be conducted in places where the people being filmed do not have a reasonable expectation of privacy. The following cases further illustrate:

McCray v. State
Maryland Court of Special Appeals, 84 Md.
App. 513, 581 A.2d 45 (1990)

The defendant was suspected of being involved in a scheme to provide false drivers' licenses for money. Investigating officers videotaped him walking from his home across the public street to the motor vehicle office. This tape was used as evidence in a trial that resulted in the defendant's conviction. In holding that a court order or search warrant was not needed, the court held that:

> . . . one walking along a public sidewalk or standing in a public park cannot reasonably expect that his activity will be immune from the public eye or from observation by the police. . . . Consequently, any justified expectation of privacy is not violated by the videotaping of activity occurring in full public view. . . .
>
> Thus, the videotape surveillance of McCray, in public view, walking across the street to the MVA poses no Fourth Amendment problem. Clearly, the videotape of McCray was captured in a public place and in public view. Consequently, McCray had no reasonable expectation of privacy when he walked on public sidewalks, streets and parking lots, since he voluntarily exposed to anyone interested the fact that he was traveling to a particular destination

A security camera showed Winona Ryder with bags of merchandise that she was found guilty of stealing.

and meeting a particular individual in a public place. See *Sponick v. City of Detroit Police Dept.,* 49 Mich. App. 162, 211 N.W.2d 674 (1973) (where police officer videotaped in bar talking with known criminals did not have a "reasonable expectation of privacy" because observations occurred in a public place).

Here, the police officers were engaged in a legitimate investigation, and upon first utilizing various investigative activities to ferret out this licensing scheme, the police officers then chose to record their own visual observations with a video camera rather than with a note pad. The officers were observing a public place and positioned the video camera to observe the activities in this public place. As such, any visual observations were not an intrusion into an area where appellant possessed a "reasonable expectation of privacy." The videotape surveillance did not, therefore, constitute a search in violation of the Fourth Amendment. The videotaping of that which is lawfully observed is not more invasive or unreasonable than personal observation and is just as lawful. Consequently, neither a court order nor a search warrant was required. The trial court, therefore, did not err in admitting into evidence the videotapes.

People v. Lynch
Michigan Court of Appeals, 445 N.W.2d 803 (1989)

Because of unlawful homosexual activity taking place in a men's public restroom on a public highway, police obtained a search warrant to install videocameras in the ceiling above the toilet stalls because a person in a toilet stall with the door closed has a right of privacy. The defendant was convicted of two counts of gross indecency between males in the common area (the open area a person walks into from outside) of the public restroom, and he appealed, arguing that a right of privacy also exists in the common area. In holding that a warrant was not needed for the common area, the court held:

> . . . This was a public bathroom in a public rest area off a public highway. Any member of the public could feel free to enter that restroom. While the structure itself preserves a certain amount of privacy to those using the facilities, it can be presumed that any member of the public would expect that in the common area of the facility their privacy is not absolute and that any activity in that area is open to public examination. . . .
>
> The common area was readily accessible to anyone needing to use the facility. The public's expectation that they were entering a public facility certainly was not extinguished because they had to open two doors rather than one. To the extent that the videotapes were made of activities in the common area of the restroom, we cannot find that they invaded a constitutionally protected expectation of privacy. . . .
>
> As applied to this case, our holding means that the police did not need a warrant to monitor or videotape the common area.

B USING PHOTOGRAPHS AS EVIDENCE

Photographs and videotapes are **demonstrative evidence** because they portray (demonstrate) objects, persons, or events not in the courtroom. Videotapes present many pictures of an event or object, whereas a photo presents only one picture. Diagrams, maps, drawings, models, and sketches are also demonstrative evidence in that they present information needed to understand events, places, or objects relevant to a case. A Texas Court of Appeals made the following statement regarding the use of photographs as evidence:

> Photographs are admissible in evidence on the theory that they are pictorial communications of a witness who uses them instead of, or in addition to, some other method of communication. Thus, they are admissible on the same grounds and for the same purposes as are diagrams, maps, and drawings of objects or places, and the same rules of admissibility applicable to objects connected with the crime apply to photographs of such objects. This is true whether they are originals or copies, black and white or colored. So, a photograph, proved to be a true representation of the person, place, or thing which it purports to represent, is competent evidence of those things of which it is material and relevant for a witness to give a verbal description.[20]

Introducing Photographs and Videotapes into Evidence

Photographs and videos are admissible into evidence, to explain or illustrate anything that a witness could testify to or describe in words. It is not necessary to have the person who has taken the photo or video introduce the picture or pictures into evidence. Any witness who can testify from firsthand knowledge that the photograph or video accurately portrays and represents the object, place, person, or event may introduce the photo or video for use in evidence. In many instances, the person who took the photo or video would introduce it into evidence, but this is not necessary.

The extent that the verifying witness would have to testify about the accuracy of a photograph might vary somewhat, depending upon the importance of each photograph to the issues before the court. Some photographs might be admitted by stipulation (agreement between the parties) or with no challenge, whereas other photographs might be sharply contested and challenged. A photograph that is incriminating to a defendant is more likely to be contested and would therefore require more testimony about verification. Conversely, minimal proof of accuracy may be sufficient for a photograph illustrating something not seriously contested.

All evidence sought to be admitted for use in criminal or civil trials must be relevant to at least one of the issues before that court. In determining the admissibility of a photograph or video, the trial judge must determine whether the photo or video has probative, or evidentiary, value and tends to prove or disprove some issue in dispute. The Supreme Court of Minnesota stated that "Photographs are admissible if they accurately portray what a witness would be permitted to describe or if they aid a description, provided they are relevant. *State v. De Zeler,* 230 Minn. 39, 46–47, 41 N.W.2d 313, 319 (1950)."[21]

After verifying the accuracy of a photograph, the officer may then be asked to state how he or she knows that the photograph is the one the officer took. The witness may show identification of the photograph by testimony showing any one or more of the following:

- Sole continuous possession of the photograph from the time of the taking up through the presentation of the photograph in court.
- The chain of possession for the period of time between the taking of the photograph and the presentation in court.
- The presence of an identifiable object in the picture that the officer placed at the scene before taking the photograph. The identifiable object could be an information data board or a measuring device with the initials of the officer and the date and place that the photograph was taken.

Gruesome Photographs and Videotapes

Photographs of some crime scenes and victims are shocking and horribly gruesome. Such videos or **gruesome photographs** could be used as evidence if they are relevant to some issue before the court. The trial judge would have a great deal of discretion in determining if such photos would be needed and how many photos could be used. In the case of *Young v. State,*[22] a Florida Court of Appeals held as follows:

The fact that the photographs are offensive to our senses and might tend to inflame the jury is insufficient by itself to constitute reversible error, but the admission of such photographs, particularly in large numbers must have some relevancy, either independently or as corroborative of other evidence. . . .

The very number of photographs of the victim in evidence here, especially those taken away from the scene of the crime, cannot but have had an inflammatory influence on the normal fact-finding process of the jury. The number of inflammatory photographs and resulting effect thereof was totally unnecessary to a full and complete presentation of the state's case. The same information could have been presented to the jury by use of the less offensive photographs whenever possible and by careful selection and use of a limited number of the more gruesome ones relevant to the issues before the jury.

The Supreme Court of North Carolina explained reasons why photographs of a victim's body could be admitted for use in evidence in the 1990 case of *State v. Robinson*:[23]

. . . Photographs are usually competent to explain or illustrate anything that is competent for a witness to describe in words . . . and properly authenticated photographs of a homicide victim may be introduced into evidence under the trial court's instructions that their use is to be limited to illustrating the witness's testimony. . . .

Thus, photographs of the victim's body may be used to illustrate testimony as to the cause of death. . . . Photographs may also be introduced in a murder trial to illustrate testimony regarding the manner of killing so as to prove circumstantially the elements of murder in the first degree . . . and for this reason such evidence is not precluded by a defendant's stipulation as to the cause of death. . . . Photographs of a homicide victim may be introduced even if they are gory, gruesome, horrible or revolting, so long as they are used for illustrative purposes and so long as their excessive or repetitious use is not aimed solely at arousing the passions of the jury. . . .

This Court has recognized, however, that when the use of the photographs that have inflammatory potential is excessive or repetitious, the probative value of such evidence is eclipsed by its tendency to prejudice the jury.

X-Ray Films as Evidence

Rule 1001(2) of the Federal Rules of Evidence (see Appendix B) defines photographs as including still photographs, X-ray films, videotapes, and motion pictures. Therefore, X-ray films, videotapes, and motion pictures are introduced into evidence upon the same basis and principles as still photographs. X-ray films—radiographs, roentgenograms, and skiagrams—are different than the ordinary type of photographs in the following respects:

- An untrained person may take a photograph, but a trained technician or a physician must take an X-ray. Therefore, the photographer of the X-ray must testify in court unless the defense stipulates or agrees to the admission of the X-ray film.

- Unlike most photographs, X-ray films require an expert to explain and interpret them. Therefore, in most situations a licensed physician who has had experience with X-rays would have to be qualified as an expert witness to testify as to the content of the X-ray film.

- Since no witness is capable of testifying to actually seeing the injury depicted by the X-ray, the picture must be admitted as original evidence in order to provide the basis for the opinion of the expert trained in the interpretation of X-rays.

Ⓒ USING DOCUMENTS AND WRITINGS AS EVIDENCE

Documents and writings are involved in practically all civil cases and in many criminal cases. Generally, anything that conveys a message is a document. In criminal cases, this could include such things as written confessions, bad checks, drug records and accounts, written evidence of fraud, business and hospital records, betting slips, altered prescriptions, incriminating statements found in notes and letters, demand notes used in kidnapping and robbery cases, and computer printouts relating to a criminal case.

The party seeking to use a **document** or writing **as evidence** must show that the document or writing is not only relevant and material but also genuine and authentic.

Some documents and writings can prove their own authenticity. A prosecutor or defense attorney seeking to use a public record, whether sealed or not, or a newspaper or periodical as evidence could use a state rule of evidence similar to Federal Rule of Evidence 902 (self-authentication; see Appendix B). Authenticity could also be agreed upon by a stipulation between the parties that the document was genuine and authentic, leaving only the question as to whether the document was relevant and material.

Although a document or writing may be shown to be authentic and genuine, this is not proof about statements and assertions made in the document or writing. For example, a newspaper may be shown to be genuine and authentic and accepted for use in evidence as such. However, a jury or judge could find that statements made in the newspaper were not true.

Using Direct Evidence to Prove that Documents Are Authentic and Genuine

Documents and writings may be proven genuine and authentic by any of the following forms of **direct evidence:**

- Testimony of a witness who observed the signing or the writing of the document— for example, an officer who observed the defendant write or sign a consent form or a confession.

- Testimony of the person who wrote or signed the document acknowledging that the writing was genuine and authentic.

- *Regularly kept business records* that are authenticated by witnesses who are custodians or supervisors of such records and who can testify that the writing offered for use in evidence is actually part of the records of the business. In such cases, the custodian or supervisor may not have actually seen the writing or document written or signed. However, the trustworthiness of the writing may be established with testimony that the writing was a regularly kept business record. The regularly kept business record exception is also sometimes referred to as the *shopbook rule* or the *business record exception.* (See Chapter 8 on "Regularly Kept Records" as a major exception to the hearsay rule.)

- Testimony establishing proof of handwriting by an expert witness who is qualified to testify as to the identity of the writer of the document or writing. For example, an expert could testify about the identity of the writer of a check, a demand note in a robbery case, or a threat found in a writing sent to a victim.

- Testimony of a person who is not a handwriting expert but is well acquainted with the handwriting of the signer or writer of the document or writing. This could be a member of the family, a friend, or other person who had seen the handwriting of the writer frequently.[24]

- The contents of the document or writing—for example, a demand note or a check may be easily recognized by the contents and form of the writing.[25]

Using Circumstantial Evidence to Prove that Documents Are Authentic and Genuine

The majority of documents and writings introduced for use as evidence in criminal trials are proven authentic and genuine by direct evidence or by the contents of the document or writing itself. If the document or writing cannot be proven authentic and genuine by direct evidence or by the contents of the document or writing itself, *circumstantial evidence* may be used. The types of circumstantial evidence that may be used include:

- Circumstantial evidence such as the fact that the writing was in the custody of defendant, the victim,[26] or the deceased; or that the defendant, victim, or deceased acted in response to the writing; or that the defendant, victim, or deceased referred to the document or writing in oral or written communications with other persons; or that the document or writing did not appear to be forged or have any other suspicious appearance.

- The **ancient documents rule,** which permits the use of circumstantial evidence where the document has been in existence for a number of years [twenty years under the Federal Rule of Evidence 901 (8)].[27]

- Circumstantial evidence derived from the fact that the document or writing was in the custody of a public official. Statements made in a will, an income tax return, a bill of sale, or a deed could be used in evidence. If there was any question as to the authenticity or genuineness of such documents, circumstantial evidence could be used.

- The reply doctrine, which permits the use of circumstantial evidence to show that a writing was in response to other communication. Writings in response to other communications often indicate this in the contents of the writing. The following case illustrates a situation in which the writing was shown to be a reply communication.

Winel v. United States
U.S. Court of Appeals, Eighth Circuit, 365 F.2d 646 (1966)

In holding that a postcard was properly admitted for use in evidence in a mail fraud case, the court held that:

> It has long been recognized that one of the principal situations where the authenticity of a letter is provable by circumstantial evidence arising out of the letter's context, other than proof of handwriting or the business records exception, is where it can be shown that the letter was sent in reply to a previous communication. . . .
>
> . . . In the instant case the inherent nature of the communication makes it absolutely certain that it is a reply communication. The only question that can then arise with respect to its admissibility would be whether there was proof of its mailing and receipt. This is clearly answered by the record. . . .
>
> . . . It is not necessary that there be direct testimony of placing in the mails or removing from the mails if there is a full showing of the customs and usage relating to this type of communication.

Regularly Kept Records

All large businesses, hospitals, law enforcement agencies, and other organizations have *regularly kept records*. Over three hundred years ago, English courts recognized the *shop book rule*, which is today a well-recognized exception to the hearsay rule. A writing is in most instances recognized as authentic and genuine if it is shown to be a regularly kept record.

Police reports and police records meet the requirements as regularly kept records. Records of illegal sales and shipments of drugs have been held to fall within the hearsay exception.[28] In recognizing computer printouts as a regularly kept business record, the Superior Court of New Jersey held:

> We hold that as long as a proper foundation is laid, a computer printout is admissible on the same basis as any other business record. . . .
>
> Computerized bookkeeping has become commonplace. Because the business records exception is intended to bring the realities of the business world into the courtroom, a record kept on computer in the ordinary course of business qualifies as competent evidence. This result is in accordance with that reached in other jurisdictions. . . . Of course, if the computer printout at issue here is admitted at trial, it will constitute only prima facie evidence of an account stated. Defendant will have the opportunity to refute plaintiff's evidence.[29]

The Best Evidence, or Original Document, Rule

The famous English lawyer and writer, Blackstone, wrote in the 1760s that "the best evidence the nature of the case will admit of shall always be required, if possible to be had; but if not possible then the best evidence that can be had shall be allowed."[30]

The Use of Writings or Documents as Evidence

Documents and writings may be admissible for use as evidence if:

- The document or writing is shown to be genuine and authentic.

- The evidence contained in the document or writing is relevant, material, and competent.

- The document or writing does not contain inadmissible hearsay. (Part of a writing may be held to be inadmissible for this reason.)

- The requirements of the best evidence or original document rules are complied with.

After the writing or document has been admitted for use as evidence, the jury or judge as fact finder would then determine:

- The author and person who wrote the writing, if this question and issue was unresolved.

- The truth and credibility of the statements and assertions made in the document or writing.

- The weight to be given to the statements and assertions made in the document or writing.

- The issue of guilt or innocence of each of the charges made against the defendant.

Federal Rules of Evidence 1002 through 1006 state the **best evidence rule** (**original document rule**) used today in federal courts and most state courts. (See Appendix B for the rules.) Rule 1002 provides that the best evidence rule applies to "writing(s), recording(s), or photograph(s)" and requires the original unless "(1) Original is lost or destroyed. . . . (2) Original is not obtainable. . . . (3) Original in possession of opponent. . . . (4) . . . the writing, recording, or photograph is not closely related to a controlling issue" (Rule 1004).

Carbon or photographic copies of an original document or writing are secondary evidence of the original. The requirement that the original be offered as evidence is an ancient requirement that originated in English law prior to the American Revolution. Some writers state that the reason for the rule was to prevent fraud. Most modern writers, however, state that the primary purpose of the rule was to ensure the most accurate written version, which is the original document or writing.

The rule requires that the best evidence available be used. This preference for the original of any document or writing is a commonsense attempt to minimize possibilities of errors or fraud in seeking the truth. Possibilities of errors certainly existed years ago when all copies of original documents were hand copied. With modern copy machines, the margin of error has been minimized but still exists. The rule, which originated centuries ago, continues to require that the best available evidence be used.

If a particular state follows the federal best evidence rule, the rule would apply only to writings, recordings, or photographs (Rule 1002). In the following case, the Supreme Court of Georgia held the best evidence rule applies only to writings and not to other evidence.

Munsford v. State
Supreme Court of Georgia, 235 Ga. 38, 218 S.E.2d 792 (1975)

The defendants were convicted of armed robbery. A police officer appeared as one of the witnesses in the case and testified that a track shoe print found at the scene of the crime matched the tennis shoe of one of the defendants. A photograph of the shoe print was admitted into evidence, but the tennis shoe was not used in evidence. The Supreme Court of Georgia held that the procedure did not violate the best evidence rule, quoting an earlier Georgia case holding: "The [best evidence] rule has nothing to do with evidence generally, but is restricted to writing alone."[31]

Failure to comply with the original (or best evidence) could create problems unless one of the reasons listed in Rule 1004 is shown. The following case illustrates:

Commonwealth v. Lewis
Pennsylvania Superior Court, 623 A.2d 355 (1993)

A shoplifting was recorded by a videocamera in a Sears retail store. At the trial, a police officer who had not viewed the theft testified about what he observed on the store videotape, but the videotape was not introduced for use as evidence.

A store security guard testified that he was unable "to locate the videotape of [defendant's] action." The court held that this explanation was unsatisfactory and reversed the conviction for a new trial holding that: "whatever knowledge [the police officer] possessed was gained from his viewing of the videotape. Thus, the original tape should have been produced."

The Fourth Amendment Protection of Writings, Records, and Documents

The Fourth Amendment provides that "The right of the people to be secure in their persons, houses, papers and effects, against unreasonable searches and seizures, shall not be violated." Therefore, law enforcement officers and other governmental officials cannot intrude into a "zone of privacy" of a person to seize documents, writings, or records without a showing of proper authority.

However, the plain-view and public-view doctrines apply to documents and writings as follows:

- *Plain view* If officers are where they have a right to be and see a document or writing in plain view that is immediately apparent to be evidence of a crime, they may seize the document or writing.

- *Public view* Handwriting, like the tone of a person's voice, is constantly exposed to public view, and therefore samples may be compelled by court or grand jury order.

In addition, the business records of banks, stock brokerage houses, and other financial institutions are available to governmental authorities because such records are not private papers of individual investors and account holders. The following two U.S. Supreme Court cases state the law concerning this.

United States v. Dionisio
United States Supreme Court, 410 U.S. 1, 93 S.Ct. 764 (1973)

The Supreme Court held that handwriting, like speech, is a characteristic that is continually on display to the public and people can have no greater expectation of privacy to their writings than to the tone quality of their voices. A grand jury can therefore order people to submit samples of their handwriting, just as a person can be requested to talk for identification purposes.[32]

United States v. Miller
United States Supreme Court, 425 U.S. 435, 96 S.Ct. 1619 (1976)

The defendant was charged with various federal offenses. Microfilms of checks, deposit slips, and other records were obtained by the government by means of subpoenas duces tecum served upon officials of two banks where the defendant had accounts. The Supreme Court held that these documents and records were properly used as evidence in the defendant's trial because:

- The evidence was business records of the banks and was not private papers of the defendant.

- The defendant had no legitimate expectation of privacy in the original checks and deposit slips because these writings were not confidential communications but negotiable instruments used in commercial transactions.

The Court ruled that:

> The depositor takes the risk, in revealing his affairs to another, that the information will be conveyed by that person to the government. . . . This Court has held repeatedly that the Fourth Amendment does not prohibit the obtaining of information revealed to a third party and conveyed by him to government authorities, even if the information is revealed on the assumption that it will be used only for a limited purpose and the confidence placed in the third party will not be betrayed.

The Fifth Amendment Protection of Writings, Records, and Documents

The Fifth Amendment provides that "No person shall . . . be compelled in any criminal case to be a witness against himself." The Fifth Amendment would therefore forbid demanding that a suspect write out a confession or otherwise incriminate himself by producing a writing. The U.S. Supreme Court stated the Fifth Amendment privilege against self-incrimination as follows:

Terms Used in the Examination of Documents and Writings

- *Questioned document* A document or writing is questioned when questions are raised about who wrote, typed, or made the writing; whether the document is genuine and authentic; or whether the writing is totally or partially forged or altered.

- *Questioned document examiner* A person with special training and experience necessary to examine questioned documents to determine the author or the genuineness of the document. To make this determination, the questioned document is often compared with one or more other documents.

- *Graphologist* A person who studies one or more documents written by a known person and concludes from the writing or penmanship personality traits of the writer of the document. Because graphology is not recognized by courts as a reliable science, such evidence would not be admissible.

- *Indented writings* A person writing on a note pad or telephone pad may leave indented writing on one or more of the sheets under the paper upon which he or she is writing. Indented writing could provide valuable information in the investigation of a crime.

- *Charred document* A writing or document that has been partially or completely burned. If the document is left undisturbed or can be preserved, the written contents can generally be determined by a document examiner.

- *Linguistics analyst* A study of language usage; could be used to determine the genuineness of a document or could be used in an effort to determine who wrote the document. [The defense in the Patty Hearst case used linguistic evidence of writings and tape recordings in an attempt to prove that she did not participate voluntarily in the bank robbery. See *United States v. Hearst,* 412 F. Supp. 893 (N.D. Calif., 1976).]

> . . . the constitutional privilege against self-incrimination . . . is designed to prevent the use of legal process to force from the lips of the accused individual the evidence necessary to convict him or to force him to produce and authenticate any personal documents or effects that might incriminate him. *Bellis v. United States,* 417 U.S. at 88, 94 S.Ct. at 2183.

Although the government cannot force a suspect to produce a document that would incriminate the suspect, this does not mean that the government cannot lawfully seize a document that would incriminate the defendant. U.S. Supreme Court Justice Holmes stated this principle of law in 1913 as follows: "A party is privileged from producing the evidence but not from its production. *Johnson v. United States,* 228 U.S. 457, 458, 33 S.Ct. 572 (1913)." The following U.S. Supreme Court case illustrates.

Andresen v. Maryland
United States Supreme Court, 427 U.S. 463, 96 S.Ct. 2737 (1976)

The defendant, an attorney who practiced alone, was convicted of real estate fraud. Business records were obtained from the defendant's office under the authority of a search warrant. The trial court permitted these records to be used as evidence, holding that the defendant had not been compelled to do anything that incriminated himself. At the trial the records were authenticated by prosecution witnesses and not by the defendant. In affirming the defendant's conviction, the Supreme Court held that

> There is no question that the records seized from petitioner's offices and introduced against him were incriminating. Moreover, it is undisputed that some of these business records contain statements made by petitioner. . . .
>
> This case thus falls within the principle stated by Mr. Justice Holmes: "A party is privileged from producing the evidence but not from its production." *Johnson v. United States,* 228 U.S. 457, 458, 33 S.Ct. 572, 57 L.Ed. 919 (1913). This principle recognizes that the protection afforded by the self-incrimination clause of the Fifth Amendment "adheres basically to the person, not to information that may incriminate him." *Couch v. United States,* 409 U.S., at 328, 93 S.Ct. at 611. Thus, although the Fifth Amendment may protect an individual from complying with a subpoena for the production of his personal records in his possession because the very act of production may constitute a compulsory authentication of incriminating information, . . . a seizure of the same materials by law enforcement officers differs in a crucial respect—the individual against whom the search is directed is not required to aid in the discovery, production, or authentication of incriminating evidence. . . .
>
> Accordingly, we hold that the search of an individual's office for business records, their seizure, and subsequent introduction into evidence does not offend the Fifth Amendment's prescription that "[n]o person . . . shall be compelled in any criminal case to be a witness against himself."

SUMMARY

Fixed surveillance cameras, handheld videocameras, closed circuit cameras, and ordinary cameras are used every day in the United States to provide evidence for police and prosecutors to use in criminal and civil cases throughout the United States.

Documents and writings are also important evidence in many criminal cases. It is hard to imagine a civil case where documents were not used as evidence.

This chapter presents cases and the law as to the use of photos, videotapes, and documents as evidence in criminal cases.

PROBLEMS

1. Federal Alcohol, Tobacco, and Firearms agents set up a sting operation in Michigan. The undercover officers used a storefront operation and pretended to be fences willing to buy stolen property. A videotape was made of the defendant selling stolen property to the agents in the store-front operation. A search warrant had not been obtained to videotape either the defendant or other persons as they sold stolen property to the federal agents.

Should the videotape, which was material and relevant to the criminal charges against the defendant, be permitted to be used as evidence against the defendant? [*People v. Barker,* 101 Mich. App. 599, 300 N.W.2d 648 (1980).]

2. An elderly woman was the victim of a "pigeon-drop" scheme, which is also known as a "flim-flam" operation or "con game." The elderly woman was persuaded to withdraw $26,000 from her bank and turn it over to the defendant, believing that she would share in money that the defendant falsely told the elderly woman had been found. Police officers investigating the crime requested bank surveillance photographs and were able to identify the defendant as the woman who accompanied the elderly woman into the bank to withdraw the money. Because the bank camera also photographed a clock and calendar, the time and date of the photographs could be determined. At the defendant's criminal trial, a bank officer testified about the source of the photographs and to the fact that the photographs showed the interior of the bank.

Was this a sufficient foundation to permit the use of photographs as evidence? [*State v. Pulphus,* 465 A.2d 153 (R.I., 1983).]

3. The defendant, Colonel Abel, was the highest-ranking Soviet spy taken into custody. Abel was arrested in a New York hotel room in the middle of the night. He was ordered to dress, pack, and then check out of his room. After Abel was taken to jail, FBI agents received consent from the hotel management to search the room. False identity papers and a coded message found in the room were used as evidence to convict Abel.

Did the U.S. Supreme Court rule that the use of these documents violated either the Fourth or Fifth Amendment rights of Abel? Explain. [*Abel v. United States,* 362 U.S. 217, 80 S.Ct. 683 (1960).]

INFOTRAC COLLEGE EDITION EXERCISES

1. Go to InfoTrac College Edition and using the search term "best evidence rule" find the 1994 article in *Managing Office Technology* titled "Will Your Records Stand Up in a Court of Law?" by Joan Mariani Andrew. This is a "how-to" article on making sure records and documents are maintained and identified so as to be admissible in court. It discusses the best evidence rule as well as other evidentiary rules that apply to the introduction of documents as evidence.

2. Go to InfoTrac College Edition and using the search term "legal documents" and the subdivision "identification" find the 1993 article in *Security Management* titled "Reading Between the Lines," by James Hayes. This article describes what forensic document examiners do and how they do it.

NOTES

1. 496 U.S. 582, 110 S.Ct. 2638.
2. 578 So.2d 698, 49 CrL 1169 (Fla.).
3. 611 So.2d 422 (Ala. Crim., App.).
4. 829 S.W.2d 407 (Tex. App., 1992).
5. 583 So.2d 740 (Fla. App., 1991).
6. 830 P.2d 193 (Okla. Crim., App.).
7. 466 N.W.2d 105 (N.D.).
8. 591 A.2d 288 (Pa. Super.).
9. 577 N.E.2d 855 (Ill. App.).
10. 464 N.W.2d 517 (Minn. App.).
11. 367 N.W.2d 546 (Minn. App., 1985).
12. 808 S.W.2d 102 (Tex. App., 1990).
13. 581 So.2d 1249 (Ala. Crim. App., 1991).
14. 561 A.2d 468 (D.C. App., 1989).
15. 562 N.E.2d 1355 (Mass., 1990).
16. 480 U.S. 709, 107 S.Ct. 1492 (1987).
17. 923 F.2d 665 (9th Cir.).
18. 856 P.2d 1265 (Hawaii 1993).
19. 848 F.Supp. 362 (E.D.N.Y., 1994).
20. *Terry v. State,* 491 S.W.2d 161 (Tex. Crim. App., 1973).
21. Quoted in *State v. Olson,* 459 N.W.2d 711 (Minn. App., 1990).
22. 234 So.2d 341 (Fla., 1970).

23. 395 S.E.2d 402.

24. See the 1990 case of *State v. Glidden,* 459 N.W.2d 136 (Minn. App.), where the Minnesota Court of Appeals quoted *McCormick on Evidence* that "generally anyone familiar with the handwriting of a given person may supply authenticating testimony in the form of his opinion that a writing or a signature is the handwriting of that person." In the *Glidden* case, an office manager who was familiar with the defendant's handwriting identified the handwriting on questioned documents as that of the defendant's.

25. Records and writings of drug transactions are often found in raids on drug houses and apartments. In the 1991 case of *United States v. Jaramillo-Suarez,* 942 F.2d 1412 (9th Cir.), a "pay/owe" sheet was held admissible; in *United States v. Lai,* 934 F.2d 1414 (9th Cir., 1991), "what appeared to be handwritten and computer summaries of drug transactions" was allowed in evidence; and in *State v. Lewis,* 567 So.2d 726 (Fla. App., 1990), writings of the drug transactions between the defendant and the undercover officers were admitted into evidence.

26. In the 1990 case of *State v. Boppre,* 453 N.W.2d 406, a dying murder victim wrote the defendant's name on the floor and on a door casement as he was dying. The Supreme Court of Nebraska held that the writing was admissible in evidence as both a dying declaration and also an excited utterance. In this case, in which the floor and the door could not be brought into court, a photograph of the writings was introduced as evidence.

For cases where the contents of a writing was used as evidence to identify the writer, see *United States v. Sutton,* 426 F.2d 1202 (D.C. Cir., 1969), where four handwritten, unsigned notes found on the body of a murdered woman revealed knowledge identifying and incriminating the defendant of the murder of the woman; *People v. Faircloth,* 599 N.E.2d 1356 (Ill. App., 1992), where letters signed using a nickname showed that the defendant sold the illegal drugs that caused the death of the victim. The letters were admitted for use as evidence in the case where the defendant was convicted of the drug-induced death of a woman.

27. See Appendix B.

28. See *United States v. Grossman,* 614 F.2d 295 (1st Cir., 1980).

29. *Sears, Roebuck & Co. v. Merla,* 361 A.2d 68 (1976).

30. *Blackstone, Commentaries,* 368.

31. Rule 1002 of the Federal Rules of Evidence, which is followed by most states, now requires "the original writing, recording, or photograph."

32. See also *United States v. Mara,* 410 U.S. 19, 93 S.Ct. 774 (1973).

18

Scientific Evidence

Ⓐ THE IMPORTANCE OF SCIENTIFIC EVIDENCE

The American criminal justice system relies upon the knowledge and equipment of many sciences and skills—chemistry, physics, mathematics, medicine, and dentistry, just to name a few. Crime laboratories with sophisticated equipment are used every day; highly skilled arts and specialized training are often required to analyze and support evidence.

In this chapter we examine a variety of kinds of **scientific evidence** and the rules used by courts for the admissibility of scientific evidence. DNA evidence is discussed in some detail, owing to the frequency and importance of that evidence in criminal prosecutions.

The Use of Scientific Evidence

Experienced law enforcement officers state that most crimes are solved through the use of common sense and hard work. An officer who is investigating a crime may obtain enough information to identify the perpetrator of the offense but may have insufficient evidence to charge and obtain a conviction. In such situations the use of scientific techniques may provide the additional evidence necessary to carry the burden of proving guilt beyond a reasonable doubt.

In some situations an investigating officer may have only the evidence obtained from crime laboratories. When no additional evidence is available, scientific evidence may be the starting point or link that leads to the solution of the crime.

For these reasons, scientific evidence has become one of the strongest weapons available for the successful prosecution of criminal offenders. However, judges and juries may overestimate the reliability of scientific evidence. This problem caused the Supreme Judicial Court of Massachusetts to state: "We are aware that scientific proof may in some instances assume 'a posture of mystic infallibility in the eyes of a jury of laymen.'"[1]

Even though scientific evidence is not infallible, it could contribute to an investigation by:

- Providing a lead or leads to head a criminal investigation in the right direction.

- Providing information eliminating a suspect as the person who committed the crime being investigated. For example, DNA evidence, regular fingerprinting, or a surveillance videotape could show that the suspect did not commit the crime.

- Proving corpus delicti, or proof that a crime was committed, such as scientific evidence that a fire was intentionally started, as in arson, or that death was caused by poisoning.

- Providing the independent corroborative evidence necessary to support a confession, or to corroborate and support other evidence presented by the prosecutor or the defense attorney.

- Establishing a link between the crime scene and the suspect or between the suspect and the victim of the crime.

- Proving one of the essential elements of the crime being investigated.

- Affirming or disproving an alibi.

- Establishing the innocence of people not involved in the crime.

- Encouraging or inducing a person to make a confession or an incriminating admission when the person is confronted with scientific evidence that incriminates them. (If such a person were being held in custody, *Miranda* warnings would have to be given before the confrontation.)

- Providing reasonable suspicion (for an investigative stop), probable cause (to make an arrest, obtain a search warrant, and so on), or sufficient proof beyond a reasonable doubt (necessary for a criminal conviction).

- Building such strong cases against defendants that the number of guilty pleas are increased, clearing court calendars and permitting faster trials of contested cases.

B THE ADMISSIBILITY OF SCIENTIFIC EVIDENCE

What Is Scientific Evidence?

Scientific evidence is most often presented in court by an expert witness testifying as to expert opinions. When, for example, a person trained in science or technology gives his or her opinion about the chemical or biological composition of a substance, the testimony is scientific evidence. If the scientist has the necessary education, training, and experience to test the substance and if the scientist has conducted suitable tests of the substance, the testimony would usually be admissible as expert testimony. Most states have rules identical or similar to Federal Rule 702 (see Appendix B), which permits such expert testimony.

Scientific evidence also includes expert testimony that goes beyond science. The scientific expert is frequently called upon to interpret results and draw conclusions about what results mean in the case being tried. This is very common in criminal trials, where experts in a wide variety of scientific disciplines offer comparison testimony linking a defendant to a crime, crime scene, or victim. For example, the fingerprint expert may testify that the defendant's fingerprints match those found on a murder weapon; the ballistics expert may testify that bullets found in the victim were fired from the defendant's pistol; the forensic odontologist may testify that bite marks on the victim's body were made by the defendant's teeth; or a voice identification expert may testify that a recorded voice matched the defendant's voice.

The central issue for this kind of scientific evidence is the reliability of the theory and testing upon which the conclusions are based. If the scientific theory is flawed or the tests unpredictable, the conclusions are unreliable and should not be admitted as evidence.

Some scientific theories and tests are so widely accepted and verified that they are virtually beyond criticism. The theory that each person's fingerprints are unique, for example, has universal acceptance. Similarly, tests used to link bullets to the gun that fired them are rarely questioned.

Other scientific theories have been rejected as unreliable. Voice-print comparisons, for example, have been found inadmissible on both theoretical and testing grounds.[2] Many courts have rejected the theory that voice prints are unique and also the tests by which experts match voice spectrograms.

Thus, an important question in the admissibility of scientific evidence is the theoretical and experimental basis of the scientific expert's testimony. Courts traditionally use one of three rules for the admissibility of scientific evidence.

THE *FRYE* TEST In *Frye v. United States*,[3] the Federal Court of Appeals refused to admit the results of a lie detector test given to a defendant in a murder trial. In rejecting the scientific basis for lie detector results, the court formulated what has become known as the *general acceptance test*:

> Just when a scientific principle or discovery crosses the line between the experimental and demonstrable stages is difficult to define. Somewhere in this twilight zone the evidential force of the principle must be recognized, and while courts will go a long way in admitting expert testimony deduced from a well-recognized scientific principle or discovery, the thing from which the deduction is made must be sufficiently established to have gained general acceptance in the particular field in which it belongs.[4]

Prior to 1993 when the U.S. Supreme Court decided *Daubert v. Merrill Dow Pharmaceuticals*,[5] the federal courts and most state courts applied the *Frye* general acceptance test to determine the admissibility of scientific evidence. The **Frye test** was subject to significant criticisms. First, some thought the test too broad, in that it permitted expert scientific testimony in areas where no real scientific methods had been followed. For example, in *Commonwealth v. Lykus*[6] the Massachusetts Supreme Judicial Court admitted voice spectrographic identification evidence, stating ". . . the requirement of the *Frye* rule of general acceptance is satisfied, in our opinion, if the principle is generally accepted by those who would be expected to be familiar with its use."[7] As critics observed, the only people "familiar with the use" of voice-print analysis are the voice-print experts themselves.

Frye was also criticized as too narrow since otherwise reliable scientific evidence might be inadmissible even though it had sound theoretical and experimental foundations. Indeed, some courts rejected *Frye* for this reason. In *State v. Hall*,[8] the Iowa Supreme Court permitted an expert witness to testify concerning blood-spatter analysis. In this analysis the expert reaches conclusions about the direction, force, and other physical characteristics of the crime, based upon the pattern of the victim's blood spatter. Though not generally accepted, the Iowa Court permitted the evidence because it was otherwise shown to be reliable.

THE *FRYE* PLUS TEST When in the 1980s prosecutors begin using DNA test results to link defendants to crime scenes, some courts modified the *Frye* test by adding additional requirements to it. In the leading case of *People v. Castro*,[9] the New York Supreme Court held that DNA evidence[10] would be admissible if (1) the theory was generally accepted (2) procedures for testing the theory were generally accepted, and (3) the testing was shown to have followed those procedures.

In the case of DNA evidence, the theory is generally accepted. Most courts and scientists agree that the DNA chain of an individual can be analyzed and compared with the DNA chain found in crime-scene evidence.[11] Moreover, general acceptance for some, but not all, procedures for testing DNA exists. The RFLP test (see next section) has general acceptance.[12] The PCR test has been found not to be generally accepted by some courts.[13]

In courts using *Frye* Plus, the admissibility question frequently turns on how accurate and faithful the testing laboratory followed accepted procedures.

THE *DAUBERT* TEST The U.S. Supreme Court decision in *Daubert v. Merrill Dow Pharmaceuticals Co.*[14] rejected the *Frye* test and held that Rule 702 of the Federal Rules of Evidence created its own standard for the introduction of scientific evidence. Under Rule 702, scientific evidence is admissible if:

> . . . the expert is proposing to testify to (1) scientific knowledge that (2) will assist the trier of fact to understand or determine a fact in issue. This entails a preliminary assessment of whether the reasoning or methodology underlying the testimony is scientifically valid and of whether that reasoning or methodology properly can be applied to the facts in issue.[15]

The *Daubert* Court suggested the trial court consider various factors to assess scientific validity. Those factors are: (1) Has the theory been tested? (2) Has it been subjected to peer review by other scientists? (3) What is the theory's or technique's known or potential rate of error? (4) Do standards controlling the application of the theory or technique exist? (5) Is the theory or technique generally accepted?

In 1999 the U.S. Supreme Court held that the **_Daubert_ test** was applicable to technical as well as scientific evidence. In *Kumho Tire Co. v. Carmichael,*[16] the Court held that an engineer's testimony concerning a tire failure was inadmissible under the *Daubert* test.

Kumho and *Daubert* are decisions interpreting Rule 702 of the Federal Rules of Evidence and are binding only in federal prosecutions. Because most states have adopted a rule similar to Rule 702, *Daubert* and *Kumho* will be influential in state cases. In 1998,[17] it was reported that thirty-three states have adopted *Daubert,* seventeen states continue to use *Frye* or *Frye* Plus, and ten have announced no final decision.[18]

As pointed out in Chapter 16, fingerprint science has reconstructed itself in recent years. New proficiency testing and new qualitative and quantitative analyses have been established. These changes can be attributed to *Daubert,* which emphasizes rigorous testing and organized skepticism and points out there are no certainties in science, only probabilistic results. While it continues to be widely accepted that no two people have the same fingerprints, it is now known that the same finger will not produce the same print twice in a row and that the impression of a small area of a fingerprint may match any number of different fingers.

In 2000 Rule 702 of the Federal Rules of Evidence was amended to incorporate reliability tests mandated by *Daubert* (the Federal Rules of Evidence appear in Appendix B). Many of the states that have adopted the *Daubert* decision will likely make similar amendments to their evidence rules. The amendment to Rule 702 has already resulted in changes on how scientific evidence is received. For example, the Horizontal Gaze Nystagmus sobriety test discussed in this chapter was once such well-regarded scientific evidence that courts took judicial notice of its reliability. See, for example, *Emerson v. State*, 880 S.W.2d 759 (Tex. Crim. App., 1994). Since the amendments to Rule 702, courts have taken a more cautious approach to that test. In *United States v. Horn,* 185 F.Supp.2d 530 (D. Md. 2002), the court refused to take **judicial notice** of the reliability of the HGN test and permitted the introduction of test results only as evidence of probable cause for arrest, not as proof of intoxication.

The Use of Judicial Notice for Accepted Scientific Techniques

After a scientific technique has been found to be reliable under Rule 702 or the standard required in a specific state, judicial notice can be made of the higher court's ruling.

In the 1993 case of *United States v. Jakobetz,*[19] a woman was abducted from a rest area along Interstate 91 in Vermont. After she was repeatedly raped, the woman was released in New York. The federal trial court used Rule 702 in admitting DNA evidence in the trial of the defendant. In holding that the scientific technique was reliable and did not unfairly prejudice the defendant's case, the Federal Court of Appeals stated:

> [I]t appears that in future cases with a similar evidentiary issue, a court could properly *take judicial notice of the general acceptability of the general theory and the use of these specific techniques.* Beyond such judicial notice, the threshold for admissibility should require only a preliminary showing of reliability of the particular data to be offered, i.e., some indication of how the laboratory work was done and what analysis and assumptions underlie the probability calculations. . . . *Affidavits should normally suffice to provide a sufficient basis for admissibility.* [emphasis added]

The extent to which judicial notice of a scientific theory will be taken can change. For example, the science of handwriting analysis has been the subject of judicial notice.[20] However, as the result of the *Daubert* case and independent handwriting analysis studies,[21] handwriting expert testimony has come under attack. One court has concluded that handwriting analysis is not scientific knowledge at all but only technical knowledge.[22] After the *Kumho* decision, which made *Daubert's* rules applicable to technical evidence, handwriting testimony will have to meet the *Daubert* reliability tests.

C A FEW OF THE SCIENCES AND SCIENTIFIC TECHNIQUES USED IN THE CRIMINAL JUSTICE SYSTEM

Scientific evidence covers a range of evidence that varies widely in probative value, weight, and persuasiveness. Some sciences permit the formulation of an opinion with almost mathematical certainty while others are less precise and become more of an art than a science. For example, polygraph testing is widely used in the United States, yet the courts in very few states permit the results of lie detector tests to be used as evidence because of the reasons stated in Chapter 12.

A scientific theory that was novel only a few years ago but is now widely accepted by the scientific, legal, and law enforcement community is the DNA test and technique. DNA easily passes the *Daubert* test. It is reported that DNA was first used as

FIGURE 18.1 *The polymerase chain reaction*

1. Collection of Samples. DNA samples can be taken from a number of sources, including saliva, blood, hair, or skin. These samples are labeled and shipped to a forensic lab.

2. Extraction and Purification. At the lab, the sample is mixed with chemicals that break open the cells and let the DNA seep out. The broken cell fragments are removed from the mixture, and the remains are placed in a test tube. This tube is then spun very quickly, which makes the pure DNA sink to the bottom.

3. Separation and Binding The double helix is then separated into two single strands. Lab technicians add "probes" to the single strands. These probes are short pieces of single-stranded DNA: A pairs with T and C pairs with G. Because the probes are tagged with radioactivity, technicians follow them as they form connections, and figure out the strand of the original DNA sample. (For example, whenever a T probe connects, it connects with an A strand, etc.)

4. Replication. DNA samples are very small and difficult to see. Consequently, scientists have invented a way to "photocopy" them using a process called polymerase chain reaction (PCR). In PCR, when a probe attaches itself to a rung in the original DNA, it very quickly creates a large number of copies of the new pair (Imagine that the probe acts like a finger pressing the "copy" button on a photocopying machine, producing repeated patterns such as ATGCTAGCAT, etc..)

5. Identification. Next, technicians place a drop containing millions of DNA fragments at one end of a sheet of gel. An electric current is then run through the sheet, a process that pulls the DNA fragments across the gel. The larger a fragment is, the slower it will move. In order to measure these movements, the DNA fragments are tagged with dye, and they show up as colored bands when exposed to ultraviolet light.

6. Machine Normally, a crime lab will analyze thirteen places on a person's DNA in the profiling process. These thirteen markers will be compared to a suspect's DNA profiles that are already on file. If a match is found for each of the thirteen markers, there is almost no chance that the two DNA samples did not come from the same person.

Source: L. Gaines, M. Kaune, and R. Miller, *Criminal Justice in Action* (Belmont, Calif.: Wadsworth, 2000), Figure 5.12.

evidence in a criminal court in 1987, and the FBI first began analyzing DNA in casework in 1996.

DNA Genetic Profiling

Deoxyribonucleic acid (DNA) testing has become an important **forensic** tool for linking suspects to a crime. Equally importantly, DNA testing has made it possible to eliminate a suspect in a crime, sometimes even after the suspect has been convicted of that crime.[23] **DNA genetic profiling** has received such wide acceptance among criminal justice professionals that it is frequently called *genetic fingerprinting*.

DNA testing is in many ways similar to fingerprint testing. In both, samples found at the crime scene or on the victim are collected and stored. In the crime of rape, where DNA testing is widely used, most police departments or hospitals have a "rape kit," in which blood or semen samples from the victim are collected and stored. This procedure begins a proper chain of custody, a vital ingredient in any DNA evidence.

Two major tests are used to test DNA: polymerase chain reaction (PCR) (see figure) and restriction fragment length polymorphism (RFLP) analysis. Although these tests are conducted differently, they have a common goal: to identify the genetic code in the crime-scene sample and compare it with the genetic code in the suspect's (and victim's) samples.

The human body consists of billions of cells, most of which carry chromosomal DNA. Human genetic information is encoded in the DNA found in chromosomes. The

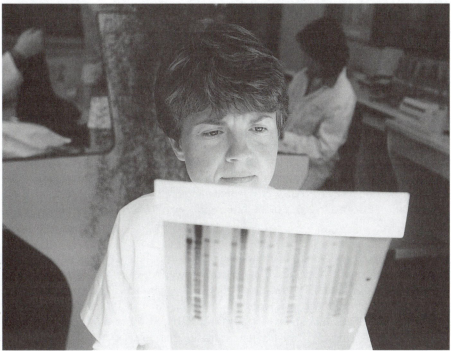

A technician examines DNA profiles. If the suspect's profile does not match the crime sample profile, it is certain that the two samples did not come from the same person. If the profiles match, an estimate of the probability that the profile could match a profile belonging to someone other than the suspect is calculated.

DNA in chromosomes is arranged in a sequence of paired, organic bases, called *base pairs,* which form the well-known twisted *double helix* DNA chain. A set of chromosomes (one from the mother, one from the father) might contain 3 billion of these base pairs arranged in sequences on the DNA chain. Knowledge about these sequences in chromosomes makes DNA matching possible.

If we compare DNA chains from two people who weren't identical twins, we discover two things. First, the chains, or sequences of base pairs, would be identical for more than 99 percent of the base pairs. Humans are, after all, more alike than different. Second, at certain identifiable sites, called **locus points,** base pairs that vary from one individual to the next can be located. At such a locus, for example, where eye color is determined, base pairs will join in a sequence that is repeated; measuring the size of a repetitive sequence of base pairs at many such locations gives a fingerprint-like picture of the DNA chain, since at these locations the sequence of base pairs varies among different individuals. Thus, like fingerprints, if we have a picture of enough of these locations where human DNA varies, we will have an individual's genetic fingerprint.

When a suspect's DNA profile matches the crime-scene sample's DNA profile, it means that the two profiles appear the same at several key points in the DNA chain where individual differences occur. Because databases do not have millions of individual DNA profiles on file, one cannot simply search a database and see if another person's DNA profile matches the suspect's. Instead, DNA profiles taken from a selected sample of the population are compared with the suspect's profile. Based upon the number of times at each of the locus points tested a match in the selected sample is found, a probability estimate can be made.

Experts who perform DNA tests and later testify to test results and meaning usually give probability estimates, taking into account different population samples, as the following example demonstrates:

> Deoxyribonucleic acid (DNA) profiles for [the specific sites tested] were developed from specimens obtained from the crime scene, from the victim, and from the suspect. Based on these results, the DNA profiles from the crime scene match those of the suspect. The probability of selecting at random from the population an unrelated individual having a DNA profile matching the suspect's is approximately 1 in 200,000 in Blacks, 1 in 200,000 in Whites, and 1 in 100,000 in Hispanics.[24]

At present, DNA profiles have a wide variety of uses. Some examples are the following:

- Identify air crash victims and other dead people from bits of bones or charred flesh. For example, casualties from Desert Storm and the Vietnam War have been identified by obtaining DNA samples from family members. Bones thought to be former Russian Czar Nicholas II and his family executed in 1917 were proven to be the remains of the Russian royal family through blood donated by British Prince Philip, who is a distant relative of the former Russian royalty.[25]

- Identify offenders from blood, semen, and hair left at the scene of a crime. The FBI reports that over 80 percent of the cases they receive from state and local police are rape cases.

- Clear suspects who are innocent. The FBI reports that in 20 to 25 percent of the cases sent to them, the suspect is cleared. An FBI official stated that in one case the standard blood tests did not eliminate the suspect and that two victims of a serial rapist had identified the suspect, with "one of them fairly positive. He certainly would have gone to trial and probably would have been convicted, but the DNA evidence eliminated him as a suspect."[26]

- Establish proof of corpus delicti, which is proof that a crime was committed. Missing persons are a problem in every American city. To charge murder, the state must prove the missing person is dead and was killed by the defendant. In the 1991 case of *State v. Davis*,[27] a woman was missing. She was last seen going to work, but her body was never found. However, DNA tests of dried blood, skull bone fragments, and blood-encrusted tissue were compared with blood from her children and husband and showed that the woman had been murdered. The conviction of her husband was affirmed.

- Establish from blood samples, the man who fathered a child.

DNA databanks and laboratories are now established or are being established in all states. In addition to government laboratories, more than twenty private forensic laboratories in the United States currently conduct DNA testing in criminal casework.

In addition to fingerprinting, it is becoming a standard practice to take blood from newly convicted felons and those serving prison terms for use in state databanks.

Rape Cases and Statutes of Limitation

Ruth Fremson/ *The New York Times*

Evidence from rape crime scenes stored in rape kits in a Queens, New York, police warehouse. Rape kits contain blood, semen, saliva, or skin samples.

The use of DNA evidence may make police warehouses like the one pictured less obsolete. In many states, including New York, legislatures passed laws, called *statutes of limitations,* that place a time limit for prosecuting certain crimes. Most states have no limit for prosecutions for murder but do for rape. These limits range from three to ten years from the date the crime was committed. For example, Texas has a 5-year limitation,[a] and Maine has a 6-year statute, unless the rape victim was under 16 years of age; in that case there is no limitation period.[b]

Statutes of limitations reflect the legislative and judicial view that after a period of years the evidence needed to convict a defendant becomes unreliable. Witnesses forget, may die, or leave the jurisdiction. Physical evidence may be lost or deteriorate. DNA tests, however, can be run on a blood or tissue sample that is hundreds of years old. As a result, rape kits like those pictured can be DNA-tested at any time. The reliability of DNA tests has led Nevada, New Jersey, and Florida to abolish limitation periods for sexual assault cases.[c]

[a]See Vernon's Ann. Texas C.C.P.A.rA. 1201 (1999).
[b]See Me.ST.T. 17-AS8 (1999).

[c]See *New York Times,* 9 February 2000, A27.

Statutes requiring such procedures have been sustained by courts when challenged. The use of DNA test results have been held admissible in all states, with some states imposing stricter foundation requirements than others.[28]

The armed forces of the United States are building a DNA databank by collecting blood and saliva from all service personnel. The reason for this databank is that military dog tags can be lost, switched, or counterfeited and that fingerprinting and dental records are not always reliable.

While many states are abolishing, extending, or ammending their statutes of limitation for rape, prosecutors are issuing John Doe criminal complaints or obtaining John Doe indictments when it is determined they have probable cause based on DNA evidence. New York obtained rape indictments against an unknown serial rapist known as the "East Side Rapist" in March 2000. In October 1999, Wisconsin prosecutors filed three rape charges against a man known only by his DNA code, to avoid the running of the Wisconsin statute of limitations, and in 1991 Kansas prosecutors filed one rape charge based only on DNA evidence.

Forensic Entomology

Entomology is the study of insects. **Forensic entomology** is used to determine the time since death on human cadavers and also other facts surrounding the death such as location, placement, movement of the body, and information on the manner of death.

Because insects can be present on a cadaver for up to $2\frac{1}{2}$ years, entomological analysis can provide useful information (evidence) concerning the cause and manner of death, as well as the approximate time of death when bodies are found or missing persons are found dead.

Entomological evidence is widely accepted as scientific evidence in courts. The May 2002 Institute of Justice publication (NCJ 191717) used the following example to illustrate. An Oklahoma woman's claim as to when she last saw her husband was disproved by the third-stage maggot accumulation on his body. In the analysis were critical climatological data, the time delay from death until colonization, the effect of the maggot mass temperature on development, and the nocturnal absence of blow flies. The woman was eventually convicted of murdering her husband.

Forensic examination and forensic entomology can provide information that could help lead to the identity of unidentified bodies that are found. Assistance in seeking the identification of unidentified bodies can also be obtained from the Forensic Anthropology Computer Enhancement Service laboratory (FACES), which will prepare a reconstructed clay model of what the victim's face may have looked like. Photographs of the clay model and any clothing, jewelry, or available personal belongings are then depicted on the FBI Web site at *http://www.fbi.gov/mostwant/seekinfo/seek.htm.* Identity can be confirmed by DNA testing.

Ballistics Fingerprinting or Firearm Fingerprinting

When the body of a shooting victim is brought into a hospital emergency room, the medical staff view the body as a "crime scene" because any bullet fragments that are recovered from a body can be important evidence to investigating law officers.

Bullet fragments from victims of the deadly sniper shootings during October 2002 in the Washington, D.C., area were rushed to the national ballistic laboratory in Rockville, Md. In only two of the cases were the fragments too badly damaged to be accurately tested. Ballistic matches were made in all of the other cases.

The rifling of the barrel of the gun leaves unique marks in the lead or steel of the bullet fragment. Technicians can then enter a digital image of the tiny markings into a computer database called the National Integrated Ballistic Information Network. The computer then spits out likely matches, which the examiners can then study further under a microscope.

This technology is often called **ballistic fingerprinting** and is used by the federal Bureau of Alcohol, Tobacco, and Firearms (AFT), and by more than 160 crime laboratories in the United States and more than 27 other countries in the world. The technology matches bullets and shell casings to a crime gun.

To have a workable system in the United States, all gun manufacturers would be required to test-fire all new firearms and provide an electronic image (fingerprint) of each firearm before sale. A national database of firearms would be built up to immediately identify firearms used in crimes. If such a system were operating, police in the Washington, D.C., area would have had the identity of the sniper rifle immediately after the first killing.

However, because this system would amount to a national gun registry, the National Rifle Association (NRA) opposes a national database. The NRA argues that the more a gun is fired, the less accurate the tracing becomes.

The Canadian company, Forensic Technology, Inc., rejected this argument, stating that they test-fired a gun "5,000 times and the technology was able to match the first round with the last round."[29]

Because the U.S. Congress is not likely to act immediately, a number of states have started state databases for firearms. But because of the limited number of guns that will be recorded, this will limit the usefulness of state systems. The police commissioner of Boston stated that he thought "it [the database] would be a great law enforcement tool."[30] The Boston police had seized a pistol in July 2002 that, when tested, showed it had been used to shoot seven people in four cities.

Sources of Other Scientific Evidence

Almost every known science and sometimes what is called "junk science"[31] has been presented to courts for use as evidence. The U.S. Supreme Court has stressed the obligation of trial judges as "gatekeepers" to screen expert witnesses to prevent the presentation of unreliable evidence to juries and judges. Since *Daubert,* the U.S. Supreme Court has issued two additional opinions dealing with the admissibility of scientific evidence.[32]

Other scientific evidence used regularly in courts throughout the United States include:

● *Tests for alcoholic intoxication.*   Used in drunk driving and other cases. It is necessary in most cases to present evidence showing that the officer had probable cause to arrest the defendant for operating under the influence. This is done by testimony of the officer and in some cases of witnesses as to what they saw and smelled. A variety

Obtaining Evidence from Drug Testing

A 2002 study by the National Highway Traffic Safety Administration and the Robert Wood Johnson Foundation estimated that 9 million Americans a year drive while under the influence of illegal drugs.

It has been recognized for some time that drunk drivers are detected far more often than drugged drivers, while both are very serious dangers on American highways. In 2003, only eight states had laws that made it illegal to drive with any measurable amount of illegal drugs in the system. In the other states, prosecutors must prove that the reckless conduct for which a driver was stopped was caused by the illegal drugs. This is very difficult to prove in many cases. The following are sources of samples that may be used for drug testing:

Sample Used for Testing	Advantages	Detection Times	Disadvantages
Urine—privacy intrusion	Most appropriate for use as evidence because of accuracy and economy; will have high concentrations of drugs used by person	Will detect within hours, up to days	Cannot indicate blood levels; is easy to falsify
Blood—highly invasive procedure	Will indicate the extent of the impairment of the person at time of taking sample	Variable limits of detection	Because of the potential for infection, this test is not recommended for use as evidence in court
Breath— noninvasive	Indicates ethanol concentrations and the extent of impairment of person from alcohol (not other drugs)	Hours only	Very short time frame for detection and only detects volatile compounds
Hair	Will indicate long-term drug use; is difficult to adulterate	Weeks to months	Can be contaminated by external products; has a potential racial bias as dark pigmented hair absorbs drugs more readily than blond or bleached hair
Sweat—obtained from patches placed on person for days	Has a longer time frame for detection than urine and is difficult to adulterate	Days to weeks	Persons differ in manner of sweat production; does indicate degree of impairment
Saliva—Can be easily obtained	Provides estimates of blood levels and indicates degree of impairment	Hours to days	Smoking and other substances will contaminate; pH changes may alter sample

Sources: "Drug Testing in a Drug Court Environment," NCJ 1811103 document (May 2000) and the November 15, 2002, *New York Times* article, "Many, Undetected, Use Drugs and Then Drive, Report Says."

Coplink and New Police Computer Systems

Large American cities now have increased computerization to include the following:[a]

- All large departments use computer-aided dispatch systems.

- Enhanced "911" emergency systems capable of pinpointing a caller's location automatically.

- Almost all large departments use in-field computers or terminals.

- Almost all have exclusive or shared ownership of an Automated Fingerprint Identification System (AFIS) that will within minutes match fingerprints from a crime scene with a known person (if the person's fingerprints are on file).

- *The National Crime Information Center (NCIC)* continues to operate effectively with information to police agencies on wanted suspects, stolen firearms, stolen property and securities, unidentified bodies, and computerized criminal histories. Information is put into the system by members for use by other law enforcement agencies.

During the 21 days in which the snipers terrorized the Washington, D.C., area, investigators from a dozen law agencies were working together sharing ballistic testing information, geographic and criminal profiling, thousands of tips from citizens, and police files and computer information.

To coordinate all of this information, an Internet-based system called Coplink was used that allows police agencies to establish links quickly to their own files and to those of other departments. With resources from the military, federal, state, and local departments, Coplink interconnected files through new computer systems.

Will Evidence Be Excluded If There Is Computer Error Attributed to Court Officials Rather than a Police Record Keeping System?

The purpose of the exclusionary rule is to deter police misconduct. The U.S. Supreme Court held in the 1995 case of *Arizona v. Evans,* 115 S. Ct. 1185, that the rule does not apply when the mistake was made by employees of a court. Evidence, therefore, can be used under the "good faith" exception when there is police reliance on computerized information.

[a]See the U.S. Department of Justice report NCJ 175703 (May 2002).

---

of field tests could include performance tests, the horizontal gaze nystagmus (HGN),[33] and alcohol screening devices that sample the air around the suspect including air from the person. Video pictures of the driver or other person could also be used as evidence.

If probable cause exists, the person is then arrested and informed that under the "implied consent" statute of that state or jurisdiction, the person is obligated to submit to either a breathalyzer test, a blood-alcohol test, or a urine test.

- *Fire and explosive science evidence.*   In arson and civil lawsuit cases.

- *Forensic pathology.*   In determining the cause of death, time of death, and identity of the deceased.

- *Chemistry, toxicology, serology, and hematology.* For identification of stains such as blood, human blood types, blood spatters, age of blood stains; for identification of seminal fluid, sperm cells, saliva, fecal matter, perspiration; for identification of opiates, hallucinogens, barbiturates, and amphetamines; and for determining narcotic addiction.

- *Microanalysis.* To identify and compare small objects and particles including hair, fibers, paint, glass, soil and dust, cosmetics, wood, and trace evidence.

- *Neutron activation analysis (NAA).* For gunshot residue testing.

- *Tests used in questioned documents.* For handwriting and typing comparisons, analysis of inks, examination of papers and watermarks, and forensic linguistics.

- *Scientific detection of speeding.* By use of radar, Vascar, and other speed detection devices.

- *Forensic odontology.* For identification by dental characteristics, bite-mark analysis, and dental comparisons.

- *Accident reconstruction techniques.* By use of skidmarks, tire imprints, and scuff marks.

- *Physical anthropology.* To determine time of death and age, sex, race, and identification of victim.

SUMMARY

Science has become a very valuable tool for law enforcement. Scientific evidence is used every day in criminal and civil courts throughout the United States.

More than a hundred years ago, the science of chemistry and physics were combined to develop photography. Over the years, the science of photography has improved techniques and skills to develop equipment that we now take for granted. DNA testing and technology are among the new sciences used as evidence in courts today. DNA profiling was first used as evidence in a courtroom in 1987.

Scientific evidence can be used effectively to convict the guilty and to exonerate the innocent. New standards have been adopted by the courts and the scientific community to increase the reliability of science that is used as evidence in criminal and civil courts.

PROBLEMS

1. A murder occurred as the victim was sitting in the backseat of a yellow 1974 Mercury sedan. The car belonged to Gerald, who, along with his brother Harold, was charged with the murder. During the murder trial, an expert witness for the state testified that he had found "hairs inside the yellow Mercury which were microscopically similar to sample hairs taken from Gerald and Harold." However, before the trial the prosecutor for the state failed to provide the defense with samples of the hair found in the car.

Should a new trial be ordered for the failure to provide samples of the hair to the defense? Give reasons for your answer. [*State v. Tillinghast*, 465 A.2d 191 (R.I., 1983).]

2. Police received a report from a motel manager that money had been stolen from coin-operated machines in the motel. The police officer investigating the theft put fluorescent powder and paste onto and around the coin box of a vending machine in an effort to identify the thief. Within a short time, money was again taken from the machine. Because coins with fluorescent powder were found in the motel cash register, suspicion then focused on motel employees who had access to vending-machine keys. These employees were told to assemble and to place their hands under an ultraviolet light. Police could then determine that traces of powder and paste were on the hands of the defendant. The defendant had not been asked to consent to the procedure but had done so without making any objections.

May the evidence obtained be used in a criminal trial of the defendant? Did the defendant have a reasonable expectation of privacy in substances on his hands whose incriminating nature was not visible to the naked eye? Explain. [*Colorado v. Santistevan*, 715 P.2d 792 (1986), review denied 479 U.S. 965, 107 S.Ct. 468, 40 CrL 4089 (1986).]

3. Police found the body of a woman in her home. The woman was severely beaten and lying in a large pool of blood. Many broken Mason jars were near the body, and there was broken glass and blood throughout the house. The woman, separated from her husband, had commenced an annulment action against him. After the body was found, a police officer telephoned the husband and asked him to drive to the house to identify the body. The husband entered the house and walked through different rooms before identifying the body of the victim. The husband then reentered his car. The next day, a search warrant was issued to search the car. Sweepings of the floor of the car produced small glass fragments and blood that matched glass and blood found on the floor of the victim's home.

What was the easy answer that the defense had to this matching of glass and blood? [*State v. Davidson*, 170 N.W.2d 755 (Wis., 1969).]

INFOTRAC COLLEGE EDITION EXERCISES

1. Go to InfoTrac College Edition and using the search term "DNA evidence" find the 2002 article in *The Economist* titled "A Pandora's Box: DNA Evidence." This article reviews the many criminal convictions overturned in this country by use of DNA evidence, including the Central Park jogger case.

2. Go to InfoTrac College Edition and using the search term "DNA testing" find the 2001 article in the *Cornell Journal of Law & Public Policy* titled "The Constitutionality of DNA Sampling on Arrest," by D. H. Kaye. Most states and the federal government are creating DNA bases similar to the FBI's fingerprint base. The bases are generally created by taking DNA samples from prisoners or convicted felons, to be used when subsequent crimes produce DNA evidence to compare to the samples. There have been some challenges to these sample programs; can you imagine what some of those challenges might entail? In this article the author considers the constitutionality of requiring persons merely arrested for a crime to give a DNA sample. Do you concur with the author's conclusions? Why or why not?

NOTES

1. *Commonwealth v. Lykus,* 327 N.E.2d 671 (Mass., 1975), quoting *United States v. Addison,* 498 F.2d 741 (D.C. Cir., 1974).

2. See, e.g., *State v. Cortarez,* 686 P.2d 1224 (Ariz., 1984) and *Cornet v. State,* 450 N.E.2d 498 (Ind., 1983).

3. 293 Fed. 1013 (D.C. Cir., 1923).

4. 293 Fed. 1013, 1014 (D.C. Cir., 1923).

5. 509 U.S. 579 (1993).

6. 327 N.E.2d 671 (Mass., 1975).

7. Idem, 677.

8. 297 N.W.2d 80 (Iowa, 1980).

9. 545 N.Y.S.2d 985 (Sup. Ct., 1989).

10. DNA, DNA tests, and probability estimates are discussed on pp. 255–258.

11. In *Hayes v. State,* 660 So.2d 257 (Fla., 1995), the Florida Supreme Court stated it could take judicial notice of the general theory of DNA. It also held that one testing procedure sometimes used to explain minor variances in DNA results, the band-width connection procedure, was not generally accepted.

12. See, e.g., *State v. Cauthron,* 846 P.2d 502 (Wash., 1993).

13. See, e.g., *State v. Carter,* 524 N.W.2d 763 (Neb., 1994). Other courts have found the PCR test generally accepted. See *State v. Russell,* 882 P.2d 742 (Wash., 1994).

14. 509 U.S. 579 (1993).

15. 509 U.S. 592–593.

16. 119 S.Ct. 1167 (1999).

17. Hamilton, "The Movement from *Frye* to *Daubert:* Where Do the States Stand," *Jurimetrics Journal,* 38 (1998): 201.

18. Ibid, 209.

19. 955 F.2d 786 (2d Cir.).

20. See, e.g., *Greenberg Gallery Inc. v. Bauman,* 817 F.Supp. 167, 172 (D.D.C., 1993).

21. See, e.g., Kam, Fielding, and Conn, "Written Identification by Professional Document Examiners," *Journal of Forensic Science,* 42 (1997): 778. The Kam study found that some, but not all, handwriting professionals were superior to laypersons on matching handwriting samples. Those professionals made mistaken matches on 6.5% of 144 samples. Laypersons made mistaken matches on 38.3% of those same samples.

22. *United States v. Starzecpyzel,* 880 F.Supp. 1027 (S.O.N.Y., 1995).

23. Between 1988 and 1998, fifty-six wrongfully convicted people were exonerated based on DNA tests that showed they could not have committed the crime for which they were charged. Ten of those exonerated were awaiting the death penalty. L. Gaines, M. Kaune, and R. Miller, *Criminal Justice in Action* (Belmont, Calif.: Wadsworth, 2000).

24. J. McKenna, J. Cecil, and P. Coukos, *Reference Manual on Scientific Evidence,* Federal Judicial Center (St. Paul: West, 1994), 278.

25. See "Scientists Identify Bones as Those of the Czar," *New York Times,* 10 July 1993, 1.

26. See *National District Attorneys Association Bulletin* (November 1990), 7.

27. 814 S.W.2d 593 (Mo.).

28. The Federal Bureau of Investigation has created a DNA database called CODIS, which stands for the "Combined DNA Index System." The U.S. Congress has enacted legislation, called the 2000 DNA Analysis Backlog Elimination Act, 42 U.S.C. 14135, that requires certain convicted felons to provide a DNA sample to the FBI for use in the CODIS database. The purpose of that requirement is to expand the database so that in subsequent investigations DNA samples can be compared to samples on file in the database. Many states have similar statutes.

The constitutionality of the federal statute has been questioned after the U.S. Supreme Court decisions in *City of Indianapolis v. Edmond,* 531 U.S. 32 (2000) (discussed in Chapter 11), and *Ferguson v. Charleston, S.C.,* 532 U.S. 67 (2001). In *Edmonds* the Court held that suspicionless roadblocks set up to discover ordinary criminal wrongdoing were unlawful under the Fourth Amendment. In *Ferguson* the Court held that a state statute requiring pregnant women being treated at a state hospital to submit to a urine test to discover cocaine use was unconstitutional under the Fourth Amendment. In both of those cases the Court held that the government could not conduct a search without "individualized" suspicion, if the purpose of the search was discovery or investigation of ordinary criminal wrongdoing.

In *United States v. Miles,* 2002 WL 31439363 (E.D. Cal., 2002), a federal district court held that the federal DNA database statute was an unconstitutional search under the *Edmond* and *Ferguson* holdings. The court concluded that the primary purpose of the CODIS database was to provide a way for investigators in subsequent crimes to match DNA samples from those crimes with DNA samples on file in the CODIS database. The court first noted that taking the DNA samples constituted a "search" under the holding of *Schmerber v. California,* 384 U.S. 757 (1966), where the Supreme Court held that compulsory administration of a blood test constituted a search under Fourth Amendment law. The court then concluded that the samples taken from persons regulated by the statute were "suspicionless searches of those persons for the purpose of discovering 'ordinary criminal activity.'"

Other courts have reached a contrary conclusion. The court in *United States v. Reynard,* 220 F.Supp.2d 1142 (S.D. Cal., 2002), held that the primary purpose of the statute was expanding the CODIS database, which is a non-law enforcement purpose. In *Groceman v. United States,* 2002 WL 1398559 (N.D. Tex., 2002), the court upheld the statute as applied to federal prison inmates. The court concluded the diminished rights to privacy afforded to prisoners, as well as the interest of the government in identifying prisoners for the purpose of avoiding recidivism, made the statute constitutional.

Virtually all the cases decided before *Edmond* and *Ferguson* upheld the constitutionality of state laws setting up DNA databases and requiring convicted felons to provide a DNA sample to the database. See, for example, *Rise v. Oregon,* 59 F.3d 1556 (9th Cir., 1995), cert. denied 517 U.S. 1160 (1996), which upheld the Oregon DNA databank law, and *Shaffer v. Saffle,* 148 F.3d 1180 (10th Cir., 1997), cert. denied 525 U.S. 1005 (1998), upholding the Colorado and Oklahoma DNA databank laws. These cases were decided before *Edmond*'s prohibition against searches for the purpose of discovery of "ordinary criminal wrongdoing." The justification in those decisions for the DNA sample requirement was that it made subsequent crime investigations easier, an interest viewed by the courts then as legitimate and justifying the minimal intrusion of the test needed to obtain the DNA sample. It re-

mains to be seen if that is a sufficient justification after *Edmond.*

29. See the *New York Times* article of October 18, 2002, entitled, "Sniper Case Renews Debate over Firearm Fingerprinting," and the *Washington Post* article of October 23, 2002, entitled, "Doctors Help Gather Evidence."

30. See the *New York Times* article of October 24, 2002, entitled, "Technology: Now, 4 States Look to Start Tracing Shells and Bullets."

31. Some or all of the following could be called "junk science" depending upon who was making the judgment call: narcoanalysis ("truth serum"), hypnosis, voice stress analysis, polygraph (lie detector), spectrographic voice recognition, and handwriting analysis.

32. The two additional cases are *General Electric v. Joiner,* 522 U.S. 136 (1997), and *Kumho Tire Co. v. Carmichael,* 526 U.S. 137 (1999).

33. When police officers stop a driver who has been drinking beer or most other alcohol, smell will cause the officer to suspect a driving violation. However, most illegal drugs do not have a smell, and the person's behavior can be tranquil and calm. It is therefore necessary to use the horizontal gaze test. Horizontal gaze nystagmus (HGN) is a field sobriety test in which a person is requested to follow an object with his eyes. When a person's central nervous system is depressed by alcohol, barbiturates, phencyclidine (PCP), and certain inhalants, rapid involuntary jerking of the eyeballs occurs as the eyes seek to follow a pencil or finger moved before them. In the 1960s California police observed this involuntary jerking in the eyes of barbiturate users. Later, East Coast law enforcement officers began applying the concept to intoxicated drivers. The HGN test is administered in conjunction with other field sobriety tests such as the one-leg-stand test and the walk-and-turn test. Many state courts have held that HGN test results can be used with other information to establish probable cause.

Sections of the U.S. Constitution

Applicable Sections of the U.S. Constitution, Ratified in 1788

Preamble

We the People of the United States, in Order to form a more perfect Union, establish Justice, insure domestic Tranquility, provide for the common defence, promote the general Welfare, and secure the Blessings of Liberty to ourselves and our Posterity, do ordain and establish this CONSTITUTION for the United States of America.

Article I

Section 1. All legislative Powers herein granted shall be vested in a Congress of the United States, which shall consist of a Senate and House of Representatives. . . .

Article II

Section 1. The executive Power shall be vested in a President of the United States of America. . . .

Article III

Section 1. The judicial Power of the United States, shall be vested in one supreme Court, and in such inferior Courts as the Congress may from time to time ordain and establish. . . .

Article IV

Section 4. The United States shall guarantee to every State in this Union a Republican Form of Government, and shall protect each of them against Invasion; and on Application of the Legislature, or of the Executive (when the Legislature cannot be convened) against domestic Violence. . . .

Article VI

This Constitution, and the Laws of the United States which shall be made in Pursuance thereof; and all Treaties made, or which shall be made, under the Authority of the United States, shall be the supreme Law of the Land; and the Judges in every State shall be bound thereby, any Thing in the Constitution or Laws of any State to the Contrary notwithstanding. . . .

American Bill of Rights, Ratified 1791

Amendment I

Congress shall make no law respecting an establishment of religion, or prohibiting the free exercise thereof; or abridging the freedom of speech or of the press; or the right of the people peaceably to assemble and to petition the Government for a redress of grievances.

Amendment II

A well-regulated Militia, being necessary to the security of a free State, the right of the people to keep and bear Arms, shall not be infringed.

Amendment III

No Soldier shall, in time of peace be quartered in any house, without the consent of the Owner, nor in time of war, but in a manner to be prescribed by law.

Amendment IV

The right of the people to be secure in their persons, houses, papers, and effects, against unreasonable searches and seizures, shall not be violated, and no Warrants shall issue, but upon probable cause, supported by Oath, or affirmation, and particularly describing the place to be searched and the persons or things to be seized.

Amendment V

No person shall be held to answer for a capital, or otherwise infamous crime, unless on a presentment or indictment of a Grand Jury, except in cases arising in the land or naval forces, or in the Militia, when in actual service in time of War or public danger; nor shall any person be subject for the same offence to be twice put in jeopardy of life or limb; nor shall be compelled in any criminal case to be a witness against himself, nor be deprived of life, liberty, or property, without due process of law; nor shall private property be taken for public use, without just compensation.

Amendment VI

In all criminal prosecutions, the accused shall enjoy the right to a speedy and public trial, by an impartial jury of the State and district wherein the crime shall have been committed, which dis-

trict shall have been previously ascertained by law, and to be informed of the nature and cause of the accusation; to be confronted with the witnesses against him; to have compulsory process for obtaining witnesses in his favor, and to have the Assistance of Counsel for his defence.

Amendment VII

In suits at common law, where the value in controversy shall exceed twenty dollars, the right of trial by jury shall be preserved, and no fact tried by jury, shall be otherwise reexamined in any Court of the United States, than according to the rules of the common law.

Amendment VIII

Excessive bail shall not be required, nor excessive fines imposed, nor cruel and unusual punishments inflicted.

Amendment IX

The enumeration in the Constitution, of certain rights, shall not be construed to deny or disparage others retained by the people.

Amendment X

The powers not delegated to the United States by the Constitution, nor prohibited by it to the States, are reserved to the States respectively, or to the people. . . .

Amendment XIV, Ratified 1868

Section 1. All persons born or naturalized in the United States, and subject to the jurisdiction thereof, are citizens of the United States and of the State wherein they reside. No State shall make or enforce any law which shall abridge the privileges or immunities of citizens of the United States; nor shall any State deprive any person of life, liberty, or property, without due process of law; nor deny to any person within its jurisdiction the equal protection of the laws. . . .

Federal Rules of Evidence

Article 1. General Provisions

Rule 101. Scope

These rules govern proceedings in the courts of the United States and before United States bankruptcy judges, to the extent and with the exceptions stated in Rule 1101.

Rule 102. Purpose and Construction

These rules shall be construed to secure fairness in administration, elimination of unjustifiable expense and delay, and promotion of growth and development of the law of evidence to the end that the truth may be ascertained and proceedings justly determined.

Rule 103. Rulings on Evidence

(a) Effect of erroneous ruling. Error may not be predicated upon a ruling which admits or excludes evidence unless a substantial right of the party is affected, and

(1) *Objection.* In case the ruling is one admitting evidence, a timely objection or motion to strike appears of record, stating the specific ground of objection, if the specific ground was not apparent from the context; or

(2) *Offer of proof.* In case the ruling is one excluding evidence, the substance of the evidence was made known to the court by offer or was apparent from the context within which questions were asked.

(b) Record of offer and ruling. The court may add any other or further statement which shows the character of the evidence, the form in which it was offered, the objection made, and the ruling thereon. It may direct the making of an offer in question and answer form.

(c) Hearing of jury. In jury cases, proceedings shall be conducted, to the extent practicable, so as to prevent inadmissible evidence from being suggested to the jury by any means, such as making statements or offers of proof or asking questions in the hearing of the jury.

(d) Plain error. Nothing in this rule precludes taking notice of plain errors affecting substantial rights although they were not brought to the attention of the court.

Rule 104. Preliminary Questions

(a) Questions of admissibility generally. Preliminary questions concerning the qualification of a person to be a witness, the existence of a privilege, or the admissibility of evidence shall be determined by the court, subject to the provisions of subdivision (b). In making its determination it is not bound by the rules of evidence except those with respect to privileges.

(b) Relevancy conditioned on fact. When the relevancy of evidence depends upon the fulfillment of a condition of fact, the court shall admit it upon, or subject to, the introduction of evidence sufficient to support a finding of the fulfillment of the condition.

(c) Hearing of jury. Hearings on the admissibility of confessions shall in all cases be conducted out of the hearing of the jury. Hearings on other preliminary matters shall be so conducted when the interests of justice require or, when an accused is a witness and so requests.

(d) Testimony by accused. The accused does not, by testifying upon a preliminary matter, become subject to cross-examination as to other issues in the case.

(e) Weight and credibility. This rule does not limit the right of a party to introduce before the jury evidence relevant to weight or credibility.

• • •

Article II. Judicial Notice

Rule 201. Judicial Notice of Adjudicative Facts

(a) Scope of rule. This rule governs only judicial notice of adjudicative facts.

(b) Kinds of facts. A judicially noticed fact must be one not subject to reasonable dispute in that it is either (1) generally known within the territorial jurisdiction of the trial court or (2) capable of accurate and ready determination by resort to sources whose accuracy cannot reasonably be questioned.

(c) When discretionary. A court may take judicial notice, whether requested or not.

(d) When mandatory. A court shall take judicial notice if requested by a party and supplied with the necessary information.

(e) Opportunity to be heard. A party is entitled upon timely request to an opportunity to be heard as to the propriety of taking judicial notice and the tenor of the matter noticed. In the absence of prior notification, the request may be made after judicial notice has been taken.

(f) Time of taking notice. Judicial notice may be taken at any stage of the proceeding.

(g) Instructing jury. In a civil action or proceeding, the court shall instruct the jury to accept as conclusive any fact judicially noticed. In a criminal case, the court shall instruct the jury that it may, but is not required to, accept as conclusive any fact judicially noticed.

• • •

Article III. Presumptions in Civil Actions and Proceedings

Rule 301. Presumptions in General in Civil Actions and Proceedings

In all civil actions and proceedings not otherwise provided for by Act of Congress or by these rules, a presumption imposes on the party against whom it is directed the burden of going forward with evidence to rebut or meet the presumption, but does not shift to such party the burden of proof in the sense of the risk of nonpersuasion, which remains throughout the trial upon the party on whom it was originally cast.

• • •

Article IV. Relevancy and Its Limits

Rule 401. Definition of "Relevant Evidence"

"Relevant evidence" means evidence having any tendency to make the existence of any fact that is of consequence to the determination of the action more probable or less probable than it would be without the evidence.

Rule 402. Relevant Evidence Generally Admissible; Irrelevant Evidence Inadmissible

All relevant evidence is admissible, except as otherwise provided by the Constitution of the United States, by Act of Congress, by these rules, or by other rules prescribed by the Supreme Court pursuant to statutory authority. Evidence which is not relevant is not admissible.

Rule 403. Exclusion of Relevant Evidence on Grounds of Prejudice, Confusion, or Waste of Time

Although relevant, evidence may be excluded if its probative value is substantially outweighed by the danger of unfair prejudice, confusion of the issues, or misleading the jury, or by considerations of undue delay, waste of time, or needless presentation of cumulative evidence.

Rule 404. Character Evidence Not Admissible to Prove Conduct; Exceptions; Other Crimes

(a) Character evidence generally. Evidence of a person's character or a trait of character is not admissible for the purpose of proving action in conformity therewith on a particular occasion, except:

(1) *Character of accused.* Evidence of a pertinent trait of character offered by an accused, or by the prosecution to rebut the same;

(2) *Character of victim.* Evidence of a pertinent trait of character of the victim of the crime offered by an accused, or by the prosecution to rebut the same, or evidence of a character trait of peacefulness of the victim offered by the prosecution in a homicide case to rebut evidence that the victim was the first aggressor;

(3) *Character of witness.* Evidence of the character of a witness, as provided in rules 607, 608, and 609.

• • •

(b) Other crimes, wrongs, or acts. Evidence of other crimes, wrongs, or acts is not admissible to prove the character of a person in order to show action in conformity therewith. It may, however, be admissible for other purposes, such as proof of motive, opportunity, intent, preparation, plan, knowledge, identity, or absence of mistake or accident, provided that upon request by the accused, the prosecution in a criminal case shall provide reasonable notice in advance of trial, or during trial if the court excuses pretrial notice on

good cause shown, or the general nature of any such evidence it intends to introduce at trial.

Rule 405. Methods of Proving Character

(a) Reputation or opinion. In all cases in which evidence of character or a trait of character of a person is admissible, proof may be made by testimony as to reputation or by testimony in the form of an opinion. On cross-examination, inquiry is allowable into relevant specific instances of conduct.

(b) Specific instances of conduct. In cases in which character or a trait of character of a person is an essential element of a charge, claim, or defense, proof may also be made of specific instances of that person's conduct.

Rule 406. Habit; Routine Practice

Evidence of the habit of a person or the routine practice of an organization, whether corroborated or not and regardless of the presence of eyewitnesses, is relevant to prove that the conduct of the person or organization on a particular occasion was in conformity with the habit or routine practice.

• • •

Rule 410. Inadmissibility of Pleas, Plea Discussions, and Related Statements

Except as otherwise provided in this rule, evidence of the following is not, in any civil or criminal proceeding, admissible against the defendant who made the plea or was a participant in the plea discussions:

(1) a plea of guilty which was later withdrawn;

(2) a plea of nolo contendere;

(3) any statement made in the course of any proceedings under Rule 11 of the Federal Rules of Criminal Procedure or comparable state procedure regarding either of the foregoing pleas; or

(4) any statement made in the course of plea discussions with an attorney for the prosecuting authority which do not result in a plea of guilty or which result in a plea of guilty later withdrawn.

However, such a statement is admissible (i) in any proceeding wherein another statement made in the course of the same plea or plea discussions has been introduced and the statement ought in fairness be considered contemporaneously with it, or (ii) in a criminal proceeding for perjury or false statement if the statement was made by the defendant under oath, on the record and in the presence of counsel.

• • •

Rule 412. Sex Offense Cases; Relevance of Alleged Victim's Past Sexual Behavior or Alleged Sexual Predisposition

(a) Evidence generally inadmissible. The following evidence is not admissible in any civil or criminal proceeding involving alleged sexual misconduct except as provided in subdivisions (b) and (c):

(1) Evidence offered to prove that any alleged victim engaged in other sexual behavior.

(2) Evidence offered to prove any alleged victim's sexual predisposition.

(b) Exceptions.

(1) In a criminal case, the following evidence is admissible, if otherwise admissible under these rules:

(A) evidence of specific instances of sexual behavior by the alleged victim offered to prove that a person other than the accused was the source of semen, injury or other physical evidence;

(B) evidence of specific instances of sexual behavior by the alleged victim with respect to the person accused of the sexual misconduct offered by the accused to prove consent or by the prosecution; and

(C) evidence the exclusion of which would violate the constitutional rights of the defendant.

(2) In a civil case, evidence offered to prove the sexual behavior or sexual predisposition of any alleged victim is admissible if it is otherwise admissible under these rules and its probative value substantially outweighs the danger of harm to any victim and of unfair prejudice to any party. Evidence of an alleged victim's reputation is admissible only if it has been placed in controversy by the alleged victim.

(c) Procedure to determine admissibility.

(1) A party intending to offer evidence under subdivision (b) must—

(A) file a written motion at least 14 days before trial specifically describing the evidence and stating the purpose for which it is offered unless the court, for good cause requires a different time for filing or permits filing during trial; and

(B) serve the motion on all parties and notify the alleged victim or, when appropriate, the alleged victim's guardian or representative.

(2) Before admitting evidence under this rule the court must conduct a hearing in camera and afford the victim and parties a right to attend and be heard. The motion, related papers, and the record of the hearing must be sealed and remain under seal unless the court orders otherwise.

Rule 413. Evidence of Similar Crimes in Sexual Assault Cases

(a) In a criminal case in which the defendant is accused of an offense of sexual assault, evidence of the defendant's commission of another offense or offenses of sexual assault is admissible, and may be considered for its bearing on any matter to which it is relevant.

(b) In a case in which the Government intends to offer evidence under this rule, the attorney for the Government shall disclose the evidence to the defendant, including statements of witnesses or a summary of the substance of any testimony that is expected to be offered, at least fifteen days before the scheduled date of trial or at such later time as the court may allow for good cause.

(c) This rule shall not be construed to limit the admission or consideration of evidence under any other rule.

(d) For purposes of this rule and Rule 415, "offense of sexual assault" means a crime under Federal law or the law of a State (as defined in section 513 of title 18, United States Code) that involved—

(1) any conduct proscribed by chapter 109A of title 18, United States Code;

(2) contact, without consent, between any part of the defendant's body or an object and the genitals or anus of another person;

(3) contact, without consent, between the genitals or anus of the defendant and any part of another person's body;

(4) deriving sexual pleasure or gratification from the infliction of death, bodily injury, or physical pain on another person; or

(5) an attempt or conspiracy to engage in conduct described in paragraphs (1)–(4).

Rule 414. Evidence of Similar Crimes in Child Molestation Cases

(a) In a criminal case in which the defendant is accused of an offense of child molestation, evidence of the defendant's commission of another offense or offenses of child molestation is admissible, and may be considered for its bearing on any matter to which it is relevant.

(b) In a case in which the Government intends to offer evidence under this rule, the attorney for the Government shall disclose the evidence to the defendant, including statements of witnesses or a summary of the substance of any testimony that is expected to be offered, at least fifteen days before the scheduled date of trial or at such later time as the court may allow for good cause.

(c) This rule shall not be construed to limit the admission or consideration of evidence under any other rule.

(d) For purposes of this rule and Rule 415, "child" means a person below the age of fourteen, and "offense of child molestation" means a crime under Federal law or the law of a State (as defined in section 513 of title 18, United States Code) that involved—

(1) any conduct proscribed by chapter 109A of title 18, United States Code, that was committed in relation to a child;

(2) any conduct proscribed by chapter 110 of title 18, United States Code;

(3) contact between any part of the defendant's body or an object and the genitals or anus of a child;

(4) contact between the genitals or anus of the defendant and any part of the body of a child;

(5) deriving sexual pleasure or gratification from the infliction of death, bodily injury, or physical pain on a child; or

(6) an attempt or conspiracy to engage in conduct described in paragraphs (1)–(5).

Rule 415. Evidence of Similar Acts in Civil Cases Concerning Sexual Assault or Child Molestation

(a) In a civil case in which a claim for damages or other relief is predicated on a party's alleged commission of conduct constituting an offense of sexual assault or child molestation, evidence of that party's commission of another offense or offenses of sexual assault or child molestation is admissible and may be considered as provided in Rule 413 and Rule 414 of these rules.

(b) A party who intends to offer evidence under this Rule shall disclose the evidence to the party against whom it will be offered, including statements of witnesses or a summary of the substance of any testimony that is expected to be offered, at least fifteen days before the scheduled date of trial or at such later time as the court may allow for good cause.

(c) This rule shall not be construed to limit the admission or consideration of evidence under any other rule.

Article V. Privileges

Rule 501. General Rule

Except as otherwise required by the Constitution of the United States or provided by Act of Congress or in rules prescribed by the Supreme Court pursuant to statutory authority, the privilege of a witness, person, government, State, or political subdivision thereof shall be governed by the principles of the common law as they may be interpreted by the courts of the United States in the light of reason and experience. However, in civil actions and proceedings, with respect to an element of a claim or defense as to which State law supplies the rule of decision, the privilege of a witness, person, government, State, or political subdivision thereof shall be determined in accordance with State law.

Article VI. Witnesses

Rule 601. General Rule of Competency

Every person is competent to be a witness except as otherwise provided in these rules. However, in civil actions and proceedings, with respect to an element of a claim or defense as to which State law supplies the rule of decision, the competency of a witness shall be determined in accordance with State law.

Rule 602. Lack of Personal Knowledge

A witness may not testify to a matter unless evidence is introduced sufficient to support a finding that he has personal knowledge of the matter. Evidence to prove personal knowledge may, but need not, consist of the witness' own testimony. This rule is subject to the provisions of Rule 703, relating to opinion testimony by expert witnesses.

Rule 603. Oath or Affirmation

Before testifying, every witness shall be required to declare that the witness will testify truthfully, by oath or affirmation administered in a form calculated to awaken his conscience and impress the witness' mind with the duty to do so.

Rule 604. Interpreters

An interpreter is subject to the provisions of these rules relating to qualification as an expert and the administration of an oath or affirmation to make a true translation.

Rule 605. Competency of Judge as Witness

The judge presiding at the trial may not testify in that trial as a witness. No objection need be made in order to preserve the point.

Rule 606. Competency of Juror as Witness

(a) At the trial. A member of the jury may not testify as a witness before that jury in the trial of the case in which the juror is sitting. If the juror is called so to testify, the opposing party shall be afforded an opportunity to object out of the presence of the jury.

(b) Inquiry into validity of verdict or indictment. Upon an inquiry into the validity of a verdict or indictment, a juror may not testify as to any matter or statement occurring during the course of the jury's deliberations or to the effect of anything upon that or any other juror's mind or emotions as influencing the juror to assent to or dissent from the verdict or indictment or concerning the juror's mental processes in connection therewith, except that a juror may testify on the question whether extraneous prejudicial information was improperly brought to the jury's attention or whether any outside influence was improperly brought to bear upon any juror. Nor may a juror's affidavit or evidence of any statement by the juror concerning a matter about which the juror would be precluded from testifying be received for these purposes.

Rule 607. Who May Impeach

The credibility of a witness may be attacked by any party, including the party calling the witness.

Rule 608. Evidence of Character and Conduct of Witness

(a) Opinion and reputation evidence of character. The credibility of a witness may be attacked or supported by evidence in the form of opinion or reputation, but subject to these limitations: (1) the evidence may refer only to character for truthfulness or untruthfulness, and (2) evidence of truthful character is admissible only after the character of the witness for truthfulness has been attacked by opinion or reputation evidence or otherwise.

(b) Specific instances of conduct. Specific instances of the conduct of a witness, for the purpose of attacking or supporting the witness' credibility, other than conviction of crime as provided in Rule 609, may not be proved by extrinsic evidence. They may, however, in the discretion of the court, if probative of truthfulness or untruthfulness, be inquired into on cross-examination of the witness (1) concerning the witness' character for truthfulness or untruthfulness, or (2) concerning the character for truthfulness or untruthfulness of another witness as to which character the witness being cross-examined has testified.

The giving of testimony, whether by an accused or by any other witness, does not operate as a waiver of the accused's or the witness' privilege against self-incrimination when examined with respect to matters which relate only to credibility.

Rule 609. Impeachment by Evidence of Conviction of Crime

(a) General rule. For the purpose of attacking the credibility of a witness,

(1) evidence that a witness other than an accused has been convicted of a crime shall be admitted, subject to Rule 403, if the crime was punishable by death or imprisonment in excess of one year under the law under which the witness was convicted, and evidence that an accused has been convicted of such a crime shall be admitted if the court determines that the probative value of admitting this evidence outweighs its prejudicial effect to the accused; and

(2) evidence that any witness has been convicted of a crime shall be admitted if it involved dishonesty or false statement, regardless of the punishment.

(b) Time limit. Evidence of a conviction under this rule is not admissible if a period of more than ten years has elapsed since the date of the conviction or of the release of the witness from the confinement imposed for that conviction, whichever is the later date, unless the court determines, in the interests of justice, that the probative value of the conviction supported by specific facts and circumstances substantially outweighs its prejudicial effect. However, evidence of a conviction more than 10 years old as calculated herein, is not admissible unless the proponent gives to the adverse party sufficient advance written notice of intent to use such evidence to provide the adverse party with a fair opportunity to contest the use of such evidence.

(c) Effect of pardon, annulment, or certificate of rehabilitation. Evidence of a conviction is not admissible under this rule if (1) the conviction has been the subject of a pardon, annulment, certificate of rehabilitation, or other equivalent procedure based on a finding of the rehabilitation of the person convicted, and that person has not been convicted of a subsequent crime which was punishable by death or imprisonment in excess of one year, or (2) the conviction has been the subject of a pardon, annulment, or other equivalent procedure based on a finding of innocence.

(d) Juvenile adjudications. Evidence of juvenile adjudications is generally not admissible under this rule. The court may, however, in a criminal case allow evidence of a juvenile adjudication of a witness other than the accused if conviction of the offense would be admissible to attack the credibility of an adult and the court is satisfied that admission in evidence is necessary for a fair determination of the issue of guilt or innocence.

(e) Pendency of appeal. The pendency of an appeal therefrom does not render evidence of a conviction inadmissible. Evidence of the pendency of an appeal is admissible.

Rule 610. Religious Beliefs or Opinions

Evidence of the beliefs or opinions of a witness on matters of religion is not admissible for the purpose of showing that by reason of their nature the witness' credibility is impaired or enhanced.

Rule 611. Mode and Order of Interrogation and Presentation

(a) Control by court. The court shall exercise reasonable control over the mode and order of interrogating witnesses and presenting evidence so as to (1) make the interrogation and presentation effective for the ascertainment of the truth, (2) avoid needless consumption of time, and (3) protect witnesses from harassment or undue embarrassment.

(b) Scope of cross-examination. Cross-examination should be limited to the subject matter of the direct examination and matters affecting the credibility of the witness. The court may, in the exercise of discretion, permit inquiry into additional matters as if on direct examination.

(c) Leading questions. Leading questions should not be used on the direct examination of a witness except as may be necessary to develop the witness' testimony. Ordinarily leading questions should be permitted on cross-examination. When a party calls a hostile witness, an adverse party, or a witness identified with an adverse party, interrogation may be by leading questions.

Rule 612. Writing Used To Refresh Memory

Except as otherwise provided in criminal proceedings by section 3500 of title 18, United States Code, if a witness uses a writing to refresh his memory for the purpose of testifying, either—

(1) while testifying, or

(2) before testifying, if the court in its discretion determines it is necessary in the interests of justice,

an adverse party is entitled to have the writing produced at the hearing, to inspect it, to cross-examine the witness thereon, and to introduce in evidence those portions which relate to the testimony of the witness. If it is claimed that the writing contains matters not related to the subject matter of the testimony the court shall examine the writing in camera, excise any portions not so related, and order delivery of the remainder to the party entitled thereto. Any portion withheld over objections shall be preserved and made available to the appellate court in the event of an appeal. If a writing is not produced or delivered pursuant to order under this rule, the court shall make any order justice requires, except that in criminal cases when the prosecution elects not to comply, the order shall be one striking the testimony or, if the court in its discretion determines that the interests of justice so require, declaring a mistrial.

Rule 613. Prior Statements of Witnesses

(a) Examining witness concerning prior statement. In examining a witness concerning a prior statement made by the witness, whether written or not, the statement need not be shown nor its contents disclosed to the witness at that time, but on request the same shall be shown or disclosed to opposing counsel.

(b) Extrinsic evidence of prior inconsistent statement of witness. Extrinsic evidence of a prior inconsistent statement by a witness is not admissible unless the witness is afforded an opportunity to explain or deny the same and the opposite party is afforded an opportunity to interrogate the witness thereon, or the interests of justice otherwise require. This provision does not apply to admissions of a party-opponent as defined in Rule 801(d)(2).

Rule 614. Calling and Interrogation of Witnesses by Court

(a) Calling by court. The court may, on its own motion or at the suggestion of a party, call witnesses, and all parties are entitled to cross-examine witnesses thus called.

(b) Interrogation by court. The court may interrogate witnesses, whether called by itself or by a party.

(c) Objections. Objections to the calling of witnesses by the court or to interrogation by it may be made at the time or at the next available opportunity when the jury is not present.

Rule 615. Exclusion of Witnesses

At the request of a party the court shall order witnesses excluded so that they cannot hear the testimony of other witnesses, and it may make the order of its own motion. This rule does not authorize exclusion of (1) party who is a natural person, or (2) an officer or employee of a party which is not a natural person designated as its representative by its attorney, or (3) a person whose presence is shown by a party to be essential to the presentation of the party's cause, or (4) a person authorized by statute to be present.

Article VII. Opinions and Expert Testimony

Rule 701. Opinion Testimony by Lay Witnesses

If the witness is not testifying as an expert, the witness' testimony in the form of opinions or inferences is limited to those opinions or inferences which are (a) rationally based on the perception of the witness and (b) helpful to a clear understanding of the witness' testimony or the determination of a fact in issue.

Rule 702. Testimony by Experts

If scientific, technical, or other specialized knowledge will assist the trier of fact to understand the evidence or to determine a fact in issue, a witness qualified as an expert by knowledge, skill, experience, training, or education, may testify thereto in the form of an opinion or otherwise.

Rule 703. Bases of Opinion Testimony by Experts

The facts or data in the particular case upon which an expert bases an opinion or inference may be those perceived by or made known to the expert at or before the hearing. If of a type reasonably relied upon by experts in the particular field in forming opinions or inferences upon the subject, the facts or data need not be admissible in evidence.

Rule 704. Opinion on Ultimate Issue

(a) Except as provided in subdivision (b), testimony in the form of an opinion or inference otherwise admissible is not objectionable because it embraces an ultimate issue to be decided by the trier of fact.

(b) No expert witness testifying with respect to the mental state or condition of a defendant in a criminal case may state an opinion or inference as to whether the defendant did or did not have the mental state or condition constituting an element of the crime charged or of a defense thereto. Such ultimate issues are matters for the trier of fact alone.

Rule 705. Disclosure of Facts or Data Underlying Expert Opinion

The expert may testify in terms of opinion or inference and give reasons therefore without prior disclosure of the underlying facts or data, unless the court requires otherwise. The expert may in any event be required to disclose the underlying facts or data on cross-examination.

Rule 706. Court Appointed Experts

(a) **Appointment.** The court may on its own motion or on the motion of any party enter an order to show cause why expert witnesses should not be appointed, and may request the parties to submit nominations. The court may appoint any expert witnesses agreed upon by the parties, and may appoint expert witnesses of its own selection. An expert witness shall not be appointed by the court unless the witness consents to act. A witness so appointed shall be informed of the witness' duties by the court in writing, a copy of which shall be filed with the clerk, or at a conference in which the parties shall have opportunity to participate. A witness so appointed shall advise the parties of the witness' findings, if any; the witness' deposition may be taken by any party; and the witness may be called to testify by the court or any party. The witness shall be subject to cross-examination by each party, including a party calling the witness.

(b) **Compensation.** Expert witnesses so appointed are entitled to reasonable compensation in whatever sum the court may allow. The compensation thus fixed is payable from funds which may be provided by law in criminal cases and civil actions and proceedings involving just compensation under the fifth amendment. In other civil actions and proceedings the compensation shall be paid by the parties in such proportion and at such time as the court directs, and thereafter charged in like manner as other costs.

(c) Disclosure of appointment. In the exercise of its discretion, the court may authorize disclosure to the jury of the fact that the court appointed the expert witness.

(d) Parties' experts of own selection. Nothing in this rule limits the parties in calling expert witnesses of their own selection.

Article VIII. Hearsay

Rule 801. Definitions

The following definitions apply under this article:

(a) Statement. A "statement" is (1) an oral or written assertion or (2) nonverbal conduct of a person, if it is intended by the person as an assertion.

(b) Declarant. A "declarant" is a person who makes a statement.

(c) Hearsay. "Hearsay" is a statement, other than one made by the declarant while testifying at the trial or hearing, offered in evidence to prove the truth of the matter asserted.

(d) Statements which are not hearsay. A statement is not hearsay if—

(1) *Prior statement by witness.* The declarant testifies at the trial or hearing and is subject to cross-examination concerning the statement, and the statement is (A) inconsistent with the declarant's testimony, and was given under oath subject to the penalty of perjury at a trial, hearing, or other proceedings or in a deposition, or (B) consistent with the declarant's testimony and is offered to rebut an express or implied charge against the declarant of recent fabrication or improper influence or motive, or (C) one of identification of a person made after perceiving the person; or

(2) *Admission by party-opponent.* The statement is offered against a party and is (A) the party's own statement, in either an individual or a representative capacity or (B) a statement of which

the party has manifested an adoption or belief in its truth, or (C) a statement by a person authorized by the party to make a statement concerning the subject, or (D) a statement by the party's agent or servant concerning a matter within the scope of the agency or employment, made during the existence of the relationship, or (E) a statement by a coconspirator of a party during the course and in furtherance of the conspiracy. The contents of the statement shall be considered but are not alone sufficient to establish the declarant's authority under subdivision (C), the agency or employment relationship and scope thereof under subdivision (D), or the existence of the conspiracy and the participation therein of the declarant and the party against whom the statement is offered under subdivision (E).

Rule 802. Hearsay Rule

Hearsay is not admissible except as provided by these rules or by other rules prescribed by the Supreme Court pursuant to statutory authority or by Act of Congress.

Rule 803. Hearsay Exceptions; Availability of Declarant Immaterial

The following are not excluded by the hearsay rule, even though the declarant is available as a witness:

(1) Present sense impression. A statement describing or explaining an event or condition made while the declarant was perceiving the event or condition, or immediately thereafter.

(2) Excited utterance. A statement relating to a startling event or condition made while the declarant was under the stress of excitement caused by the event or condition.

(3) Then existing mental, emotional, or physical condition. A statement of the declarant's then existing state of mind, emotion, sensation, or physical condition (such as intent, plan, motive, design, mental feeling, pain, and bodily health), but not including a statement of memory or belief to prove the fact remembered or believed unless it relates to the execution, revocation, identification, or terms of declarant's will.

(4) Statements for purposes of medical diagnosis or treatment. Statements made for purposes of medical diagnosis or treatment and describing medical history, or past or present symptoms, pain, or sensations, or the inception or general character of the cause or external source thereof insofar as reasonably pertinent to diagnosis or treatment.

(5) Recorded recollection. A memorandum or record concerning a matter about which a witness once had knowledge but now has insufficient recollection to enable the witness to testify fully and accurately, shown to have been made or adopted by the witness when the matter was fresh in the witness' memory and to reflect that knowledge correctly. If admitted, the memorandum or record may be read into evidence but may not itself be received as an exhibit unless offered by an adverse party.

(6) Records of regularly conducted activity. A memorandum, report, record, or data compilation, in any form, of acts, events, conditions, opinions, or diagnoses, made at or near the time by, or from information transmitted by, a person with knowledge, if kept in the course of a regularly conducted business activity and if it was the regular practice of that business activity to make the memorandum, report, record, or data compilation, all as shown by the testimony of the custodian or other qualified witness, unless the source of information or the method or circumstances of preparation indicate lack of trustworthiness. The term "business" as used in this paragraph includes business, institution, association, profession, occupation, and calling of every kind, whether or not conducted for profit.

(7) Absence of entry in records kept in accordance with the provisions of paragraph (6). Evidence that a matter is not included in the memoranda reports, records, or data compilations, in any form, kept in accordance with the provisions of paragraph (6), to prove the nonoccurrence or nonexistence of the matter if the matter was a kind of which a memorandum report, record, or data compilation was regularly made and preserved, unless the sources of information or other circumstances indicate lack of trustworthiness.

(8) Public records and reports. Records, reports, statements, or data compilations, in any form, of public offices or agencies, setting forth (A) the activities of the office or agency, or (B) matters observed pursuant to duty imposed by law as to which matters there was a duty to report, excluding, however, in criminal cases matters observed by police officers and other law enforcement personnel, or (C) in civil actions and proceedings and against the Government in criminal cases, factual findings resulting from an investigation made pursuant to authority granted by law, unless the sources of information or other circumstances indicate lack of trustworthiness.

(9) Records of vital statistics. Records or data compilations, in any form, of births, fetal deaths, deaths, or marriages, if the report thereof was made to a public office pursuant to requirements of law.

(10) Absence of public record or entry. To prove the absence of a record, report, statement, or data compilation, in any form, or the nonoccurrence or nonexistence of a matter of which a record, report, statement, or data compilation, in any form, was regularly made and preserved by a public office or agency, evidence in the form of a certification in accordance with Rule 902, or testimony, that diligent search failed to disclose the record, report, statement, or data compilation, or entry.

(11) Records of religious organizations. Statements of births, marriages, divorces, deaths, legitimacy, ancestry, relationship by blood or marriage, or other similar facts of personal or family history, contained in a regularly kept record of a religious organization.

(12) Marriage, baptismal, and similar certificates. Statements of fact contained in a certificate that the maker performed a marriage or other ceremony or administered a sacrament, made by a clergyman, public official, or other person authorized by the rules or practices of a religious organization or by law to perform the act certified, and purporting to have been issued at the time of the act or within a reasonable time thereafter.

(13) Family records. Statements of fact concerning personal or family history contained in family Bibles, genealogies, charts, engravings on rings, inscriptions on family portraits, engravings on urns, crypts, or tombstones, or the like.

(14) Records of documents affecting an interest in property. The record of a document purporting to establish or affect an interest in property, as proof of the content of the original recorded document and its execution and delivery by each person by whom it purports to have been executed, if the record is a record of a public office and an applicable statute authorizes the recording of documents of that kind in that office.

(15) Statements in documents affecting an interest in property. A statement contained in a document purporting to establish or affect an interest in property if the matter stated was relevant to the purpose of the document, unless dealings with the property since the document was made have been inconsistent with the truth of the statement or the purport of the document.

(16) Statements in ancient documents. Statements in a document in existence twenty years or more the authenticity of which is established.

(17) Market reports, commercial publications. Market quotations, tabulations, lists, directories, or other published compilations, generally used and relied upon by the public or by persons in particular occupations.

(18) Learned treatises. To the extent called to the attention of an expert witness upon cross-examination or relied upon by the expert witness in direct examination, statements contained in published treatises, periodicals, or pamphlets on a subject of history, medicine, or other science or art, established as a reliable authority by the testimony or admission of the witness or by other expert testimony or by judicial notice. If admitted, the statements may be read into evidence but may not be received as exhibits.

(19) Reputation concerning personal or family history. Reputation among members of a person's family by blood, adoption, or marriage, or among a person's associates, or in the community, concerning a person's birth, adoption, marriage, divorce, death, legitimacy, relationship by blood, adoption, or marriage, ancestry, or other similar fact of personal or family history.

(20) Reputation concerning boundaries or general history. Reputation in a community, arising before the controversy, as to boundaries of or customs affecting lands in the community, and reputation as to events of general history important to the community or State or nation in which located.

(21) Reputation as to character. Reputation of a person's character among associates or in the community.

(22) Judgment of previous conviction. Evidence of a final judgment, entered after a trial or upon a plea of guilty (but not upon a plea of nolo contendere), adjudging a person guilty of a crime punishable by death or imprisonment in excess of one year, to prove any fact essential to sustain the judgment, but not including, when offered by the Government in a criminal prosecution for purposes other than impeachment, judgments against persons other than the accused. The pendency of an appeal may be shown but does not affect admissibility.

(23) Judgment as to personal, family, or general history, or boundaries. Judgments as proof of matters of personal, family or general history, or boundaries, essential to the judgment, if the same would be provable by evidence of reputation.

(24) [Transferred to Rule 807]

Rule 804. Hearsay Exceptions; Declarant Unavailable

(a) Definition of unavailability. "Unavailability as a witness" includes situations in which the declarant—

(1) is exempted by ruling of the court on the ground of privilege from testifying concerning the subject matter of the declarant's statement; or

(2) persists in refusing to testify concerning the subject matter of the declarant's statement despite an order of the court to do so; or

(3) testifies to a lack of memory of the subject matter of the declarant's statement; or

(4) is unable to be present or to testify at the hearing because of death or then existing physical or mental illness or infirmity; or

(5) is absent from the hearing and the proponent of a statement has been unable to procure the declarant's attendance (or in the case of a hearsay exception under subdivision (b)(2), (3), or (4), the declarant's attendance or testimony) by process or other reasonable means.

A declarant is not unavailable as a witness if exemption, refusal, claim of lack of memory, inability, or absence is due to the procurement or wrongdoing of the proponent of a statement for the purpose of preventing the witness from attending or testifying.

(b) Hearsay exceptions. The following are not excluded by the hearsay rule if the declarant is unavailable as a witness:

(1) *Former testimony.* Testimony given as a witness at another hearing of the same or a different proceeding, or in a deposition taken in compliance with law in the course of the same or another proceeding, if the party against whom the testimony is now offered, or, in a civil action or proceeding, a predecessor in interest, had an opportunity and similar motive to develop the testimony by direct, cross, or redirect examination.

(2) *Statement under belief of impending death.* In a prosecution for homicide or in a civil action or proceeding, a statement made by a declarant while believing that the declarant's death was imminent, concerning the cause or circumstances of what the declarant believed to be impending death.

(3) *Statement against interest.* A statement which was at the time of its making so far contrary to the declarant's pecuniary or proprietary interest, or so far tended to subject the declarant to civil or criminal liability, or to render invalid a claim by the declarant against another, that a reasonable person in the declarant's position would not have made

the statement unless believing it to be true. A statement tending to expose the declarant to criminal liability and offered to exculpate the accused is not admissible unless corroborating circumstances clearly indicate the trustworthiness of the statement.

(4) *Statement of personal or family history.* (A) A statement concerning the declarant's own birth, adoption, marriage, divorce, legitimacy, relationship by blood, adoption, or marriage, ancestry, or other similar fact of personal or family history, even though declarant had no means of acquiring personal knowledge of the matter stated; or (B) a statement concerning the foregoing matters, and death also, of another person, if the declarant was related to the other by blood, adoption, or marriage or was so intimately associated with the other's family as to be likely to have accurate information concerning the matter declared.

(5) [Transferred to Rule 807]

(6) *Forfeiture by wrongdoing.* A statement offered against a party that has engaged or acquiesced in wrongdoing that was intended to, and did, procure the unavailability of the declarant as a witness.

Rule 805. Hearsay Within Hearsay

Hearsay included within hearsay is not excluded under the hearsay rule if each part of the combined statements conforms with an exception to the hearsay rule provided in these rules.

Rule 806. Attacking and Supporting Credibility of Declarant

When a hearsay statement, or a statement defined in Rule 801(d)(2)(C), (D), or (E), has been admitted in evidence, the credibility of the declarant may be attacked, and if attacked may be supported, by any evidence which would be admissible for those purposes if declarant had testified as a witness. Evidence of a statement or conduct by the declarant at any time, inconsistent with the declarant's hearsay statement, is not subject to any requirement that the declarant may have been afforded an opportunity to deny or explain. If the party against whom a hearsay statement has been admitted calls the declarant as a witness, the party is entitled to examine the declarant on the statement as if under cross-examination.

Rule 807. Residual Exception

A statement not specifically covered by Rule 803 or 804 but having equivalent circumstantial guarantees of trustworthiness, is not excluded by the hearsay rule, if the court determines that (A) the statement is offered as evidence of a material fact; (B) the statement is more probative on the point for which it is offered than any other evidence which the proponent can procure through reasonable efforts; and (C) the general purposes of these rules and the interests of justice will best be served by admission of the statement into evidence. However, a statement may not be admitted under this exception unless the proponent of it makes known to the adverse party sufficiently in advance of the trial or hearing to provide the adverse party with a fair opportunity to prepare to meet it, the proponent's intention to offer the statement and the particulars of it, including the name and address of the declarant.

Article IX. Authentication and Identification

Rule 901. Requirement of Authentication or Identification

(a) General provision. The requirement of authentication or identification as a condition precedent to admissibility is satisfied by evidence sufficient to support a finding that the matter in question is what its proponent claims.

(b) Illustrations. By way of illustration only, and not by way of limitation, the following are examples of authentication or identification conforming with the requirements of this rule:

(1) *Testimony of witness with knowledge.* Testimony that a matter is what it is claimed to be.

(2) *Nonexpert opinion on handwriting.* Nonexpert opinion as to the genuineness of handwriting, based upon familiarity not acquired for purposes of the litigation.

(3) *Comparison by trier or expert witness.* Comparison by the trier of fact or by expert witnesses with specimens which have been authenticated.

(4) *Distinctive characteristics and the like.* Appearance, contents, substance, internal patterns, or other distinctive characteristics, taken in conjunction with circumstances.

(5) *Voice identification.* Identification of a voice, whether heard firsthand or through mechanical or electronic transmission or recording, by opinion based upon hearing the voice at any time under circumstances connecting it with the alleged speaker.

(6) *Telephone conversations.* Telephone conversations, by evidence that a call was made to the number assigned at the time by the telephone company to a particular person or business, if (A) in the case of a person, circumstances, including self-identification, show the person answering to be the one called, or (B) in the case of a business, the call was made to a place of business and the conversation related to business reasonably transacted over the telephone.

(7) *Public records or reports.* Evidence that a writing authorized by law to be recorded or filed and in fact recorded or filed in a public office, or a purported public record, report, statement, or data compilation, in any form, is from the public office where items of this nature are kept.

(8) *Ancient documents or data compilation.* Evidence that a document or data compilation, in any form, (A) is in such condition as to create no suspicion concerning its authenticity, (B) was in a place where it, if authentic, would likely be, and (C) has been in existence 20 years or more at the time it is offered.

(9) *Process or system.* Evidence describing a process or system used to produce a result

and showing that the process or system produces an accurate result.

(10) *Methods provided by statute or rule.* Any method of authentication or identification provided by Act of Congress or by other rules prescribed by the Supreme Court pursuant to statutory authority.

Rule 902. Self-Authentication

Extrinsic evidence of authenticity as a condition precedent to admissibility is not required with respect to the following:

(1) Domestic public documents under seal. A document bearing a seal purporting to be that of the United States, or of any State, district, Commonwealth, territory, or insular possession thereof, or the Panama Canal Zone, or the Trust Territory of the Pacific Islands, or of a political subdivision, department, officer, or agency thereof, and a signature purporting to be an attestation or execution.

(2) Domestic public documents not under seal. A document purporting to bear the signature in the official capacity of an officer or employee of any entity included in paragraph (1) hereof, having no seal, if a public officer having a seal and having official duties in the district or political subdivision of the officer or employee certifies under seal that the signer has the official capacity and that the signature is genuine.

(3) Foreign public documents. A document purporting to be executed or attested in an official capacity by a person authorized by the laws of a foreign country to make the execution or attestation, and accompanied by a final certification as to the genuineness of the signature and official position (A) of the executing or attesting person, or (B) of any foreign official whose certificate of genuineness of signature and official position relates to the execution or attestation or is in a chain of certificates of genuineness of signature and official position relating to the execution or attestation. A final certification may be made by a secretary of an embassy or legation, consul general, consul, vice consul, or consular agent of the United States, or a diplomatic or consular official of the foreign country assigned or accredited to the United States. If

reasonable opportunity has been given to all parties to investigate the authenticity and accuracy of official documents, the court may, for good cause shown, order that they be treated as presumptively authentic without final certification or permit them to be evidenced by an attested summary with or without final certification.

(4) Certified copies of public records. A copy of an official record or report or entry therein, or of a document authorized by law to be recorded or filed and actually recorded or filed in a public office, including data compilations in any form, certified as correct by the custodian or other person authorized to make the certification, by certificate complying with paragraph (1), (2), or (3) of this rule or complying with any Act of Congress or rule prescribed by the Supreme Court pursuant to statutory authority.

(5) Official publications. Books, pamphlets, or other publications purporting to be issued by public authority.

(6) Newspapers and periodicals. Printed materials purporting to be newspapers or periodicals.

(7) Trade inscriptions and the like. Inscriptions, signs, tags, or labels purporting to have been affixed in the course of business and indicating ownership, control, or origin.

(8) Acknowledged documents. Documents accompanied by a certificate of acknowledgment executed in the manner provided by law by a notary public or other officer authorized by law to take acknowledgments.

(9) Commercial paper and related documents. Commercial paper, signatures thereon, and documents relating thereto to the extent provided by general commercial law.

(10) Presumptions under Acts of Congress. Any signature, document, or other matter declared by Act of Congress to be presumptively or prima facie genuine or authentic.

Rule 903. Subscribing Witness' Testimony Unnecessary

The testimony of a subscribing witness is not necessary to authenticate a writing unless required by the laws of the jurisdiction whose laws govern the validity of the writing.

Article X. Contents of Writings, Recordings, and Photographs

Rule 1001. Definitions

For purposes of this article the following definitions are applicable:

(1) Writings and recordings. "Writings" and "recordings" consist of letters, words, or numbers, or their equivalent, set down by handwriting, typewriting, printing, photostating, photographing, magnetic impulse, mechanical or electronic recording, or other form of data compilation.

(2) Photographs. "Photographs" include still photographs, X-ray films, video tapes, and motion pictures.

(3) Original. An "original" of a writing or recording is the writing or recording itself or any counterpart intended to have the same effect by a person executing or issuing it. An "original" of a photograph includes the negative or any print therefrom. If data are stored in a computer or similar device, any printout or other output readable by sight, shown to reflect the data accurately, is an "original."

(4) Duplicate. A "duplicate" is a counterpart produced by the same impression as the original, or from the same matrix, or by means of photography, including enlargements and miniatures, or by mechanical or electronic re-recording, or by chemical reproduction, or by other equivalent techniques which accurately reproduces the original.

Rule 1002. Requirement of Original

To prove the content of a writing, recording, or photograph, the original writing, recording, or photograph is required, except as otherwise provided in these rules or by Act of Congress.

Rule 1003. Admissibility of Duplicates

A duplicate is admissible to the same extent as an original unless (1) a genuine question is raised as to the authenticity of the original or (2) in the circumstances it would be unfair to admit the duplicate in lieu of the original.

Rule 1004. Admissibility of Other Evidence of Contents

The original is not required, and other evidence of the contents of a writing, recording, or photograph is admissible if—

(1) Originals lost or destroyed. All originals are lost or have been destroyed, unless the proponent lost or destroyed them in bad faith; or

(2) Original not obtainable. No original can be obtained by any available judicial process or procedure; or

(3) Original in possession of opponent. At a time when an original was under the control of the party against whom offered, that party was put on notice, by the pleadings or otherwise, that the contents would be a subject of proof at the hearing, and that party does not produce the original at the hearing; or

(4) Collateral matters. The writing, recording, or photograph is not closely related to a controlling issue.

Rule 1005. Public Records

The contents of an official record, or of a document authorized to be recorded or filed and actually recorded or filed, including data compilations in any form, if otherwise admissible, may be proved by copy, certified as correct in accordance with rule 902 or testified to be correct by a witness who has compared it with the original. If a copy which complies with the foregoing cannot be obtained by the exercise of reasonable diligence, then other evidence of the contents may be given.

Rule 1006. Summaries

The contents of voluminous writings, recordings, or photographs which cannot conveniently be examined in court may be presented in the form of a chart, summary, or calculation. The originals, or duplicates, shall be made available for examination or copying, or both, by other parties at reasonable time and place. The court may order that they be produced in court.

Rule 1007. Testimony or Written Admission of Party

Contents of writings, recordings, or photographs may be proved by the testimony or deposition of the party against whom offered or by that party's written admission, without accounting for the nonproduction of the original.

Rule 1008. Functions of Court and Jury

When the admissibility of other evidence of contents of writings, recordings, or photographs under these rules depends upon the fulfillment of a condition of fact, the question whether the condition has been fulfilled is ordinarily for the court to determine in accordance with the provisions of rule 104. However, when an issue is raised (a) whether the asserted writing ever existed, or (b) whether another writing, recording, or photograph produced at the trial is the original, or (c) whether other evidence of contents correctly reflects the contents, the issue is for the trier of fact to determine as in the case of other issues of fact.

Glossary

abandoned property A person who abandons or throws property away disclaims his or her interest in the property. Therefore, abandoned property may be used as evidence against the former owner. See section D, Chapter 10.

administrative functions Evidence of crimes may be uncovered not only in police work but also in administrative functions such as screening at airports and courthouses. Many fire, health, housing, and school services are also administrative functions.

adversary system The judicial system in which opposing parties present evidence and an impartial judge or jury weighs evidence. In contrast to the inquisitorial system, where the judge actively questions the accused and witnesses.

affirmative defense A defense that admits the defendant committed the crime charged but asserts that the defendant should not be convicted. Examples of affirmative defenses include the insanity defense, double jeopardy, immunity, and entrapment.

Alford guilty plea A guilty plea that permits the accused to maintain innocence.

ancient document rule Circumstantial evidence may be used to prove ancient documents to be authentic and genuine. See section C, Chapter 17.

anonymous tips A tip (information) from an unknown person, which could be received in a 911 call or other telephone call.

arraignment The formal proceeding following the indictment or information, where a plea is entered and the case is bound over for trial.

arrest Arrest was defined in 1760 by Sir William Blackstone as "the apprehending or restraining of one's person, in order to be forthcoming to answer an alledged or suspected crime."

arrest warrant An order signed by a judge or magistrate authorizing the arrest of a named person or persons. See Chapter 14.

assertive statement A statement in which the person making the statement intends to communicate a thought or belief.

attorney–client privilege The attorney–client privilege is the oldest of the privileges. See Chapter 6 and the statutes in your state.

ballistic fingerprints Unique marks in the lead or steel of bullet fragments can be entered into a computer database in a search for a likely match with a firearm. Firearms can be "fingerprinted" in the effort to build a national database of firearms that could immediately identify firearms used in crimes. See Chapter 18.

best evidence rule The rule that requires the original of a writing, photograph, or other document, unless the original is unavailable. Also known as "original document rule."

beyond a reasonable doubt The burden that the prosecution must meet in proving guilt in criminal cases; applies to every element of crime charged.

Bill of Rights The first Ten Amendments to the U.S. Constitution.

***Brady* rule** The rule that requires the prosecution to disclose upon request evidence favorable to the accused.

***Bruton* rule** Use of a confession or incriminating statement against a defendant in a criminal trial that was made by another party to the crime without producing the speaker is a *Bruton* violation. See section E, Chapter 12.

burden of persuasion That part of the burden of proof that requires a party to persuade the jury that a fact exists.

burden of production That part of the burden of proof that requires a party to produce sufficient evidence to establish the fact at issue.

chain of custody Foundation evidence tracing evidence from the time it was obtained to the time it is offered at trial.

circumstantial evidence Evidence from which proof of the fact in question may be inferred.

closely regulated businesses Some businesses because of their nature are closely regulated by laws and codes. Liquor, firearms, coal mines, and pharmacies are among the businesses closely regulated. See section E, Chapter 11.

common law Legal rules that evolved over many years in English and American court opinions.

competency of witnesses The competency of a witness can be challenged by the opposing lawyer. See section A, Chapter 5.

competent evidence Any evidence that is relevant and reliable and not otherwise excludable.

confession A confession is generally viewed the same as a guilty plea in open court. It is a direct acknowledgment of guilt.

Confrontation Clause The clause in the U.S. Constitution that entitles a defendant to demand witnesses to testify against him in his presence.

conspiracy An agreement by two or more people to commit an illegal act.

corpus delicti The body of the crime. The requirement that the government must prove that the crime charged has been committed. In a rape case where the defendant acknowledges that the parties had sex but alleges that both parties consented to the sex, you then have a corpus delicti case. If there was mutual consent, there was no crime.

courtroom identification In every criminal trial there must be an identification of the defendant as the person who committed the crime or was a party to the crime charged.

credibility Fact finders (juries or judges) determine the credibility (believability) of witnesses. Juries not only determine whether statements made by witnesses are true but also what weight should be given them.

crime-fraud exception When a client consults with an attorney for the purpose of committing a future crime such as perjury, the attorney–client privilege does not protect communication and documents relating to this fraud. See section C, Chapter 6.

crime scene Crimes can occur in public or private places. If a drug house (crime scene) is raided, law officers must have a valid search warrant or one of the authorities listed in Chapter 16 to enter the premises.

criminal complaint The formal charge made by the prosecution against a defendant, which begins criminal proceedings; usually found in misdemeanor cases.

criminal indictment The formal charge issued by a grand jury, listing crimes believed to have been committed by the named defendant.

cross-examination After the direct examination of a witness, the witness may then be cross-examined by the opposing attorney. Cross-examination is one of the safeguards of the accuracy and completeness of testimony given by a witness.

curtilage Curtilage is that area close to a home where persons have a right of privacy. See section E, Chapter 10.

custody Under police control, whether or not physically constrained.

Daubert test The 1993 *Daubert* case (see Chapter 18) was used by the U.S. Supreme Court to reject the old *Frye* test. The *Daubert* test emphasizes rigorous testing and organized skepticism. *Daubert* points out there are no certainties in science, only probabilistic results.

declarant A person who makes a statement, either in or out of court.

demonstrative evidence Evidence that demonstrates objects, persons, or events not in the courtroom. Photographs and videotapes are demonstrative evidence.

direct evidence Evidence that proves or disproves a fact in question with no need for inferences.

direct examination The lawyer who subpoenaed a witness would call the witness to take the witness stand and conduct the direct examination of the witness. See section E, Chapter 5.

discovery Formal procedures used by prosecution and defense attorneys to gather documents, witnesses, and other evidence.

DNA genetic profiling A very important scientific forensic tool for identifying the person who committed a crime and clearing innocent suspects. First used as

evidence in 1987 and now used extensively throughout the world. See Chapter 18.

documents as evidence Generally, anything that conveys a message is a document. See section C, Chapter 17, for rules governing the use of documents as evidence.

due process The minimum procedural protections courts must afford those charged with crimes; guaranteed by the Fifth and Fourteenth Amendments to the U.S. Constitution.

dying declaration exception Statements made by a victim or other person under the belief of impending death (dying declarations) are admissible evidence under Rule 804(2).

electronic surveillance Secret interception of communications by wiretapping or "bugging," which "typically is accomplished by installation of a small microphone in the room (or vehicle) to be bugged." U.S. Supreme Court in *Dalia v. United States*, 99 S. Ct. 1682 (1979).

evidence Evidence is ordinarily defined as the means of establishing the truth or untruth of any fact that is alleged. See section A, Chapter 4.

exclusionary rule A judicial rule that makes inadmissible evidence obtained in violation of the U.S. Constitution, state or federal laws, or court rules.

exigency situations An emergency situation such as "hot pursuit," now-or-never, or emergency aid. See Chapter 16.

expert witness A witness with special knowledge or training in a specialized area.

federalism Division of power between state governments and the federal government, in which the federal government has specified powers delegated to it, with the remaining powers vested in the states.

Federal Rules of Evidence Codification in 1975 of common-law rules of evidence; applicable only in federal courts, but is the model for most state evidence codes.

forensic Belonging to or connected with a court. For example, forensic fingerprints are fingerprints that will be or have been used as evidence in a civil or criminal trial.

forensic entomology Entomology is the study of insects. Entomological evidence (such as maggots) is widely accepted as scientific evidence. See Chapter 18.

free-to-leave test If a person is free to leave the presence of a law officer, there is no detention of that person. If the person is not free to leave, the officer must then show legal authority to detain the person. See Chapter 14.

fruit of the poisonous tree Evidence obtained legally through the use of evidence obtained illegally. See Chapter 9.

Frye test The 1923 case of *Frye v. United States* established the *Frye* test that was used until 1993. The old *Frye* test determined the admissibility of scientific evidence until the U.S. Supreme Court held that Rule 702 created its own standard for the introduction of scientific evidence. See Chapter 18.

good faith exception Most states permit the use of evidence obtained under a search warrant that has a technical error unknown to the law officers executing the warrant. See section F, Chapter 10.

grand jury Jury that hears evidence presented by the prosecution and makes a determination to charge persons with crimes; used in federal and many state criminal proceedings.

grand jury secrecy requirement Persons serving on grand juries are required to take an ancient oath not to disclose "matters occurring before" the grand jury on which they serve. Federal and state laws protect disclosure of such matters. See section K, Chapter 6.

gruesome photographs Photographs that are shocking and gruesome. See Chapter 17 for the use of such photographs as evidence.

habeas corpus Latin name of the writ used to compel a government official, such as a prison warden, to show cause why a person is held by the official.

hearsay Secondhand testimony; reports by one person about what another person said.

honest mistake rule The U.S. Supreme Court held that courts must "allow some latitude for honest mistakes that are made by officers in the dangerous and difficult process of making arrests and executing search warrants," 107 S. Ct. 1013. See section F, Chapter 10.

hypnosis Many (but not all) persons can be placed in a sleeplike condition where they become subject to many of the suggestions and orders of the hypnotizer. Rulings of courts in most states forbid hypnotically refreshed testimony from a witness. See section I, Chapter 5.

impeachment Calling into question the truth or accuracy of direct testimony by cross-examination or introduction of contradictory evidence.

impermissible inferences An inference a fact finder may not draw; examples include an inference of guilt because the defendant does not testify.

incriminating statement "Is any statement or conduct from guilt of the crime can be inferred." *People v. Stanton*, 158 N.E. 2d 47 (Ill.1959).

independent source doctrine Evidence obtained lawfully by one source is admissible even though another source (law officers) obtained the same evidence improperly. See section C, Chapter 9.

"indicia of reliability" Signs or indications of reliability required for a law officer to make an investigative detention or arrest of a person based upon an anonymous tip or other information. The term denotes facts that give rise to inferences.

inevitable discovery rule Limitation on the exclusionary rule, where illegally discovered evidence would certainly have been discovered legally.

inferences An inference is a conclusion that can be drawn from a fact. Direct evidence can be used to directly prove a fact, while circumstantial evidence requires a fact finder to draw inferences from fact. See section C, Chapter 4.

informants Informants are persons who provide information to law officers. The informant's privilege is stated in section K, Chapter 6, and U.S. Supreme Court cases having to do with the use of evidence obtained from informant's tips are found in Chapter 11.

initial appearance The first appearance by an accused before a judge or magistrate; a plea is entered, and bail is set at this hearing.

insanity plea Entering a plea to a criminal charge of not guilty because of mental disease or defect is commonly called the insanity plea. In most states and the federal government, the burden of proof for this plea in criminal cases is upon the defendant or person entering the plea.

inventory searches Law officers must inventory property of others that is in their custody. Evidence discovered during a proper inventory is admissible. See Chapter 14.

judgment NOV A posttrial judgment made by a judge changing or reversing the jury decision; literally, *non obstante veredicto* ("notwithstanding the verdict").

judicial notice All states and the federal government have statutes permitting the admission as evidence of facts where there is no real necessity to prove the facts. Judicial notice is a judicial shortcut. See Chapter 6.

latent fingerprints Fingerprints left by a person on a surface other than one designed for recording fingerprints.

lineups Viewing of six or more persons for purposes of identification under the conditions described in Chapter 13.

locus point A point in the sequence of base pairs in human DNA where individual DNA chains vary.

Magna Carta The Great Charter signed by King John of England and his great barons in 1215; created the first standards for arresting and imprisonment of those accused of crimes.

***Massiah* limitation** After a person has been charged with a crime, law officers cannot question the person regarding that crime without the person's attorney. See section D, Chapter 12.

materiality A fact is material if it will affect the results of a trial. To be admissible, evidence must be relevant, material, and competent. See section F, Chapter 5.

***Miranda* requirements** The requirements established by the U.S. Supreme Court in 1966, which are presented in section C, Chapter 12.

motion to suppress evidence A motion is a written or oral request to a court for an order. Therefore, a motion to suppress evidence is a request that the court suppress specified evidence.

mug shots Photographs taken by law enforcement agencies to identify persons arrested or charged with a crime. Such photos often have an identification number and name of the law agency printed on the photograph.

news reporter privilege Many states have enacted laws creating a news reporter privilege. This privilege does not exist at common law. See Chapter 6.

nolo contendere plea A plea in which the accused neither contests nor admits the charges against him; treated as a guilty plea.

objections Formal statements made by attorneys during trials, objecting to the form or substance of a question or to the answer given by a witness to a question.

open fields Objects found in an open field may be used as evidence as the owner of the property has no right of privacy in an open field. See section E, Chapter 10.

ordeal A medieval method of proof that was an appeal to God to determine guilt or innocence.

ordinary witness A witness with firsthand information about a fact gained by personal observation.

partner-in-crime exception If a husband and wife are committing a crime together, the marital privilege (wife and husband) would not apply. See section D, Chapter 6.

passage of time rule (attenuation) If a significant period of time goes by after improper police conduct, the U.S. Supreme Court held in the 1963 case of *Wong Sun v. United States* that the "taint" from the improper conduct could be dissipated. See section C, Chapter 9.

permissible inference An inference from proof of facts that a fact finder may but need not draw.

photographic arrays Victims and witnesses to crimes often look at photographic arrays, which must comply with conditions described in Chapter 13.

physical evidence Evidence in the form of physical objects, such as weapons, drugs, and clothing.

physician–patient privilege The physician–patient privilege did not exist at common law but is created by state law for state courts. The privilege belongs to the patient and can be waived by the patient. See Chapter 6.

plain view or open view If a law officer is where the officer has a right to be and sees evidence or contraband in plain view, the evidence may be seized and can be used in a criminal trial. See Chapter 10.

plea bargaining Agreement to enter a guilty plea in return for a reduction in the charge or sentence. For example, first offense shoplifters are often given the opportunity to plea to disorderly conduct in a municipal court instead of going to trial for a theft charge. First offense drunk drivers are often permitted to enter a guilty plea in return for the dropping of one of the three or four criminal charges that they face.

preliminary hearing Full adversarial hearing with a lawyer present; the judge determines if probable cause exists to try the accused for the crime charged.

presentment jury The English procedure for determining when crimes had been committed; forerunner to the grand jury.

presumption of innocence All criminal trials must start with the legal presumption that the defendant is innocent until sufficient credible evidence is produced to carry the burden of proving guilt beyond a reasonable doubt.

prima facie case A civil or criminal case that is so strong that the opponent must respond with rebutting evidence to avoid losing the case is called a prima facie case.

private searches A private search by a private person is not subject to the exclusionary rule. The exclusionary rule applies only to evidence obtained improperly by law officers. See section A, Chapter 10.

privilege A benefit or right enjoyed by a person. The privilege of a witness not to answer a question might be based upon the privilege against self-incrimination or the marital privilege.

probable cause The quantum (amount) of evidence required by the Fourth Amendment to make an arrest or to issue a search warrant is probable cause. Probable cause is greater than reasonable suspicion but can be less than proof or reasonable doubt.

proof Proof is the result of evidence, and evidence is the means of attaining proof. See section A, Chapter 4.

protective search A protective search is limited to discovering threatening weapons as it is "unreasonable to require police officers to take unnecessary risks in the performance of their duties." U.S. Supreme Court, 88 S. Ct. 1868.

protective sweep or safety check A check or sweep of a building or vehicle to determine if other persons or weapons are present that could jeopardize safety.

psychotherapist–patient privilege Many states have laws creating this privilege. See Chapter 6.

real evidence Physical objects, such as weapons and drugs; also called *physical evidence*.

reasonable doubt standard Fact finders (juries or judges) in criminal cases must use the reasonable doubt standard to find a defendant guilty of the crime charged. See section B, Chapter 4.

reasonable suspicion That quantum of evidence (information) needed by a law enforcement officer to make an investigative stop (a *Terry* stop). Reasonable suspicion is less than probable cause, but it is more than a hunch or mere suspicion. See Chapter 14.

regularly kept records exception Rule 803 allows the use of regularly kept business records and public, religious, and family records.

relevancy Evidence is relevant if it has a tendency to make a material issue that is before the court more or less probable. See section F, Chapter 5.

reliable evidence Evidence that possesses a sufficient degree of likelihood that it is true and accurate.

scientific evidence Evidence, usually in the form of expert testimony, concerning scientific theory, experiments, or tests.

search warrant An order signed by a judge or magistrate authorizing the place to be searched and the persons or things to be seized. See Chapter 14.

sexual assault counselor's privilege Counseling is often needed for victims in sexual assault cases and crimes of violence. Many states protect these records and forbid testimony by counselors without the consent or the victim or patient. See Chapter 6.

showups A one-on-one identification procedure that should only be used under conditions described in Chapter 13.

sketches There must always be an in-court identification of the defendant as the person who committed or was a party to the crime charged.

special needs of government Administrative functions are related to the "special needs" of government necessary to provide safety, health, and educational services. See Chapter 11.

spectrograms or voiceprints Voice graphs made on a spectrograph, which analyzes voice recordings based on intensity, frequency, and time gaps in the recording.

standing Possessing the necessary relationship to an issue to be permitted to raise that issue in a court of law.

statement against-penal-interest exception A statement against penal interest that exposes the speaker to criminal liability is admissible under Rule 804(3).

statements for the purpose of medical diagnosis or treatment exception Rule 803(4) defines the statements for the purposes of medical diagnosis or treatment exception. Doctors and nurses may testify as such statements that are particularly important in child abuse cases.

subpoena An order compelling a person to appear as witness is called a subpoena. Defense lawyers and prosecutors may have subpoenas issued for witnesses needed in either criminal or civil cases.

subpoena duces tecum A subpoena that not only requires the appearance of a witness but also requires the witness to bring documents or writings that may be in his or her possession is called a subpoena duces tecum. The subpoenaed documents must be relevant and competent to the matters before the court.

sufficiency-of-evidence requirement A jury's verdict and a judge's finding must be supported and must be based upon a sufficiency of evidence. Therefore the sufficiency-of-evidence requirement requires a reasonably substantial foundation of evidence to support the verdict or finding. See section E, Chapter 4.

Terry stop An investigative street detention named after the 1968 U.S. Supreme Court case of *Terry v. Ohio*. See Chapter 14.

then existing mental, emotional, or physical exception Rule 803(3) defines the then existing mental, emotional, or physical exception. Testimony that the victim stated that she was going to visit a friend and then her boyfriend is admissible evidence under this exception to show intent.

totality-of-the-circumstances test The test that looks at the whole picture—all of the factors—in determining whether a confession, incriminating statement, or consent was freely and voluntarily given.

trace evidence Usually small evidence a suspect would leave when he or she comes in contact with another object. See section D, Chapter 16.

truth of the matter asserted To fall within the hearsay rule, the declarant's statement must be an assertive statement. See Rule 801(c) and Chapter 7.

verbal communication Not only verbal statements but nonverbal acts can be assertive and therefore hearsay. See Chapter 7.

videotape surveillance Surveillance by use of videotape. See Chapter 17 for the law governing this practice.

voir dire The preliminary examination of prospective jurors or a child who is going to be a witness to determine qualifications.

voluntariness test The requirement that confessions, incriminating statements, and consent be shown to be voluntary and freely given and were not obtained by means that overwhelmed the will of the accused or another person.

wiretapping "Interception of communication by telephone and telegraph." U.S. Supreme Court in *Dalia v. United States*, 99 S. Ct. 1682 (1979).

witnesses Witnesses are persons who appear and testify under oath or affirmation before civil and criminal courts and other hearings. See section A, Chapter 5.

work-related searches If a city or state worker is sick and does not show up for work, another employee often fills in for the sick worker. To do this, the employee and the supervisor will have to go into the sick worker's desk and work station. This is a work-related search for the necessary records or equipment. See section F, Chapter 11.

writ of certiorari The formal notice by the U.S. Supreme Court to a lower federal or state court that the case will be reviewed by the Supreme Court.

Table of Cases

Index